Handbook to Saville Consulting Wave Professional Styles

First Published in October 2009. Saville Consulting Group, Jersey, CI.
Copyright ©2009 Saville Consulting. All rights reserved.

ISBN: 978-0-9562875-1-9

Acknowledgments

Saville Consulting would like to thank the many individuals, charities and organizations that helped to make the development of Saville Consulting Wave® possible. We would like to recognize the contribution each person made from the 50 countries involved in the development in giving their time to complete and review the questionnaires. We would also like to thank every person who completed the early versions of Saville Consulting Wave® Styles online and every individual who provided an independent rating which allowed us to select the most valid items for use in Saville Consulting Wave® Styles assessments. Since the initial development of Professional and Focus Styles many more individuals have completed and many more independent ratings of performance at work have been collected allowing us to cross validate the results in other groups. We thank you all.

Citation

Citation: Saville, P., MacIver, R., & Kurz, R. (2009). Handbook to Saville Consulting Wave® Professional Styles. Saville Consulting Group, Jersey.

The main contributors to this Handbook were:

Saville, P.
MacIver, R.
Kurz, R.
Parry, G.
Herridge, K.
Mitchener, A.
Becker, S.
Oxley, H.
Tonks, K.
Rojon, C.
Hopton, T.
Schmidt, G.
Schmidt, S.
Henley, S.
Staddon, H.

info@savilleconsulting.com
www.savilleconsulting.com

Handbook Designed by Katrina Haberfield

CONTENTS

3

CONTENTS

CONTENTS

CONTENTS

CONTENTS

ABOUT THIS HANDBOOK

This handbook is designed to provide users of Saville Consulting Wave® Styles assessments with technical information regarding design, development and validation. The handbook also provides guidance on the applications and recommended use of the Saville Consulting Wave Styles assessments.

PART 1

OVERVIEW

1.0 Introducing Saville Consulting Wave® Styles

Saville Consulting Wave Styles assessments are built around one integrated model based on a rich understanding of personal motives, talents, competency potential and preferred culture. The concepts of motive and talent are central to the structure and have real implications for selection, individual development, career planning and performance management.

Saville Consulting Wave Styles are part of the multidimensional assessment suite. The styles assessments measure motivation, talent, competency potential and preferred culture in one questionnaire. They provide value in both recruitment and development, transforming the quality of the assessment process through the use of technology and well researched, performance-driven models of effectiveness in the workplace.

The Saville Consulting Wave Professional Styles questionnaires have 216 questions measuring 108 behavioral facets. The Professional Styles questionnaire takes about 40 minutes to complete. The ultra-compact Saville Consulting Wave Focus Styles questionnaires have 72 items measuring 36 behavioral facets that were selected for their strong validity. Focus Styles is typically completed in 13 minutes.

Professional Styles have been developed from first principles as work relevant, high validity, international tools available in many languages and suitable for a range of job roles across different industry sectors.

Saville Consulting Wave Styles questionnaires were designed specifically for the Internet. Rather than taking a paper questionnaire and putting it on the internet, Wave Styles assessments form an innovative suite of self-report measures developed with the opportunities and challenges of the internet at the heart of their design. They operate as both trait and type instruments and rely on a new hierarchical model of work performance developed by Saville Consulting. The model is aligned to the Big Five personality factors and the Great Eight competencies but provides more information than either of these models.

The development of the questionnaires has benefited from a performance-driven methodology we call "validation-centric." The methodology maximizes the validity of the questionnaires by selecting the most valid items from our item pools so only the best predictors were included in the final questionnaires.

A new dynamic online format integrates rating and ranking responses and results in a combined profile that highlights differences between the ipsative and normative scores on the profile. This new scaling technology also allows unprecedented levels of detail to be tapped, yet with radically reduced completion times.

The research matching the questionnaire to the preferred culture, environment and job demands allows individuals (and their managers) to gain new perspectives on what they can take from their job and what will motivate them.

Saville Consulting Wave Styles Approach

Saville Consulting Wave Styles are based on a unique perspective which makes it different from many other popular assessments. Some of these unique properties and features of Wave Professional Styles are outlined below.

1.1 Performance Driven

Saville Consulting Wave Styles questionnaires have been developed (and continue to be developed) using a variety of development strategies, but at the core is a *performance driven, validation-centric strategy*.

This strategy is based on starting with what a questionnaire is designed to predict, i.e., the criteria. This is to take a *criterion centric* rather than *predictor centric* perspective on measurement. To be *performance driven* is to adopt a validation-centric strategy which selects items with the best criterion-related validity into the questionnaire (i.e., selects the best predictors of the criteria and removes the weaker predictors in order to maximize prediction of the criteria).

11

For the initial development of the Professional Styles questionnaires, 214 work constructs were written (each with separate motive and talent components, 428 work constructs in total). 108 of these constructs (facets) made it into the final questionnaire with item/facet selection based first and foremost on criterion validity. Items were correlated with external ratings on relevant work behavior competencies as well as overall job proficiency and potential for promotion.

Saville Consulting Wave Styles are therefore based on the work constructs which are the best indicators of performance and underpin not only effectiveness in terms of key behaviors but also in terms of overall performance.

The Criterion Centric and Performance Driven foundation is a central feature of the Wave Styles model. Wave Styles is not like other questionnaires that are based on parsimonious factor structures of self-report variables or solely measuring a particular deductive or theoretical model.

This approach is designed to have the impact of not only making the validity clearer and more transparent to the assessment user but also maximizing the validity and the return on investment from Wave Styles assessments.

Further discussion on the rationale for performance driven, criterion centric development is given in the Validity chapter.

1.2 The Saville Consulting Wave® Performance Culture Framework

At the heart of Saville Consulting Wave assessment tools is the Wave Performance Culture Framework model. The Saville Consulting Wave Performance Culture Framework is an extensively researched model of the key characteristics that underpin success at work across different occupations. It is the starting point for Saville Consulting's new product development, because validation evidence has demonstrated its elements are important correlates of work performance.

The Saville Consulting Wave Performance Culture Framework is made up of Behavior, Ability and Global areas (see Figure 1.1).

Figure 1.1 An Overview of the Structure of the Wave Performance Culture Framework

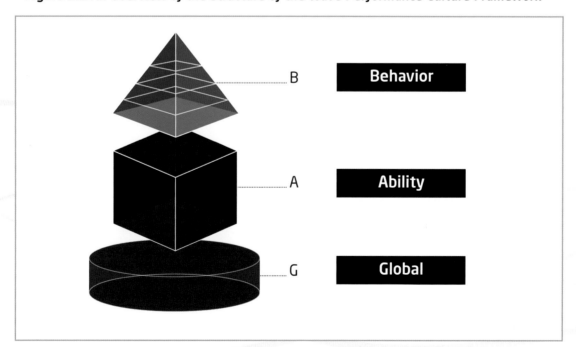

'**Behavior**' refers to work behavioral styles and competencies. The Saville Consulting Wave model has a hierarchical structure consisting of four clusters, 12 sections, 36 dimensions and 108 facets. These behavioral areas can be directly assessed using Saville Consulting Wave Performance 360. Saville Consulting Wave Professional and Focus Styles have been developed to indicate individuals' potential to perform in these behavioral areas.

'**Ability**' assesses a person's abilities to perform certain intellectual or cognitive tasks. Many areas of cognitive ability can be assessed such as verbal comprehension, numerical reasoning or strengths in working with designs or systems. These abilities can be assessed using the Saville Consulting portfolio of Aptitude Assessments (for more information see www.savilleconsulting.com). These abilities can also be assessed in practice in the workplace, with a 360 degree approach using the Saville Consulting Wave Performance 360.

'**Global**' describes broad overall effectiveness characteristics of performance at work. These refer to a person's overall performance at work in key areas such as Applying Expertise, Accomplishing Objectives and Demonstrating Potential. The Saville Consulting Wave Performance Culture Framework includes a hierarchical model of Global work performance consisting of three sections and nine dimensions. These can also be assessed with Saville Consulting Wave Performance 360.

The importance of work requirements for individuals or teams to demonstrate superior performance on these behavior, ability and global elements of effectiveness can be assessed in a small group using a deck of cards from the Saville Consulting Wave Performance Culture Framework. They can also be rated online with Saville Consulting Wave Job Profiler.

For more information on the Saville Consulting Wave Performance Culture Framework please refer to the User Guide provided with the Saville Consulting Performance Culture Card Deck.

1.3 Aligned Model of Potential and Performance

The Saville Consulting Wave model of potential and performance consists of two models that are aligned with each other. Work performance criteria are aligned with the Styles predictors that best measure them. Figure 1.2 shows the Saville Consulting Wave Aligned Criterion and Predictor Model.

Figure 1.2 Saville Consulting Aligned Model of Performance (Criteria) and Potential (Predictors)

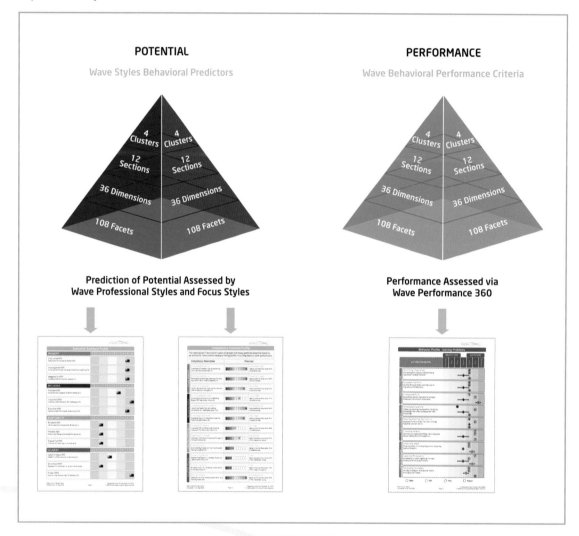

The final model therefore clearly aligns each predictor with a matched criterion. Every component at every level in the criterion (or competency) model has a corresponding component in the predictor (or styles) model. However, the matched components in the two models are not identical. For example, Inventive is one of the 36 Styles dimensions with items selected that specifically predict effectiveness on the competency/criterion of Generating Ideas. Hence, Inventive and Generating Ideas are aligned in the model.

The aligned model is designed to increase the empirical validity available to the user by providing a direct link between the motive and talent components measured in the Wave Styles questionnaires and effective performance at work. This link is explicitly shown in the Wave Styles report.

Cross validated prediction equations of Competency Potential are also provided. This was accomplished using empirical validation evidence and the aligned performance model. The creation of these prediction equations maximizes the validity in predicting a person's competency potential from the Wave Professional Styles assessments. For more information about validity refer to the Validity chapter and for more information about predicting competency potential, refer to the Construction chapter section on 'Development of Competency Potential Equations.'

The aligned model is also designed to help individuals realize and develop their potential. This can be done by contrasting results from the self-report Professional Styles or Focus assessments with the assessment of performance using the Saville Consulting Wave Performance 360.

In addition, the aligned model allows for Job Profiling in organizational competency language down to the 108 facet level using tools such as the Saville Consulting Wave Performance Culture Framework and the Saville Consulting Wave Job Profiler.

1.4 Integrated Model and Application

The Saville Consulting Wave Performance Culture Framework is assessed using a variety of tools for a range of human resource applications. Figure 1.3 gives an overview of what is measured by each of the assessment tools.

Figure 1.3 Integrated Saville Consulting Wave Assessments

The Applications chapter of this handbook and the Saville Consulting Performance Culture Framework User Guide give more information on the integrated model and its application.

From this point on, this handbook will focus on the Behavior segment of the Wave Performance Culture Framework as predicted by Wave Professional Styles and Wave Focus Styles.

1.5 New Levels – New Insights

The Wave Behavioral Model is hierarchical in that there are four levels that, starting from the highest level, include: Clusters (4), Sections (12), Dimensions (36) and Facets (108). The levels and the number of components at each level are the same in both the Styles and the aligned Competency model. Users can focus on the cluster level for a quick and simple view of a profile or dig for deeper insights by focusing on the facet level of a profile.

The hierarchical approach allows for a broad measurement and understanding of how each of the four clusters in the predictor domain (measured by Wave Styles) is directly linked to the criterion domain. For example, Thought is a Styles cluster and Solving Problems is its aligned Competency cluster. This matching applies to every component at all the levels in the hierarchy. Colors are associated with the four sections to aid differentiation and ease interpretation.

Styles Cluster	Competency Cluster	Associated Color
Thought	Solving Problems	Blue
Influence	Influencing People	Red
Adaptability	Adapting Approaches	Gold
Delivery	Delivering Results	Green

The hierarchy allows the user the opportunity to have a broad overview of an individual. It may indicate, for example, that the person profiled is strong on 'Delivering Results' (Green) and 'Influencing People' (Red), but less strong on 'Solving Problems' (Blue) and 'Adapting Approaches' (Gold). These four clusters provide a simple overview of an individual that relies on the aggregated validity of the Wave scales.

Figure 1.4 The Saville Consulting Wave Types Report

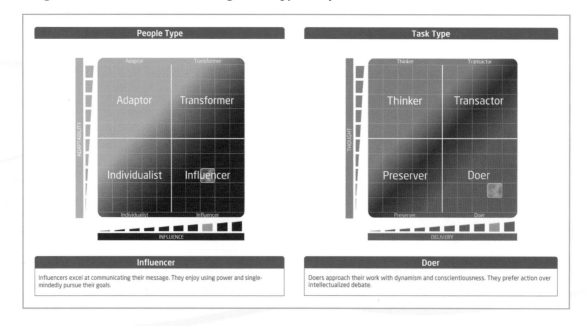

This forms the basis of the Types report.

Figure 1.5 The four 'People' types and four 'Task' types combine to create 16 overall Saville Consulting Wave Types

Saville Consulting Wave Overview of the 16 Types

PEOPLE ORIENTATION				
High	Transformer-Preserver	Transformer-Thinker	Transformer-Doer	Transformer-Transactor
	Influencer-Preserver	Influencer-Thinker	Influencer-Doer	Influencer-Transactor
	Adaptor-Preserver	Adaptor-Thinker	Adaptor-Doer	Adaptor-Transactor
Low	Individualist-Preserver	Individualist-Thinker	Individualist-Doer	Individualist-Transactor
	Low	**TASK ORIENTATION**		**High**

This level is also particularly useful when comparing and contrasting individuals in exercises such as Team Profiling or Relationship Management. The Types chapter of this handbook provides more information on the Types reports and model.

Figure 1.6 Multi Graph Types

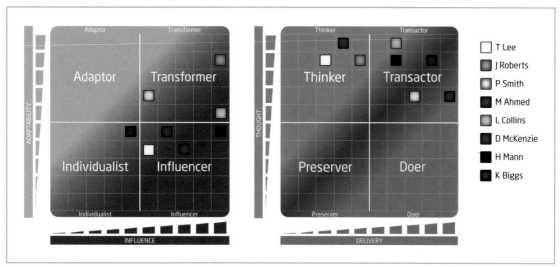

The next level in the hierarchy is the twelve sections which provide more detail and form the basis of the Saville Consulting Wave Wheel.

Figure 1.7 The Wave Wheel

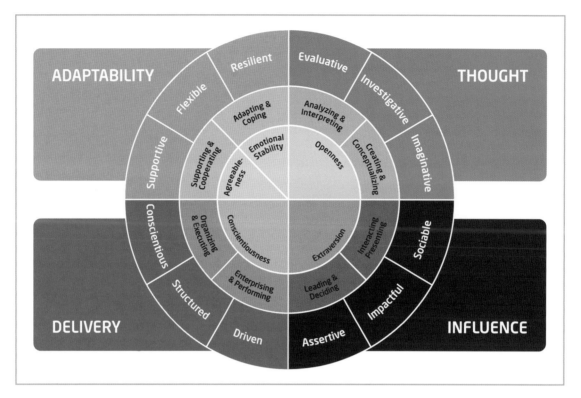

The "Wave Wheel" provides a mechanism for understanding how Wave compares with other major models of personality and performance in its structure (Musek's Big One, Digman's Alpha and Beta, The Great Eight Competencies, The Big Five).

Refer to the Construction chapter for further discussion on the Wave Wheel and how it integrates previous research and models of both personality and performance at work (and see Kurz et al. (2008) for a discussion on the use of the Wave Wheel in coaching).

Each of the four clusters then breaks down into three sections to create 12 sections (four clusters x three sections) as follows:

Figure 1.8 The Saville Consulting Wave Work Hierarchy

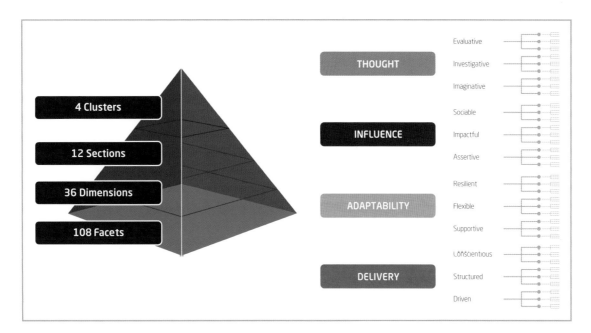

Clusters:

- **Thought** encompasses the sections Evaluative, Investigative and Imaginative. This cluster is focused on developing ideas, from analyzing problems and showing interest in underlying principles through to being more expansive and divergent in thought by being creative and strategic.

- **Influence** encompasses the sections Sociable, Impactful and Assertive. This cluster relates to communication and working with others. It is concerned with establishing positive relationships with people and demonstrating positive leadership behaviors.

- **Adaptability** encompasses the sections Resilient, Flexible and Supportive. This cluster covers areas of emotional, behavioral and social adaptability, respectively.

- **Delivery** encompasses the sections Conscientious, Structured and Driven. This cluster is focused on implementation and delivery of results, from ensuring high standards of delivery through to proactively making things happen.

The 12 sections then break down into the more detailed level of 36 dimensions. This is the level of fidelity that would be expected from a trait instrument that typically takes 40 minutes to complete. However, the new form of scaling developed with Wave's dynamic online format allows for a further level of detail to be assessed. Both the styles predictor and the criterion models finish at the most detailed level of 108 facets.

In Wave Styles, these 108 facets are measured with two item scales to allow for narrow, clearly defined specific behaviors to be assessed. While these short facet scales of two items do not give sufficient coverage of a broader trait, this is overcome by building short precise scales (facets) that measure each concept specifically that group together to form larger, broader scales higher up the hierarchy - Wave Professional Styles dimensions (6 items from three facet scales), sections (18 items from 6 facet scales), and clusters (54 items from 27 facet scales).

19

A benefit of this approach is that it avoids extremely similar or tautologous items being repeated to cover a trait. At the dimension level and higher, this approach leads to scales which have a degree of breadth and are multifaceted and are not just similar items repeated again and again with no unique contribution to improved prediction.

This 108 level enables a richer degree of insight and understanding of where an individual's strengths and weaknesses lie within the context of the overall Wave hierarchy.

Figure 1.9 Example of Wave Cluster to Facet Structure

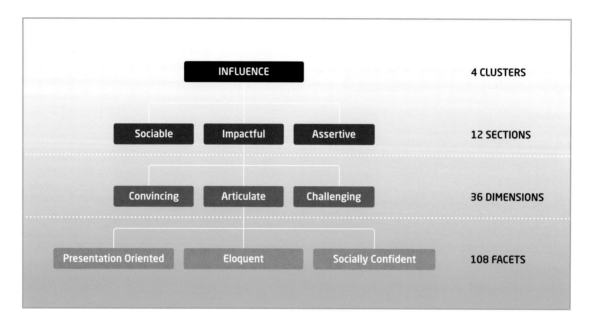

For an example, see Figure 1.9 highlighting one small part of the four level Wave hierarchy. The cluster 'Influence' breaks down into sections 'Assertive', 'Impactful' and 'Sociable.' If we follow the section 'Impactful' further down the hierarchy, it can be seen that it is composed of the dimensions 'Convincing', 'Challenging' and 'Articulate.' At the lowest level of the hierarchy, the 108 facet level, the dimension 'Articulate' is made up of the facets 'Presentation Oriented,' 'Eloquent' and 'Socially Confident.'

Scale descriptions of the 36 Dimensions of Wave Professional Styles can be found in the Scale Descriptions chapter of this handbook.

1.6 Aiding Interpretation with Dynamic Scores Description

The Psychometric Profile of the Wave report is also designed to aid interpretation by providing a narrative description of each of the 108 facets that varies according to the score the individual received on each facet. The description varies according to the sten score. There are five categories which give different statements (based on sten 1-2, 3-4, 5-6, 7-8, 9-10).

Fig 1.10 Example of Dynamic Facet Score Description

Articulate Styles dimension scale from Psychometric Profile of Wave Professional Styles Expert Report

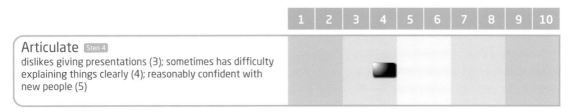

In the excerpt from the profile above the individual has a sten score of three on Presentation Oriented, four on Eloquent and five on Socially Confident. The examples that will be presented for the other features of the Wave assessment will demonstrate how the narrative text changes according to the level of the three facets within the Articulate dimension.

1.7 Facet Range

Rather than profiling every score of the 108 facets on the Styles Psychometric Profile, only non-alignment of the facet scores is highlighted to the Wave user in the Wave report. When the facets are not aligned, and there is a difference between the facet scores of three or more stens, this constitutes a facet range and allows the user to delve deeper into the scores. The facet range is indicated by a series of horizontal lines on the profile running from the lowest to highest facet score.

Fig 1.11 Example of a Facet Range

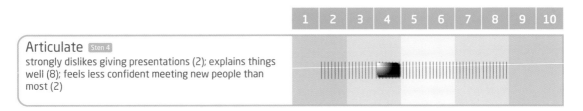

In the facet range above, the individual's score of four on the Articulate dimension is the same as in the previous example, but the large facet range provides a very different picture for the Wave user to investigate. In this case, while the profile indicates the individual is more eloquent than others (8) it also indicates that the individual has less confidence in social situations (2) and feel much less positive than others about giving presentations (2).

Facet ranges are common on profiles with an average profile of 36 dimensions possessing 17 dimensions with facet ranges.

1.8 Motive - Talent Splits

Saville Consulting Wave Styles questionnaires have been developed to separate out talents from underlying predispositions or motives. For every Styles section or dimension measured there is a motive component and a talent component underlying it. At the lowest level of the hierarchy each facet is composed of one motive item and one talent item.

e.g.,   wants to give others encouragement – (motive)
          is good at encouraging others – (talent)

Items were created to specifically measure Motive (will do) and Talent (can do). When differences between these exist they are indicated on the profile chart making it easy for a user to spot when Motive may be greater than Talent, or vice versa. Hence, a report may indicate that a person is higher on Motive than on Talent, which may indicate a development opportunity for this person. Alternatively, the report may show a person to be higher on Talent than on Motive, indicating that the person "can do" the task, but may not want to.

The motive-talent concept is designed to provide additional information which has important implications for selection, development and talent management. The model matches every talent component with a motive component, making it easy for the user to understand the impact of motivation on work performance.

The Expert Report Psychometric Profile indicates where 'Motive-Talent splits' occur. Where there is a difference of three stens or more between the three normed motive items within a dimension and the three normed talent items within a dimension this is shown with M and T symbols on the profile.

Fig 1.12 Example of a Motive-Talent Split

The above example indicates that the individual is higher on motive than talent, potentially opening up the prospect that this is an area for development – i.e., the individual is motivated to develop this area of strength.

Motive-Talent Splits are rarer on profiles than Facet Ranges with the average profile of thirty-six dimensions typically having three or four Motive-Talent splits. The presence of many Motive-Talent Splits may indicate that there is a mismatch between the individual's motives, talents and the demands of the work environment.

1.9 Dynamic Normative-Ipsative "Ra-Ra" Response Format

Saville Consulting Wave Styles assessments use a new dynamic response format that combines a free choice rating response format with a forced-choice ranking response format (our new rate-rank or "ra-ra" format). This can help to identify where on a profile a person's behavior may be underestimated or where a person may be responding in a socially desirable manner.

The online Saville Consulting Wave Styles questionnaires present a page of six statements (see figure 1.13).

Figure 1.13 Screenshot of Online Normative Rating Task of Professional Styles

After the six statements are rated by the respondent, the system records the normative ratings and then calculates the ipsative rankings automatically. If a respondent has tied certain ratings, the system immediately re-presents the tied items to be placed in rank order by the respondent using a forced-choice response format. If there are no tied items, then a new page of six items is presented.

Figure 1.14 Screenshot of Online Ipsative Ranking Task of Professional Styles

N.B. The ipsative score comes from both the order of the normative rating and the ranking task.

Where there are differences of three stens or more between the normative and ipsative scores within a dimension these are highlighted on the profile to allow the user to explore the reasons for this, perhaps during a feedback session or during an interview. Unlike a scale of social desirability, this feature can help to quickly spot the specific dimensions where socially desirable responding (or overly self-critical responding) may have occurred to allow for verification.

23

There are benefits and weaknesses to both ipsative and normative scaling. At the practitioner level, however, it is often useful to have both sources of information.

Figure 1.15 Example of Normative - Ipsative Split

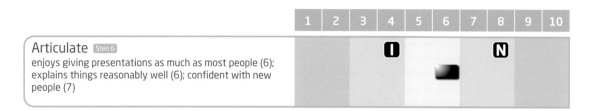

In the example, the individual has an overall sten score of six on the Articulate dimension, but their Normative score is eight and the Ipsative is four. The reason for the difference is not immediately clear without further investigation. One hypothesis is that the normative score is more a reflection of how they like to present themselves and the ipsative is more a reflection of their behavior when they have to choose between competing commitments at work or when under pressure.

1.10 Clear Interpretation

A criticism that can be fairly leveled at many self-report questionnaires is that, despite their reliability and validity, there is still a degree of subjectivity in their interpretation.

Even with proper training subject matter experts in assessment believe that poor interpretation is a significant source of error in the use of personality questionnaires (Smith & Foley, 2006). A lack of consistency between interpreters is much more likely where an aspect of work performance is predicted by a complex combination of predictor scales, which is the situation with many multi-scale self-report personality instruments.

Is inconsistency a given? Can we do anything about it? With the performance driven approach, the work constructs that best predict a work competency are brought together to form a scale. This largely removes the need to look around the profile for what scales relate to a particular competency (i.e., we move from predictor centric models to criterion centric models of work performance so users have to work less hard to "join-the-dots.")

Better interpretation inevitably leads to improved validity in decision-making based on questionnaire data. Clearer interpretation means fewer selection errors and better identification of talent in selection processes. In career development situations, it means clearer feedback and finer understanding of development needs. Ultimately, the higher the validity, the greater the return on investment from using psychometric assessments.

1.11 Configurable Competency Reporting

The level of detail that Saville Consulting Wave Styles achieves also enables a more detailed match with client models of performance (such as competency, capability or value frameworks) allowing for fast configuration of output reports to predict organizational client models.

This detailed configuration has enabled Saville Consulting Wave to partner with Entrecode®, the model of successful entrepreneurs developed by Professor David Hall and his associates. The Entrepreneurial Potential Report is available to all qualified Wave Styles users following completion of Professional Styles or Focus Styles questionnaires. The configuration of Wave Professional Styles scales to Entrecode is an example of the precision and flexibility of the Wave model in mapping onto other competency models.

More information about configurable competency reporting is available from any Saville Consulting office.

1.12 Culture Match

The Saville Consulting Wave development program has also developed measures of work culture that are parallel to the Saville Consulting Wave Styles model. This empirical research allows a prediction of the preferred culture/environment and job demands that would suit an individual based on completion of Saville Consulting Wave Styles questionnaires.

From the perspective of Positive Psychology, Dr. Seligman, the author of Learned Optimism, has argued that work can be changed to suit the employee (rather than just finding an employee that fits the job or trying to develop the individual to better match/meet job demands). Assessment can be constructed to support this approach.

With our unique model which ties together motive, talent, competency and culture, we can help individuals understand what work demands (culture, job and environment) they are most likely to favor.

Figure 1.16 The Saville Consulting Model of Work Performance Effectiveness

Performance Enhancers
(Culture, Job & Environment)

Individual
Motives

Individual
Talents

Work
Competency

Performance Inhibitors
(Culture, Job & Environment)

Armed with this understanding it becomes easier to discuss what enhances or inhibits individuals' performance at work. It also facilitates constructive discussions about how a job could better reflect a person's motives and talents.

This approach can help managers think about how to tailor work to suit individual employees in order to retain staff by keeping them satisfied and motivated.

1.13 Enhanced Security

Wave Styles questionnaires are available in two parallel forms: Invited Access and Supervised Access. Invited Access means the Wave Styles questionnaire is completed remotely on the internet without supervision. Supervised Access is an online version completed on-site under the supervision of a test administrator.

The internet offers great convenience in allowing individuals to respond at great geographical distance (without an administrator present) by sending a link to the questionnaire directly to an email address. This so called "controlled" mode does present security concerns, for example, not being certain that the questionnaire is completed by the person you emailed it to (and not by a group of the person's friends one evening). We believe that as well as "controlled" (or "Invited Access" forms) a self-report questionnaire (particularly questionnaires that can be used for selection or other decision-making processes) can benefit from having a separate supervised secure form.

The need for separate versions of online ability tests is essential, and Saville Consulting offers both Invited Access and Supervised Access versions of our Aptitude Assessment tests.

2.0 Applications of Saville Consulting Wave® Styles

Saville Consulting Wave Styles have been designed to be used throughout the employee life-cycle. Below are some of the applications of Saville Consulting Wave Styles giving an insight into where they can make a difference. The advanced features and models that aid interpretation and decision-making are critical to Wave Styles' success in these applications, as well as the improved validity offered by the measures *(see Validity chapter)*.

Recruitment Selection

Saville Consulting Wave Styles are designed to create a platform for much better decision-making from a self-report questionnaire, leading to increases in the caliber of employees. Saville Consulting Wave gives more valid data in less time and can be administered before conducting an interview or as a source of information to cross reference with other data. Person-Job Fit Reports can also be generated when the competency requirements of a job have been profiled.

Career Planning

Self-insight is important when career planning. It is therefore useful for the individual to understand what things they like to do and what things they are good at. It is also helpful to identify characteristics in a work culture that will help bring out their full potential and enhance satisfaction. Saville Consulting Wave Styles provides that insight.

Coaching and Development

Saville Consulting Wave Styles provide insights that are useful to those being coached and provide a clear link to understanding the impact of their personal style (motive and talent) on their performance at work. Facet splits provide greater detail and interesting contrasts that lead to a precise understanding of the individual's approach to work. In development, it is also extremely useful to know where an individual is intrinsically motivated to develop, and where they are not (which is provided by motive-talent splits).

Self-Selection

Self-selection can be aided by showing job applicants how well they fit with specific job demands and work culture. It may be that self-selection happens before a formal application is made by candidates or as part of the selection process itself. Supplying each applicant with a culture prediction report can enable applicants to make their own decision about how compatible they are with the work culture.

Individualized Induction and On-boarding

Saville Consulting Wave Styles can be used after hire to accelerate induction and development. Despite new hires reporting to be satisfied in general, their satisfaction ratings are relatively weak when they are asked about the feedback of (or lack of feedback of) assessment data collected during the selection process (Miles, 2006). The culture prediction report provides new hires with a picture of what is most likely to enhance their performance in their specific work environment and can help them consider how best to make the most of their talents within that setting.

Team Development

The Saville Consulting Types Model helps members of teams see how they complement one another (e.g., Thinker Influencers are complemented by Adaptor Doers). Group profile reporting is available for team building to explore how two or more people are likely to interact. The detail provided on the full Saville Consulting Wave Expert reports can also provide deeper insight into how people interact with each other.

Organizational Talent Audit/Benchmark

Saville Consulting Wave provides a vehicle for benchmarking groups in terms of their perceived motives and talents. This information can be combined with Saville Consulting organizational surveys of preferred and actual culture to give a unique insight into how the motives and talents of employees are aligned to the organizational culture which can help inform future organizational development strategy.

2.1 Misuse of Saville Consulting Wave Styles

Saville Consulting Wave Styles questionnaires provide a wealth of information about job applicants and employees to the user for a wide range of applications, but there are uses and target populations for which Wave Styles assessments are not appropriate. A sample of these include the following:

Mental Health or Clinical Assessment

Wave Styles questionnaires are not designed as an assessment or diagnostic for mental health disorders. This could include assessment for emotional or psychological stability, substance abuse, eating disorders, physiological disorders, depression, or for creating a treatment program. In these cases a clinical assessment should be used.

Forensic Assessment

Assessments are sometimes used in a forensic setting to determine the suitability of a person to keep custody of a child or to help to decide if a person should go to jail. The Wave Styles questionnaires are not appropriate for these types of decisions as they are not designed or validated to be an assessment of a person's general mental health or emotional well being.

Intelligence Testing

The Wave Styles questionnaires are a measure of work behaviors and personality, not cognitive or mental ability. While the Wave Styles questionnaires measure aspects of behavior related to cognitive performance (i.e., Evaluation), it is an indirect measure only and does not provide an IQ score or similar index of intellectual capacity. We recommend Saville Consulting Aptitude tests for measuring work-related aptitudes. These aptitude tests are frequently used with a Wave Styles questionnaire for a more comprehensive assessment of a person's style and aptitudes.

Parenting Advice or School Eligibility

Wave Styles questionnaires are useful tools for working adults to think about the occupations and work settings that they may be best suited for (career counseling.) However, the questionnaires were not designed or intended for use with children to determine if they qualify to attend a particular school, are eligible for a particular curriculum or can be assigned to a specific classroom, e.g., whether a child be put into a special school, program or class. Likewise, Wave Styles questionnaires are not designed to be used by parents for advice on parenting behavior. The questionnaires were designed for use by individuals who are 16 years or older.

Relationship Compatibility

The Wave Styles questionnaires measure behaviors important for success at work for many different occupations, and as such measure many "normal personality" traits that are important for compatibility in non-work settings. However, the Wave Styles questionnaires have not been designed or validated for use in assessing compatibility between persons for dating, marriage or other non-work oriented relationships.

Workforce Reductions or Firing a Problem Employee

Some line managers prefer to use a tool to help them identify which employees to let go during a staff reduction initiative. Likewise, they may want a tool to decide that a person should be fired – providing a "pass or fail" score to make the decision for them. These are inappropriate uses of a personality questionnaire and will not provide an optimum business outcome from a workforce planning viewpoint. There are other more effective methods that yield better results (contact Saville Consulting for information).

Workforce reduction decisions should be based on appropriate organizational criteria with appropriate consultation, and not based primarily on the results of a personality questionnaire, especially if the job itself remains unchanged. If there is a redesign of a job, then a Wave Styles questionnaire may be appropriate to help inform decision makers about an employee's potential to succeed in the newly designed job along with other known information about the employee.

3.0 Target Users

Saville Consulting Wave® Professional Styles and Focus Styles were developed to assess styles of individuals across different jobs and levels.

The questionnaire was designed specifically for the age of 16 and over and for use in a work context.

To give an appreciation of the range of job levels for which Wave Styles are appropriate, Wave Styles can be used with the following:

- **Enterprise/Corporate Manager**
  (Board member of large, multinational enterprise, e.g., Chairperson, Corporate Chief Executive Officer of multinational corporation or enterprise)

- **Group Manager**
  (Regional Managing Director or President/Vice President with a portfolio of businesses/geographies/product lines, e.g., Managing Director of Eastern Europe, Managing Director of Energy Division, President of Global Software Company, Vice President of Americas Region)

- **Business Manager**
  (Managing Director or President of a single country or product line or owner of small to mid-size organization, e.g., Managing Director of Poland, President Solar Power Division, Executive Chair/Principal Shareholder Power Trends)

- **Functional Manager**
  (Manages a business function such as finance or sales, e.g., Information Technology Director, Chief Financial Officer, Vice President of Sales)

- **Senior Manager**
  (Manages a number of business units or sub functions, e.g., Regional Sales Director, Marketing Brand Director - Product Division, Head of Information Technology - Commercial Systems)

- **Manager**
  (Manages a business unit, e.g., Bank Branch Manager, Store Manager, Sales Manager, Marketing Product Manager, Shipping Manager)

- **Team Leader**
  (Manages a small team of individual contributors, e.g., Supervisor, Team Controller, Charge Hand, Customer Service Supervisor, Shift Supervisor)

- **Individual Contributor - Professional**
  (Manages own work with professional qualification, e.g., Accountant, Electrical Engineer, Research Scientist, Sales Executive)

- **Individual Contributor - Non-Professional**
  (Manages own work with no professional qualification, e.g., Retail Sales Associate, Customer Service Representative, Machine Operator)

4.0 Available Versions of Saville Consulting Wave® Styles

Version	Administration Mode	Format	Items	Average Time*
Professional Styles (IA)	Invited Access	Online	216	40 minutes
Professional Styles (SA)	Supervised Access	Online	216	
Focus Styles (IA)	Invited Access	Online	72	13 minutes
Focus Styles (SA)	Supervised Access	Online	72	

* This is based on the average (modal) completion time for 35,626 completions of Professional Styles (IA) and 33,262 completions of Focus Styles (IA).

Invited Access versions are for use on the internet by individuals who are invited to complete the questionnaire unsupervised. The standard process is that participants receive an "invitation email" to log into the Saville Consulting Oasys site and complete the assessment in their own time and from any location where they have internet access. This is a very convenient and efficient method of administration. However, it is also important that the administrator is aware of the potential risk of identity deception, e.g., there is a risk that the person who received the invitation asks someone else to complete the questionnaire.

Supervised Access versions are also administered online, but only under supervised conditions. No invitation email is sent to the participant. Instead, a test administrator is assigned the task of supervising the assessment at a secure location. This requires that the supervisor logs into the Saville Consulting Oasys site to start the administration of Wave. This is not the same Invited Access version of Wave Styles, but rather an alternative Supervised Access form. This is a more secure and controlled mode of administration.

Both Invited Access and Supervised Access forms measure the same Wave sections, dimension and facets and the same reports can be generated.

5.0 Administration and Security

5.1 A Note on Security for Administrators

Saville Consulting Wave Styles were built from first principles to be internet assessment tools. There are two modes of administration available for Wave Styles assessment which represent two different levels of security.

Invited Access mode is where an individual has been prequalified to be assessed. This prequalification could take many forms. For example, it may be that the individual is an existing member of staff attending an internal development event or a candidate having passed previous qualification stages of a selection procedure. The typical form of administration in Invited Access mode is the individuals receive a link and username and password to their email address and then complete Wave Styles online with no supervision.

Supervised Access mode is a more secure form of administration, with an administrator present and the individual being assessed online. Supervised Administration offers greater safeguards over identity deception (i.e., getting someone else to complete).

In practice, the Supervised Access mode is used much more rarely than the Invited Access mode, but it provides the reassurance of a separate version where there is any concern over misrepresentation.

A second form is also useful as it provides evidence of Wave Styles Alternate Form Reliability. When a separate supervised alternative form of a self-report assessment is not available it may be appropriate to complete the invited access form under supervised conditions.

We recommend that Saville Consulting Wave® should be supported by an analysis of the components of the job critical to job success from sources such as local validation studies, formal job analysis, competency models, role profiles, person specifications and job descriptions.

The Saville Consulting Wave Job Profiler can be completed by appropriate stakeholders and subject matter experts to indicate the relevance or importance of different characteristics for the job. Alternatively, a parallel process can be accomplished person-to-person or in focus groups with Saville Consulting Wave Performance Culture Framework.

A local validation study can also be commissioned and completed using our short online performance rating tools to establish criterion-related validity job relevance. Wave Job Profiler typically takes 15 minutes to complete per stakeholder/subject matter expert and is a quick and efficient way to establish job relevance.

5.2 Administration

Saville Consulting Wave Styles questionnaires are online questionnaires with instructions and examples given as part of the administration. This means that in both Supervised Access and Invited Access administration modes the questionnaires do not require the support of an administration card.

We do advise that prior to administration assessees are sent a Professional Styles Preparation Guide. The preparation guide provides a short description of the assessment process, along with example screen shots and tips for proper preparation. Digital versions of the preparation guides are available as complimentary downloads on the Saville Consulting Website www.savilleconsulting.com.

Assessees are not allowed to go back to previous items that have already been answered. In the event that an assessee notices that the response scale has been used incorrectly, the questionnaire may be reset and the assessee can start over. A reset can only be done by an Oasys Project Administrator (e.g., client project administrator or Saville Consulting Bureau Services).

This should be completed under the direction of a Saville Consulting Wave qualified user. During supervision, the supervisor should check the speed of completion of each assessee. We recommend aiming to get every assessee to complete the questionnaire within one hour. As a rule of thumb, if someone has completed six blocks of six items within the first 10 minutes they are on course for completion in approximately 60 minutes. If someone has not reached this point, it is worth encouraging them to work faster.

5.3 A Note on Completion Time for Administrators

Saville Consulting Wave Styles have no time limit. We recommend that they are completed in 35 minutes for Professional Styles and 15 minutes for Focus Styles.

When allowing time for completion of Wave Styles questionnaires on a timed event such as an Assessment or Development Center it is worth bearing in mind that there can be a wide range of completion times. We would recommend that you allow an hour to complete Wave Professional Styles and 30 minutes for Wave Focus on a timed event, and that individuals are scheduled to complete the assessment before a coffee or meal break.

5.4 Administration to Accommodate Disabilities

If you have established that an individual who will be completing a Wave Styles questionnaire has a disability that you may need to accommodate in the administration, then you can make contact with your local Saville Consulting contact to go through issues and considerations in making any necessary accommodations to an administration.

Some of the common accommodations you have to make in three areas are given below to help Wave Users have an understanding of some of the common accommodations for disability.

Visual

While some people with visual disabilities may be able to complete Wave Styles without the need for accommodation, others may wish to have the support of additional accessibility software or hardware they have been set up to use. In other cases, it may be appropriate to have a trained reader to read the questions and note the answers for an individual assessee. Often this can be successfully accomplished on the telephone rather than needing to have the individual present in person. Clearly, this raises issues of confidentiality for the reader who should be given clear instructions not to disclose the individual's responses from the administration session and be suitably trained in test and questionnaire administration. It may be that an administration will be longer than usual, so typically no instruction is given on the speed of completion to individuals with visual impairments. Ask the assessee what accommodation would be effective.

Auditory

Individuals with hearing impairments are unlikely to need accommodation in an invited access administration (although if they require technical support this may need to be accommodated). In a supervised administration, accommodation may be needed to ensure that the hearing impaired individual gets any initial instruction on logging in and using the computer. It may be that an individual signing in the appropriate language or the administrator taking care to allow the hearing impaired individual to lip read are appropriate accommodations. Communicate with the assessee on what accommodation would be effective.

Movement

Individuals with disabilities that are related to movement and coordination may have their own devices and software to allow them to use the computer and as a result this may require no accommodation when using Saville Consulting Wave Styles in Invited Access format. In other cases, in either Invited or Supervised Access modes a suitable accommodation may include providing an administrator to record the responses to the assessment. Ask the assessee what accommodation would be effective.

5.5 Online Administration Instructions

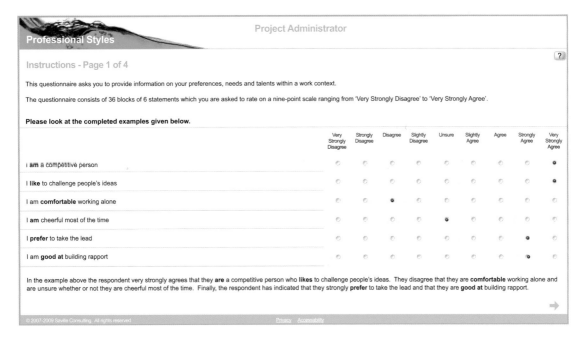

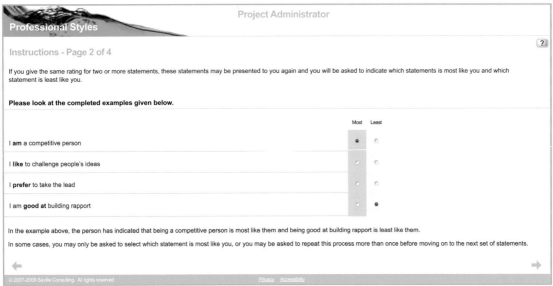

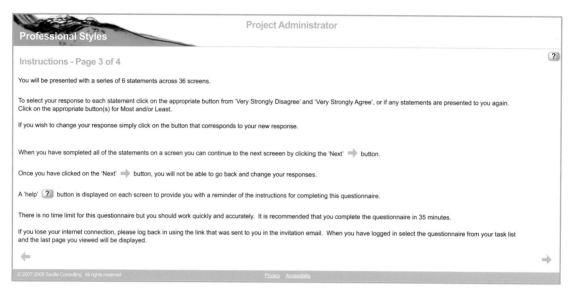

You will be presented with a series of 6 statements across 36 screens.

To select your response to each statement click on the appropriate button from 'Very Strongly Disagree' and 'Very Strongly Agree', or if any statements are presented to you again. Click on the appropriate button(s) for Most and/or Least.

If you wish to change your response simply click on the button that corresponds to your new response.

When you have completed all of the statements on a screen you can continue to the next screen by clicking the 'Next' button.

Once you have clicked on the 'Next' button, you will not be able to go back and change your responses.

A 'help' [?] button is displayed on each screen to provide you with a reminder of the instructions for completing this questionnaire.

There is no time limit for this questionnaire but you should work quickly and accurately. It is recommended that you complete the questionnaire in 35 minutes.

If you lose your internet connection, please log back in using the link that was sent to you in the invitation email. When you have logged in select the questionnaire from your task list and the last page you viewed will be displayed.

Privacy Accessibility

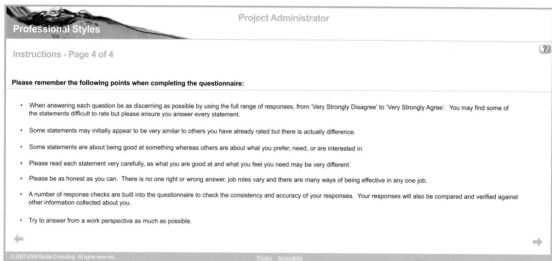

Please remember the following points when completing the questionnaire:

- When answering each question be as discerning as possible by using the full range of responses, from 'Very Strongly Disagree' to 'Very Strongly Agree'. You may find some of the statements difficult to rate but please ensure you answer every statement.

- Some statements may initially appear to be very similar to others you have already rated but there is actually difference.

- Some statements are about being good at something whereas others are about what you prefer, need, or are interested in.

- Please read each statement very carefully, as what you are good at and what you feel you need may be very different.

- Please be as honest as you can. There is no one right or wrong answer, job roles vary and there are many ways of being effective in any one job.

- A number of response checks are built into the questionnaire to check the consistency and accuracy of your responses. Your responses will also be compared and verified against other information collected about you.

- Try to answer from a work perspective as much as possible.

Privacy Accessibility

5.6 Preparation Guides

The preparation guide is available for download at www.savilleconsulting.com.

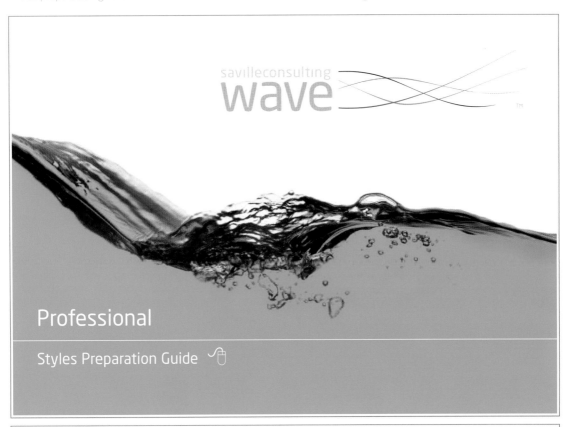

Professional

Styles Preparation Guide

Introducing Professional Styles

This preparation guide is designed to help you understand how to approach the Professional Styles questionnaire. The questionnaire explores a person's motives, preferences, needs and talents within a work context. Research has demonstrated that Saville Consulting Wave questionnaires are powerful predictors of a wide variety of performance and behavior at work.

Professional Styles can help you to:

- understand your motives, preferences, needs and talents in a work context
- find ways to make better use of your preferred working style in your current job, or identify future jobs, environments and cultures suited to your style
- increase your awareness of how your work style impacts your experiences at work

Professional Styles can help employers to:

- understand the motives, preferences, needs and talents of their employees and applicants
- place individuals in positions best suited to their style and the organization's style
- identify areas where individuals might benefit from further development

Completing Professional Styles

The questionnaire is presented on-screen in blocks of six statements which you are asked to rate on a nine-point scale, ranging from 'Very Strongly Disagree' to 'Very Strongly Agree'. Please enter your responses by clicking on the appropriate rating for each statement. You must respond to every statement to progress to the next screen. If you give the same rating for two or more statements, these statements may be presented to you again and you will be asked to indicate which statement is most like you and which statement is least like you.

Look at the completed example on the next page.

39

Example

	Very Strongly Disagree	Strongly Disagree	Disagree	Slightly Disagree	Unsure	Slightly Agree	Agree	Strongly Agree	Very Strongly Agree
It is **important** to me to know how well I have done	○	○	○	○	○	○	○	○	⊙
I **am** an optimist	○	○	○	○	○	○	○	○	⊙
I am **good** at generating ideas	○	○	⊙	○	○	○	○	○	○
Using technology is one of my **strong** points	○	○	○	○	⊙	○	○	○	○
I am **good** at understanding how others feel	○	○	○	○	○	○	○	⊙	○
I am someone who **is** confident when meeting new people	○	○	○	○	○	○	○	⊙	○

In the example, the respondent has indicated that they:

- *very strongly agree* that it is **important** to know how well they have done
- *very strongly agree* that they **are** an optimist
- *disagree* that **they** are **good at** generating ideas
- are *unsure* whether or not technology is one of their **strong** points
- *strongly agree* that they are **good** at understanding how others feel
- *strongly agree* that they are someone who **is** confident when meeting new people

Because the respondent has given the same rating to two pairs of statements, these are presented again, and the respondent is asked to indicate which statement is **most** like them and which statement is **least** like them.

	Most	Least
It is **important** to me to know how well I have done	◉	○
I **am** an optimist	◉	○
I am **good** at understanding how others feel	◉	○
I am someone who **is** confident when meeting new people	◉	○

How to approach Professional Styles

When completing the questionnaire, it is important you consider the following points:

- When answering each question be as discerning as possible by using the full range of possible responses, from 'Very Strongly Disagree' to 'Very Strongly Agree'. Please try to respond from a work perspective.

- Read each statement carefully, as what you are good at and what you feel you need may be very different.

- Respond to the statements as honestly as you can. There are no right or wrong answers; jobs vary and there are ways of being effective in any one job.

- A number of response checks are built into the questionnaire to validate the consistency of your responses. Your responses will also be verified against other information collected.

- Before you complete the questionnaire, you may find it useful to reflect on your own work style. You may also find it useful to consider any feedback you have received from others on your style at work.

- The questionnaire is best completed when you are alert and free from interruptions.

- If you have any special requirements it is important that you make these known immediately to allow appropriate accommodations to be made.

PROF-ST-PG-MTS1-USE
© 2006 Saville Consulting. All rights reserved.

info@savilleconsulting.com
www.savilleconsulting.com

PART 2

INTERPRETATION

6.0 Scale Descriptions

43

6.1 Scale Descriptions – Notes for Interpretation

The likelihood is given of having a significant **Facet Range, Motive-Talent Split** or **Normative-Ipsative Split** on each dimension. This is based on the percentage of the Professional Styles comparison group who had a significant Facet range, Motive-Talent or Normative-Ipsative split.

Interpreting Trends

The Trends section on each page provides information on gender and age differences. *(Please note that as this is based on cross sectional data, 'age' refers to the age of participants at the time of completing the questionnaire).* Those participants who were 39 years of age or less were categorized into the 'younger' group and those over 40 years in the 'older' group. Moderate effect sizes (Cohen, 1988) of .50 of a standard deviation (SD) are shown to indicate differences in terms of gender and age. This section also highlights whether the dimension has a relatively high or low distribution, for example, the Principled dimension has a particularly high mean – people rate themselves highly in this area because being principled is generally considered desirable. Consequently, because the results are relative people may find that they have scored lower than they might have expected, which should be taken into account when giving feedback.

With regards to age group trends, where there is a stated trend in favor of younger or older participants, care must be taken in how this is interpreted. We can say that there *is* a difference between how younger people and older people respond, but we cannot account for *why* this difference exists. It is difficult to separate out 'cohort' effects from 'maturational' effects. In other words, do older people respond differently as a product of growing up in a certain generation (cohort effects) or whether people's personalities show certain changes as they get older. These differences in interpretation must be taken account of when considering age group trends. Group differences and fairness are dealt with in greater detail in the Fairness chapter.

Normative-Ipsative Splits

Where between 10% and 13% of the group had a split on a given dimension, having a split is categorized as a 'moderately common' occurrence, less than 10% as 'less common' and over 13% as 'more common.'

Motive-Talent Splits

Where between 10% and 13% of the group had a split on a given dimension, having a split is categorized as a 'moderately common' occurrence, less than 10% as 'less common' and over 13% as 'more common.'

Facet Range

Where below 40% of the group had a significant facet range on a given dimension, having a facet range is classified as a 'less usual' occurrence. Where 40% to 50% of the group had a facet range, this is categorized as 'common,' and where over 50% of the group had a significant facet range, this is classified as a 'frequent' occurrence.

6.2 How to Use the Scale Descriptions Section

Wave Styles Dimension Scale Name

The left hand side of the pyramid Wave Professional Styles hierarchy displays from top to bottom: cluster, section, dimension, facets

The right hand side of the pyramid displays the competency criterion that the styles scales have been built to predict

This displays from top to bottom: cluster, section, dimension, facets

Possible interpretations of high, low and mid-scorers on the Styles dimension are given

This graph shows the Mean Sten Scores for gender across age groups. Note. This is based on international data (N=10,783)

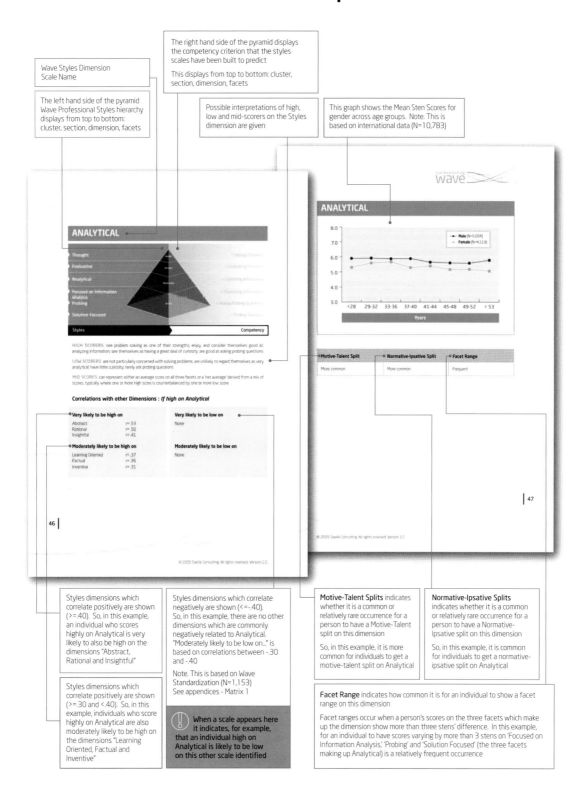

Styles dimensions which correlate positively are shown (>=.40). So, in this example, an individual who scores highly on Analytical is very likely to also be high on the dimensions "Abstract, Rational and Insightful"

Styles dimensions which correlate positively are shown (>=.30 and <.40). So, in this example, individuals who score highly on Analytical are also moderately likely to be high on the dimensions "Learning Oriented, Factual and Inventive"

Styles dimensions which correlate negatively are shown (<=-.40). So, in this example, there are no other dimensions which are commonly negatively related to Analytical. "Moderately likely to be low on..." is based on correlations between -.30 and -.40

Note. This is based on Wave Standardization (N=1,153) See appendices - Matrix 1

When a scale appears here it indicates, for example, that an individual high on Analytical is likely to be low on this other scale identified

Motive-Talent Splits indicates whether it is a common or relatively rare occurrence for a person to have a Motive-Talent split on this dimension

So, in this example, it is more common for individuals to get a motive-talent split on Analytical

Normative-Ipsative Splits indicates whether it is a common or relatively rare occurrence for a person to have a Normative-Ipsative split on this dimension

So, in this example, it is common for individuals to get a normative-ipsative split on Analytical

Facet Range indicates how common it is for an individual to show a facet range on this dimension

Facet ranges occur when a person's scores on the three facets which make up the dimension show more than three stens' difference. In this example, for an individual to have scores varying by more than 3 stens on 'Focused on Information Analysis,' 'Probing' and 'Solution Focused' (the three facets making up Analytical) is a relatively frequent occurrence

ANALYTICAL

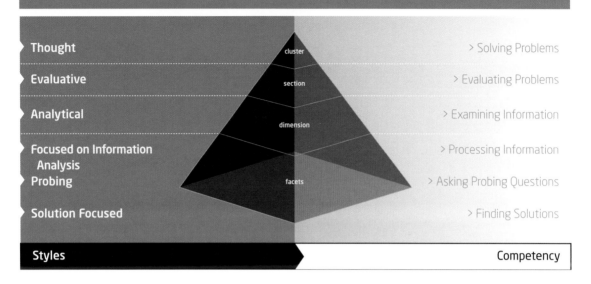

Styles	Competency
Thought	> Solving Problems
Evaluative	> Evaluating Problems
Analytical	> Examining Information
Focused on Information Analysis	> Processing Information
Probing	> Asking Probing Questions
Solution Focused	> Finding Solutions

HIGH SCORERS: see problem solving as one of their strengths; enjoy, and consider themselves good at, analyzing information; see themselves as having a great deal of curiosity; are good at asking probing questions

LOW SCORERS: are not particularly concerned with solving problems; are unlikely to regard themselves as very analytical; have little curiosity; rarely ask probing questions

MID SCORES: can represent *either* an average score on all three facets *or* a 'net average' derived from a mix of scores, typically where one or more high score is counterbalanced by one or more low score

Correlations with other dimensions: *If high on Analytical*

Very likely to be high on		**Very likely to be low on**
Abstract	r= .53	None
Rational	r= .50	
Insightful	r= .41	

Moderately likely to be high on		**Moderately likely to be low on**
Learning Oriented	r= .37	None
Factual	r= .36	
Inventive	r= .31	

ANALYTICAL

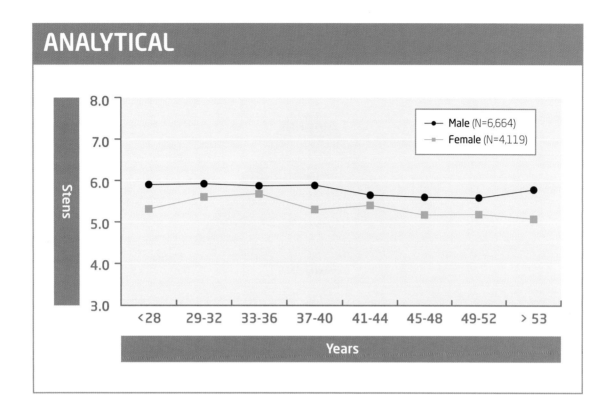

Motive-Talent Split	Normative-Ipsative Split	Facet Range
More common	More common	Frequent

FACTUAL

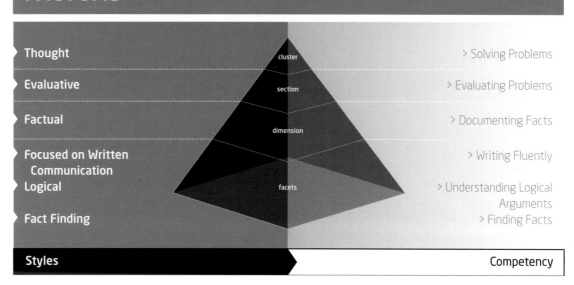

Styles		Competency
Thought	cluster	> Solving Problems
Evaluative	section	> Evaluating Problems
Factual	dimension	> Documenting Facts
Focused on Written Communication		> Writing Fluently
Logical	facets	> Understanding Logical Arguments
Fact Finding		> Finding Facts

HIGH SCORERS: consider that they communicate well in writing; readily understand the logic behind an argument; go to some lengths to ensure that they have all the relevant facts

LOW SCORERS: tend not to communicate well in writing; show less need than most people to understand the logic behind an argument; are happy to work without full information

MID SCORES: can represent *either* an average score on all three facets a 'net average' derived from a mix of scores, typically where one or more high score is counterbalanced by one or more low score

Correlations with other dimensions: *If high on Factual*

Very likely to be high on	Very likely to be low on
None	None
Moderately likely to be high on	**Moderately likely to be low on**
Analytical r= .36	None

FACTUAL

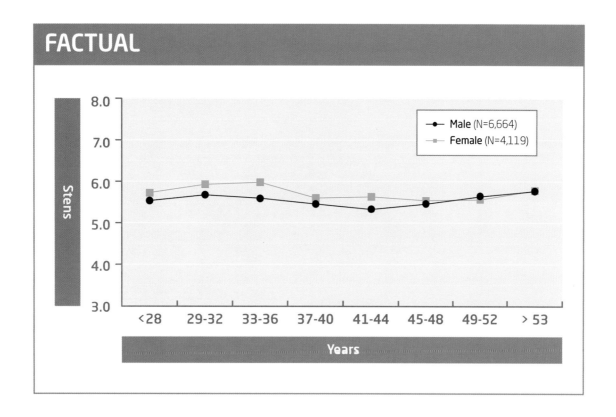

Motive-Talent Split	Normative-Ipsative Split	Facet Range
More common	More common	Frequent

RATIONAL

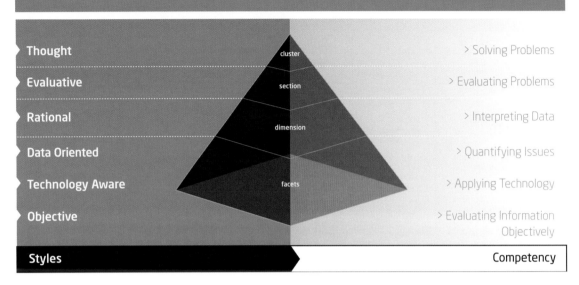

Styles		Competency
Thought	cluster	> Solving Problems
Evaluative	section	> Evaluating Problems
Rational	dimension	> Interpreting Data
Data Oriented		> Quantifying Issues
Technology Aware	facets	> Applying Technology
Objective		> Evaluating Information Objectively

HIGH SCORERS: are very comfortable working with numerical data; are interested, and regard themselves as well versed in information technology; rely heavily on facts and hard, objective data in making decisions

LOW SCORERS: are less comfortable working with numerical data; do not consider using information technology to be one of their strengths; recognize that their decisions are seldom based solely on hard, objective facts

MID SCORES: can represent *either* an average score on all three facets *or* a 'net average' derived from a mix of scores, typically where one or more high score is counterbalanced by one or more low score

Correlations with other dimensions: *If high on Rational*

Very likely to be high on

Analytical   r= .50

Moderately likely to be high on

Abstract   r= .33
Learning Oriented   r= .30

Very likely to be low on

None

Moderately likely to be low on

None

RATIONAL

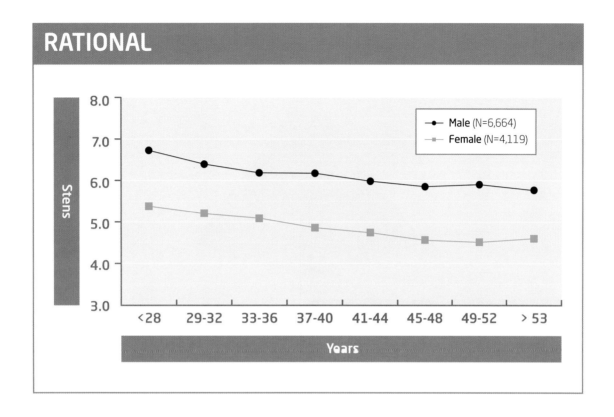

Motive-Talent Split	Normative-Ipsative Split	Facet Range
Less common	Less common	Frequent

LEARNING ORIENTED

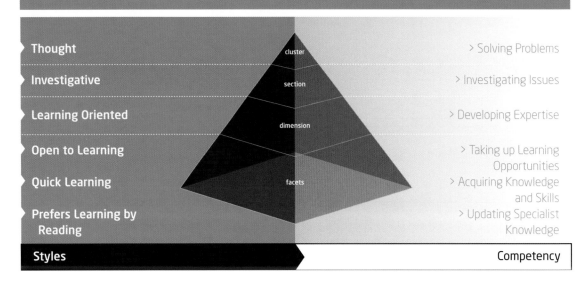

Styles		Competency
Thought	cluster	> Solving Problems
Investigative	section	> Investigating Issues
Learning Oriented	dimension	> Developing Expertise
Open to Learning		> Taking up Learning Opportunities
Quick Learning	facets	> Acquiring Knowledge and Skills
Prefers Learning by Reading		> Updating Specialist Knowledge

HIGH SCORERS: are motivated by, and actively seek opportunities for learning new things; enjoy, and believe they learn a great deal through reading; consider themselves to be very quick learners

LOW SCORERS: are less motivated by, and are unlikely to actively seek, opportunities for learning; consider that they learn relatively little through reading; take time to learn

MID SCORES: can represent *either* an average score on all three facets *or* a 'net average' derived from a mix of scores, typically where one or more high score is counterbalanced by one or more low score

Correlations with other dimensions: *If high on Learning Oriented*

Very likely to be high on

Abstract   r= .49

Moderately likely to be high on

Analytical   r= .37
Rational   r= .30
Change Oriented   r= .30

Very likely to be low on

None

Moderately likely to be low on

None

LEARNING ORIENTED

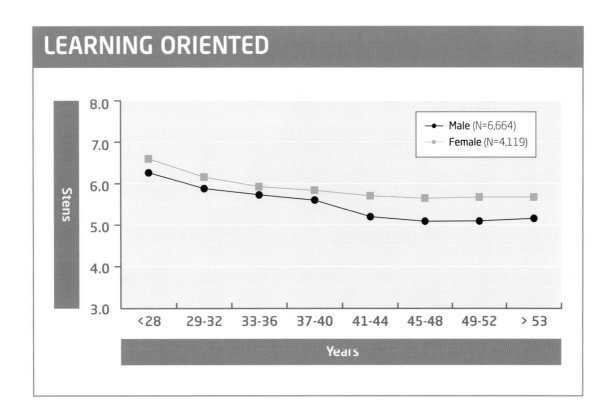

Motive-Talent Split	Normative-Ipsative Split	Facet Range
Less common	Less common	Frequent

PRACTICALLY MINDED

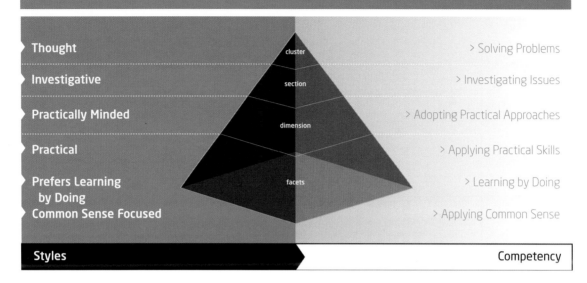

Styles	Competency
Thought	> Solving Problems
Investigative	> Investigating Issues
Practically Minded	> Adopting Practical Approaches
Practical	> Applying Practical Skills
Prefers Learning by Doing	> Learning by Doing
Common Sense Focused	> Applying Common Sense

HIGH SCORERS: are very oriented towards practical work; enjoy, and consider themselves good at, practical tasks; much prefer to learn by doing; like to apply common sense

LOW SCORERS: avoid practical work where possible; tend not to favor learning by doing; recognize that they do not always show common sense

MID SCORES: can represent *either* an average score on all three facets *or* a 'net average' derived from a mix of scores, typically where one or more high score is counterbalanced by one or more low score

Correlations with other dimensions

No high or moderate degree of correlation with other dimensions

PRACTICALLY MINDED

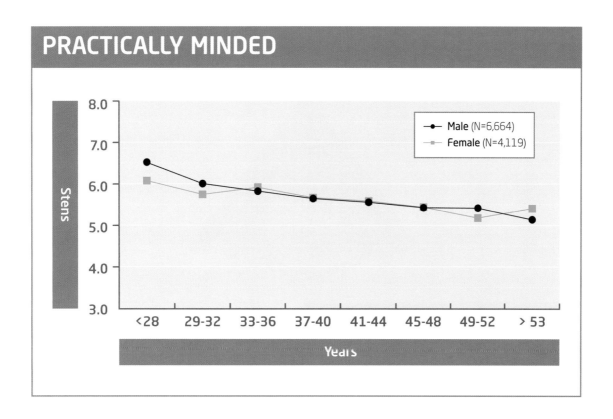

Motive-Talent Split	Normative-Ipsative Split	Facet Range
Moderately common	Moderately common	Frequent

INSIGHTFUL

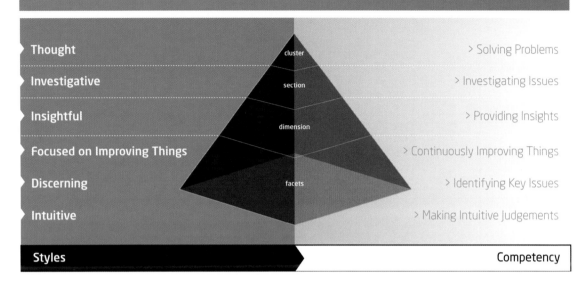

Styles	Competency
Thought — cluster	> Solving Problems
Investigative — section	> Investigating Issues
Insightful — dimension	> Providing Insights
Focused on Improving Things	> Continuously Improving Things
Discerning — facets	> Identifying Key Issues
Intuitive	> Making Intuitive Judgements

HIGH SCORERS: consider themselves very quick at getting to the core of a problem; have a constant need to improve things and believe they are good at identifying ways in which things can be improved; very much trust their intuition about whether things will work

LOW SCORERS: take time to get to the core of a problem; seldom identify ways in which things can be improved; tend to accept things as they are; rarely rely on intuition to guide their judgments

MID SCORES: can represent *either* an average score on all three facets *or* a 'net average' derived from a mix of scores, typically where one or more high score is counterbalanced by one or more low score

Correlations with other dimensions: *If high on Insightful*

Very likely to be high on		Very likely to be low on
Strategic	r= .47	None
Inventive	r= .41	
Analytical	r= .41	

Moderately likely to be high on		Moderately likely to be low on
Purposeful	r= .39	None
Dynamic	r= .38	
Abstract	r= .37	

INSIGHTFUL

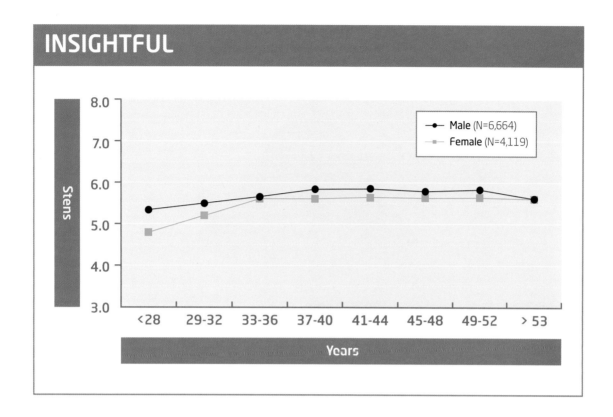

There is a high average self-rating on Insightful. This indicates that in general this is seen as a particularly desirable characteristic. As the results are relative, please bear in mind that that some people may be surprised at scoring as low in this area as their profile indicates as many people consider themselves to be highly Insightful.

Motive-Talent Split	Normative-Ipsative Split	Facet Range
More common	More common	Frequent

INVENTIVE

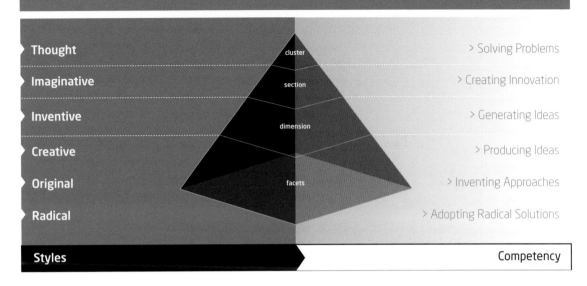

Styles	Competency
Thought	> Solving Problems
Imaginative	> Creating Innovation
Inventive	> Generating Ideas
Creative	> Producing Ideas
Original	> Inventing Approaches
Radical	> Adopting Radical Solutions

HIGH SCORERS: are fluent in generating ideas, produce lots of ideas; are confident in their ability to generate unusual ideas; favor radical solutions to problems; very much enjoy the creative process

LOW SCORERS: do not regard themselves as creative; generate few ideas; seldom come up with original ideas; favor conventional solutions to problems; are less likely to enjoy the creative process

MID SCORES: can represent *either* an average score on all three facets *or* a 'net average' derived from a mix of scores, typically where one or more high score is counterbalanced by one or more low score

Correlations with other dimensions: *If high on Inventive*

Very likely to be high on

Strategic	r= .49
Abstract	r= .44
Insightful	r= .41

Moderately likely to be high on

Change Oriented	r= .36
Empowering	r= .34
Dynamic	r= .34
Convincing	r= .31
Analytical	r= .31

Very likely to be low on

Conforming	r= -.50

Moderately likely to be low on

None

INVENTIVE

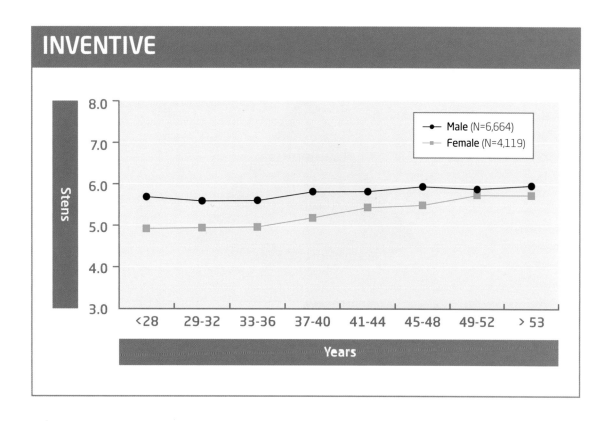

Motive-Talent Split	Normative-Ipsative Split	Facet Range
Less common	Less common	Less usual

ABSTRACT

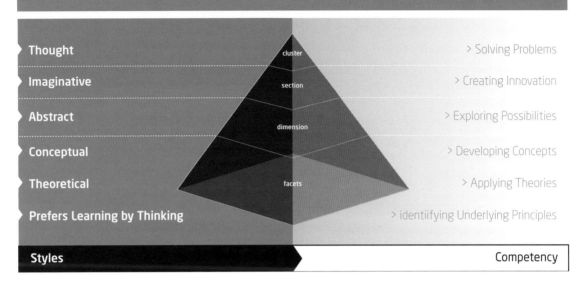

Styles		Competency
Thought	cluster	> Solving Problems
Imaginative	section	> Creating Innovation
Abstract	dimension	> Exploring Possibilities
Conceptual		> Developing Concepts
Theoretical	facets	> Applying Theories
Prefers Learning by Thinking		> identiifying Underlying Principles

HIGH SCORERS: enjoy thinking about and developing concepts; develop concepts well; apply theories a lot; like applying theories and believe they do this effectively; need to understand the underlying principles to learn effectively

LOW SCORERS: have little interest in thinking about or developing concepts; are not interested in applying theories; do not need to understand the underlying principles to learn effectively

MID SCORES: can represent *either* an average score on all three facets *or* a 'net average' derived from a mix of scores, typically where one or more high score is counterbalanced by one or more low score

Correlations with other dimensions: *If high on Abstract*

Very likely to be high on

Analytical	r= .53
Learning Oriented	r= .49
Inventive	r= .44

Moderately likely to be high on

Strategic	r= .38
Insightful	r= .37
Rational	r= .33

Very likely to be low on

None

Moderately likely to be low on

None

ABSTRACT

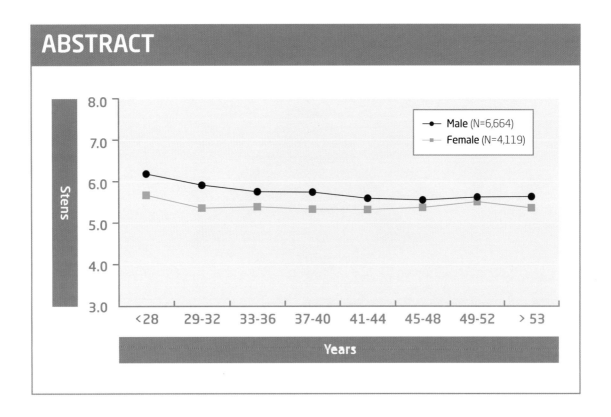

Motive-Talent Split	Normative-Ipsative Split	Facet Range
Moderately common	Moderately common	Common

STRATEGIC

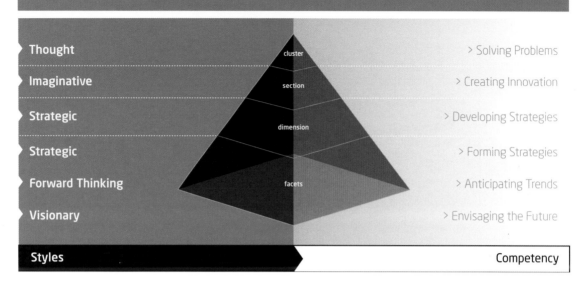

Styles		Competency
Thought	cluster	> Solving Problems
Imaginative	section	> Creating Innovation
Strategic	dimension	> Developing Strategies
Strategic		> Forming Strategies
Forward Thinking	facets	> Anticipating Trends
Visionary		> Envisaging the Future

HIGH SCORERS: are good at developing effective strategies and derive real satisfaction from this; need to have, and feel able to create, an inspiring vision for the future; think long term; are likely to be seen as visionary

LOW SCORERS: show limited interest in developing strategies and do not regard this as their strong point; have some difficulty creating an inspiring vision for the future; take a relatively short term view and prefer to concentrate on the here and now

MID SCORES: can represent *either* an average score on all three facets *or* a 'net average' derived from a mix of scores, typically where one or more high score is counterbalanced by one or more low score

Correlations with other dimensions: *If high on Strategic*

Very likely to be high on

Inventive	r= .49
Insightful	r= .47
Dynamic	r= .41
Striving	r= .41
Empowering	r= .40

Moderately likely to be high on

Abstract	r= .38
Directing	r= .37
Convincing	r= .35
Self-assured	r= .35
Enterprising	r= .35
Purposeful	r= .32
Change Oriented	r= .31

Very likely to be low on

None

Moderately likely to be low on

Conforming	r= -.38

62

STRATEGIC

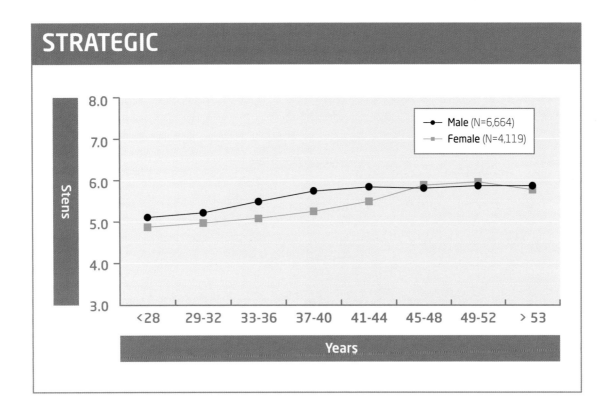

Motive-Talent Split	Normative-Ipsative Split	Facet Range
More common	Moderately common	Common

INTERACTIVE

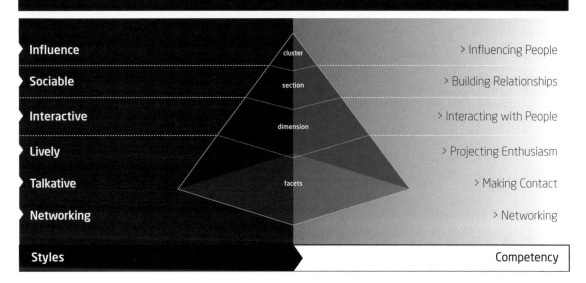

Styles	Competency
Influence	> Influencing People
Sociable	> Building Relationships
Interactive	> Interacting with People
Lively	> Projecting Enthusiasm
Talkative	> Making Contact
Networking	> Networking

HIGH SCORERS: attach a high degree of importance to networking and believe they network very well; are extremely talkative; consider themselves to be very lively

LOW SCORERS: attach little importance to networking; spend little time networking; are very quiet; see themselves as less lively than most people

MID SCORES: can represent *either* an average score on all three facets *or* a 'net average' derived from a mix of scores, typically where one or more high score is counterbalanced by one or more low score

Correlations with other dimensions: *If high on Interactive*

Very likely to be high on		Very likely to be low on
Engaging	r= .58	None
Self-promoting	r= .41	

Moderately likely to be high on		Moderately likely to be low on
Articulate	r= .39	None
Convincing	r= .31	

INTERACTIVE

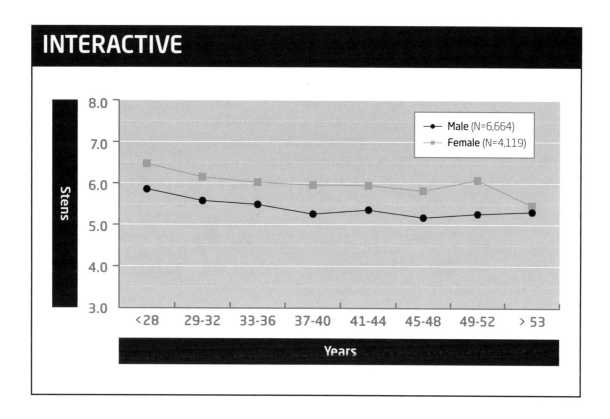

Motive-Talent Split	Normative-Ipsative Split	Facet Range
Less common	Less common	Frequent

ENGAGING

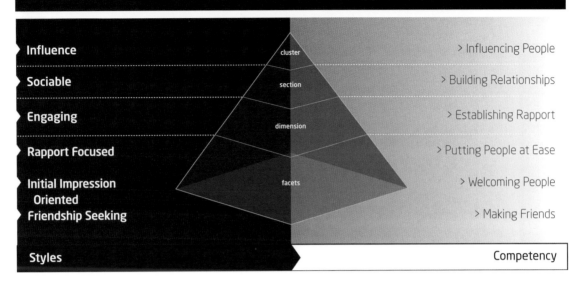

Styles		Competency
Influence	cluster	> Influencing People
Sociable	section	> Building Relationships
Engaging	dimension	> Establishing Rapport
Rapport Focused		> Putting People at Ease
Initial Impression Oriented	facets	> Welcoming People
Friendship Seeking		> Making Friends

HIGH SCORERS: very quickly establish rapport with people; like making new friends and find making friends easy; attach importance to, and believe they are effective in making a good first impression

LOW SCORERS: can take considerable time to establish rapport with people; have limited interest in making new friends; are unlikely to make strong first impression

MID SCORES: can represent *either* an average score on all three facets *or* a 'net average' derived from a mix of scores, typically where one or more high score is counterbalanced by one or more low score

Correlations with other dimensions: *If high on Engaging*

Very likely to be high on		Very likely to be low on
Interactive	r= .58	None
Articulate	r= .40	

Moderately likely to be high on		Moderately likely to be low on
Positive	r= .31	None
Self-promoting	r= .30	

ENGAGING

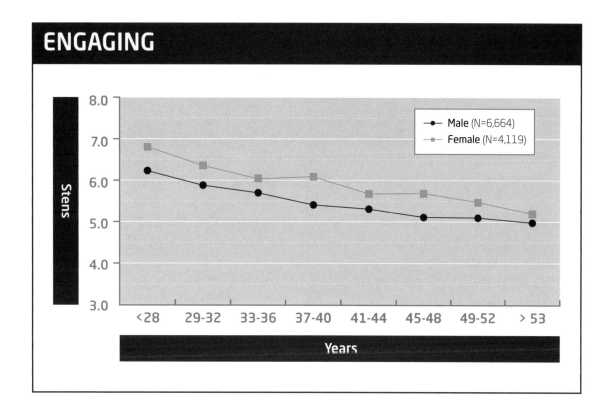

Motive-Talent Split	Normative-Ipsative Split	Facet Range
More common	Less common	Common

SELF-PROMOTING

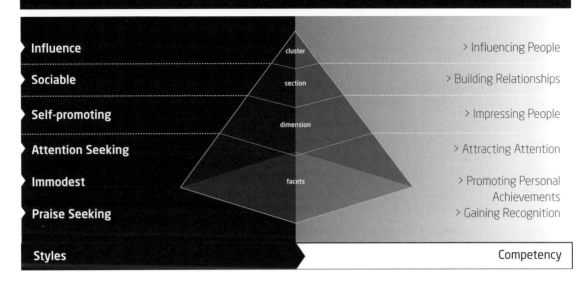

Styles	Competency
Influence	> Influencing People
Sociable	> Building Relationships
Self-promoting	> Impressing People
Attention Seeking	> Attracting Attention
Immodest	> Promoting Personal Achievements
Praise Seeking	> Gaining Recognition

HIGH SCORERS: want people to know about their successes and go to some lengths to bring their achievements to others' attention; like to be, and often find themselves, the center of attention; have a strong need for praise and seek praise when they have done well

LOW SCORERS: are reserved about their achievements and rarely bring them to people's attention; dislike and avoid, becoming the center of attention; seldom look for praise, even when they have done very well

MID SCORES: can represent *either* an average score on all three facets *or* a 'net average' derived from a mix of scores, typically where one or more high score is counterbalanced by one or more low score

Correlations with other dimensions: *If high on Self-promoting*

Very likely to be high on		Very likely to be low on	
Interactive	r= .41	None	

Moderately likely to be high on		Moderately likely to be low on	
Enterprising	r= .33	None	
Engaging	r= .30		

SELF-PROMOTING

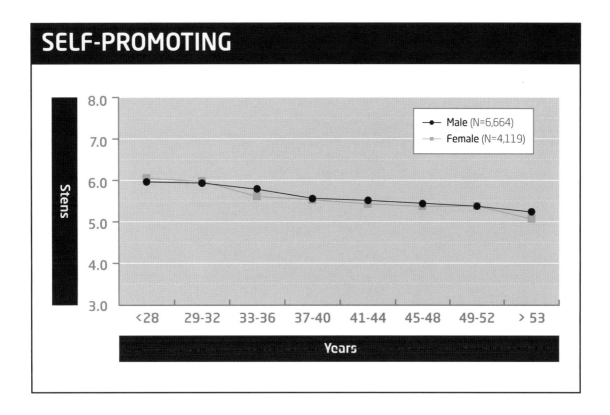

Note: There is a low average self-rating on Self-promoting. This indicates that in general this is not seen as a particularly desirable characteristic. As the results are relative, please bear in mind that some people may be surprised at scoring as high in this area as their profile indicates.

Motive-Talent Split	Normative-Ipsative Split	Facet Range
Moderately common	Less common	Common

CONVINCING

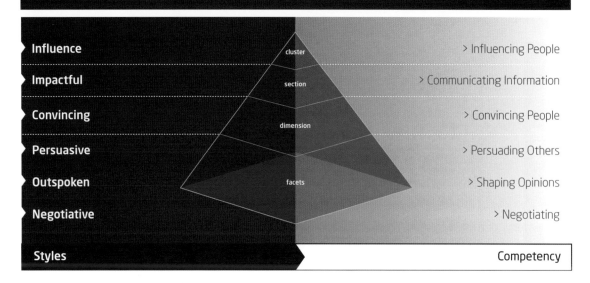

Styles	Competency
Influence	> Influencing People
Impactful	> Communicating Information
Convincing	> Convincing People
Persuasive	> Persuading Others
Outspoken	> Shaping Opinions
Negotiative	> Negotiating

HIGH SCORERS: are eager to bring people round to their point of view and see themselves as very persuasive; are eager to get the best deal and believe they negotiate well; are determined to make people listen to their views and put their point across forcibly

LOW SCORERS: consider themselves to be less persuasive; do not consider themselves strong at negotiation; are less forceful in putting their points across

MID SCORES: can represent *either* an average score on all three facets *or* a 'net average' derived from a mix of scores, typically where one or more high score is counterbalanced by one or more low score

Correlations with other dimensions: *If high on Convincing*

Very likely to be high on

Challenging	r= .55
Enterprising	r= .47
Purposeful	r= .46
Directing	r= .43

Very likely to be low on

None

Moderately likely to be high on

Dynamic	r= .36
Striving	r= .35
Strategic	r= .35
Inventive	r= .31
Interactive	r= .31
Articulate	r= .31

Moderately likely to be low on

Conforming	r= -.30

CONVINCING

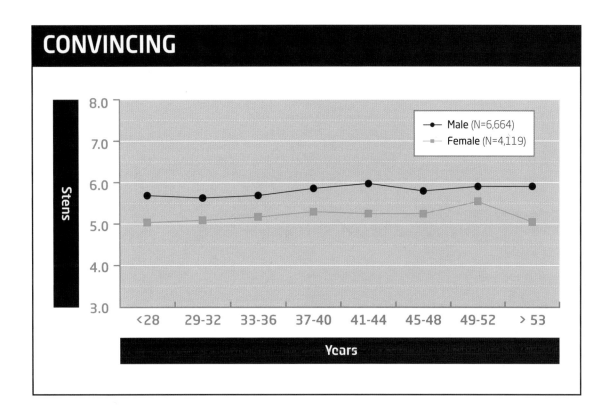

Motive-Talent Split	Normative-Ipsative Split	Facet Range
More common	More common	Common

71

Saville Consulting. All rights reserved. Version 1.0.

ARTICULATE

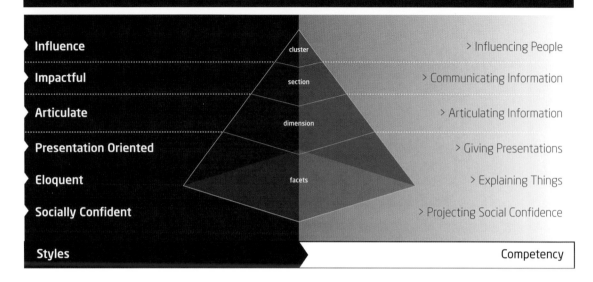

Styles	Competency
Influence	> Influencing People
Impactful	> Communicating Information
Articulate	> Articulating Information
Presentation Oriented	> Giving Presentations
Eloquent	> Explaining Things
Socially Confident	> Projecting Social Confidence

HIGH SCORERS: enjoy, and believe they are good at, giving presentations; enjoy explaining things and consider that they do this well; enjoy meeting and are confident with new people

LOW SCORERS: tend to avoid giving presentations; do not enjoy, nor consider themselves effective at, explaining things; lack confidence when meeting and mixing with new people

MID SCORES: can represent *either* an average score on all three facets *or* a 'net average' derived from a mix of scores, typically where one or more high score is counterbalanced by one or more low score

Correlations with other dimensions: *If high on Articulate*

Very likely to be high on		Very likely to be low on
Engaging	r= .40	None

Moderately likely to be high on		Moderately likely to be low on
Interactive	r= .39	None
Empowering	r= .35	
Composed	r= .35	
Directing	r= .31	
Convincing	r= .31	

ARTICULATE

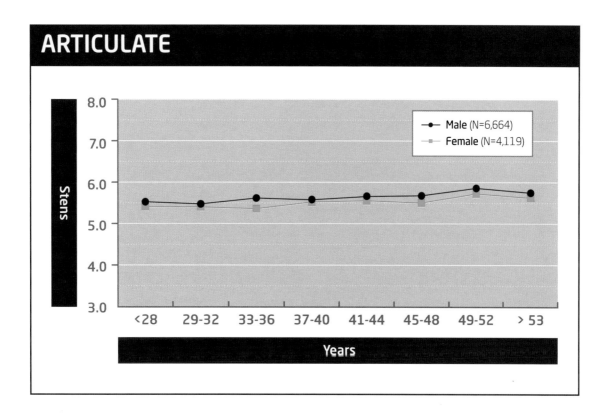

Motive-Talent Split	Normative-Ipsative Split	Facet Range
Moderately common	Less common	Frequent

CHALLENGING

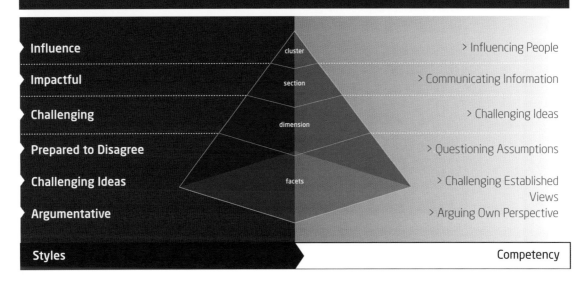

Styles		Competency
Influence	cluster	> Influencing People
Impactful	section	> Communicating Information
Challenging	dimension	> Challenging Ideas
Prepared to Disagree		> Questioning Assumptions
Challenging Ideas	facets	> Challenging Established Views
Argumentative		> Arguing Own Perspective

HIGH SCORERS: frequently challenge other people's ideas; want people to know when they disagree with them and are open in voicing disagreements; really enjoy arguing with people and regularly get involved in arguments

LOW SCORERS: seldom challenge other people's ideas; avoid expressing disagreements openly, preferring to keep their views to themselves; rarely get involved in arguments

MID SCORES: can represent *either* an average score on all three facets *or* a 'net average' derived from a mix of scores, typically where one or more high score is counterbalanced by one or more low score

Correlations with other dimensions: *If high on Challenging*

Very likely to be high on		Very likely to be low on	
Convincing	r= .55	None	
Moderately likely to be high on		**Moderately likely to be low on**	
None		Conforming	r= -.31

CHALLENGING

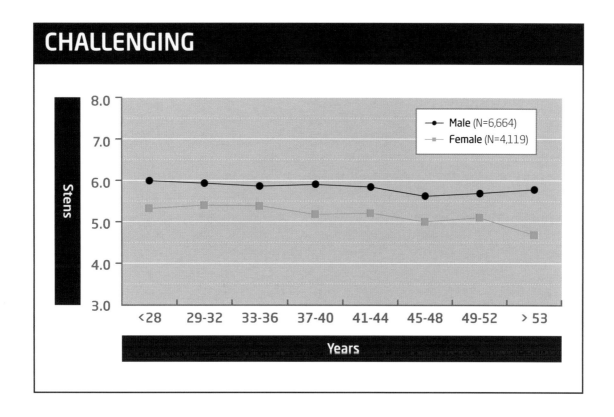

Note: There is a low average self-rating on Challenging. This indicates that in general this is not seen as a particularly desirable characteristic. As the results are relative, please bear in mind that some people may be surprised at scoring as high in this area as their profile indicates.

Motive-Talent Split	Normative-Ipsative Split	Facet Range
Moderately common	Less common	Common

PURPOSEFUL

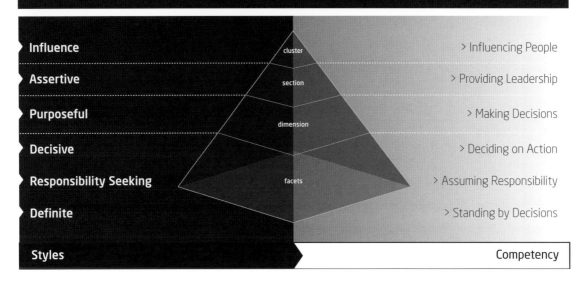

Styles	Competency
Influence	> Influencing People
Assertive	> Providing Leadership
Purposeful	> Making Decisions
Decisive	> Deciding on Action
Responsibility Seeking	> Assuming Responsibility
Definite	> Standing by Decisions

HIGH SCORERS: are very comfortable making quick decisions; relish the responsibility for, and are prepared to make, big decisions; hold definite opinions on most issues and rarely change their minds

LOW SCORERS: take their time over decision making; prefer to let others take responsibility for big decisions; hold few strong opinions and are prone to change their minds

MID SCORES: can represent *either* an average score on all three facets *or* a 'net average' derived from a mix of scores, typically where one or more high score is counterbalanced by one or more low score

Correlations with other dimensions: *If high on Purposeful*

Very likely to be high on		Very likely to be low on	
Directing	r= .50	Conforming	r= -.40
Convincing	r= .46		
Dynamic	r= .45		

Moderately likely to be high on		Moderately likely to be low on	
Enterprising	r= .39	Involving	r= -.30
Insightful	r= .39		
Striving	r= .38		
Composed	r= .36		
Strategic	r= .32		

PURPOSEFUL

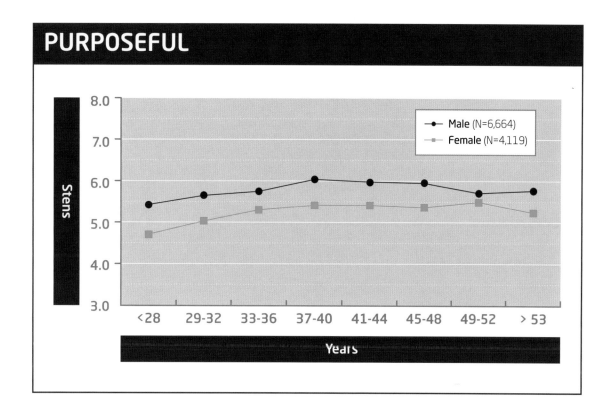

Motive-Talent Split	Normative-Ipsative Split	Facet Range
More common	Less common	Frequent

DIRECTING

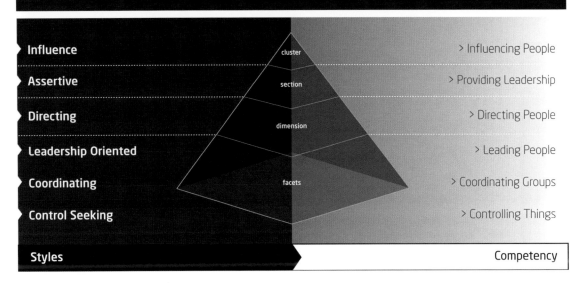

Styles	Competency
Influence	> Influencing People
Assertive	> Providing Leadership
Directing	> Directing People
Leadership Oriented	> Leading People
Coordinating	> Coordinating Groups
Control Seeking	> Controlling Things

(cluster, section, dimension, facets)

HIGH SCORERS: definitely want to take the lead and see leadership as one of their key strengths; are very much inclined to take control of things; enjoy, and believe they are good at, coordinating people

LOW SCORERS: prefer to let other people take the lead; have little desire to take control of things; do not enjoy coordinating people nor regard this as one of their strengths

MID SCORES: can represent *either* an average score on all three facets *or* a 'net average' derived from a mix of scores, typically where one or more high score is counterbalanced by one or more low score

Correlations with other dimensions: *If high on Directing*

Very likely to be high on		Very likely to be low on
Empowering	r= .55	None
Purposeful	r= .50	
Dynamic	r= .47	
Convincing	r= .43	
Enterprising	r= .40	

Moderately likely to be high on		Moderately likely to be low on	
Strategic	r= .37	Conforming	r= -.31
Striving	r= .36		
Articulate	r= .31		

DIRECTING

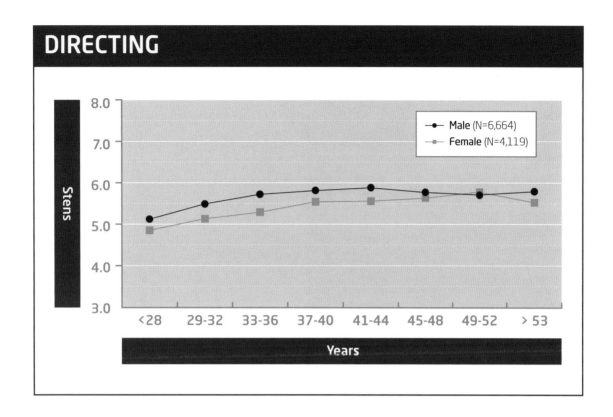

Motive-Talent Split	Normative-Ipsative Split	Facet Range
Moderately common	Less common	Common

EMPOWERING

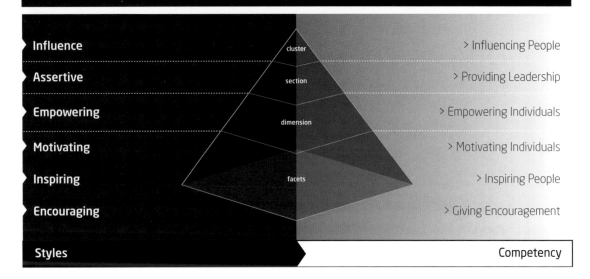

Styles	Competency
Influence	> Influencing People
Assertive	> Providing Leadership
Empowering	> Empowering Individuals
Motivating	> Motivating Individuals
Inspiring	> Inspiring People
Encouraging	> Giving Encouragement

HIGH SCORERS: attach importance to being able to motivate other people and consider themselves adept at finding ways to do this; want, and believe they are able, to be inspirational to others; go out of their way to encourage others

LOW SCORERS: show limited interest in finding ways to motivate others; do not consider themselves to be inspirational to other people; do not go out of their way to encourage others

MID SCORES: can represent *either* an average score on all three facets *or* a 'net average' derived from a mix of scores, typically where one or more high score is counterbalanced by one or more low score

Correlations with other dimensions: *If high on Empowering*

Very likely to be high on		Very likely to be low on	
Directing	r= .55	None	
Strategic	r= .40		

Moderately likely to be high on		Moderately likely to be low on	
Enterprising	r= .37	Conforming	r= -.30
Articulate	r= .35		
Inventive	r= .34		
Dynamic	r= .34		

EMPOWERING

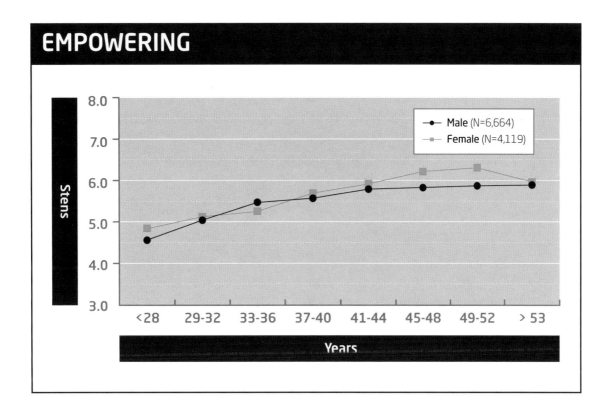

Motive-Talent Split	Normative-Ipsative Split	Facet Range
Less common	Less common	Less usual

SELF-ASSURED

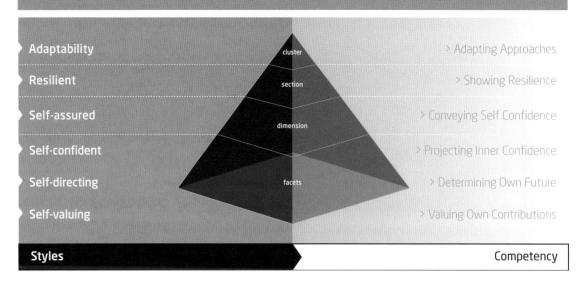

Styles	Competency
Adaptability	> Adapting Approaches
Resilient	> Showing Resilience
Self-assured	> Conveying Self Confidence
Self-confident	> Projecting Inner Confidence
Self-directing	> Determining Own Future
Self-valuing	> Valuing Own Contributions

HIGH SCORERS: are self confident; feel very positive about themselves; have a strong sense of their own worth; feel in control of their own future

LOW SCORERS: are less self confident; are less positive about themselves; have a limited sense of their own worth; feel a limited sense of control over their own future

MID SCORES: can represent *either* an average score on all three facets *or* a 'net average' derived from a mix of scores, typically where one or more high score is counterbalanced by one or more low score

Correlations with other dimensions: *If high on Self-assured*

Very likely to be high on	**Very likely to be low on**
None	None
Moderately likely to be high on	**Moderately likely to be low on**
Strategic r= .35	None
Positive r= .35	

SELF-ASSURED

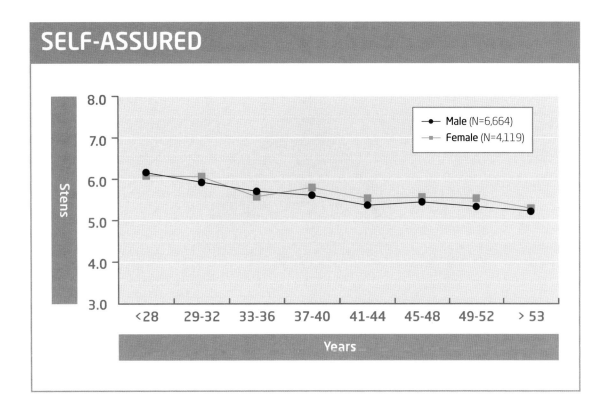

Motive-Talent Split	Normative-Ipsative Split	Facet Range
More common	Moderately common	Frequent

COMPOSED

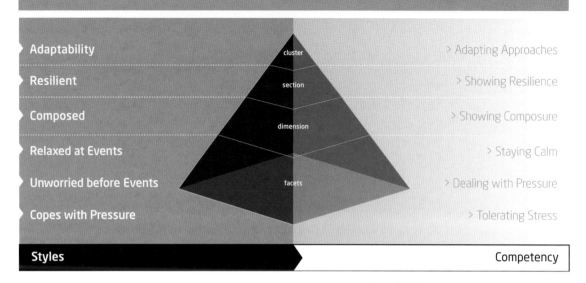

Styles		Competency
Adaptability	cluster	> Adapting Approaches
Resilient	section	> Showing Resilience
Composed	dimension	> Showing Composure
Relaxed at Events		> Staying Calm
Unworried before Events	facets	> Dealing with Pressure
Copes with Pressure		> Tolerating Stress

HIGH SCORERS: are calm; see little point in worrying before important events; rarely get anxious during important events; work well under pressure

LOW SCORERS: feel tense before important events; get anxious during important events; do not cope well with pressure

MID SCORES: can represent *either* an average score on all three facets *or* a 'net average' derived from a mix of scores, typically where one or more high score is counterbalanced by one or more low score

Correlations with other dimensions: *If high on Composed*

Very likely to be high on		Very likely to be low on	
Change Oriented	r= .43	None	

Moderately likely to be high on		Moderately likely to be low on	
Purposeful	r= .36	Conforming	r= -.39
Articulate	r= .35		
Positive	r= .31		

COMPOSED

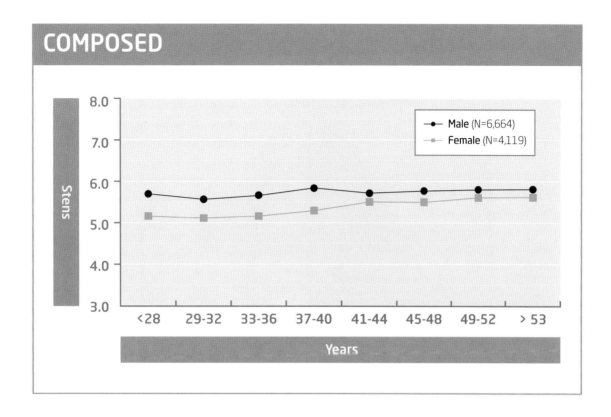

Motive-Talent Split	Normative-Ipsative Split	Facet Range
Less common	Less common	Common

RESOLVING

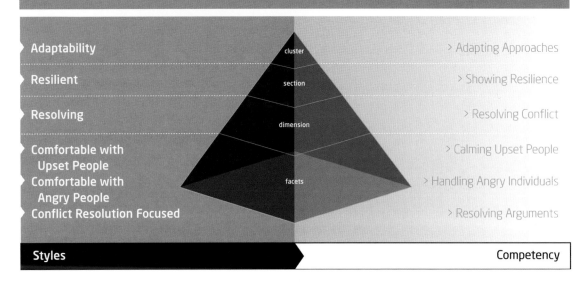

Styles	Competency
Adaptability	> Adapting Approaches
Resilient	> Showing Resilience
Resolving	> Resolving Conflict
Comfortable with Upset People	> Calming Upset People
Comfortable with Angry People	> Handling Angry Individuals
Conflict Resolution Focused	> Resolving Arguments

Pyramid labels: cluster, section, dimension, facets

HIGH SCORERS: quickly resolve disagreements; consider themselves effective at calming angry people down; believe they cope well with people who are upset

LOW SCORERS: do not consider resolving disagreements to be one of their strengths; see themselves as having some difficulty dealing with angry people; recognize that they do not cope well with people who are upset

MID SCORES: can represent *either* an average score on all three facets *or* a 'net average' derived from a mix of scores, typically where one or more high score is counterbalanced by one or more low score

Correlations with other dimensions: *If high on Resolving*

Very likely to be high on		Very likely to be low on
Attentive	r= .47	None

Moderately likely to be high on	Moderately likely to be low on
None	None

RESOLVING

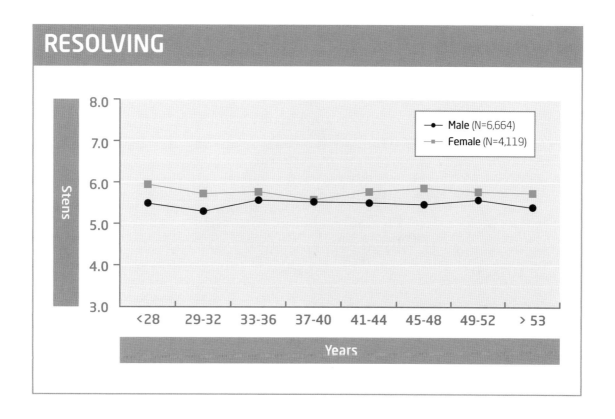

Motive-Talent Split	Normative-Ipsative Split	Facet Range
Moderately common	Moderately common	Common

POSITIVE

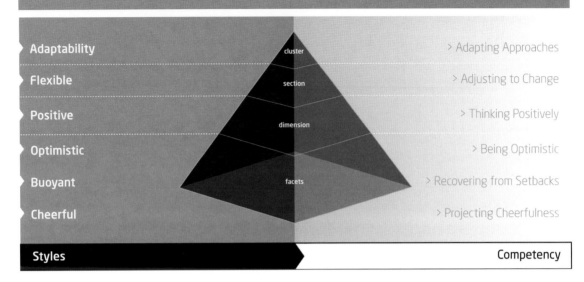

Styles	Competency
Adaptability	> Adapting Approaches
Flexible	> Adjusting to Change
Positive	> Thinking Positively
Optimistic	> Being Optimistic
Buoyant	> Recovering from Setbacks
Cheerful	> Projecting Cheerfulness

HIGH SCORERS: are optimistic; are very cheerful; recover quickly from setbacks

LOW SCORERS: are inclined to be pessimistic; are less cheerful than most people; take time to recover from setbacks

MID SCORES: can represent *either* an average score on all three facets *or* a 'net average' derived from a mix of scores, typically where one or more high score is counterbalanced by one or more low score

Correlations with other dimensions: *If high on Positive*

Very likely to be high on	**Very likely to be low on**
None	None

Moderately likely to be high on		**Moderately likely to be low on**
Change Oriented	r= .35	None
Self-assured	r= .35	
Composed	r= .31	
Engaging	r= .31	

POSITIVE

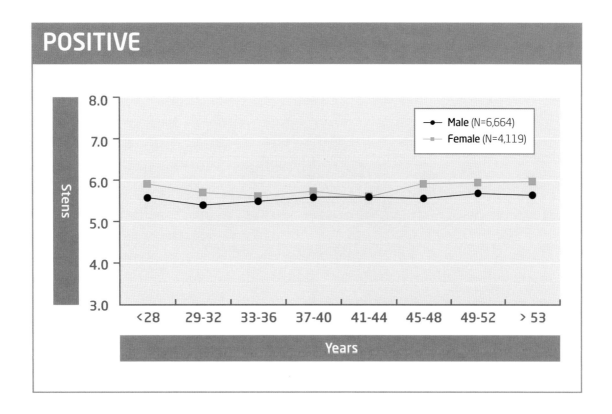

Motive-Talent Split	Normative-Ipsative Split	Facet Range
Less common	Moderately common	Common

CHANGE ORIENTED

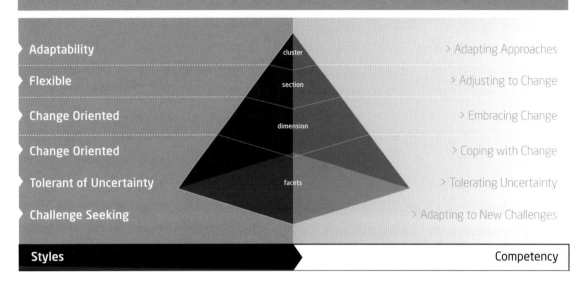

Styles	Competency
Adaptability	> Adapting Approaches
Flexible	> Adjusting to Change
Change Oriented	> Embracing Change
Change Oriented	> Coping with Change
Tolerant of Uncertainty	> Tolerating Uncertainty
Challenge Seeking	> Adapting to New Challenges

HIGH SCORERS: enjoy new challenges and adapt readily to new situations; are positive about and cope well with change; cope well with uncertainty

LOW SCORERS: take time to adapt to new situations; are uncomfortable with change; have difficulty dealing with uncertainty

MID SCORES: can represent *either* an average score on all three facets *or* a 'net average' derived from a mix of scores, typically where one or more high score is counterbalanced by one or more low score

Correlations with other dimensions: *If high on Change Oriented*

Very likely to be high on

Composed	r= .43

Moderately likely to be high on

Inventive	r= .36
Positive	r= .35
Dynamic	r= .33
Strategic	r= .31
Learning Oriented	r= .30

Very likely to be low on

Conforming	r= -.44

Moderately likely to be low on

None

CHANGE ORIENTED

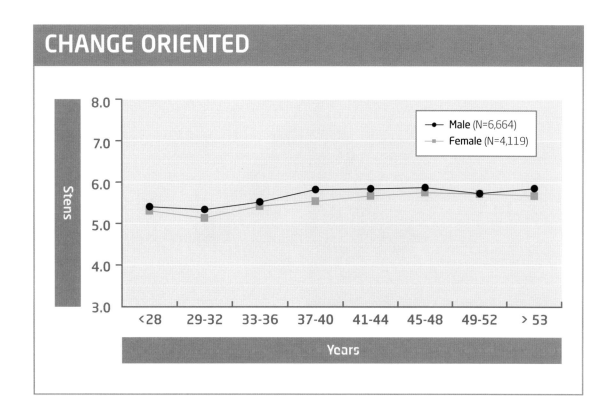

Motive-Talent Split	Normative-Ipsative Split	Facet Range
Moderately common	Less common	Common

RECEPTIVE

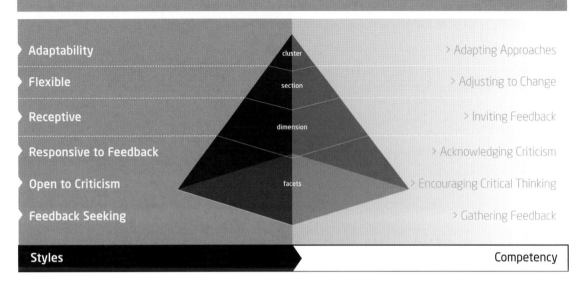

Styles	Competency
Adaptability	> Adapting Approaches
Flexible	> Adjusting to Change
Receptive	> Inviting Feedback
Responsive to Feedback	> Acknowledging Criticism
Open to Criticism	> Encouraging Critical Thinking
Feedback Seeking	> Gathering Feedback

HIGH SCORERS: respond well to feedback from others; encourage people to criticize their approach; actively seek feedback on their performance

LOW SCORERS: respond less well to feedback from others; are reluctant to accept criticism; seldom ask for feedback on their performance

MID SCORES: can represent *either* an average score on all three facets *or* a 'net average' derived from a mix of scores, typically where one or more high score is counterbalanced by one or more low score

Correlations with other dimensions

No high or moderate degree of correlation with other dimensions

RECEPTIVE

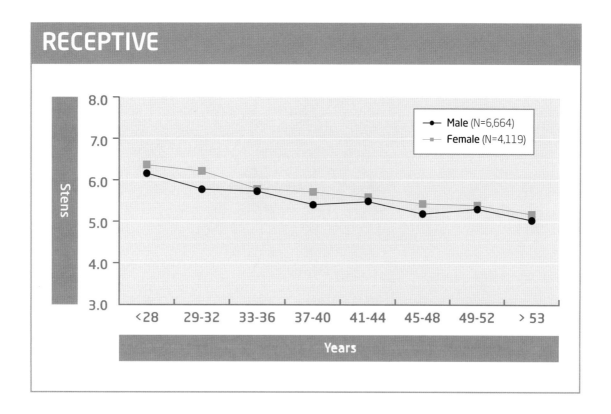

Motive-Talent Split	Normative-Ipsative Split	Facet Range
More common	More common	Frequent

ATTENTIVE

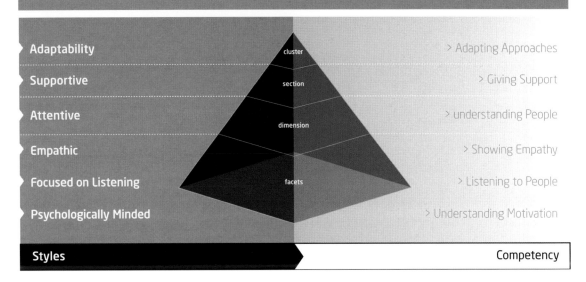

Styles	Competency
Adaptability	> Adapting Approaches
Supportive	> Giving Support
Attentive	> understanding People
Empathic	> Showing Empathy
Focused on Listening	> Listening to People
Psychologically Minded	> Understanding Motivation

HIGH SCORERS: attach importance to, and believe that they are good at, understanding how others are feeling; regard themselves as good listeners; are interested in, and consider themselves adept at, understanding why people behave as they do

LOW SCORERS: show limited interest in and awareness of how others are feeling; recognize that listening to other people is not one of their strong points; show limited interest in understanding people's behavior

MID SCORES: can represent *either* an average score on all three facets *or* a 'net average' derived from a mix of scores, typically where one or more high score is counterbalanced by one or more low score

Correlations with other dimensions: *If high on Attentive*

Very likely to be high on		Very likely to be low on
Accepting	r= .53	None
Involving	r= .51	
Resolving	r= .47	

Moderately likely to be high on	Moderately likely to be low on
None	None

ATTENTIVE

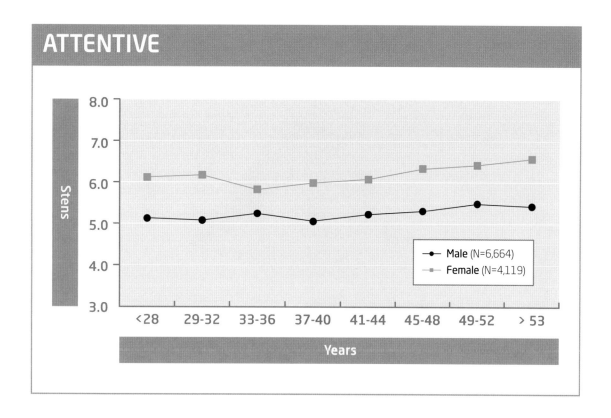

Motive-Talent Split	Normative-Ipsative Split	Facet Range
More common	Moderately common	Common

INVOLVING

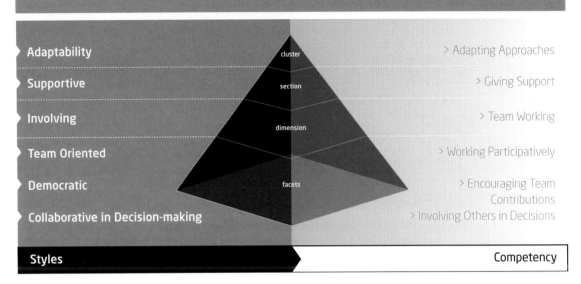

Styles		Competency
Adaptability	cluster	> Adapting Approaches
Supportive	section	> Giving Support
Involving	dimension	> Team Working
Team Oriented		> Working Participatively
Democratic	facets	> Encouraging Team Contributions
Collaborative in Decision-making		> Involving Others in Decisions

HIGH SCORERS: believe they work well in, and enjoy being in, a team; take full account of other people's views; go to considerable lengths to include others in the final decision

LOW SCORERS: prefer, and see themselves as more effective working alone than as part of a team; take limited account of other people's views; prefer to make decisions independently of others

MID SCORES: can represent *either* an average score on all three facets *or* a 'net average' derived from a mix of scores, typically where one or more high score is counterbalanced by one or more low score

Correlations with other dimensions: *If high on Involving*

Very likely to be high on		Very likely to be low on	
Accepting	r= .53	None	
Attentive	r= .51		

Moderately likely to be high on		Moderately likely to be low on	
None		Purposeful	r= -.30

INVOLVING

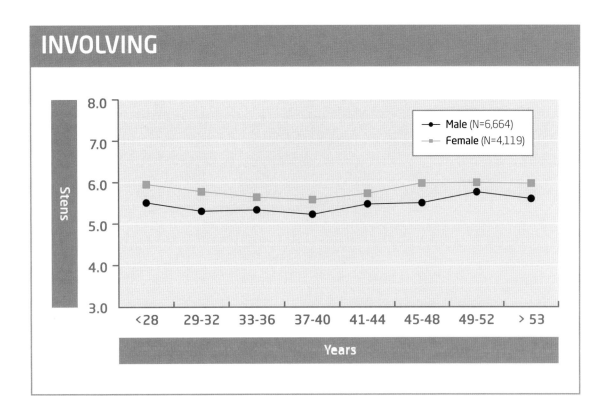

Motive-Talent Split	Normative-Ipsative Split	Facet Range
Moderately common	More common	Frequent

ACCEPTING

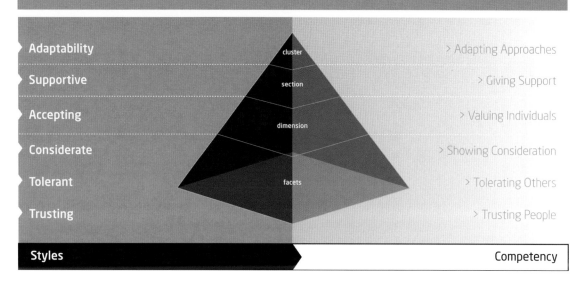

Styles		Competency
Adaptability	cluster	> Adapting Approaches
Supportive	section	> Giving Support
Accepting	dimension	> Valuing Individuals
Considerate		> Showing Consideration
Tolerant	facets	> Tolerating Others
Trusting		> Trusting People

HIGH SCORERS: are very trusting of people; are tolerant; place great emphasis on being considerate towards other people

LOW SCORERS: do not readily trust other people; are inclined to be intolerant; show a lack consideration for others at times

MID SCORES: can represent *either* an average score on all three facets *or* a 'net average' derived from a mix of scores, typically where one or more high score is counterbalanced by one or more low score

Correlations with other dimensions: *If high on Accepting*

Very likely to be high on		Very likely to be low on
Involving	r= .53	None
Attentive	r= .53	

Moderately likely to be high on		Moderately likely to be low on
Principled	r= .31	None

ACCEPTING

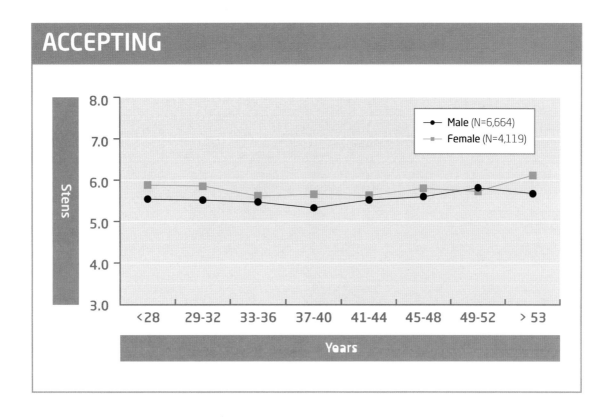

Motive-Talent Split	Normative-Ipsative Split	Facet Range
Moderately common	Less common	Common

RELIABLE

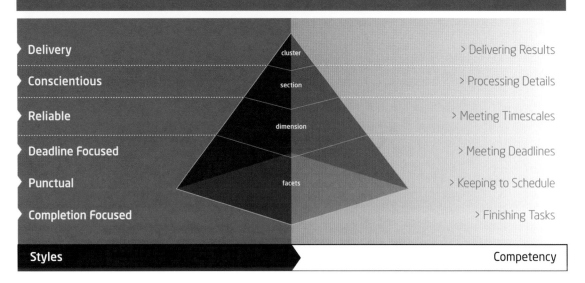

Styles		Competency
Delivery	cluster	> Delivering Results
Conscientious	section	> Processing Details
Reliable	dimension	> Meeting Timescales
Deadline Focused		> Meeting Deadlines
Punctual	facets	> Keeping to Schedule
Completion Focused		> Finishing Tasks

HIGH SCORERS: are conscientious about meeting deadlines; believe they rarely leave things unfinished; consider themselves highly punctual

LOW SCORERS: acknowledge that they have difficulty keeping to deadlines; recognize that finishing tasks is not one of their strengths; do not attach great importance to being punctual and acknowledge that they are often late

MID SCORES: can represent *either* an average score on all three facets *or* a 'net average' derived from a mix of scores, typically where one or more high score is counterbalanced by one or more low score

Correlations with other dimensions: *If high on Reliable*

Very likely to be high on		Very likely to be low on
Organized	r= .59	None
Meticulous	r= .49	
Conforming	r= .47	

Moderately likely to be high on	Moderately likely to be low on
None	None

RELIABLE

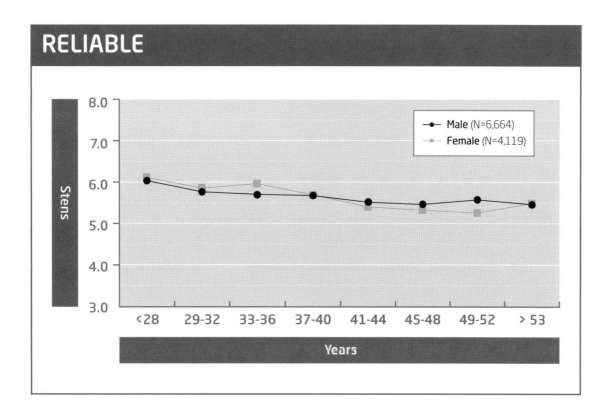

Motive-Talent Split	Normative-Ipsative Split	Facet Range
Less common	Less common	Common

METICULOUS

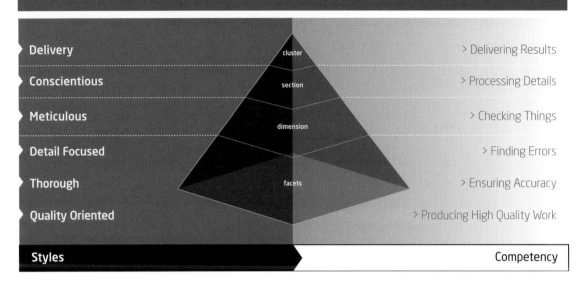

Styles		Competency
Delivery	cluster	> Delivering Results
Conscientious	section	> Processing Details
Meticulous	dimension	> Checking Things
Detail Focused		> Finding Errors
Thorough	facets	> Ensuring Accuracy
Quality Oriented		> Producing High Quality Work

HIGH SCORERS: regard themselves as perfectionists; ensure a high level of quality; want things done properly and consider themselves very thorough in their approach; see themselves as highly attentive to detail

LOW SCORERS: acknowledge that they are prepared to compromise on quality; recognize that they are less thorough than most people; do not regard attention to detail as their strong point

MID SCORES: can represent *either* an average score on all three facets *or* a 'net average' derived from a mix of scores, typically where one or more high score is counterbalanced by one or more low score

Correlations with other dimensions: *If high on Meticulous*

Very likely to be high on	
Organized	r= .50
Reliable	r= .49
Conforming	r= .42

Moderately likely to be high on

None

Very likely to be low on

None

Moderately likely to be low on

None

METICULOUS

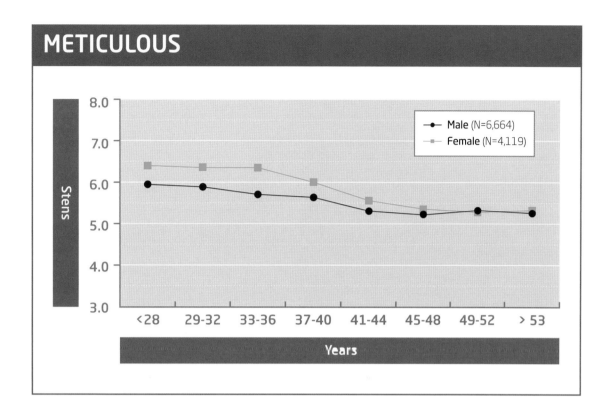

Motive-Talent Split	Normative-Ipsative Split	Facet Range
Less common	Less common	Less usual

CONFORMING

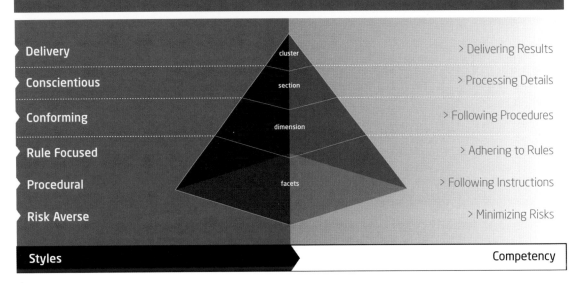

Styles	Competency
Delivery	> Delivering Results
Conscientious	> Processing Details
Conforming	> Following Procedures
Rule Focused	> Adhering to Rules
Procedural	> Following Instructions
Risk Averse	> Minimizing Risks

HIGH SCORERS: need to have rules and adhere strictly to them; like to follow set procedures; regard themselves as decidedly risk averse

LOW SCORERS: are much more likely to deviate from the rules; depart from set procedures; believe they are prepared to take risks in decision making

MID SCORES: can represent *either* an average score on all three facets *or* a 'net average' derived from a mix of scores, typically where one or more high score is counterbalanced by one or more low score

Correlations with other dimensions: *If high on Conforming*

Very likely to be high on		Very likely to be low on	
Reliable	r= .47	Inventive	r= -.50
Meticulous	r= .42	Change Oriented	r= -.44
Organized	r= .40	Purposeful	r= -.40

Moderately likely to be high on		**Moderately likely to be low on**	
None		Composed	r= -.39
		Strategic	r= -.38
		Dynamic	r= -.38
		Enterprising	r= -.32
		Directing	r= -.31
		Challenging	r= -.31
		Empowering	r= -.30
		Convincing	r= -.30

CONFORMING

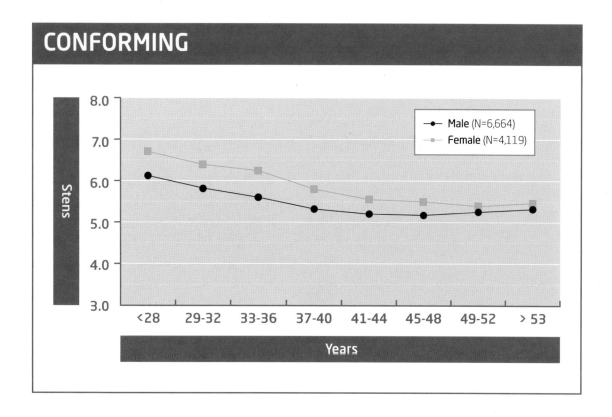

Note: There is a low average self-rating on Conforming. This indicates that in general this is not seen as a particularly desirable characteristic. As the results are relative, please bear in mind that some people may be surprised at scoring as high in this area as their profile indicates.

Motive-Talent Split	Normative-Ipsative Split	Facet Range
Less common	Less common	Less usual

ORGANIZED

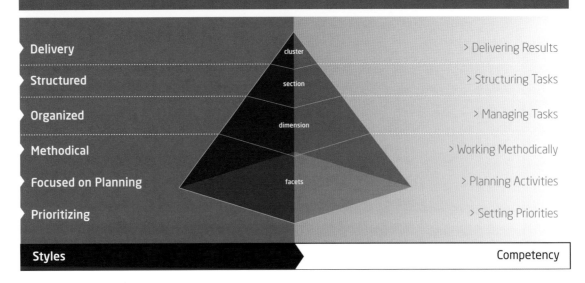

Styles		Competency
Delivery	cluster	> Delivering Results
Structured	section	> Structuring Tasks
Organized	dimension	> Managing Tasks
Methodical		> Working Methodically
Focused on Planning	facets	> Planning Activities
Prioritizing		> Setting Priorities

HIGH SCORERS: are well organized; attach importance to planning; make effective plans; establish clear priorities

LOW SCORERS: are rather disorganized; rarely make plans; seldom establish clear priorities

MID SCORES: can represent *either* an average score on all three facets *or* a 'net average' derived from a mix of scores, typically where one or more high score is counterbalanced by one or more low score

Correlations with other dimensions: *If high on Organized*

Very likely to be high on		Very likely to be low on
Reliable	r= .59	None
Meticulous	r= .50	
Conforming	r= .40	

Moderately likely to be high on	Moderately likely to be low on
None	None

ORGANIZED

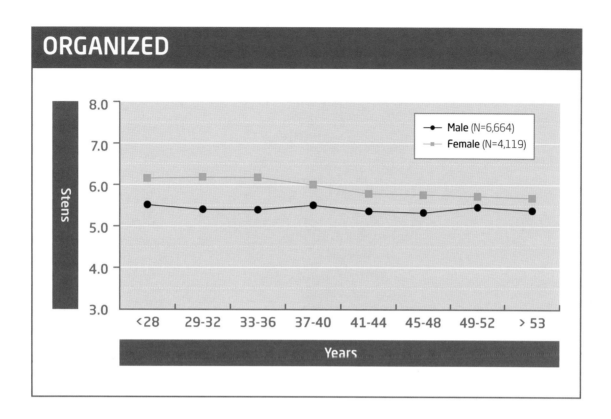

Motive-Talent Split	Normative-Ipsative Split	Facet Range
More common	Less common	Less usual

PRINCIPLED

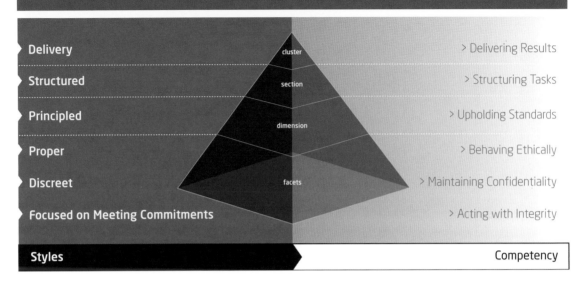

Styles	Competency
Delivery	> Delivering Results
Structured	> Structuring Tasks
Principled	> Upholding Standards
Proper	> Behaving Ethically
Discreet	> Maintaining Confidentiality
Focused on Meeting Commitments	> Acting with Integrity

HIGH SCORERS: are concerned with ethical matters and believe they behave in an ethical fashion; consider maintaining confidentiality to be among their key strengths and can be relied upon to be discreet; view themselves as honoring the commitments they have agreed to

LOW SCORERS: consider themselves to be less focused on ethical matters than most people; attach less importance to maintaining confidentiality than many; recognize that they are prone to be indiscreet; place less emphasis on honoring commitments than others

MID SCORES: can represent *either* an average score on all three facets *or* a 'net average' derived from a mix of scores, typically where one or more high score is counterbalanced by one or more low score

Correlations with other dimensions: *If high on Principled*

Very likely to be high on	Very likely to be low on
None	None
Moderately likely to be high on	**Moderately likely to be low on**
Accepting r= .31	None

PRINCIPLED

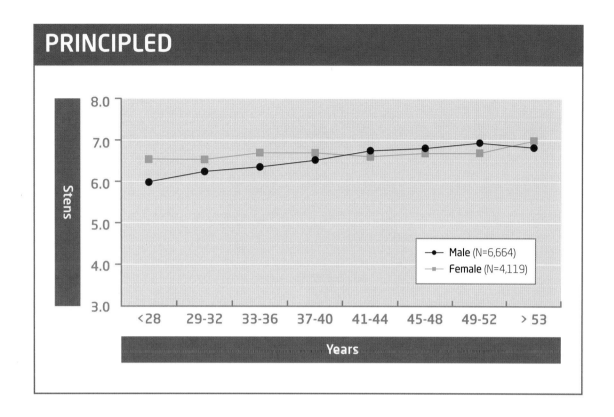

There is a high average self-rating on Principled. This indicates that in general this is seen as a particularly desirable characteristic. As the results are relative, please bear in mind that that some people may be surprised at scoring as low in this area as their profile indicates as many people consider themselves to be highly Principled.

Motive-Talent Split	Normative-Ipsative Split	Facet Range
Moderately common	Less common	Common

ACTIVITY ORIENTED

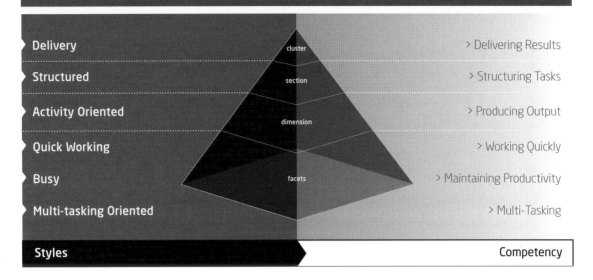

Styles		Competency
Delivery	cluster	> Delivering Results
Structured	section	> Structuring Tasks
Activity Oriented	dimension	> Producing Output
Quick Working		> Working Quickly
Busy	facets	> Maintaining Productivity
Multi-tasking Oriented		> Multi-Tasking

HIGH SCORERS: work at a fast pace; work well when busy; cope well with multi-tasking

LOW SCORERS: prefer to work at a relatively slow pace; work best when not too busy; much prefer to do one thing at a time

MID SCORES: can represent *either* an average score on all three facets *or* a 'net average' derived from a mix of scores, typically where one or more high score is counterbalanced by one or more low score

Correlations with other dimensions

No high or moderate degree of correlation with other dimensions

110

ACTIVITY ORIENTED

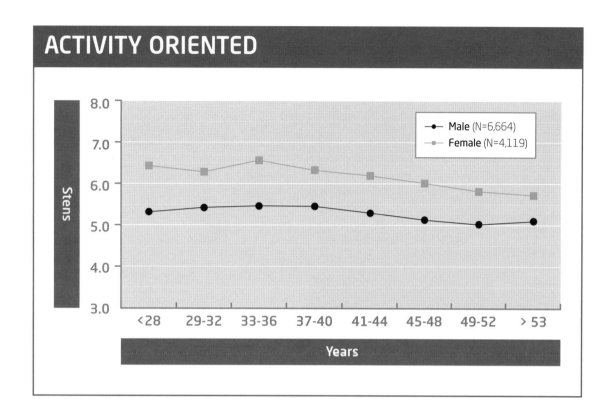

Motive-Talent Split	Normative-Ipsative Split	Facet Range
More common	More common	Common

DYNAMIC

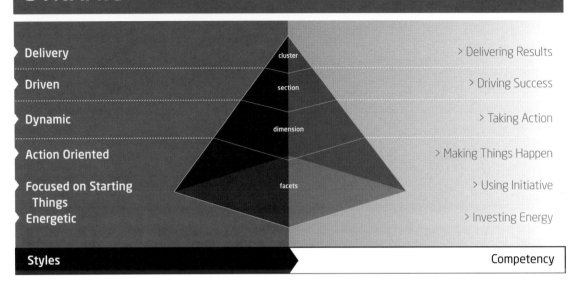

Styles	Competency
Delivery	> Delivering Results
Driven	> Driving Success
Dynamic	> Taking Action
Action Oriented	> Making Things Happen
Focused on Starting Things	> Using Initiative
Energetic	> Investing Energy

Labels within pyramid: cluster, section, dimension, facets

HIGH SCORERS: consider themselves to be very energetic; see themselves as impatient to get things started and good at starting things off; are focused on making things happen

LOW SCORERS: see themselves as less energetic than many people; seldom start things off; seldom see it as their responsibility to make things happen

MID SCORES: can represent *either* an average score on all three facets *or* a 'net average' derived from a mix of scores, typically where one or more high score is counterbalanced by one or more low score

Correlations with other dimensions: *If high on Dynamic*

Very likely to be high on

Directing	r= .47
Purposeful	r= .45
Striving	r= .42
Enterprising	r= .42
Strategic	r= .41

Moderately likely to be high on

Insightful	r= .38
Convincing	r= .36
Empowering	r= .34
Inventive	r= .34
Change Oriented	r= .33

Very likely to be low on

None

Moderately likely to be low on

Conforming	r= -.38

DYNAMIC

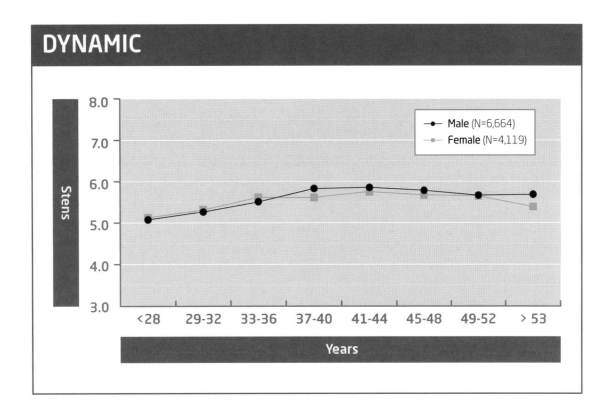

Motive-Talent Split	Normative-Ipsative Split	Facet Range
More common	Moderately common	Frequent

ENTERPRISING

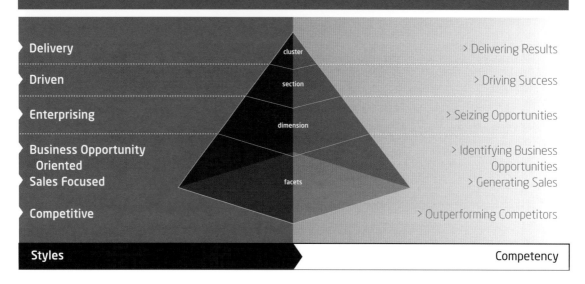

Styles	Competency
▸ Delivery	cluster	> Delivering Results
▸ Driven	section	> Driving Success
▸ Enterprising	dimension	> Seizing Opportunities
▸ Business Opportunity Oriented		> Identifying Business Opportunities
Sales Focused	facets	> Generating Sales
▸ Competitive		> Outperforming Competitors

HIGH SCORERS: regard themselves as highly competitive, with a strong need to win; believe they are good at, and derive real satisfaction from, identifying business opportunities; see themselves as very sales oriented

LOW SCORERS: do not consider themselves to be competitive; acknowledge that they seldom identify good business opportunities; do not see themselves as sales oriented

MID SCORES: can represent *either* an average score on all three facets *or* a 'net average' derived from a mix of scores, typically where one or more high score is counterbalanced by one or more low score

Correlations with other dimensions: *If high on Enterprising*

Very likely to be high on		Very likely to be low on	
Striving	r= .54	None	
Convincing	r= .47		
Dynamic	r= .42		
Directing	r= .40		

Moderately likely to be high on		Moderately likely to be low on	
Purposeful	r= .39	Conforming	r= -.32
Empowering	r= .37		
Strategic	r= .35		
Self-promoting	r= .33		

114

ENTERPRISING

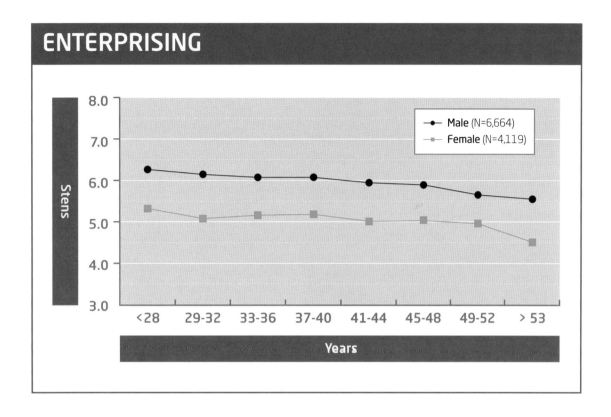

Motive-Talent Split	Normative-Ipsative Split	Facet Range
Less common	Less common	Common

STRIVING

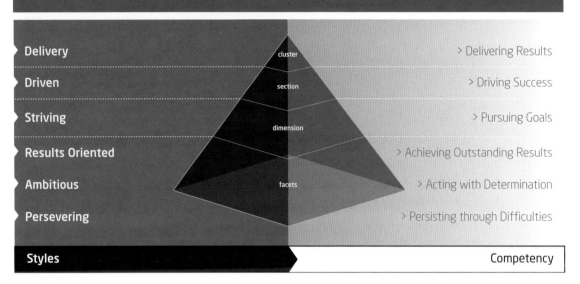

Styles	Competency
Delivery	> Delivering Results
Driven	> Driving Success
Striving	> Pursuing Goals
Results Oriented	> Achieving Outstanding Results
Ambitious	> Acting with Determination
Persevering	> Persisting through Difficulties

HIGH SCORERS: see themselves as very ambitious and want to be successful; attach great importance to achieving outstanding results and believe they do so; are very persevering and keep going no matter what

LOW SCORERS: do not see themselves as ambitious; are not driven to achieve outstanding results; are less inclined than many people to persevere in the face of difficulty

MID SCORES: can represent *either* an average score on all three facets *or* a 'net average' derived from a mix of scores, typically where one or more high score is counterbalanced by one or more low score

Correlations with other dimensions: *If high on Striving*

Very likely to be high on		Very likely to be low on
Enterprising	r= .54	None
Dynamic	r= .42	
Strategic	r= .41	

Moderately likely to be high on		Moderately likely to be low on
Purposeful	r= .38	None
Directing	r= .36	
Convincing	r= .35	

STRIVING

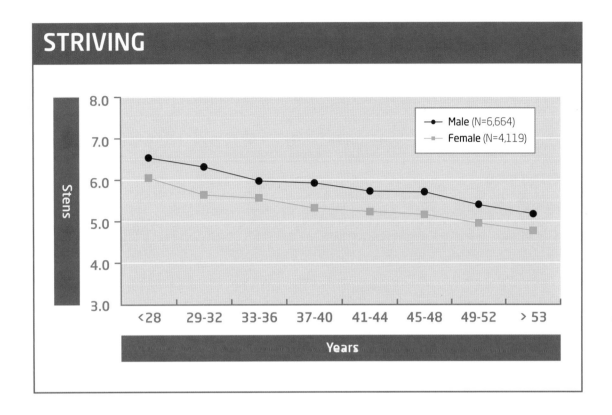

There is a high average self-rating on Striving. This indicates that in general this is seen as a particularly desirable characteristic. As the results are relative, please bear in mind that that some people may be surprised at scoring as low in this area as their profile indicates as many people consider themselves to be highly Striving.

Motive-Talent Split	Normative-Ipsative Split	Facet Range
More common	Less common	Frequent

6.3 Response Style Summary Scales

RATINGS ACQUIESCENCE

- **A measure of how positive or self-critical a person has been in terms of rating themselves (using the normative 1 to 9 scale) across the 36 dimensions**

HIGH SCORERS: have high self-esteem, need to please, or demonstrate a lack of self-criticism

LOW SCORERS: have low self-esteem, a low need to please, or are highly self-critical

MID SCORES: represent individuals who have neither portrayed themselves in a highly critical or highly positive way. They may have used the extremes at both ends of the scale, or tended towards the mid-point of the rating scale

Correlations with dimensions: *If high on Ratings Acquiescence*

Very likely to be high on		Very likely to be low on
Striving	r= .58	None
Directing	r= .53	
Strategic	r= .53	
Empowering	r= .52	
Dynamic	r= .51	
Convincing	r= .50	
Enterprising	r= .49	
Purposeful	r= .46	
Articulate	r= .43	
Inventive	r= .43	
Insightful	r= .43	
Self-assured	r= .42	
Moderately likely to be high on		**Moderately likely to be low on**
Change Oriented	r= .38	None
Composed	r= .35	
Analytical	r= .33	
Interactive	r= .33	
Learning Oriented	r= .32	
Engaging	r= .31	

Note: High Ratings Acquiescence can be indicative of high self-belief. A person with high Ratings Acquiescence may therefore demonstrate artificially high scores in their Wave report. It is important to remember that people can correctly or incorrectly represent themselves on Wave Styles assessments and it is the job of the interpreter to corroborate the indications of the Wave Styles report with further evidence of an individual's work performance.

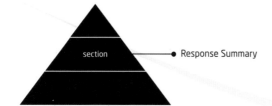

section ————● Response Summary

CONSISTENCY OF RANKINGS

- **A measure of how consistently a person has rank ordered characteristics across the 36 dimensions**

HIGH SCORERS: have been highly consistent in the way they rank ordered items

LOW SCORERS: may have had difficulty rank ordering items, possibly indicating a situational style or low motivation towards the task

MID SCORES: demonstrate that an individual has been as consistent as most people in their rank ordering of items

Correlations with dimensions: *If high on Consistency of Rankings*

Very likely to be high on	Very likely to be low on	
None	None	
Moderately likely to be high on	**Moderately likely to be low on**	
None	Enterprising	r= -0.31
	Convincing	r= -0.30

NORMATIVE-IPSATIVE AGREEMENT

- **The degree of alignment between an individual's Normative and Ipsative scores across the 36 dimensions**

HIGH SCORERS: demonstrate a high degree of alignment in their normative and ipsative scores

LOW SCORERS: have less agreement between their normative and ipsative scores. Low agreement scores on this scale combined with high Rating Acquiescence indicates a very positive self-portrait which may broadly reflect superior work performance across a wide array of behaviors (or over-estimation or exaggeration of one's capabilities, perhaps to portray oneself in an overly favorable light)

Low scores on this agreement scale with low Rating Acquiescence may indicate lower work performance or performance restricted to a more limited set of work behaviors. It may also be representative of individuals under-rating their own capabilities

MID SCORES: demonstrate that individuals has shown a typical degree of alignment between their ratings and rankings of items

Correlations with dimensions

No high or moderate degree of correlation with dimensions

Response Summary •———— section

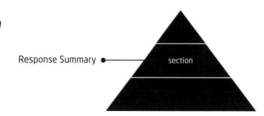

| 119

MOTIVE-TALENT AGREEMENT

- **The degree of alignment between Motive and Talent scores across the 36 dimensions**

HIGH SCORERS: have aligned talents and motives, are 'self-actualized' in that they are good at things that matter to them

LOW SCORERS: demonstrate a high degree of discrepancy between their reported talents and motives; may report feeling 'burnt out' or find little enjoyment in areas where they are talented

MID SCORES: demonstrate that an individual has reported a typical degree of alignment between their talents and motives

Correlations with dimensions

No high or moderate degree of correlation with dimensions

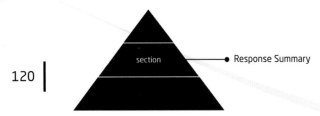

section — Response Summary

7.0 Feedback

Wave Styles assessments are used in a variety of contexts where feedback is an integral part of the process. This chapter starts with examples of three key applications of Wave where feedback is likely to be given. Feedback should only be given by appropriately trained users, so please contact Saville Consulting for more information.

7.1 Applications and Giving Feedback

The application of Wave Styles and exactly how the assessment is used in conjunction with other Wave assessments has a large number of different possible permutations. To give some insight into how Wave Styles can be applied in different contexts, three common applications of Wave are used to highlight some of the issues that should be considered. By the very nature of these applications this is designed to give the user some additional insight from experienced users rather than provide an exhaustive list of what should be considered.

Selection

When giving feedback in a selection context, it is not always necessary to give feedback of the full psychometric profile. Different levels of detail will be appropriate for different situations. For example, if the selection scenario involves having administered Wave to 20 job applicants, it may be appropriate to give two different types of feedback - one to those applicants who are selected for an interview and another to those that were not.

For those not chosen for an interview, it might be more appropriate to give a brief feedback session via telephone and to send them their Personal Report for their own self-awareness/development. For those applicants selected for an interview, the Wave Expert Reports (including their Motive-Talent and Normative-Ipsative splits) can be used to feed into a Competency Based Interview, with particular emphasis on their areas of strength and limitation with relation to the job description/job profile and on verifying areas where there could be potential exaggeration or even false modesty (from normative and ipsative splits).

It also may be appropriate to arrange a session to feedback to the candidates which is separate from the interview, to build self-awareness of the whole profile for the candidate. Again, the format of the feedback may vary significantly for individuals that are appointed and those that are not. For those that are appointed, the Wave Expert report and particularly the preferred culture can help new appointees and their manager think of how best to bring the individual 'on-board' by identifying areas for the new appointee and their manager to focus on in the first 100 days.

Points to consider when giving Wave feedback as part of selection:

- Not always giving full feedback at interview stage – focusing on areas which are particularly relevant to the role
- Look in particular at strengths on the profile to verify
- Or limitations to consider impact on performance
- Feed questions into Competency Based Interview*
- Consider Normative-Ipsative splits as areas for further investigation at interview stage
- Integrate with other information – for example from Assessment Center, etc.*

*If integrating Wave into an Assessment or Development Center matrix or Competency Based Interview, Wave users typically benefit from mapping the criteria they are assessing to the 147 components of Behavior, Ability, Global model of the Saville Consulting Wave Performance Culture Framework. This allows clarity on where each Wave component will relate to performance on the assessment center or interview.

121

Development

When giving feedback for development purposes, it is always important to set aside enough time to give full and thorough feedback on the assessee's or developee's Wave Expert Report Profile. Adequate time should also be allowed for any questions the person may have and for discussion of implications and future development plans stemming from the results of the profile. For Wave Professional Styles, initial development feedback sessions often are timed to run for an hour and a half (although the length of these sessions is highly dependent on the process).

The Saville Consulting Wave model is built on a strengths perspective; the focus should be on identifying areas of strength and building on these. While Saville Consulting emphasize building strengths as the most effective development model for the majority of people, it is also often important for individuals being developed to understand where their strengths are most lacking and could adversely impact on their effectiveness at work. For this reason, the Expert Report profile can also be used to discuss areas of relative weakness and how these can be incorporated into a development plan.

It may be useful in Development settings, to complement the feedback of the Expert Report with the Saville Consulting Wave Development Report. This development report is driven by the same questionnaire which drives the Expert Report and gives an output which is compatible with Development planning. The Development Report was designed to help bridge the gap between diagnosis and action planning.

The Development report contains four sections:

- **Building Strengths** – bullet point advice is given on ways to develop and make the most of existing strengths.
- **Possible Overplayed Strengths** – the potential pitfalls of possessing strengths are outlined followed by an example of an action to avoid the pitfall or unwanted consequence.
- **Managing Limitations** – areas of limitation are areas where it is important that an individual is realistic about and can manage them (rather than attempt to change them).
- **Development Tips** – finally these are areas where the individual lacks strength and could choose to develop these. Bullets are provided to develop these strengths.

The 'Possible Overplayed Strengths' category is often particularly powerful in practice for high performing individuals.

Points to consider when giving Wave feedback for Development:

- Identify and discuss areas of strength on the profile
- Discuss how individuals can 'play to' these (e.g., by selecting work which suits their talents) or develop these further
- Identify and discuss possible limitations and areas for development ('Development Tips' and 'Managing Limitations' on the Development Report)
- Discuss how these areas can be managed and developed and whether they should be, and realistically can be, developed or simply managed
- Explore the implications of areas of strength and areas for development for the individual on work performance
- Work to create a clear picture with the individuals of what impact development or the lack of it could have on their core personal objectives e.g., getting promoted, changing job
- Consider using the Saville Consulting Development Report to complement the development discussion
- Make sure that follow up action and a system of continued development support is in place (e.g., action learning set, individual coaching session, review of development actions)

Wave for Team Development

When giving feedback in a Team Development setting, it is common to use the Saville Consulting Wave Types report – refer to the Types chapter. This provides the opportunity for individuals to understand where their own style will impact on performance and where there are likely synergies with others and potential clashes.

Points to consider when giving Wave feedback for Team Development:

- Before feeding back the results to individuals it is important that the team is clear on its purpose, aims and objectives
- Consider whether team members receive feedback on their results individually before being given Team feedback? If feeding back Wave Expert as well as Types then giving individual feedback before giving group feedback is recommended
- Consider whether each individual will be identified – using a different symbol color when plotting a group profile
- Profile the whole team against the types model (on flipchart or Microsoft® PowerPoint, available from Saville Consulting), by adding each member's four type scores – this can be done anonymously or as part of the facilitation if naming individuals (they can add the scores)
- Ask the team members to consider, what are their combined strengths and potential limitations
- Get the team members to work out what things it will need to manage carefully and where they may benefit from extra resources
- Ask the team members to reflect on past examples if they are an established team
- Get the team members to think about the challenges they are about to face
- Ask the team members what actions they need to take and how they will review the team's actions and performance going forward

7.2 Rich Interpretation - The Deep Dives

Interpreting Facet Ranges - Deep Dive 1

- *Where the range of facet scores within any dimension is of three stens or more, this is indicated by hatching on the dimension scale. Individual facet scores in brackets alongside each verbal facet description are also provided.*

Facet ranges on any dimension provide useful information to the user about an individual's breadth of interest/talent within that dimension. For example, the dimension of 'Articulate' is made up of the facets 'Presentation Oriented,' 'Eloquent' and 'Socially Confident.' Where individuals come out as a sten eight on 'Eloquent' and 'Socially Confident' but as a sten two on 'Presentation Oriented,' it demonstrates that they do not feel their strength lies in this area of Articulate. Their overall score on the dimension 'Articulate' would still be relatively high but they will show a facet range on this dimension.

The overall dimension level score (e.g., Articulate) tends to give a good indication of the level of an individual on a trait (and is a good indicator of performance in the aligned behavioral criterion). The facets and facet ranges give more information as to what that behavior will look like at a detailed behavioral level.

Interpreting Motive-Talent Splits - Deep Dive 2

- *If an individual shows a difference of three stens or more between the Motive and Talent score on a dimension, this is highlighted in the Psychometric Profile of the Expert Report and may indicate a point of interest.*

If Motive higher than Talent:

If Motive is higher than Talent on a particular dimension, this demonstrates that individuals have more interest and motivation than they perceive to have talent in this area. It may be that they would like to be better at this area, but feel their talent is not as high as they would wish.

Individuals may well consider this area as a motivated development need. For example, they want to be more Analytical or Self-assured. There are many reasons why individuals may report such a discrepancy, for instance their work environment or culture might be preventing them from developing this talent or they may simply lack the appropriate skills. This highlights a particular area for development or training to help individuals to achieve their potential in this area.

- **Giving Feedback:**

  - Explore the discrepancy, discuss the potential development need and discuss ways in which the individual could be helped to develop in this area.

  - In a Coaching or Development setting, for example, three points could be considered:

    1. How much of a development need is this area?
    2. How will developing this area impact upon work performance?
    3. To what degree is it possible to develop this area?

If Talent higher than Motive:

If Talent is higher than Motive, this indicates that individuals may feel that they have a high level of effectiveness in this area but they are not particularly interested in or motivated by this area. For example, individuals who showed a Motive-Talent split in this direction on the dimension 'Directing' may feel they are good at being in control of a group and directing others but this is not an area that they are motivated by.

It is important to understand whether the individual finds the talent easy or difficult to display. If displaying this talent is challenging for the individual, this may lead to becoming strained or even mentally drained or stressed by constantly having to push him or herself to demonstrate a talent they have little motivation to display. In such cases external rewards and encouragement may help sustain performance as this behavior is not intrinisically rewarding. For example, showing lower Motive than Talent on the dimension of Organized may lead to burnout if the work environment continuously demands use of such attributes. Another, alternative is to change the demands of the job or change to a job with different demands.

A discrepancy between Motive and Talent could be caused by a number of factors. It is possible that it is due to environmental factors or personal factors. Environmental factors could include unrealistic expectations of the current work environment, e.g., being required to constantly demonstrate behaviors related to a certain attribute, or alternatively feeling de-motivated by the demands of the current work environment. On the personal factors side, this could simply be an area which the individual is not interested in and wishes to avoid working in for future roles.

- **Giving Feedback:**

  - Explore the discrepancy, try to understand why motive is lower (e.g., work environment? Lack of interest in this area?) and what impact this may have on performance (e.g., only rare or occasional display of effective behavior?)

  - In a selection setting, in a structured interview, for example, it may be useful to:

    1. Seek a behavioral example of this dimension
    2. Discuss the underlying motivation
    3. Probe of the frequency of demonstrating this or similar behaviors

Interpreting Normative-Ipsative Splits - Deep Dive 3

- *If individuals show a difference of three stens or more between their Normative and Ipsative score on a dimension, this is highlighted in the Psychometric Profile of the Expert Report and may represent a point of interest*

Normative-Ipsative splits are useful in that they target specifically where there may be some response distortion in the profile. Rather than have a single measure of 'Social Desirability' or even 'Lie scale' which attempts to give an overall indication of whether there was an attempt to distort results, Normative-Ipsative splits pin-point where individuals give more than one version of the truth.

Normative-Ipsative splits on a profile highlight specific areas for further verification. In other words, Normative-Ipsative splits in Saville Consulting Wave allow the Wave user to understand the specific areas where socially desirable responding (or overly self-critical responding) may have occurred.

Differential interpretations of Normative-Ipsative Splits in both directions are discussed on the next page.

If Normative score higher than Ipsative score

Where individuals have a higher normative score than ipsative score, it may mean that they have been less self critical and have possibly exaggerated their normative description. This means that when individuals were asked to rate themselves on this dimension, they have rated themselves relatively highly, in comparison to when they were asked to rank this dimension against other dimensions. Individuals may be responding normatively by answering how they would like to see themselves if given free reign (no constraints on their behavior). For example, they may like to think of themselves as highly 'Attentive' to others. However, when presented with the choice of other areas, the importance of being attentive may be relatively weak (if there are tasks to complete, people to influence, ideas to generate, etc., then being Attentive is less of a priority). One hypothesis in feedback that could be explored is that this may follow through into them acting more like their Normative description when there is no pressure or constraint, but more like their Ipsative score when there is less freedom or more pressure.

It is important to understand the reasons for an individual receiving a Normative-Ipsative split in this direction. It could demonstrate high self-confidence in this area. However, in a recruitment situation, Normative-Ipsative splits in this direction could demonstrate an attempt to distort or 'fake' results consciously or unconsciously in favor of what an individual thinks the interviewer or recruiter is looking for.

> • **Giving Feedback:**
>
>   • Check/Verify for potential exaggeration/distortion
>   • Ask which of the two markers (N or I), they feel is most representative of them
>   • Ask for examples of times when they've demonstrated this attribute. This may help you to build up a clearer picture of if and when each of the two scores is more representative of their behavior.

If Ipsative score higher than Normative score

If individuals have a higher Ipsative score than Normative score, this highlights an area in which they may have been overly modest or self-critical. This area could be one in which the individuals are higher than the rating portrays.

In this situation individuals have rated themselves as lower on this dimension than they have ranked it in a forced-choice situation. So, although individuals may feel that they are not particularly strong in this area, they may have more talent or motive than they initially give themselves credit for. One hypothesis to explore is that they may have a negative stereotype of themselves in this area but that they can give positive, concrete examples of where they have risen to the challenge and demonstrated strong performance in this area. This could lead to them demonstrating better performance on this dimension in the workplace than would be expected from their psychometric profile. A component of feedback which may result from one or more Normative lower than Ipsative splits is helping to build confidence in the area identified.

> • **Giving Feedback:**
>
>   • Check/Verify for potential false modesty/self-criticism
>   • Ask which of the two markers (N or I), individuals feel is most representative of them
>   • Ask for examples of times when individuals have demonstrated this attribute. This may help you to build up a clearer picture of which of the two scores is more representative and which is more distorted (or when effective behavior is more likely to be seen).

7.3 A Note on Scores

It is possible on Wave Professional Styles or Wave Focus Styles to receive a sten score of, for example, nine on an overall dimension, while all three facets that make up the dimension are sten scores of eight. This is to be expected and is a normal property of standardizing scores in a hierarchical scale structure.

The individual facets each measure similar, related, but not perfectly correlated constructs. It is, therefore, more unusual for someone to be high on all three facets of a dimension than to have a combination of scores with some high and low variation. The presence of three consistently high facet scores, therefore, is more unusual than the presence of a mixture of facet scores. The summing and norming of three facet scores into one dimension score may result in a higher score than the simple average of the three facets.

Figure 7.1 An example of Standardizing Sten Scores

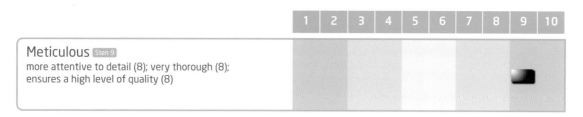

This is also true at the other end of the sten scale where someone has three scores of two on the underlying facets which leads to a dimension sten score of one.

Borderline scores can also create similar effects. The facet scores could all be high sten '8's leading to their sum reading a '9' or even a '10'.

7.4 Feedback Process

This section provides some guidance to users on approaches to delivering feedback based on Wave Styles reports.

Preparing to Give Feedback

Step 1: Consider the purpose

Step 2: Understand job requirements and identify key Wave dimensions or competencies

Step 3: Review entire report(s); think through 'splits' in the Expert Report if appropriate

Step 4: Take notes and/or use highlighter pens to guide feedback discussion

Step 5: Schedule protected time and location for feedback meeting

Step 6: You may choose to integrate with other assessment data (e.g., track record/resume, interview results, aptitude assessments) during the feedback session to look for themes and explore any 'red flags' in more depth. Alternatively, you may decide to keep the information from this report independent from other assessments to avoid 'contamination' until it is time to integrate as part of the decision making process.

Introduction to Feedack

Feeding Back with the Expert Report

1. Completion atmosphere

    "Was there anything when you completed that would lead to the results being unrepresentative?"

    - how did you find it?
    - how long did it take you?
    - anything happening at the time of completion?
    - any distractions during completion?
    - where were you completing it?

2. Review points covered in the 'About this Report' section on page 2 of the report:

    a) Report will look at motives, preferences, needs and talents in work-specific areas

    b) Results are compared against a comparsion group, e.g., 1,000 professionals

    c) Stens = standardized 10 point scale on normal curve with scores of 5 or 6 typical and 1 and 10 highly unusual/rare

    e) Results are based on self-report data so will reflect the individual's own self-perceptions

    d) Report is confidential (explain who will see results)

    e) Data has shelf life of 12 to 24 months, depending on circumstances

3. Introduce Saville Consulting Wave Model hierarchy (4 clusters, 12 sections, 36 dimensions and 108 facets), using page 4 of report as a demonstration (if preferred)

4. Feedback the Executive Summary Profile on page 4 of report

5. Feedback the Response Styles Summary on page 5 of the report (if appropriate)

    NB. This may not be necessary in some situations (e.g., recruitment) as this page is intended to provide detailed information on an individual's response styles and possible inconsistencies (see Scale Descriptions chapter for interpretation of the Response Style Summary scales) for users of the assessment, in order to highlight areas that may need probing in interview.

6.   Feedback detail of the report using the Psychometric Profile on pages 6 to 9 of the report

7.   Explain M-T splits and N-I splits *(see Richer Interpretation section in this chapter for information on interpreting splits)*

8.   Make links – particularly to the impact on performance – i.e., this can be to the performance clusters and sections that the scales are based in.

9.   Use the sandwich approach (i.e., present strengths, areas to develop, then close with strengths)

10.   Summarize key points

10.   Conclusion and next steps

Feedback Approach

- Encourage inputs – ask open questions, ask probing questions; avoid closed, hypothetical and multiple questions
- Be attentive
- Be sensitive
- Be objective – avoid value judgments
- Be specific
- Have the courage to confront all the data

Discussion Process

Use the mnemonic EAT PEAS to guide you through the feedback session.

E   Explain/introduce dimension/facet

A   Ask, or

T   Tell the position/scores on the dimension/facet and splits

P   Probe with behavioral questions

E   Example (ask for examples of times when the individual has demonstrated this approach)

A   Advantages/Disadvantages (more for developmental applications)

S   Summarize

Self-Report Descriptors

Useful terms for Feedback sessions:

- "You describe yourself as..."
- "You suggest that..."
- "You have indicated that..."
- "You see yourself as..."
- "Your responses indicate..."

129

Sten Descriptions

Useful terms for describing sten scores:

Sten 10	"Extremely ..."
Sten 9	"Very ..."
Sten 8	"More Clearly ..."
Sten 7	"Fairly, quite ..."
Sten 6	"Moderately, neither ... nor, average, typical ..."
Sten 5	"Moderately, neither ... nor, average, typical ..."
Sten 4	"Slightly less ..."
Sten 3	"Less inclined ..."
Sten 2	"Shows limited interest in ..."
Sten 1	"Seldom, rarely, disinclined ..."

7.5 Faking and Distortion

An issue that is often raised as a concern when using personality measures, particularly for assessment, is that of 'distortion.' Distortion can take the form of candidates attempting to 'fake' their results by second guessing what a desirable profile would be for a particular job and trying to complete the questionnaire in a way that may achieve the desired result.

Saville Consulting Wave® uses a variety of techniques to help reduce and identify candidate attempts at distortion, both in terms of prevention and detection.

Prevention:

Prior warnings

To reduce the risk of faking or distortion, candidates are encouraged to be honest in their answering of the assessment and prior warnings are given that faking can be detected. For example, the following points are included in Wave administration:

- "Please be as honest as you can. There is no one right or wrong answer; job roles vary and there are many ways of being effective in any one job."

- "A number of response checks are built into the questionnaire to check the consistency and accuracy of your responses. Your responses will also be compared and verified against other information collected about you."

In order to decrease the likelihood of distortion or faking, you should ideally repeat this advice in any supporting emails that you send out prior to the assessment or at the beginning of the session in a supervised administration.

More information is provided in the Administration and Security chapter.

These points are particularly important to reinforce where there is a high stakes selection scenario where the motivation to fake may be greater.

Feedback & Integration of results

To reduce the risk of faking or distortion, it is also advised that prior to completion it is made clear to the candidates that their results will be considered and cross-referenced with other assessment information collected and that their results are likely to be further explored with behavioral examples in a feedback session.

Detection:

Normative-Ipsative Splits

These are built into every dimension of the Wave questionnaires and are designed to detect inconsistencies in responding style. These provide a local means of detecting potential distortion within individual behavioral areas (rather than one scale of "social desirability").

Response Style

The Response Summary Page provides an overview of the individual's style of responding. For example, this will show if an individual has responded in a self-confident way (high Ratings Acquiescence) and has a low Normative-Ipsative Agreement overall (which could suggest potential exaggeration or distortion). It is worth noting that while high Ratings Acquiescence may indicate an overly positive self-view of capability, on average high Ratings Acquiescence scores do show a relationship to higher overall effectiveness at work. In other words, a high Ratings Acquiescence score does not always indicate distortion on the part of the respondent.

In order to establish whether the high Ratings Acquiescence score is a fair reflection of high capability and motivation across many behaviors or whether this reflects distortion, it is important to explore whether there is behavioral evidence to support the high Ratings Acquiescence score. If in the course of the feedback interview, behavioral evidence to support high self-belief such as strong track record of exceptional delivery or performance is not found, this could indicate distortion on the part of the individual. This could take the form of either unconscious distortion – where individuals have an overly positive view of themselves, or conscious distortion – where individuals are making a deliberate, conscious attempt to make themselves look better on the profile.

For more details on interpreting Response Summary Scales see Scale Descriptions chapter.

131

An Example of Faking - Low Motivation Responses

Despite all of these measures, gross distortion can occur and this can be highlighted by several features of the Wave Report.

Gross distortion in a candidate's responses can manifest in an extreme Response Summary overview. See Figure 7.2 below.

Figure 7.2 An example of an invalid administration on the Response Summary

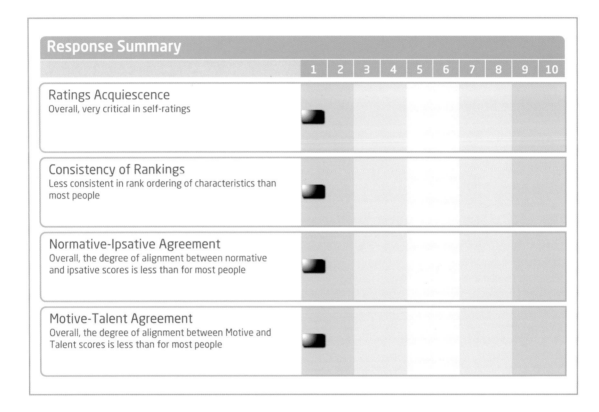

Such a Response Style also results in the following features on the Wave Psychometric Profile:

Figure 7.3 An example of an invalid administration on the Psychometric Profile

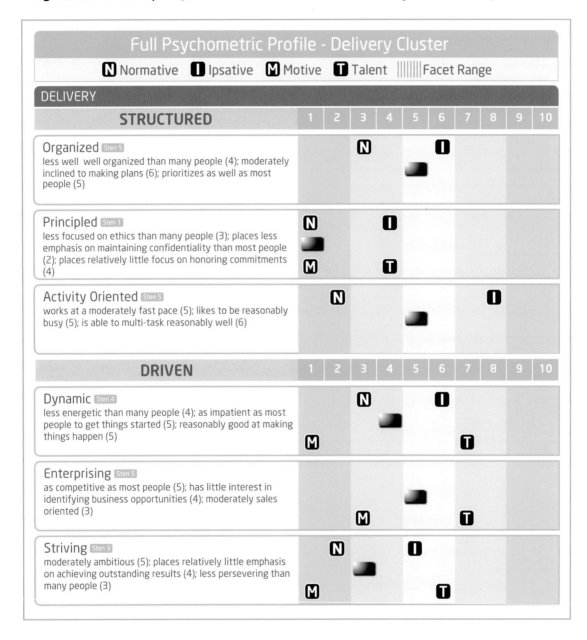

As can be seen from the above example, an invalid administration or attempts at distortion often result in lots of M-T splits and N-I splits on the profile.

Upon further investigation of the candidate in this example, it was found that the responses had followed a clear pattern throughout completion of the questionnaire. By looking at the detailed response pattern, it was found that the candidate had responded to items using a similar pattern across the page. An example of the individual responses to one set of items is given below.

Figure 7.4 An example of the responding pattern of a faking candidate

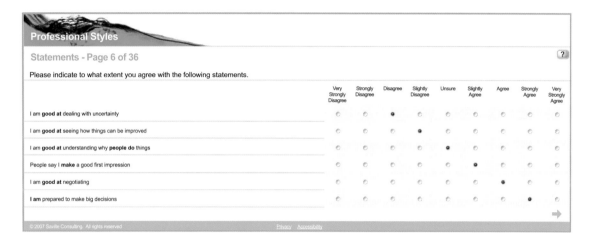

The same pattern was found across all this candidate's responses to the questionnaire.

This individual appears to be poorly motivated and probably did not even read the statements when quickly completing the questionnaire. This administration was not done in a selection setting. However, in a selection or workplace setting, where motivation is high, faking or distortion can still be detected through looking at sections such as the Response Style and Psychometric Profile for evidence of a large number of splits.

8.0 Case Studies

On the following case studies either UK or US Reports have been used.

8.1 Case Study 1

Ronald J. Stouffer

Co-Winner Nobel Peace Prize,
Global Warming

Ronald J. Stouffer is a US meteorologist and contributor towards the Nobel Peace Prize 2007. He was co-author of the 2007 Intergovernmental Panel for Climate Change (IPCC) Report. The IPCC won the Nobel prize along with the former Vice President of the United States, Al Gore. Ron's research formed part of the foundational science featured in the documentary "An Inconvenient Truth".

Ron is a senior research meteorologist in the Climate Dynamics Group of the Geophysical Fluid Dynamics Laboratory (GFDL). This is the US federal research laboratory within the Office of Oceanic and Atmospheric Research and is part of the National Oceanic and Atmospheric Administration. He is one of the leading climate modelers in the world and uses complex numerical models run on supercomputers to study and predict the behavior of the earth's climate system. Thanks to his scientific contributions to climate research over the past three decades, Ron has been a central contributor to each of the assessment reports for the Intergovernmental Panel for Climate Change (IPCC) and was a chapter author for the three most recent reports.

Ron was raised in the small community of Middletown, Pennsylvania. His father worked shifts as a laborer on jet engines for the Federal Government on the local Air Force base. His mother was also employed there as a secretary. With both parents working full time, Ron grew very close to his grandparents, who lived a few blocks up the hill. In his early teens, the Air Force base closed and his father found work in New Jersey. He only came home at weekends until the family relocated to join him when Ron was thirteen.

It was the extreme snow and rain storms that hit central Pennsylvania during his childhood which led Ron to develop into a "weather weenie" and sparked teenage ambitions of becoming a weather forecaster. Ron remembers a snow drift that buried a 35 foot tree in his back yard one winter and his family contended with rain blown in around the front door during a hurricane. Consequently, he went to study meteorology as an undergraduate at the local Penn State University. Interestingly, when he first arrived, an assessment showed that he was most suited to being an earth scientist, secondly a chemist and thirdly a minister. As a first year student he took a second year chemistry course and scored very close to the top in his class. However, meteorology remained his first love.

Ron was excited about going off to university and having the freedom to "eat, drink and be merry". Although he attended the local Lutheran church on a regular basis as a child, he went out of tradition rather than conviction. However, his first two months at Penn State were "easily the most miserable" months of his life. "You could eat and drink but you certainly couldn't be merry, at least not my definition of merry".

That Halloween he was "saved" by a friend's brother from the Campus Crusade for Christ which started him down a path of relying on God and the Bible to answer life's questions. Ron shared that since then his Christian faith has been "a core foundation of who I am". After finishing his BSc in 1976, he made two further discoveries that directed his career trajectory away from weather forecasting and into research. Firstly, he learned that forecasters worked shifts. He knew he didn't want that lifestyle after seeing the effect it had on his father. Secondly, there "were virtually no jobs because of a Federal hiring freeze going on... so I went into graduate school by default".

Ron got married the following year during his Masters program at Penn State. Upon graduation he opted for the financial stability of full time employment rather than pursuing a further degree. Ron was the only person in his extended family to get an undergraduate degree and getting a PhD was considered "beyond the realm". While he had potential job offers from NASA's prestigious Goddard Institute for Space Studies and AccuWeather, Ron chose the Geophysical Fluid Dynamics Laboratory (GDFL) in Princeton. In large part, this was because of the opportunity to work with Syukuro (Suki) Manabe, the most celebrated scientist in his field. Critically, Suki also struck Ron as a "people person" and the location allowed him to raise a family close to both his parents and his in-laws.

Suki was very influential on Ron's career, particularly in terms of mathematical modeling. Suki was the first scientist to join the atmosphere and ocean into a single coupled model to represent the earth's climate system. Ron had referenced Suki's widely-cited 1967 paper on the impact of carbon dioxide on climate change in his Master's program. Within 18 months of joining the GFDL, the two wrote a seminal paper that further reinforced Suki's reputation and also made Ron famous. This publication coincided with changes that flattened the hierarchical organizational structure and Ron was given the opportunity to move from the "support staff" to "scientist" career ladder.

In 1989, the first Intergovernmental Panel for Climate Change (IPCC) was formed in an attempt to gain more recognition of the implications of global warming. Prior to that, Suki had invested considerable time writing climate change reports, including some from the US National Academy of Sciences. Suki was naturally a key player for the IPCC but was rather skeptical about whether the panel would get the traction it hoped. Suki didn't want to travel to the second meeting in Australia. Ron eagerly volunteered to stand in and was catapulted onto the international climate change stage, making his first flight overseas and appearing live on the "Good Morning Australia" TV show. Since then he has written a number of groundbreaking papers on global climate change and has presented to various international dignitaries. He estimates that he has written around 140 peer reviewed papers and "probably built more coupled models, run more simulations and got more data to archive" than anyone else in his field.

A number of Ron's clearest areas of strength in his Wave Professional Styles profile lie in the "Thought" cluster. The whole of this cluster has been included below, to give an overall appreciation of Ron's thought styles.

Ron's "Thought" Styles

THOUGHT											
EVALUATIVE	1	2	3	4	5	6	7	8	9	10

Analytical Sten 10
extremely interested in analyzing information (9); very frequently asks probing questions (9); inclined to seek solutions to problems (8)

Factual Sten 9
likely to communicate well in writing (7); very readily understands the logic behind an argument (9); explores the facts comprehensively (8)

Rational Sten 10
very much likes working with numerical data (9); makes full use of information technology (9); makes decisions largely on the basis of the facts alone (8)

INVESTIGATIVE	1	2	3	4	5	6	7	8	9	10

Learning Oriented Sten 5
moderately focused on learning about new things (5); strongly dislikes having to learn things quickly (2); inclined to learn through reading (8)

Practically Minded Sten 5
oriented towards practical work (7); very little interest in learning by doing (1); shows a great deal of common sense (9)

Insightful Sten 6
moderately focused on constantly improving things (6); very quick to get to the core of a problem (9); unlikely to trust intuition to guide judgment (3)

IMAGINATIVE	1	2	3	4	5	6	7	8	9	10

Inventive Sten 7
generates ideas (7); produces original ideas (8); likely to adopt radical solutions (7)

Abstract Sten 9
good at developing concepts (8); applies theories more than most people (9); very interested in studying the underlying principles (9)

Strategic Sten 7
very inclined to develop strategies (9); takes a long term view (8); unlikely to create a clear vision for the future (3)

137

As we might expect given Ron's significant accomplishments as an earth scientist, his profile suggests particular strengths across all three of the dimensions within the "Evaluative" section. Specifically, he is extremely interested in analyzing information, very often asks probing questions and is inclined to look for solutions. Ron is quick to grasp the underlying logic and explores facts comprehensively. He is also very inclined to work with data and IT, and generally lets the facts guide his decisions.

The Performance Culture Framework reveals specific aspects of the work context that Ron finds the most stimulating. His top three performance enhancers are shown below. Again, these emphasize how much he values the opportunity for problem analysis, using hard data and comprehensive research.

Performance Enhancers

 where there is an emphasis on analyzing and solving problems and problem solving ability is really valued

 where there is an emphasis on quantification and the use of information technology, and decisions are based on hard objective data

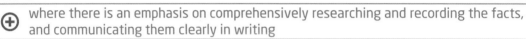 where there is an emphasis on comprehensively researching and recording the facts, and communicating them clearly in writing

Commenting on the skills shown in his "Inventive" dimension, Ron explains that he generally tries to solve technical problems with his modeling by going through a long process of making little incremental tweaks. However, if these don't work he gets frustrated and goes into a "weird space" in which he is willing to explore all angles. It doesn't happen often: some years not at all, occasionally twice in a year. When he does need to "get free ranging", he goes for a walk with no distractions. Then he becomes very creative and will try completely new things. He seeks inspiration from others, past experiences, and finding out "what would happen if I do this…"

This is also tied into the facet range under "Insightful". Ron is very quick to get to the core of a problem. At the same time he reveals that he seldom uses his intuition, preferring to base his judgment on his analysis of facts and data. However, this completely changes when that approach doesn't solve the problem and he gets in his creative zone. Then he completely trusts his intuition to make that leap. Linking this to the "Abstract" dimension, he steps as far as he can away from the problem to view it abstractly. He goes back to first principles, challenges all his assumptions and generally tries to rearrange the puzzle pieces to arrive at a new outcome. He thinks "physically" (i.e. conceptually) about things, in order to figure out what the model is doing. He also considers the implications of the changes he is evaluating: "I might create a mess of new problems!"

Ron shows an interesting facet range on "Strategic". He is unlikely to create a clear vision for the future ("In my business, nobody has a clear vision for the future – there's no such thing"). Although past carbon dioxide emissions have put the world on a course for certain kinds of environmental changes, it is hard to predict how and when nations will react to the warnings, making it impossible to anticipate the net effects. However he does take a long term view. In fact, his models look hundreds or thousands of years out into the future.

The "Practically Minded" dimension highlights that Ron shows a great deal of common sense. He sees this as one of his key strengths. Having said that, his wife has told him his common sense "isn't all that common", because he sees connections and solutions that others don't. He also prefers not to learn by doing but through his research, with input from others and through reading. This clearly ties in with his strong inclination to learn through reading shown under "Learning Oriented". Added to this, Ron emerges as strongly disliking having to learn things rapidly. "The things I'm learning are hard to learn. Having to learn them quickly is awful and in my business there's almost never a reason to learn things quickly". In fact, it is much more important for him to be accurate. He described how in his role in the IPCC he has been quizzed by representatives from 140 countries about his field's research, including the supporting literature, so he must be completely up to date with current research.

138

The strengths Ron displayed across the entire "Thought" cluster are also translated into high levels of competency potential in all three dimensions relating to his skills in solving problems.

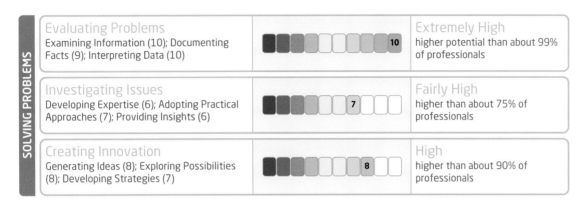

SOLVING PROBLEMS

Evaluating Problems		Extremely High
Examining Information (10); Documenting Facts (9); Interpreting Data (10)	**10**	higher potential than about 99% of professionals

Investigating Issues		Fairly High
Developing Expertise (6); Adopting Practical Approaches (7); Providing Insights (6)	**7**	higher than about 75% of professionals

Creating Innovation		High
Generating Ideas (8); Exploring Possibilities (8); Developing Strategies (7)	**8**	higher than about 90% of professionals

Next, looking at the "Purposeful" dimension (see below), Ron explains that he prefers to take time over decision making: "I don't trust making quick decisions...there has to be a lot of brick work laid before I'm comfortable".

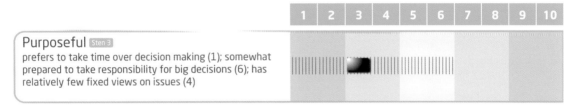

Purposeful Sten 3
prefers to take time over decision making (1); somewhat prepared to take responsibility for big decisions (6); has relatively few fixed views on issues (4)

Notably, Ron came across as fairly comfortable challenging others. "That's what science is – you argue". He joked that he and a close scientist friend agree on 95% of things but spend 95% of their time arguing about the remaining 5%. He also observed that with politicians it's the opposite. "That's what makes the IPCC so hard because scientists focus on their disagreements, but the IPCC is designed to focus on agreements".

Challenging Sten 7
reasonably open in voicing disagreement (6); inclined to challenge others' ideas (8); occasionally gets involved in arguments (6)

Ron's profile (see "Articulate" below) also suggests he can explain things very well, which is clearly a huge asset both in his role and outside of work. For instance, he said that when he explained baseball to a Chinese person he was complimented by a stranger in the crowd for his explanatory skills. "But I'd thought about it beforehand... I made a framework and explained it... then it all makes sense". Despite this, Ron feels very uncomfortable meeting new people. He has worked at the GDFL for over 30 years and so is very familiar with his work colleagues. Despite this, his role in the IPCC has involved considerable international travel and interaction with new contacts, so Ron has had to deal with such situations. It seems his extensive job knowledge helps him convey expertise and confidence.

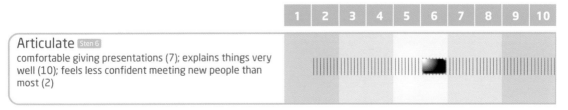

Articulate Sten 6
comfortable giving presentations (7); explains things very well (10); feels less confident meeting new people than most (2)

139

Regarding his flexibility, we can see below that Ron is very receptive: "I don't just ask for feedback, I demand it. I want to know if I'm doing a good job and how to do it better". He also emerges as being quite optimistic, moderately cheerful and recovers reasonably quickly from setbacks. He explained that the times in his career when he suffered big setbacks nearly always led to big breakthroughs. For instance, in the first coupling climate model he ran at GFDL he made a coding error so that the ocean froze by Hawaii and this resulted in his model blowing up. However, when he figured out the coding error, he also realized his framework was wrong. This ultimately resulted in him publishing a key paper in *Nature* with Suki Manabe.

When discussing his sizeable facet range on "Change Oriented", Ron says that "you live in an uncertain world when you are at the cutting edge of science". He associated being less positive about change than most people with his conservative nature: "Change isn't necessarily better".

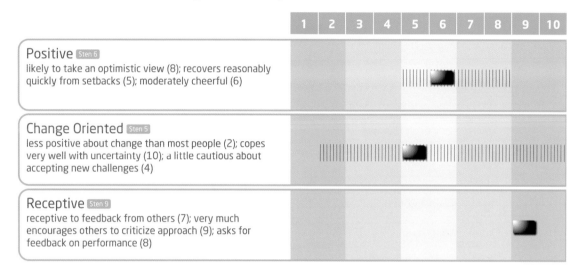

Finally, Ron describes working in an environment of "friendly competition". His coworkers and international colleagues are extremely bright, good problem solvers, pretty competitive and motivated in terms of getting credit for new research findings. "Being competitive, I want to get ahead, but I care about the people around me. I'm not going to get ahead by beating on them". For him, getting ahead involves outworking others, having better judgment and good fortune, but he also commented that once you reach the top levels (where it's a "24/7 kind of deal"), hard work is no longer a differentiator. As far as career goals go, Ron said there were no other research positions he would rather have: "I've achieved nirvana."

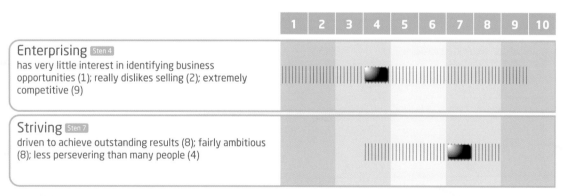

8.2 Case Study 2

Bob Wilson OBE

Soccer Legend, BBC TV Personality

Bob Wilson OBE is a former goalkeeper for Arsenal Football Club, an ex-Scotland international player and an iconic television sports presenter. Through natural talent, burning desire, self-belief, inspirational mentors and sheer graft, he became a world class soccer goalkeeper. Later, he was the voice of Saturday sport in the UK for an entire generation.

© Chris George, 24SE7EN

Bob, the youngest of six children, was born in 1941 in the English market town of Chesterfield. At Christmas in 1949 he was given a Scottish goalkeeping shirt as a present from a relative, igniting a dream to play for his father's country. Sport dominated his early life and came easily to him. His brother Hugh, his elder by three years, honed his competitive spirit by challenging him at cricket, tennis, football, boxing and other sports. Hugh's stake in the footballing success of his brother was profound. Bob concludes: "I could never accept defeat easily as a kid. The more I lost, the more I hated it". Goalkeeping became his obsession, although he admits that he never went to the extremes of one peer, Peter Shilton, who hung from a stair banister for long periods of time in order to grow taller.

At school, Bob's football playing flourished as sport took precedence. At 15 he was picked to play for England schoolboys and so patriotically Scottish was Bob's father that he couldn't watch his son's second match against their northern neighbors. On the strength of his performances, Bob was offered a football apprenticeship at Manchester United but his father refused and encouraged Bob to get an education first.

Bob applied to study Physical Education and History at Loughborough College. Back then, it was one of the best sports colleges in the country. Now, it is a university with an international reputation for sporting excellence. Maintaining a constant ambition to make the most of his football talent, Bob played initially for the college and enjoyed a giant killing run in the English Football Association's Amateur Cup. At 21 he was invited down to Arsenal Football Club for an interview with their manager, former England legend Billy Wright. The David Beckham of his day, Wright was married to one of the Beverley Sisters.

Bob accepted Arsenal's offer and played as an amateur, at the same time holding down a job as a PE teacher. However, stories quickly emerged in the press about unsettled Arsenal players piqued at playing "top-grade soccer with someone who couldn't attend training sessions because he was a schoolmaster". As Bob notes: "I was tolerated, not respected". In fact, he became the last amateur to play soccer in the English first division, signing a professional contract for Arsenal at the age of 22. It was the start of an epic ten year journey which took him from being a desperately keen amateur to a seasoned professional. It also saw him achieve his ambition to play for Scotland – becoming the first English-born player to do so - and Bob made two appearances for Scotland in 1972.

Now loyal to Arsenal for 45 years, Bob played 532 games for the club, 309 of them in the first team. In 1971 he became a legend when he helped them win both the English Football Association Cup and the first division league title. In doing so, he established himself as one of the world's best goalkeepers and earned himself the title of Arsenal's Player of the Year. In 1976, Bob became the UK's first specialist goalkeeping coach at his home club. His legacy is that every top-level English football club now has a full-time goalkeeping coach.

By this stage, Bob had also become the first professional soccer player to make the switch to television. He was the enthusiastic, expert and friendly face of BBC Sports, a role which he retained for two decades. He also found time to establish one of Britain's first goalkeeping schools and in 1998 presided over the most watched TV football match in the UK, the World Cup match between England and Argentina.

But it is not only in sport where father of three Bob has made a difference. The loss of his daughter Anna to a rare form of cancer in 1998 led to the establishment, in 1999, of the Willow Foundation. The charity, which inherited its name from Anna's nickname, organizes special days for seriously ill adults. It was set up in a back bedroom at home by his wife Megs in memory of (and "under instruction" from) their daughter, who entreated her parents to make use of what they had learned from the dreadful experience. Anna suffered a five year illness and sixteen lifesaving operations before her untimely death. The Willow Foundation helps young adults, between the ages of 16 and 40, who live with life-threatening conditions. Previously, little or no attention had been paid to this group of people. Through the Willow Foundation, they are given a chance to escape the pressures of their daily routine and to share quality time with family and friends.

Bob retired from television in 2002 and is now an accomplished author. One of his first books was a history of goalkeeping entitled *You've Got to Be Crazy*. His acclaimed autobiography *Behind The Network* was published in October 2003 and was shortlisted for sports book of the year. In 2008, Bob released *Life in the Beautiful Game*, a personal look at the footballing greats he has met in the course of his career. In 2007 he was awarded the Order of the British Empire (OBE) in recognition of his charitable services through the Willow Foundation.

The Wave Professional Styles questionnaire that Bob completed offers insights into the inspirations, turning points and key talents that enabled him to make the grade from amateur to professional footballer and develop from TV pundit to TV broadcasting professional. Bob called his first book on goalkeeping *You've Got To Be Crazy*. Gordon Banks, one of England's greatest keepers, believed that every match as a goalkeeper was like facing a firing squad and any who did it without preparation were crazy. Bob's preparation skills, seen from the "Delivery" cluster of the Wave Styles questionnaire, are central to his successful style. Three of these dimensions, "Organized", "Reliable" and "Meticulous", are shown below.

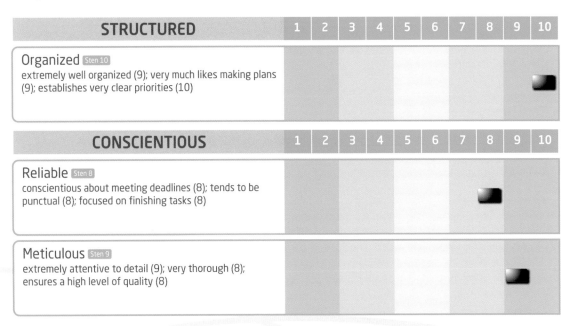

Many top class goalkeepers have been characterized as perfectionists and workaholics. Of himself, Bob says: "I had a natural agility, was quick, had a good pair of hands but had to work and work at the other key areas required of a top class keeper". Bob believes that it is preparation and consistency which separate the good from the great. As his profile indicates, he is supremely well organized, attaches importance to planning, makes effective plans and establishes very clear priorities. He is amongst the top one or two per cent of professionals in this respect. He ensures a high level of quality in wanting things done properly and considers himself very thorough in approach.

142

Bob is also extremely attentive to detail and will rarely leave things unfinished. Essential for goalkeeping success, his meticulous approach was a foundation of his progress and success in the TV world. Throughout his media career, Bob explains that every week was "planned like a military operation".

Over his twenty years broadcasting with the BBC, Bob was responsible for producing logs of every goal, close-up, save or worthwhile camera moment, while also making the time to work as Arsenal's goalkeeping coach. Bob considers himself conscientious about meeting deadlines, and is highly punctual. These are both attributes he needed in his time on commercial television with the ITV network. Then, overrunning into a commercial break by just a few seconds risked considerable loss of advertising revenue.

Goalkeeping is for many people the most dangerous and lonely position in soccer. As well as physical attributes, says Bob, it also relies on daring, courage and judgment. The "Insightful" dimension of his profile, which concerns his ability to make such intuitive judgments, is shown below.

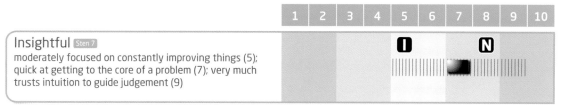

	1	2	3	4	5	6	7	8	9	10
Insightful Sten 7 moderately focused on constantly improving things (5); quick at getting to the core of a problem (7); very much trusts intuition to guide judgement (9)							**I**	**N**		

Bob is discerning and quick at getting to the core of a problem. He very much trusts his intuition to guide his judgment. A good example of his strength in this area is his coverage of the controversial 1986 Soccer World Cup "Hand of God" incident between long term rivals England and Argentina.

For non-fans, this was the moment when Argentine legend Maradona scored a goal which helped knock England out of the World Cup. At the post-match conference, Maradona described the goal as being "a little with the head of Maradona and a little with the hand of God". Immediately on seeing it live, Bob announced that Maradona had handled the ball, thus committing a clear foul. Soccer pundits accused him of his "usual goalkeeping bias" but replays insisted on by Bob and Maradona's later confession both proved his original judgment to be correct. Bob has also prioritized "Insightfulness" rather more in the normative (free rating) task than the ipsative (forced ranking) task. This has resulted in the separate N (normative) and I (ipsative) markers in the "Insightful" dimension of his profile. One of several possible interpretations for this normative-ipsative split is that in some situations, Bob is able to be more insightful than others. Bob may, for example focus more on the facts than on his insight when under pressure and when there is little or no pressure he may be more comfortable relying on his instincts.

It is also important to consider Bob's leadership style. Below are three dimensions relating to this, "Purposeful", "Directing" and "Empowering".

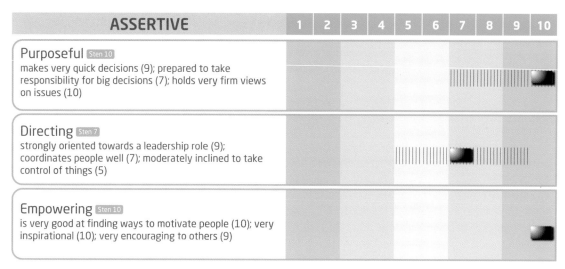

ASSERTIVE	1	2	3	4	5	6	7	8	9	10
Purposeful Sten 10 makes very quick decisions (9); prepared to take responsibility for big decisions (7); holds very firm views on issues (10)										■
Directing Sten 7 strongly oriented towards a leadership role (9); coordinates people well (7); moderately inclined to take control of things (5)							■			
Empowering Sten 10 is very good at finding ways to motivate people (10); very inspirational (10); very encouraging to others (9)										■

143

Goalkeeping for Bob is all about decision making. The soccer goalkeeper makes split-second decisions that affect the outcome of the game. Indecision costs goals and loses matches. As demonstrated by the profile, Bob is purposeful, makes quick decisions, and is very comfortable making quick decisions. He tends to relish responsibility and is prepared to make big decisions. Bob rarely changes his mind and holds very firm views on most issues. On the pitch, though, he kept opinions in check and never recorded a serious foul during his entire career. Bob is also strongly oriented to a leadership role. He coordinates people well and is moderately inclined to take control of things.

Commenting on teamwork and his leadership skills, Bob points to the Willow Foundation. "I look at Willow now compared to when we started in a back bedroom with just Megs and I. We are now 32 staff and provide 1400 special days. People think of the Willow Foundation as Bob Wilson. I might be the front man but it would be nothing without Megs and everyone else who is now making it what it is". Bob is an ethical man who honors his commitments and obligations to others and this is shown in the "Principled" dimension of his profile. Nevertheless, his profile also reveals him to be persuasive and good at negotiating the best deals (as shown in the "Convincing" dimension from his profile) so there is no doubt that he is a good leader and front man for the organization.

For Bob the diamond in his goalkeeping game was the ability to dive at feet, which he sees as a "God-given asset". He is clear that his quasi-kamikaze style wasn't deliberate, rather instinct. "Some elements of my game I had to work hard to be able to do, like kicking a ball over a long distance and becoming proficient on high crosses. But the one natural thing, absolutely natural, was the ability to dive head first at feet like my hero Bert Trautmann".

Whilst a sportsperson needs talent and determination, a third invaluable factor for Bob is choosing an idol. "It can speed the learning process by providing unlimited inspiration which, when allied with natural talent and determination, can provide an unstoppable force". The German Bert Trautmann, a former prisoner of war, was Bob's goalkeeping hero. A Luftwaffe Paratrooper in World War Two, Trautmann was captured by the Russians and escaped. He was then caught by the French resistance and escaped again. He learned goalkeeping as a British prisoner of war and in 1956 was the first foreigner to win the Football Writers' Association Footballer of the Year award in the English league. Trautmann famously broke his neck in the 1956 FA Cup Final but carried on playing and saved a crucial goal, winning his team the game. Amid a bitter Anglo-German row over wartime responsibilities, he was awarded an Order of the British Empire in 2004 for his work fostering relations between Germany and the UK. He now has his own charitable foundation in Germany.

Even before he had seen him play, Bob emulated Trautmann's diving style. With his sportsmanship and daring, Bob believes that "Trautmann did more than any politician to bring two countries at war with each other together". While Trautmann holds a special place in Bob's heart as his idol, so too does his courageous daughter Anna. "In the five years of her dying, she taught us all how to live", he remarks.

As a footballer Bob was, in his own words, blessed with "enthusiasm" and a "massively competitive" nature. He had the will to have a go and faced the consequences. Over twenty stitches in his face, an eye almost torn out, a chipped shoulder bone, six broken ribs, five cracked ribs, a punctured lung, torn cartilage and ligaments, a broken arm, a dislocated elbow, several broken fingers and a broken ankle were proof of his desire to win. Such was his determination that he once played with a dislocated shoulder. The match report recommended a medal for "gallantry above and beyond the call of duty" should be awarded to "Wilson the keeper". Bob jokes that had he fought in a war, he would have been one of the first casualties.

Being a goalkeeper is not simply technically demanding: it can also make its exponents psychologically vulnerable. As the last line of defense, their errors are a pundit's paradise, ready to spark controversy. A drop in concentration and they can go from hero to zero. When a goal is scored, goalkeepers have to move on. They have to stay positive and cannot dwell on errors. For many years Bob did not see himself as the best. It took until 1968 before he was able to break through a psychological sense of inferiority when playing for Arsenal. As he says, initially "I didn't believe in me".

Two areas concerning Bob's self-belief are shown below, "Receptive" and "Self-assured".

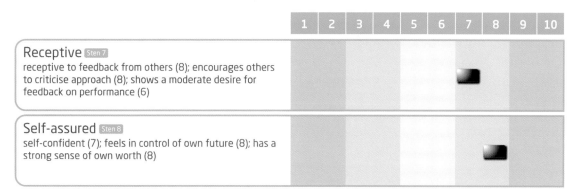

Receptive Sten 7
receptive to feedback from others (8); encourages others to criticise approach (8); shows a moderate desire for feedback on performance (6)

Self-assured Sten 8
self-confident (7); feels in control of own future (8); has a strong sense of own worth (8)

Bob may have felt an inferiority complex during the early stages of his career but it shouldn't be confused with fundamental insecurity. As the profile indicates, Bob is self-confident, has a strong sense of his own worth and feels in control of his own future. He has always been receptive to feedback from others. Throughout his career in football and broadcasting he made the most of opportunities and his mentors. Even now he encourages others to criticize his approach. Added to that he is self-assured, highly positive, likely to take an optimistic view and quickly recovers from setbacks. These areas can be seen below in the "Positive" dimension of Bob's profile.

Positive Sten 8
likely to take an optimistic view (7); quickly recovers from setbacks (8); cheerful (8)

In Bob's own words: "You cannot survive forty years in the spotlight in the world of football, or thirty in television, without facing the sort of criticism that challenges even the most hardened and optimistic spirit. I have always had a natural basic enthusiasm and determination to prove people wrong".

Below can be seen Bob's "Composed" dimension from his Wave profile which looks at how he responds to pressure.

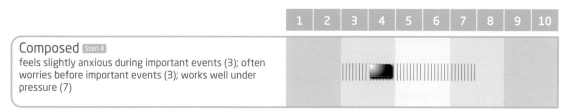

Composed Sten 4
feels slightly anxious during important events (3); often worries before important events (3); works well under pressure (7)

As the profile shows, Bob often worries before important events and feels slightly anxious during important events. Yet, he works well under pressure. He explains his tense approach in this way: "I had a nervous disposition as a footballer. I was desperate in the dressing room, and almost out of control coming on to the pitch. But from the moment I stepped on the field then there was this feeling that this is what I had chosen to do; and I had to now go out and prove I could do it".

There were other personality characteristics that also made Bob stand out. As his friend Sir Michael Parkinson notes in the introduction to his autobiography, what set Bob apart from the mob of footballers was that he was charming, socially adept and articulate. Below, we can see evidence that Bob is an "Engaging" individual.

Engaging Sten 9
quickly establishes rapport (8); extremely focused on making a good first impression (9); makes new friends easily (8)

Most importantly, Bob was popular and had an affinity with the public. He is extremely focused on making a good first impression, quickly establishes rapport, and makes new friends easily. As a television personality, this engaging approach, combined with his systematic preparation, helped Bob get the best out of all the legends that he interviewed. An empathetic approach, a naturally supportive style and tendency to ask probing questions made Bob a balanced interviewer and sympathetic listener.

As a coach there is a difference between knowing where a player has to improve, and enabling the player to learn for himself. As borne out by research, an involving style combined with empathy and supportive behaviors pays dividends in the art of persuasion. The best coaches and the best salespeople are interested in what makes people tick. Through their empathy and sensitivity they are able to help people and teams change. This is Bob's approach, seen below in the "Supportive" area of his Wave profile. Bob is highly involving and extremely team oriented. He is sensitive to others' needs and readily understands how others are feeling. He regards himself as an extremely good listener and is very interested in why people do things. He is trusting of people (sometimes too much so, according to his wife Megs) and considerate towards others.

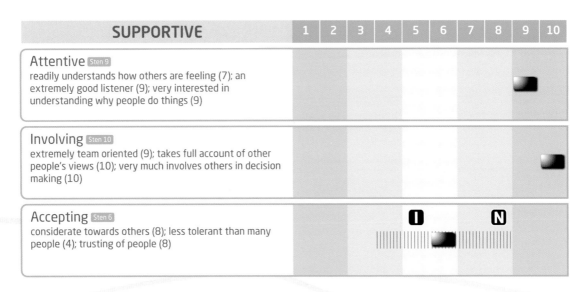

SUPPORTIVE

Attentive Sten 9
readily understands how others are feeling (7); an extremely good listener (9); very interested in understanding why people do things (9)

Involving Sten 10
extremely team oriented (9); takes full account of other people's views (10); very much involves others in decision making (10)

Accepting Sten 6
considerate towards others (8); less tolerant than many people (4); trusting of people (8)

These strengths align closely to Bob's own perspective on goalkeeper coaching. In his view, getting to understand what motivates players was (and is) the starting point for goalkeeper coaching. As one of the most psychologically demanding positions in soccer, it was critical for him to be able to get to know his goalkeepers and to act as their mentors.

What emerges from his Wave Professional Styles profile is that Bob is able to modify his coaching strategy to different personalities. He is equally at home coaching schoolchildren and emerging talent, as he is with evergreen veterans. His disciplined and meticulous approach is balanced by passionate communication skills and

146

natural enthusiasm. These combine with natural empathy and his supportive skills. This combination helps him to translate ideas and visions into structured step-by-step guidelines. There is also an element of the old fashioned teacher in Bob. Those he coaches know where they stand. The normative-ipsative split shown in the "Accepting" dimension of Bob's profile could suggest that while he is rather considerate and trusting of others in ideal conditions, when he comes under pressure (for example, if people try his patience), Bob may be less accepting of people. Given that Bob is less tolerant than many people and is likely to challenge others, there is a probability that he will neither suffer fools gladly, nor put up with those who do not meet his high standards.

With formative skills developed at Loughborough College, Bob is a natural coach and mentor. He encourages others to give of their best with his enthusiasm and warmth. There was never an obvious dark side to his self-confessed "burning desire to succeed". This helped Bob navigate the challenge of being an outsider. He was the gentleman amateur amongst established professionals in both the sporting and TV world. Talent, a desire to improve his abilities, increasing self belief and supportive mentors helped him to achieve the pinnacle of both his professions as a goalkeeper and as a sports presenter. Natural talent also helped make him a great coach and teacher.

Existential philosopher and fellow goalkeeper Albert Camus once wrote: "All that I know most surely about morality and the obligations of man, I owe to football". Camus was simply emphasizing a belief in sticking up for your friends, of valuing courage and fair-play. He felt that people may do better to look to the simple morality of the football field than to politicians. Looking at the personality, life and times of Bob Wilson, he has a point. Bob is a hard act to follow.

147

8.3 Case Study 3

Ajaz Ahmed

Entrepreneur, Founder of the £9 Billion
Company Freeserve

Ajaz Ahmed is a man on a quest for his next eureka moment. He had his first ten years ago in a computer store in the north of England. He discovered that having just bought a new PC, none of the staff could explain to him how to get onto the internet. To solve this problem, which he rightly assumed to be widespread, Ajaz set up the company Freeserve with his employer, The Dixons Group. This allowed people to simply and quickly install the internet on their computer. Freeserve rapidly became the UK's largest internet service provider. Within a year it floated on the London Stock Exchange at £1.5 billion. Six months later, it had entered the FTSE 100. At its peak it had a value of £9 billion.

Although born in Lahore, Pakistan, Ajaz moved to the Yorkshire town of Huddersfield in the north of England at the age of three. He grew up in the humblest of surroundings. His father worked at a textile mill and his family lived in a terraced house with an outside toilet. Neither luxury nor success was forthcoming at an early age. Ajaz left school with nothing to show for himself, having failed every exam and without a hope of getting into university. Today he points to other very successful entrepreneurs who also failed to get a degree - individuals such as Sir Richard Branson, Bill Gates and Larry Ellison - and is keen to make a clear distinction between academic prowess and business savvy.

Despite any academic shortcomings, the young Ajaz needed to earn a living and in 1979 he was offered a £30-per-week sales assistant's job at British high street electronics retailer, Dixons. He was a successful salesman and in his twenties he became a manager, rising to take charge of the biggest store in the area within one year.

It was here that he received his inspiration for the idea that would make him one of the most successful internet entrepreneurs of his time. He recalls having heard about "this thing called the internet" which he felt he had to try. But he soon discovered, much to his personal frustration, that there was no simple way for the average person with a limited technological understanding to get online. The idea that was to become Freeserve began to crystallize. Ajaz realized that at Dixons he could do something that none of his competitors could do. He could physically talk to the customer about the internet at the point of sale. His team could get to those customers first. Ajaz worked hard to convince his seniors of the growing importance of the internet as a revolutionary technological medium. He conceived a simple system for getting people online. At a time when all internet access in the UK was via dial-up through telephone lines, Freeserve was one of the first service providers to dispense with a monthly subscription fee. Customers typically had to pay a monthly fee and then the price of a local rate phone call for every minute they were connected to the internet. But Freeserve customers could just pay the local rate and the company collected a share of that call cost.

When Freeserve was bought in 2001 by the France Telecom owned group Wanadoo, Ajaz had the opportunity to turn his attention to other areas. Since then, he has remained a successful entrepreneur working particularly with a number of companies in the science and technology fields. Having started in electronics, Ajaz feels his understanding of this area is a useful strength and prefers to focus his efforts into such businesses. He now sits on the boards of several technology companies.

Ajaz is also involved in a project called Jumble Aid, an eBay style operation which encourages people and businesses to post unwanted items on a website (www.jumbleaid.com). When a customer buys an item on the site, all the money goes to a charity nominated by the seller. It is a simple and effective way to both raise money for charity and to reduce landfill.

Notwithstanding his earlier academic shortcomings, Ajaz also sits on the Governing Council of the University of Huddersfield. In another role which affords him something of an opportunity to return to his retail roots, he is also a partner in Abdul's, a chain of Asian restaurants.

Ajaz completed the Wave Professional Styles questionnaire and his profile provides a fascinating insight into an immensely successful individual. He is extremely inventive and creative and also has exceptional abilities which help him influence and interact with people. From his responses, we can probe more deeply into what motivations and talents underlie entrepreneurial success using Professor David Hall's Entrecode® Model of Entrepreneurial Potential. The Entrecode® is validated against a model developed to identify successful entrepreneurs. In order to do this, it predicts potential in six core areas of importance to entrepreneurs. Notably, Ajaz has a higher indicated potential than 99% of people who complete the Wave Professional Styles questionnaire in two of these key areas: "Seeing Possibilities" and "Opening Up to the World". "Seeing Possibilities" refers to the ability to take in information and create insights. Below is shown three of the ways by which Ajaz achieves this.

SEEING POSSIBILITIES

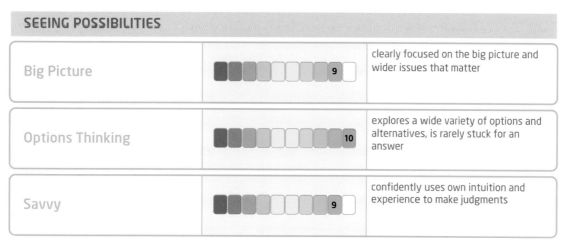

Big Picture	9	clearly focused on the big picture and wider issues that matter
Options Thinking	10	explores a wide variety of options and alternatives, is rarely stuck for an answer
Savvy	9	confidently uses own intuition and experience to make judgments

Ajaz is clearly focused on seeing the full extent of issues. From his Wave Professional Styles profile it can be seen that he nurtures a very clear vision for the future and takes a very long term view. He is also able to explore a wide range of different options. All of these are skills that would no doubt be of crucial importance to a self-made entrepreneur whose role requires him to work out which ideas are worth pursuing and which are not.

It is an example of Ajaz's commercial savvy and ingenuity that when he and his friend Abdul set up their restaurant chain, Ajaz made the radical decision to invite British comedian Bernard Manning to officially open the venture. The presence of Manning, who was well-known for a stage act that many felt to be racist and intolerant of other cultures, ensured that national press coverage was devoted to the simple opening of a restaurant. The headline in best-selling British newspaper The Sun the following morning quipped: "Who's a cheeky chapatti?"

Inviting Bernard Manning to open an Asian restaurant exemplifies how Ajaz can clearly "think outside of the box". He evidently considers a variety of options to work to his advantage. His responses place him in the top 1% of people for "Options Thinking", according to the Entrecode® model. Ajaz and Abdul also marketed an aphrodisiac-themed curry for Valentine's Day, having discovered that many of the ingredients in curry did have aphrodisiac qualities. This enterprise had people queuing around the block and proved so successful that they subsequently extended the offer to include the two days either side of February 14th. Ever since, this has been their busiest time of the year and nobody has ever denied their claim that curry is an aphrodisiac. Ajaz confirmed this with a glint in his eye. "Well, they couldn't, could they?"

149

Ajaz's profile highlights another aspect of his behavioral style: his ability to use his own intuition and experience when making decisions. Ajaz particularly embodies this principle of successful entrepreneurship. He likes to focus on companies specializing in science and technology, as he has considerable experience in this area. Ajaz is keen to emphasize the importance of his extensive retail experience in guiding his decisions, as his grounding in this field allows him to speak to customers in jargon-free, succinct terms. He is mindful of the importance of mirroring a customer's language when dealing with them, regardless of the context. In his role, Ajaz often needs to take people's ideas and articulate them in a way that customers understand. He also demonstrates an aptitude for recognizing opportunities and the signals people give off when they are about to make a purchase. As a salesman at Dixons, for example, he recognized that customers who put their bags down were more likely to make a purchase than those who did not.

While he is savvy and prepared to use his own experience to guide judgments, Ajaz is also receptive to feedback from others. He recovers quickly from setbacks, as can be seen in the "Receptive" and "Positive" dimensions of his profile below.

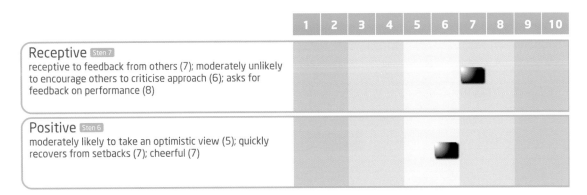

This combination of using one's own experience to make judgments, while at the same time being prepared to listen to others and learn from mistakes, could be of great use to a self-made entrepreneur. Many truly successful individuals learn just as much from their failures as they do from their triumphs. Certainly, Ajaz was keen to ask for feedback from others as a manager at Dixons. He frequently monitored and sought reactions from his salespeople about their communications with customers. He even recalls asking staff to find out from prospective customers where they might have gone wrong in their dealings. He sometimes asked salespeople to go out and bring customers back into the store so a deal could be closed that day, rather than letting them "go away and think about it".

Furthermore, while Ajaz admits that he has lost hundreds of thousands of pounds and has had some failures, his outlook is such that he is keen to learn something from every experience. We can see that he is adept at recovering from poor performances and has a flexible, adaptive style. He takes this ability to adapt and learn and also applies it in his personal life. Ajaz's world was profoundly changed when he discovered he had oral cancer on his tongue, despite never having been a drinker or a smoker. Happily, this was successfully treated by laser surgery. But the experience prompted him to make some lifestyle changes. He started going to the gym and lost a total of 30 pounds in weight. Ajaz regards his healthy lifestyle as a contributing factor to his business success.

The second of the six core Entrecode® competencies where Ajaz demonstrates higher potential than 99% of people is "Opening Up to the World". This reflects his ability to present appropriate information to the appropriate people. It also concerns building networks and forming those relationships that enable a business to develop.

Ajaz has a very high potential for networking purposefully and is skilled at negotiating with people. He builds strong commercial partnerships. However, what must be of particular use to him is that he is skilled at conveying passion for what he does. He is therefore able to express his ideas persuasively and inspires people. The particular methods by which Ajaz is able to effectively open up to the world are shown in the diagram below.

OPENING UP TO THE WORLD

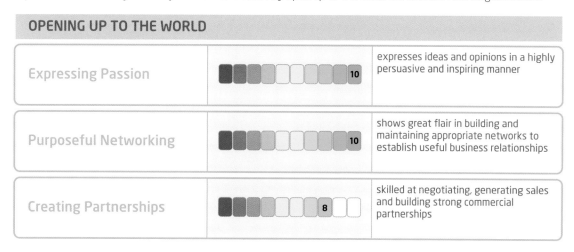

Expressing Passion	10	expresses ideas and opinions in a highly persuasive and inspiring manner
Purposeful Networking	10	shows great flair in building and maintaining appropriate networks to establish useful business relationships
Creating Partnerships	8	skilled at negotiating, generating sales and building strong commercial partnerships

We have seen that Ajaz is adept at seeing possibilities, influencing people appropriately and can also use his own intuitions and experiences when judging a wide-range of options. However, he reports that he is less organized, meticulous and reliable than most people. As Ajaz is so successful, it is clear that these areas aren't so important to his success. In his job, Ajaz makes judgments about whether something will be successful or not and forms profitable relationships with others. He is not required to pay close attention to detail or to work to regular deadlines. Ajaz believes in the principles of Monkey Management. If a problem is represented as a monkey, it is important to prevent other people passing their monkeys on to you for feeding. Ajaz is the ideas man. His skill is in persuading and empowering people to get their own monkeys off their backs.

When considered with his ability to create a clear vision for the future, it would be interesting to see whether developing his planning abilities would help Ajaz further improve his already formidable capacity for recognizing business opportunities. Ajaz's interest in identifying business opportunities can be seen in the "Enterprising" dimension of his profile (below), so this may well prove to be an area he would be keen to develop. For example, he might find that planning could enhance his ability to identify the goals he wants to achieve from a particular project.

| | 1 | 2 | 3 | 4 | 5 | 6 | 7 | 8 | 9 | 10 |

Enterprising Sten 9
Identifies business opportunities effectively (10); fairly sales oriented (8); competitive (8)

As has already been touched upon, Ajaz's interpersonal skills are a key factor in his successful behavioral style. He is very persuasive and assertive in putting his points across and explains things well. Combined with his very strong networking skills, it appears that Ajaz projects himself to the appropriate people as an articulate and convincing individual. He remains very liberal and likes to be tolerant of other people and cultures and there is no doubt that this outlook also helps him to interact well with others. Ajaz also knows when to tell people about his achievements and is comfortable being the centre of attention if necessary, as indicated by the "Self-Promoting" dimension of his profile. Such useful skills, employed judiciously, no doubt aid Ajaz in his interactions with others.

151

It is interesting to explore further the exact nature of Ajaz's influence over others. He reports that he is adept at finding ways to influence people, is inspirational and is clearly oriented towards leadership. But he also says that he is less team-oriented than many people and has little desire to co-ordinate people. Ajaz affirms that he wouldn't want to be a CEO again, because his interests lie in vision and creativity, rather than in co-ordinating people and "their monkeys", which he can find frustrating. In his day-to-day work he is primarily responsible only for himself and doesn't actually have much involvement with teams of people. His profile responses seem to reflect that team working skills are not important to Ajaz, rather than that he lacks these skills per se.

In his Wave profile, an interesting motive-talent split becomes apparent in the "Purposeful" dimension. As shown below he is rather more motivated by, rather than talented in, this area. His talent for making quick decisions and taking responsibility for decisions is typical of many people, but he is somewhat more motivated by this than many people are. It may well be appropriate for Ajaz to consider this as an area for further development.

| 1 | 2 | 3 | 4 | 5 | 6 | 7 | 8 | 9 | 10 |

Purposeful Sten 5
makes reasonably quick decisions (6); somewhat prepared to take responsibility for big decisions (6); has definite views on some issues (5)

What is perhaps so fascinating about Ajaz's profile is that he demonstrates many areas of strength which interact in striking ways. As we have seen, he combines a powerful set of skills that allow him to influence people effectively. Yet, while he is quick to state that his work involves articulating other people's ideas in a persuasive way, it is eminently clear that Ajaz excels at generating his own ideas too. Perhaps his greatest strength as illustrated in his Wave profile is his inventive and strategic thought style. Ajaz generates many original ideas and is prepared to adopt radical solutions to problems. This makes him far more inventive than most people report they are. He develops concepts, theories and strategies with ease. Ajaz's personal view is that it is the ideas that matter, not the business plan. As we have already seen from his Entrepreneurial Potential profile, Ajaz creates a compelling future vision. The prevailing areas of his thought style are summarized below.

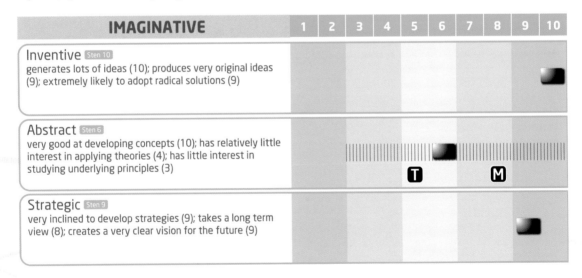

| IMAGINATIVE | 1 | 2 | 3 | 4 | 5 | 6 | 7 | 8 | 9 | 10 |

Inventive Sten 10
generates lots of ideas (10); produces very original ideas (9); extremely likely to adopt radical solutions (9)

Abstract Sten 6
very good at developing concepts (10); has relatively little interest in applying theories (4); has little interest in studying underlying principles (3)

Strategic Sten 9
very inclined to develop strategies (9); takes a long term view (8); creates a very clear vision for the future (9)

In the "Abstract" dimension, Ajaz has indicated that while he is very good at developing concepts, he is much less interested in studying the principles and underlying issues. Most people find that developing concepts, theories and underlying principles are allied much more closely than Ajaz sees them. Consequently, his profile highlights a unique aspect of his preferred behavioral style. Taken in conjunction with the motive-talent split in the "Abstract" dimension, this suggests that he has a distinct motivation to develop his conceptual and theoretical

thought skills. Because his reported understanding of underlying principles is somewhat lower than for the other areas, this might be an area that Ajaz could choose to focus on in order to further develop his capability for abstract thought.

Being practically-minded, factual and rational is quite different from being good at abstract thought. These practical areas are prioritized a good deal lower in Ajaz's responses and he is much less inclined to follow the rules of others. We can see that Ajaz has creative ideas and is talented at empowering people. His empowering skills may be the key to explaining how he is so good at realizing creative ideas despite being less interested in the practicalities of those ideas. Ajaz himself corroborates this hypothesis. He believes that many people are capable of having "eureka" moments, but that a key skill is acting appropriately on these ideas. For him, entrepreneurs are those who are able to do this and direct others to align with their vision. He read and studied how other people achieved success and believes aspiring individuals should do the same.

It is also interesting to speculate how Ajaz's clear thought style might contribute to his success. Perhaps the fact that he is less rule-bound, factual and risk-averse than many people helps him to produce exceptionally creative ideas, unconstrained in the ways that many people are. Ajaz's "Conforming" dimension of his profile can be seen below.

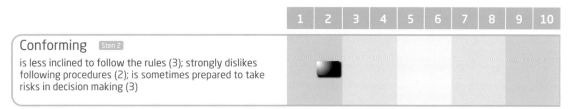

In Ajaz's view: "History is littered with examples of ordinary people achieving extraordinary things because they could see things that were completely obvious before anyone else could. That's what life is about, doing the obvious before everyone else and not trying to complicate everything". It seems this combination of a lack of constraint by rules and a very strong creative vision helps Ajaz to see things that are "obvious" before other people do. Ajaz muses: "How many times have I heard people say to me 'I had that idea!'? But the problem is that they didn't do anything about their idea. That's the tragedy".

We can also use the various reports from the Wave Professional Styles questionnaire as tools for guiding feedback in a variety of ways. For example, we have seen that Ajaz's Entrecode® Entrepreneurial Potential profile indicates that he has great flair for maintaining the networks needed for business and that he is inspiring and persuasive. However, while Ajaz's reported talent for resolving situations is lower than that for many people, his reported motivation to resolve situations is somewhat higher. He may therefore already be inclined to focus on these supportive skills. Ajaz is an immensely successful individual, so it is likely that he can effectively self-regulate changes in his behavioral styles in order to maximize success in a range of different situations.

From Ajaz's profile, we can consider areas where his success might be used to extend advice to others. There is a large facet range on "Composed", where Ajaz reports that he is very calm before important events. He is only slightly anxious during important events, but dislikes having to work under pressure. This is illustrated in the diagram below.

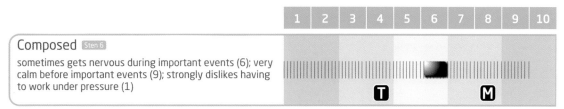

It would be enlightening to know when such anxiety can be a help and when it is a hindrance, because Ajaz is certainly very comfortable giving presentations. He reports disliking working under pressure and in a busy working environment, but appears able to flourish in other situations such as networking and giving presentations. In addition, there is a large motive-talent split in this section of Ajaz's profile. Here, he reports wanting to be a good deal more composed than he feels he is currently capable of being. It appears that Ajaz would like to be able to work even better under pressure and it is probable that if he focused on developing this skill, his impressive range of skills here would appear even stronger. Ajaz likely has the necessary insight to bring about such self-development. Crucially, he believes that "success is an attitude" so if you can go into a difficult situation believing that you will be successful, that is half of the battle.

The Wave Professional Styles reports for Ajaz Ahmed are a fascinating case-study into the very individual behavioral styles of an immensely successful and self-motivated entrepreneur. Clear strengths for Ajaz are indicated in his creative thought and interpersonal skills, which allow him to effectively influence people in order to develop his business. He also demonstrates a remarkable ability to invoke his own experience and intuitions to make discerning commercial judgments. The importance of this skill is something he is at pains to stress.

However, what is perhaps heartening for others is that Ajaz believes that ordinary people can do extraordinary things given the right motivations. He explains how one famous British television commercial affected him profoundly. An advertisement for Hovis bread showed a millworker walking down a cobbled street as he retires from a hard life's work. He clutches the clock that has been given him as a leaving gift and looks back at the mill where he has faithfully served his whole life. He returns home and cuts a slice of Hovis bread, when the advert reveals that Hovis is "as good today as it has always been". The message is meant to be one of good old-fashioned values and tradition, but Ajaz saw it in a rather different light.

Millworkers like his father left with nothing but a token gift to show for their life's work. He wasn't going to retire with nothing to show for his toil. For him, success is about wanting to have something to show for your life's work. Ajaz believes that most workers spend six months of the year thinking about the holiday they're going to take and then another six months talking about what they did on holiday. They don't try to make a difference. The desire to make a difference was the driving force of his success.

Ironically, Ajaz's colleagues at Dixons did present him with a clock as a leaving gift, but his drive, determination, creativity and influencing skills have carried him much further than that humble millworker. For many people, the advice, beliefs and behaviors demonstrated by Ajaz Ahmed form the cornerstone of a successful entrepreneur. There is no doubt that he embraces them with verve and aplomb.

8.4 Case Study 4

Kathryn McCusker

Australian Opera Star

Kathryn McCusker is a celebrated opera singer from Perth, Australia. She was Principal Soprano at the Sydney Opera for seven years, a position seen by many as the highest accolade in Australian opera. Her numerous awards and prestigious roles include first prize in the 1991 National Finals of the ABC Young Performers Award and the Remy Martin Australian Opera Award 1994. Kathryn has had a variety of eminent roles including Tytania in the acclaimed production of *A Midsummer Night's Dream*, directed by *Strictly Ballroom* and *Moulin Rouge* director Baz Luhrmann, which was performed at the 1994 Edinburgh Festival. She also played Susanna in John Copley's production of *Le nozze di Figaro* and Iphigénie in a new production of *Iphigénie en Tauride*.

Kathryn came from a family where art, creativity and music formed an integral part of her childhood. Her father was a barrister who is "a good singer, even though he never did it professionally" and her mother is an artist who runs a gallery in Perth. Her elder sister was a lawyer who is now raising a family and her younger brother is involved in the wine business.

For Kathryn, music was always a part of her and a way of finding joy in life. From an early age, she sang and played the piano and flute. However, she remembers specifically and vividly the conception of her love of classical music: "I saw at my high school a woman who came to perform and she sang an aria to us. I felt incredibly inspired". She recognized her encounter with this woman, Marybeth Williamson, as "one of those pivotal moments". Upon meeting Marybeth, they both realized that Kathryn had "a talent that needed to be nurtured". Marybeth soon went on to become Kathryn's singing teacher.

A further important step in nurturing this talent was taken when Kathryn completed a Bachelor of Music degree at the Western Australian Conservatorium of Music. She describes how she was very fortunate to have another teacher there who encouraged her and recognized her gift. It was this teacher, Janice Taylor-Warne, who urged Kathryn to audition for the Australian Opera after finishing her degree. Kathryn's considerable ability clearly shone through and she won a scholarship into the young artist program. "They say I was the youngest or maybe the second youngest they have ever had on their young artist program. I had a very mature voice for my age. Even I was sometimes a little bit surprised by it".

In 1991 she was awarded first prize in the National Finals of the ABC Young Performers Award and took part in the 1993 and 1995 Opera Foundation of Australia's National Vocal Symposium. After only three years in the young artist program, Kathryn was honored not only with the Remy Martin Award but also the position of Principal Soprano with Opera Australia. In 1999 her "mature voice" won her the Vienna State Opera award in Australia and as a result she spent four months working as a Company Principal with the Vienna State Opera.

Kathryn covered the role of Donna Elvira in *Don Giovanni* for Glyndebourne Festival Opera in their 2000 season and, at very short notice, sang the second performance to the delight of the conductor Sir Andrew Davis and a very enthusiastic audience. In 2001 she debuted with the English National Opera. In the UK, concert performances have included *The Messiah* in Swansea, Handel's *Belshazzar* at the Dartington International Summer School and a tour of major UK concert venues performing Handel arias with the London Chamber Orchestra. Kathryn has performed in Bath Abbey and recently was a soloist in the debut concert of The Australian Classical Era Orchestra, performing Mozart arias.

155

Now based in London, Kathryn is also a certified teacher of Kundalini Yoga and shares her skills in the UK capital, as well as running retreats overseas. As the new millennium dawned, Kathryn discovered this yoga of awareness in the Yucatan, Mexico. Kundalini is considered to be one of the most potent and effective systems of self-transformation and personal development. It aims to create emotional balance and to enhance intuition by harnessing the energy of the mind and the emotions, rather than being controlled by thoughts and feelings.

Kathryn completed the Wave Professional Styles questionnaire and was intrigued to explore how the work-based profile would relate to her holistic approach to life. From her profile, Kathryn presents herself as an inspirational individual, who is encouraging and engages well with others. She is also dynamic and driven in her activities. Moreover, she combines these areas with a thoroughly adaptable style, possessing an overall self-assured and positive manner. Yet, she remains very interested in understanding why people do things. Along with her appetite for yoga and her desire to unlock potential, Kathryn's profile demonstrates a fusion of interest in other people's behaviors and thoughts. She has the ability to question and challenge beliefs and, as we shall see, she does all of this in an intuitive, rather than mechanistic, manner.

On first inspection, and unsurprisingly given the emphasis of Kundalini Yoga on the energies of the body, one of Kathryn's greatest areas of strength is her dynamism. Her responses to questions relating to her energy levels suggest she is more energetic than 99% of people who complete the same questionnaire. While she is also slightly more inclined to initiate action than many people are, one of the most important features of the "Dynamic" dimension of Kathryn's profile (shown below) is her high level of motivation to be dynamic.

In Kathryn's "Dynamic" dimension, she has rated the questions relating to her motivation to be a dynamic individual as more important to her than the questions about how dynamic she feels she really is (her talent). This is consistent with the "Activity Oriented" dimension of her profile, which indicates that she likes to be busy and to work at a fast pace.

She is also ready to accept new challenges and copes well with uncertainty. One of the behavioral areas which seems common in many successful people is their ability to respond flexibly and to adapt to different situations. Kathryn shows strength across all sections relating to her "Adaptability" and particularly as regards her responses to change. She is likely to take an optimistic view and quickly recovers from setbacks. Kathryn also feels she works well under pressure, as it keeps her busy and inspires her to perform. The "Positive" and "Change Oriented" dimensions of her profile are shown below.

Kathryn is so energetic, optimistic and ready to accept challenges that one gets a sense that when she focuses her energy, she *will* achieve. This is further reinforced by the fact that Kathryn is striving and likely to persevere through difficult challenges. The normative-ipsative split shown in the "Change Oriented" dimension of her profile suggests that she may actually have been quite self-critical in this regard. When forced to rank the statements in the Wave questionnaire, Kathryn prioritized statements about her orientation to change somewhat higher than when she was given the choice to freely rate how oriented to change she was. The separate normative and ipsative measures provide two different perspectives on an individual's work styles and are a useful mechanism for investigating how people view themselves in different contexts and situations. For example, separate normative-ipsative measures help indicate when an individual is likely to have been overly-positive or overly-self-critical in their responses. Here, it appears that Kathryn may be more strongly oriented towards change than she has indicated in her free rating response. Two possible hypotheses here are that the ipsative score is more representative of how oriented to change Kathryn is under pressure, or instead that Kathryn is not certain of the extent of her orientation to change.

Kathryn's profile indicates that she readily accepts new challenges. She recognizes that the challenges she undertakes allow her to further refine her expertise and technique. Dame Joan Sutherland, one of Kathryn's inspirations, also made this point in an interview, emphasizing that "technique is the basis of every pursuit. If you are a sportsman, a swimmer or a singer, you have to develop a basic technique to know what you are doing at any given time".

Kathryn points out that she was very good at sport when at school and agrees "it is that same kind of psychology behind it". She explains that when you go out on stage it is like going out on track as a sportsperson. "There are sacrifices too in your social life with the way you maintain yourself; your physical, emotional, and vocal sides. You can't have gone out 'socializing' until four in the morning when you know you have to sing a major role at the Sydney Opera House the next day".

Like many successful people, Kathryn can also name specific individuals who have inspired her to make these sacrifices and keep focused. Dame Joan Sutherland, Björk, Katherine Hepburn and Audrey Hepburn all spring to her mind. "They're strong female artists who are passionate about what they do and are true to their art form", she says.

The late Franz Schalk, an early-twentieth century conductor of the Vienna State Opera, commented that "every theatre is an insane asylum, but an opera theatre is the ward for the incurables". With so many sacrifices and so much discipline required in the demanding environment of professional opera, Kathryn is acutely aware how temperamental artistic individuals can be. Many creative people and artists have, as she puts it, "fragile egos". When an opera singer is working in a rehearsal room, they have to deal with a conductor, a director and different singers: sopranos, baritones, tenors and basses. She says, "Everyone should come in with the purpose to create a great product, a great piece of theatre and music, but sometimes people's egos get in the way. People, artists, can be very vulnerable, very sensitive. When you work you have to be sensitive because you collaborate collectively and creatively. You have to be conscious that everyone adds to the mix".

In this respect Kathryn is good at resolving difficulties and disagreements with others and for her own part is self-assured and reasonably composed. Below are the "Self-assured" and "Composed" dimensions of Kathryn's profile.

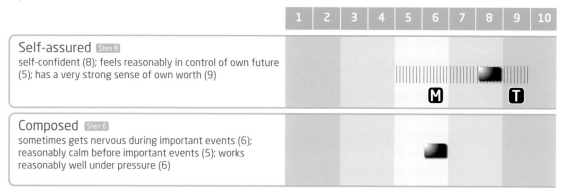

Interestingly, Kathryn has only a moderate motivation to be self-assured. She is evidently comfortable with herself and has a very strong sense of self worth. She is reasonably calm before important events and likes her space to prepare. This helps add to the "adrenaline rush" of performing and that can give her "the edge" in performance. As she points out, she performs well in front of an audience and likes to visualize what she does before she does it.

Kathryn takes what she does seriously and wants to get things exactly right. She has a good technical knowledge of what she does and enjoys gaining that technical understanding. It is apparent, moreover, that through her meticulous approach Kathryn is able to deliver when it counts. She recognizes that concentration matters and focuses totally on what needs to be done. Her desire to ensure a high level of quality is illustrated below in the "Meticulous" dimension of her profile.

From the "Self-assured" dimension of Kathryn's profile presented earlier, we can see that she has a very strong sense of self-worth. John Berry, artistic director for the English National Opera, recently commented that many people turn down the opportunity to work in opera because they fear it will be too difficult: "If a director doesn't have a real inner confidence, you know you're in trouble from the beginning. The film industry is tough, but all of the film directors I've spoken to can't believe how tough and savage the opera world can be. It stops a lot of very fine artists from coming in". For Kathryn, this resonates: "Opera is a challenging and costly art form and this applies worldwide. In any performance art form you have to have a very strong inner core and confidence. You have also to be able to tolerate high levels of physical, emotional, and mental stress".

Reiterating the fact that some of the artists she has dealt with are sensitive by nature, Kathryn describes her valuable talent of "juggling all of those different temperaments and personalities in one space". She adds, "It's important to be able to blend and mould people to work together to deliver on stage". From Kathryn's profile, her skills for dealing with upset or angry people and multi-tasking well would also be useful in this context. She is able to work well with a diverse group of people. She adds that she has worked with people who are insecure and who crave and need to be the centre of attention, but she finds that those who create themselves as "prima donnas" are those who are really insecure with themselves. But that's okay by Kathryn: "I'm not judging that, I just choose not to be that person".

Kathryn sees opera as a team activity and as a principal protagonist, she is clearly oriented towards a leadership role (see "Directing" dimension below). Her skills lie very much in empowering and encouraging individuals to find their own approaches. This is demonstrated directly in the "Empowering" dimension below.

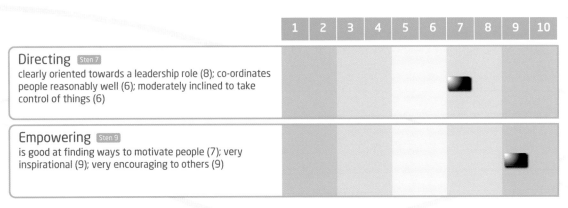

For many people this is one of the most acceptable styles of leadership and, when deployed appropriately, should be expected to earn Kathryn respect. It could also help her to realize the results she seeks. This style of "team leadership" seems to be shared by a large number of successful individuals. Kathryn, for one, thinks that "being able to collaborate in a team is important for opera, as in sports; that's always been one of my strengths".

While Kathryn is clearly skilled at managing diverse personalities, she likes to "live in the moment" and this is attested to by several areas of her profile. For example, she rarely focuses on long-term issues, is ready to accept change and only has a moderate inclination to make plans. Far from this being a weakness, however, it may well help Kathryn deliver results more effectively and to adapt to changing situations. She emphasizes that she does like to have goals and projects on the go, but not "five year goals" or to project "too much into the future". Certainly, she creates a clear vision for the future, but isn't so focused on long term issues. This can be seen below in the "Strategic" dimension.

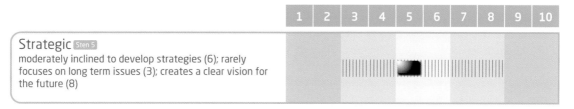

Here, the facet range, illustrated by the hatching marks, stems from the fact that Kathryn creates a clear vision for the future but rarely focuses on long term issues. For most people who complete the Wave Professional Styles questionnaire, these two issues are more closely related. One possible reason for this might be that Kathryn's vision is not simply business oriented, but comes from a more spiritual perspective than most. To appreciate this distinction, we have to look a little deeper into her philosophy.

Kathryn finds having a coherent understanding of a situation critical. "When I work with directors or when I work with people on a project, I need to know what the motivation is. It's method acting, I suppose. It's important for me to understand why I am doing something. I need to have a depth of understanding. I need to have a deep insight into the psychological complexities of the character. It helps me create a much more profound character". Central to her views too are major existential questions. This helps explain why Kathryn is less concerned about the underlying logic and facts of a situation, instead favoring a more intuitive or "instinctive" approach. Kathryn is interested in deeper issues. Reflecting on both the origins of opera and the essence of yoga, she asks: "How do we evolve through our lives? What motivates us? Why do we do things that we do? How are we governed by fate and destiny? All of these things I find fascinating". She combines her love of yoga with interest in the Dharmic traditions of Indian religions - a set of philosophies considering the ultimate reality of the universe - which help her reflect on these deeper issues.

Dr Johnson once described opera as an exotic and irrational entertainment. Looking at the "Rational" dimension from Kathryn's profile (below), we can see that she has less interest in numerical data ("I was never good at math. Good at humanities, theatre, art, music, but never math") and prefers not to base her decisions on the facts alone.

1	2	3	4	5	6	7	8	9	10

Rational Sten 1
very much dislikes working with numerical data (1); has little interest in information technology (3); unlikely to base decisions on the facts alone (3)

However, while Kathryn isn't so interested in analyzing information, she is likely to combine her intuitive approach with probing questions and a desire to learn. This orientation towards enquiry is shown below in the "Analytical" dimension of her psychometric profile.

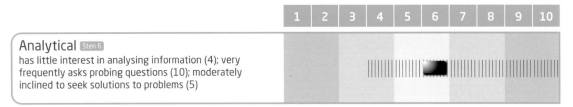

| 1 | 2 | 3 | 4 | 5 | 6 | 7 | 8 | 9 | 10 |

Analytical Sten 6
has little interest in analysing information (4); very frequently asks probing questions (10); moderately inclined to seek solutions to problems (5)

In her own words, Kathryn says: "I am very curious. Directors always say that about me. They say 'Kathryn, you're like a child. You want to know everything'". And through her questioning Kathryn is better able to understand the nuances of the character she is playing, as well as the perspective of the director. Kathryn's roots in opera also govern her approach to life. Opera combines music, theatre and dance and yet it remains a specialized form of art:. "It's a heightened form of emotion. Through music, through the voice, you can access those kinds of heightened emotions, those dimensions, as you would through yoga and exploring the meaning of life. There is something very primal about the voice, whether it's communication through music or just speaking. It's one of the most creative centers in the human body".

For Kathryn, individual voices are very revealing. They show "many different colors and layers, many different complexities". She says she "really tunes to people's different timbres and colors", adding: "I work on a sensory level. I am more in tune with the way someone speaks; the way someone walks; their rhythm; the way someone smells; the way someone looks; the way someone feels; their energy levels".

While Kathryn is very much in tune with other people, she also demonstrates an independent streak where she does take account of the views of others, but is unlikely to involve them in the final decision: "I was talking to a friend on the phone who is very similar to me," she says. "We were saying we like to get the opinions of others, but at the end of the day I will do exactly what I want to do".

She is less rule-conscious than many people and is prepared to question something if she doesn't believe in it. If a maverick is someone who stays true to their vision and will break rules if necessary, Kathryn is comfortable with this epithet. She is also pragmatic and points out that to be on stage you have to be able to take direction from the conductor, the language coach and from the director. "If you can't, you are not going to be able to get on well in that ensemble". Like a number of successful people, Kathryn scores lower on conforming than much of the general population, but also retains an awareness that sometimes you have to be compliant, manageable and flexible.

Although she does not see herself as an entrepreneur in the conventional sense, she shares a good deal of characteristics with "classic" entrepreneurs. Based on David Hall's Entrecode® model of Entrepreneurial Potential, Kathryn demonstrates high potential for areas such as "Getting in the Zone" and "Staying in the Zone". These relate to her ability to focus energy on a very specific target in order to help herself and others. She is also good at "Creating Superior Opportunities". Kathryn herself has been approached by others who recognize her entrepreneurial potential. "People have said to me 'Kathryn, you are really assertive and you have this incredible conviction, so do you like selling?'". The answer is a resounding "no".

But while Kathryn doesn't have the motivation to sell herself (and her profile indicates very little interest in networking, as in the "Interactive" dimension on the next page) she does like selling something she believes in. She believes in and sells "principles or philosophies; techniques or creative ideas". As she explains, she makes a choice: "I can network, I have the capacity to approach people, but I am not driven by that force".

160

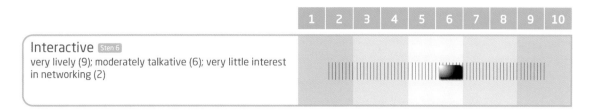

| | 1 | 2 | 3 | 4 | 5 | 6 | 7 | 8 | 9 | 10 |

Interactive `Sten 6`
very lively (9); moderately talkative (6); very little interest in networking (2)

Below are some of the key areas where Kathryn demonstrates high entrepreneurial potential.

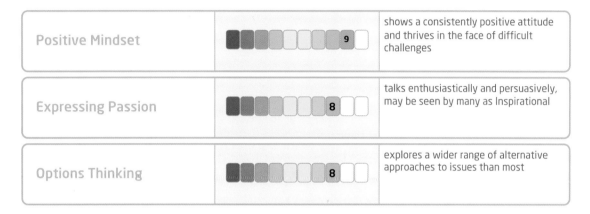

Positive Mindset	9	shows a consistently positive attitude and thrives in the face of difficult challenges
Expressing Passion	8	talks enthusiastically and persuasively, may be seen by many as Inspirational
Options Thinking	8	explores a wider range of alternative approaches to issues than most

If one were to sum up Kathryn McCusker's behavioral style in just two words, perhaps "creative passion" would be a good starting point. It is immediately apparent on meeting her that she has a breadth and depth of perception. She possesses an insight into the nature of individuals and also her own journey through life. This is backed up by a repertoire of competencies which underline the demands of performing at the highest level.

Kathryn achieved early success in her profession and has enjoyed some of the most prestigious roles within it. She has been blessed with creative vision, spirituality and an interpersonally sensitive approach which has facilitated her opera career and yoga teaching alike. Kathryn also possesses a drive for success which makes her an assertive and self-assured individual, capable of investing considerable amounts of time and effort in ensuring excellence. Success has not been accidental. Kathryn perceives a strong link between opera and her role as a teacher of Kundalini Yoga: the two complement each other. One of the aims of Kundalini Yoga is to increase radiance and the impact the practitioner has on others. There are few yoga teachers who have commanded the stage at Sydney Opera House. For Kathryn, teaching is performing too. It is important to do both authentically.

Kathryn is currently writing a book about Kundalini Yoga, meditation and her journey through this as a successful performer. She's also producing a mantra CD which helps her integrate her perspective on yoga through classical music. As she summarizes, there are issues that count in life and as you get older they get more significant. "For me it is important to live life in a certain way and value system, to question what you are here for, what you stand for". Kathryn wants to "live life consciously with awareness and the understanding of why you do something and what effect that has on another person".

Like those people who inspired her, not only is Kathryn true to herself but also to her art form. Whatever path she follows in life, it will be the Dharmic Way.

161

162

PART 3

OUTPUTS

9.0 Entrepreneurial Potential Report

9.1 Introducing the Entrepreneurial Potential Report

This report is powered by Entrecode® – a model of how successful entrepreneurs create and lead high value businesses. The report is powered by either Wave Professional Styles or Wave Focus Styles.

The Entrecode model is based on nearly twenty years of research undertaken by Professor David Hall and his associates (www.entrecode.com). Early on, Professor Hall's team discovered that the entrepreneurial business building process was much more of a personal process than the traditional business school marketing methods. Networking, building alliances and delighting customers are much more important than business models, branding or business plans.

After researching what entrepreneurs did to be successful, David Hall set out to understand how they approached each of these key activities. For example, it was acknowledged that networking was important to business growth, but how they networked was a mystery. Indeed one early insight was that successful entrepreneurs are often unable to articulate how they do things because they are 'unconsciously competent.'

However, Olympic coach Wyatt Woodsmall provided an insight enabling 'modeling' to identify 96 characteristics shared by a group of entrepreneurs. In order to narrow the list, he then surveyed 250 entrepreneurs in the UK and Australia and validated the results against job performance dating back 10 years. Effectively, Professor Hall's research 'cracked the code' of entrepreneurial success and encapsulated this in the Entrecode model.

In 2005, Entrecode and Saville Consulting collaborated to create the Entrepreneurial Potential Report, an instrument designed to rigorously assess entrepreneurial talent.

The Entrepreneurial Potential Report assesses individuals against the six core areas from the Entrecode® model below that drive entrepreneurial success.

Figure 9.1 The Entrecode® Model

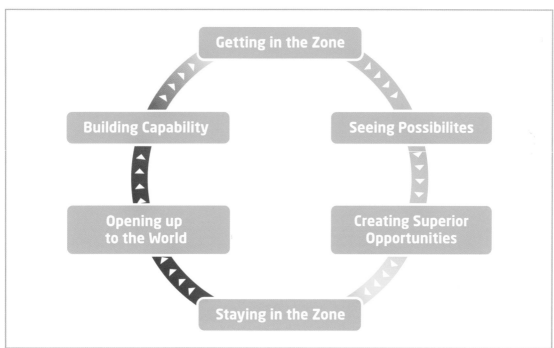

The model then breaks down into subcomponents under each of these six areas. There is a total of twenty-one subcomponents underpinning Entrepreneurial success in the Entrepreneurial Potential Report. Each of these scales is measured by a mapping to the 108 competency facets in the Wave performance model. This allows the competency potential facets of Wave Professional or Focus Styles to power the Entrepreneurial Potential Report. This report was the first example of Saville Consulting Wave research and model measuring an external model of effectiveness at work.

9.2 Development of the Entrepreneurial Potential Report

A four-step process was used to link Wave Professional Styles to the Entrecode model and then generate the Entrepreneurial Potential Report:

Step 1:	Rational links were made between the Saville Consulting Work Performance model *(at the most detailed, 108 facet level)* and the Entrecode® model
Step 2:	The competency potential facets were chosen and weighted based on these rational links. Competency potential facets themselves are weighted combinations of Wave Styles facets which maximize the validity in predicting the Saville Consulting Work Performance model *(see Construction chapter)*.
Step 3:	The Entrepreneurial equations were run on the standardization group to check for construct separation and overlap. The equations were subsequently refined.
Step 4:	Finally, an individual's results are compared against the benchmark norm group used to generate that report. *(A description of this norm group is provided at the bottom of each page within the report)*.

9.3 Applications

Assess Entrepreneurial Potential

The Entrepreneurial Potential Report allows the assessment user to see at a glance whether an individual has what it takes to be a successful entrepreneur. The graphics and narrative text quickly and easily highlight relative strengths and gaps, providing valuable insights for coaching or selection. In parallel, the Expert Report from Professional or Focus Styles can then help to understand why the person has emerged with a given pattern of strengths or development needs at a deeper behavioral style level.

Help Venture Capitalists and New Business Incubators

Venture Capitalists and other business support organizations are generally able to evaluate business plans very effectively. However, they tend to struggle with the question 'does this person with the good idea have the prerequisite skills to take the idea off the page and make it an economic success?'

The Entrepreneurial Potential Report allows a better understanding of the extent to which an individual has the traits of highly successful entrepreneurs who have created high growth businesses. This makes it possible to weigh up the probability that the business will thrive and prosper. Where there are traits missing, an organization can make an informed decision about managing the risks involved in backing a new venture.

Build on Entrepreneurial Strengths

The Entrepreneurial Potential Report will identify the raw talent, but for this potential to convert into performance, the individuals need the right environment, the tools for the job and the coaching support that recognizes that they are different from the majority of other workers in the organization. Harnessing this entrepreneurial talent has huge potential benefits, since these individuals have the ability to grow the business faster, with fewer resources and more effectively than the organization's other staff. More information on Entrecode support materials and toolkit can be found at www.entrecode.com.

Coach Entrepreneurs to Build High Growth, High Value Businesses

Entrepreneurs have specific approaches to learning and developing, primarily from active experimentation, trial-and-error, and from peers, family and friends. The EntreCoaching approach maximizes learning by leveraging these insights, including:

- Encouraging and modeling action taking
- Minimizing power and control, i.e., bureaucracy
- Focusing on strengths not weaknesses
- Helping to remove blockages to progress

Drive Corporate Entrepreneurship and Innovation

Corporate organizations struggle to innovate and this is backed up by research that highlights that 95% of all major innovations in products and services in the 20th century originated in companies employing fewer than twenty people (Timmons & Spinelli, 2003). The Entrepreneurial Potential Report enables corporate business to highlight and utilize their internal entrepreneurs in a way that maximizes their personal strengths.

167

A corporation's internal entrepreneurs are often pivotal to an organization's future success. They tend to be the people who can make step-changes and deliver breakthrough thinking. However, individuals with strong entrepreneurial characteristics are likely to make up less than 10% of most workforces. So business leaders must identify them and empower them to operate within a more entrepreneurial culture, e.g., 'just do it,' 'success or learning,' and 'take calculated risks.' Entrepreneurial people may come from unexpected places and yet will have the capacity and mindset to deliver results beyond expectations.

Revitalize and Transform the Business

Business transformation utilizes the same individual traits that would be used by an entrepreneur when setting up and delivering a new proposition; it needs people with vision, focus and a strong drive to achieve and make a difference. The Entrepreneurial Potential Report can be used to identify the people who would be most likely to drive through significant organizational change. These potential change agents can be brought together from across the organization.

Business transformation requires the organization and its employees to refocus on what is most important and ditch other activities that are not creating sufficient value. A business transformation team can be made up of internal entrepreneurs which will kick-start revitalization, and their vision and optimism will re-energize others in the organization to implement the necessary changes.

Spot Opportunities for New Products or Markets

Traditionally companies hire sales managers and product developers because of their qualifications, technical knowledge, and their experience. By contrast, the Entrepreneurial Potential Report identifies those people with the talent and motivation to shine in the development of superior commercial opportunities. Successful entrepreneurs often have served a lengthy apprenticeship in their chosen field, so they have an in-depth understanding and a network of useful contacts. However, the most successful entrepreneurs also have a distinctive style, as measured by the Entrepreneurial Potential Report. By using this tool specifically with customer facing staff (particularly key account managers), you can identify those who will be most likely to spot the new business opportunities that offer sustainable high value returns.

Retain and Liberate your Innovators

Many high growth companies are started by refugees from large corporate business. The reality is that many businesses do not appreciate that they have internal entrepreneurs who, if not managed correctly, will leave and create value for themselves rather than staying and delivering value for their employer. The key is to highlight these people before it is too late and nurture them, so that they develop ideas linked to their own company's strategy.

The Entrepreneurial Potential Report helps to identify likely innovators. Using the Entrecode process and principles, companies can then create a sub-culture within which innovators will prosper. Providing additional coaching and support will enable them to create new perspectives and spot superior opportunities. In this way business owners take their innovators and their ideas on a journey to enhance the company's competitive advantage, while at the same time making them feel valued and less likely to leave.

9.4 Interpreting the Scales

In the following section we explain how the six core areas of the Entrecode® model presented in the Entrepreneurial Summary Profile dimensions breaks down into twenty-one aspects of entrepreneurial potential. We then provide an interpretation of both high and low scores for each of these aspects, and share the four Professional Styles dimension(s) that correlate the highest with each of the Entrepreneurial Potential scales. These are listed in rank order starting with the Professional Styles dimension with the strongest correlation with the given Entrepreneurial Potential scale.

GETTING IN THE ZONE

- Achievement Drive
- Compelling Vision
- Energy
- Action Oriented

Achievement Drive

HIGH SCORERS: show total commitment to succeeding and achieving results
LOW SCORERS: place little personal emphasis on achieving results

Most highly correlating Professional Styles Dimensions:

- Striving
- Directing
- Enterprising
- Purposeful

Compelling Vision

HIGH SCORERS: create a strong, compelling vision of what they would like the future to look like
LOW SCORERS: tend to focus on the here-and-now rather than creating a vision for the future

Most highly correlating Professional Styles Dimensions:

- Convincing
- Strategic
- Directing
- Empowering

169

Energy

HIGH SCORERS: consistently put lots of energy into making things happen
LOW SCORERS: may appear quite laid-back and unconcerned about making things happen

Most highly correlating Professional Styles Dimensions:

- Dynamic
- Directing
- Purposeful
- Change Oriented

Action Oriented

HIGH SCORERS: display a strong preference for acting quickly and decisively, being impatient to move things on
LOW SCORERS: may not feel comfortable taking the initiative and may find it difficult to take action quickly

Most highly correlating Professional Styles Dimensions:

- Purposeful
- Dynamic
- Directing
- Insightful

SEEING POSSIBILITIES

- Big Picture
- Options Thinking
- Savvy

Big Picture

HIGH SCORERS: clearly focused on the big picture and the wider issues that matter
LOW SCORERS: likely to focus on a narrow set of issues and may lose sight of the big picture

Most highly correlating Professional Styles Dimensions:

- Strategic
- Insightful
- Inventive
- Dynamic

Options Thinking

HIGH SCORERS: explore a wide variety of options and alternatives, are rarely stuck for an answer
LOW SCORERS: may consider only a limited number of approaches to issues

Most highly correlating Professional Styles Dimensions:

- Inventive
- Strategic
- Abstract
- Insightful

Savvy

HIGH SCORERS: confidently use own intuition and experience to make judgments
LOW SCORERS: seldom rely on own intuition and experience to guide judgments

Most highly correlating Professional Styles Dimensions:

- Purposeful
- Insightful
- Directing
- Dynamic

Problem Seeking

HIGH SCORERS: put significant effort into finding out which problems customers really want to address
LOW SCORERS: may show a lack of interest in understanding the issues that customers face

Most highly correlating Professional Styles Dimensions:

- Interactive
- Empowering
- Engaging
- Articulate

Synthesis

HIGH SCORERS: highly skilled at integrating information from diverse sources to develop new approaches
LOW SCORERS: may not make the connection between insights gained from different sources

Most highly correlating Professional Styles Dimensions:

- Abstract
- Analytical
- Inventive
- Strategic

Problem Solving

HIGH SCORERS: produce very strong commercial solutions to customer problems that lead to new business opportunities

LOW SCORERS: unlikely to produce solutions quickly and may lack interest in identifying new business opportunities

Most highly correlating Professional Styles Dimensions:

- Enterprising
- Purposeful
- Directing
- Convincing

172

Customer Delivery

focused on personally delivering a high quality service to customers
less focused on personally delivering a high quality service to customers

Most highly correlating Professional Styles Dimensions:

- Meticulous
- Reliable
- Organized
- Principled

STAYING IN THE ZONE

- Focus
- Positive Mindset
- Self-determining
- Persistence

Focus

HIGH SCORERS: show a single-minded focus on priorities, refusing to be distracted
LOW SCORERS: may be easily distracted and lose sight of the key priorities

Most highly correlating Professional Styles Dimensions:

- Directing
- Purposeful
- Dynamic
- Strategic

Positive Mindset

HIGH SCORERS: show a consistently positive attitude and thrive in the face of difficult challenges
LOW SCORERS: may show a tendency to dwell on the negative side of things, becoming disheartened in the face of challenges

Most highly correlating Professional Styles Dimensions:

- Positive
- Change Oriented
- Dynamic
- Composed

Self-determining

HIGH SCORERS: take firm, unwavering control of shaping their own destiny
LOW SCORERS: may feel uncomfortable making decisions that will shape their own destiny

Most highly correlating Professional Styles Dimensions:

- Self-assured
- Purposeful
- Directing
- Strategic

174

Persistence

HIGH SCORERS: show strong persistence in seeing things through to the end despite difficulties, recovering very quickly from setbacks

LOW SCORERS: show less persistence than others, particularly when faced with difficulties or setbacks

Most highly correlating Professional Styles Dimensions:

- Striving
- Directing
- Positive
- Purposeful

OPENING UP TO THE WORLD

- Expressing Passion
- Purposeful Networking
- Creating Partnerships

Expressing Passion

HIGH SCORERS: express ideas and opinions in a highly persuasive and inspiring manner
LOW SCORERS: show little inclination to inspire and persuade others

Most highly correlating Professional Styles Dimensions:

- Empowering
- Directing
- Convincing
- Enterprising

Purposeful Networking

HIGH SCORERS: show great flair in building and maintaining appropriate networks to establish useful business relationships

LOW SCORERS: likely to find networking uncomfortable and avoid making time for building business relationships

Most highly correlating Professional Styles Dimensions:

- Interactive
- Articulate
- Engaging
- Self-promoting

Creating Partnerships

HIGH SCORERS: highly skilled at negotiating, generating sales and building strong commercial partnerships
LOW SCORERS: may not be comfortable generating sales or negotiating deals with potential commercial partners

Most highly correlating Professional Styles Dimensions:

- Enterprising
- Convincing
- Directing
- Empowering

176

BUILDING CAPABILITY

- Building Up the Team
- Experiential Learning
- Staying on Track

Building Up the Team

HIGH SCORERS: very focused on building a strong team by coordinating and motivating the right people
LOW SCORERS: may show a lack of interest in taking on responsibility for coordinating and motivating the team

Most highly correlating Professional Styles Dimensions:

- Empowering
- Directing
- Dynamic
- Strategic

Experiential Learning

HIGH SCORERS: show a strong preference for learning through pragmatic experimentation and drawing on experience
LOW SCORERS: unlikely to choose active experimentation as the primary method of learning

Most highly correlating Professional Styles Dimensions:

- Learning Oriented
- Inventive
- Insightful
- Change Oriented

Staying on Track

HIGH SCORERS: consistently strive for continuous improvement to ensure the business stays ahead of the competition
LOW SCORERS: may become complacent, and not put great effort into keeping things on track

Most highly correlating Professional Styles Dimensions:

- Activity Oriented
- Striving
- Dynamic
- Insightful

177

9.5 Further Reference Material

Further information can be found in the Case Studies and Reports chapters of this handbook .

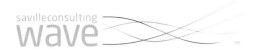

10.0 Types

10.1 Introduction to Saville Consulting Wave® Types

Typologies are essentially summaries of combinations of characteristics.

The Saville Consulting Wave types are based on the four higher level clusters in the Professional Styles assessment. These cover the areas of Thought, Influence, Adaptability and Delivery which underpin the performance areas of Solving Problems, Influencing People, Adapting Approaches and Delivering Results. The Wave Types Report integrates results on the 'People' Clusters (Influence and Adaptability) into four 'People Types' and on the 'Task' Clusters (Thought and Delivery) into four 'Task Types.'

Figure 10.1 People Types and Task Types display charts

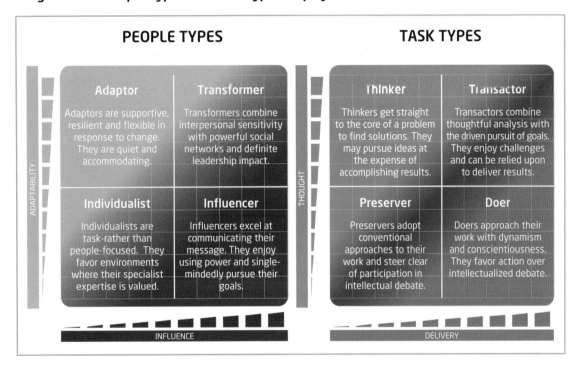

Figure 10.2 The four 'People' types and four 'Task' types combine to create 16 Saville Consulting Wave Types

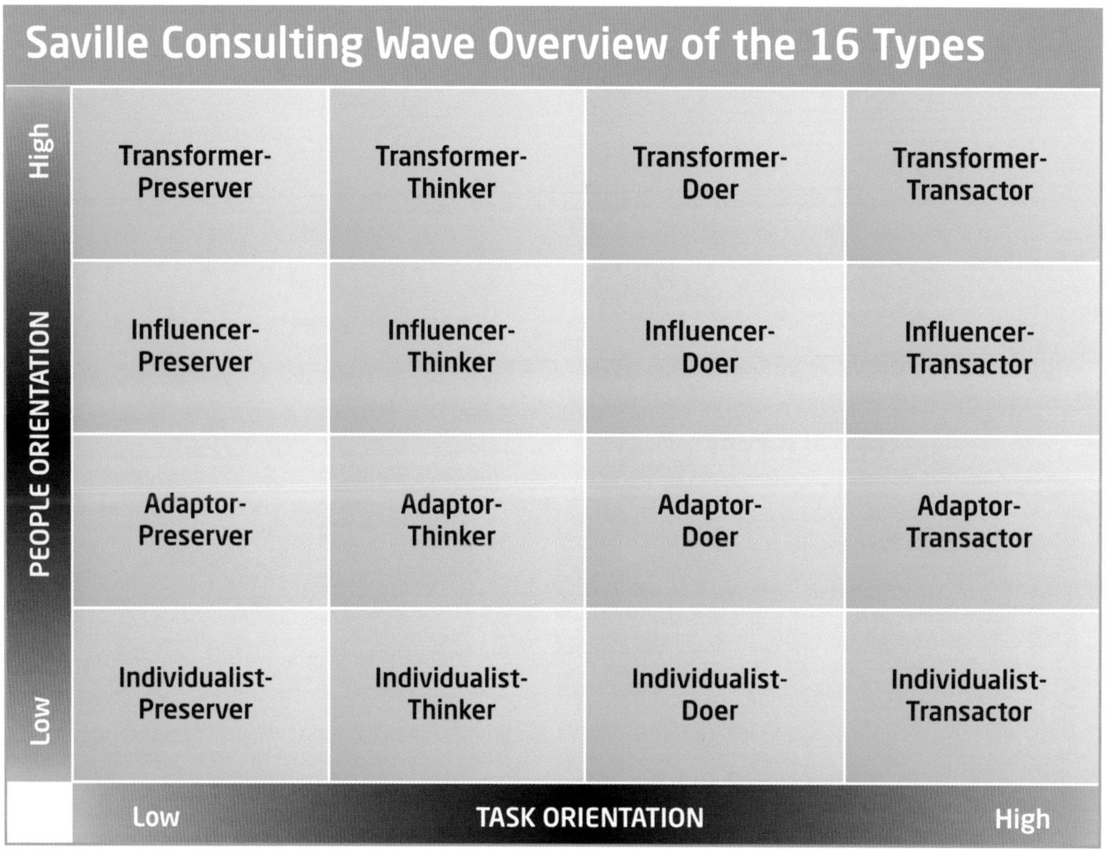

Saville Consulting Wave Overview of the 16 Types

	Low TASK ORIENTATION → High			
High	Transformer-Preserver	Transformer-Thinker	Transformer-Doer	Transformer-Transactor
	Influencer-Preserver	Influencer-Thinker	Influencer-Doer	Influencer-Transactor
	Adaptor-Preserver	Adaptor-Thinker	Adaptor-Doer	Adaptor-Transactor
Low	Individualist-Preserver	Individualist-Thinker	Individualist-Doer	Individualist-Transactor

PEOPLE ORIENTATION (vertical axis: High to Low)

TASK ORIENTATION (horizontal axis: Low to High)

Types are, by their nature, generalizations and thus will not fit every respondent equally well.

The likelihood that a person will fit a type description increases as the scores on the relevant dimensions become more extreme. For example, in the People domain, a person with both high Adaptability and high Influence scores is more likely than someone who scores at the midpoint on each of these scores to fit the description of a Transformer. By the same token, a person with very low scores on both Adaptability and Influence is more likely than someone at the midpoint of these clusters to fit the description of an Individualist.

People who score on the corridor close to the mid-point on one or both clusters can be described as less 'differentiated' in terms of type than those who score at the extremes.

When People and Task Types are combined a person could be highly differentiated in terms of People Type and undifferentiated in terms of Task Type, or vice versa. Thus, individuals with the same nominal overall Wave Type may differ quite substantially in terms of the characteristics that are most prominent.

Familiarity with the characteristics associated with each Type will facilitate understanding of these differences.

10.2 Performance Driven Types

The Saville Consulting Wave Types model directly links to performance both for individuals and teams. This gives it a sharper edge in building effectiveness, distinguishing it from other team development models which tend to focus on the advantages of particular types and type combinations rather than their direct impact on effectiveness.

The Value of Different Types to Team Effectiveness

The Wave Types model helps to identify the four high level behavioral clusters that predict different areas of effectiveness (Solving Problems, Influencing People, Adapting Approaches and Delivering Results). As each Wave type has a different combination of these behaviors, they will not all impact on team effectiveness to the same degree.

The Wave types approach is underpinned by the performance driven Wave model so that the type combinations that are the most effective contributors to overall effectiveness can be easily identified. The model allows individuals to be high or low on all four clusters relating to effectiveness. Those who combine high scores in all four areas, Transformer-Transactors, will consequently be the most effective in terms of overall performance and potential. Conversely, those who are low in all four areas, Individualist-Preservers, will likely have the smallest contribution to effectiveness.

Although effectiveness relates to an individual's score on the four behavior areas, Transformer-Transactors may still make serious errors (in many respects they leave themselves open to this due to a tendency to be less risk averse yet prepared to make big decisions). Similarly, Individualist Preservers still have a crucial role to play within a team, from doing the necessary, everyday tasks that no one else favors, and as is possible with other types providing the 'golden nugget' that improves efficiency and output. However, in general Transformer-Transactors are likely to be more effective than Individualist-Preservers. Note: It is important to consider that the Wave type bestowed on an individual is a result of their self-reported potential and effectiveness. Some people are more likely to over or under exaggerate their responses than others, either as a deliberate attempt to mislead or due to their genuine misperception.

The Benefits of Performance Centric Types and The One Person Team Concept

The key benefit of Wave Types linking directly to effectiveness is that it allows users to be clearer on what is missing from a team and what a team has in abundance (and potentially over-abundance). An Influencer-Thinker is likely to have the analysis, ideas and the powers of persuasion to get an idea put into action, but when complemented by an Adaptor-Doer, the two individuals in combination could improve the effectiveness of the team. The Adaptor-Doer brings stability and flexibility in dealing with people and a clear focus on high quality delivery, whilst the Influencer-Thinker has the ability to see a solution and influence others. These two complementary Wave types combine to cover the four behavioral clusters of effectiveness. An individual's type may be strong in all four behavioral clusters and in effect this individual can be seen as having the potential to be a one person team. The one person team is the Transformer-Transactor Type; they are likely to work constructively with any other type, although they may find the less assertive and driven types more frustrating to work with. In this way, any working partnership can be looked at in terms of the complementary, aligned and shared behaviors.

In general, a working partnership will be more effective to the extent that all four behavioral clusters are covered by its members. An individual may cover all these alone, or a team of four may still be lacking in a particular area. Where a number of individuals share common behaviors, this is not necessarily wasted resource. Three Influencer-Thinkers can be a fiery combination in terms of intellectual debate, but they have the potential to create groundbreaking solutions when they have an agreed goal to work towards. The intention of the Wave Types model is to highlight that several similar types may lead to strengths in a certain area, or that other behavioral areas are not equally represented and the team may benefit from the input of others who have strengths in this domain.

The ideal composition of the team in terms of Wave types should be determined by its core purpose. A Think Tank Team delivering a 20 year vision of product ideas may benefit from quite a different make up from a team tasked with improving process efficiency for instance, although they may share some common elements. The identification of the team's purpose is a critical early step and can be facilitated by the use of the Saville Consulting Wave Performance Culture Framework Card Deck to clarify which are the areas of most importance to the team's future effectiveness.

Performance Centric Types in Practice

The Wave types approach utilises validation evidence to suggest that certain Wave types contribute more to effectiveness, and as such has the potential pitfall that they classify the Transformer-Transactor as lacking nothing and the Individualist-Preserver as lacking everything.

To overcome this issue we recommend the Wave user utilises the Wave Expert report, creating a more detailed balance of strengths and limitations from the detailed profile (e.g., from sections, dimensions and splits). In the case of Individualist-Preservers, for example, any other key strengths or specialist skills the individual contributes to the team are identified. Finally when sharing results on a combined chart highlighting the different type combinations, the individual's particular area of strength or expertise can be charted and shared.

10.3 Development and Validation of Types

The idea for the Types model originated in an attempt to conceptualize a componential model of overall performance in the workplace to create a simple framework which would look at the key components that underpinned this criterion.

The Great Eight competencies (Kurz & Bartram, 2002) represented a componential model of work performance, but lacked an explicit higher-order structure. The four Leadership Functions described by Bartram, Kurz & Baron (2004) and Bartram (2004) clearly pointed towards a higher-order structure. Empirical modeling of competency data presented by Kurz (2005) suggested a simultaneous breakdown of performance into People and Task aspects as in the original Ohio leadership studies under the titles of Consideration and Initiating Structure, respectively. The other critical conceptualization was related to Alpha and Beta personality characteristics (Digman, 1997) as opposed to work criteria. The resulting '2 x 2' model of task, people and alpha and beta created the blueprint for the Wave Types model and what became the Wave clusters, which integrate personality and competency models in an aligned structure which underpins overall performance at work.

The 'Task Type' 2 x 2 matrix is comprised of the Wave clusters of Thought and Delivery, which form the axes of the matrix. The four cells inside the Task Type matrix are labeled Preserver, Thinker, Doer, and Transactor. The 'People Type' 2 x 2 matrix is comprised of the Wave clusters of Influence and Adaptability. These are shown on the axes of this matrix. The four cells in the People Type matrix are labeled Individualist, Influencer, Adaptor, and Transformer. This combination of four Task Types and four People Types combine to make up a total of 16 Wave Types shown in Figure 10.2.

The Construction chapter describes the development of the Wave model. In a nutshell, the Wave model was developed using both a deductive modeling approach combined with a validation-centric methodology in order to maximize validity. The 108 facets comprising the Wave model had to demonstrate empirical validity with measures of overall performance and behavioral effectiveness. Each 'style' measure in the Wave model is aligned with a behavioral 'competency' measure. This rigorous methodology was also applied to the Types model. Each of the Wave clusters that form the basis of the Wave Types model had to demonstrate empirical validity with not only its matched competency (i.e., Influence cluster score correlates with Influencing People competency rating), but also with measures of overall work performance.

Fullman (2005) demonstrated the point-to-point validities for the Professional Styles cluster trait scores (i.e., unit weight sum of 27 styles facets measured normatively) against its aligned behavior competency model (i.e., unit sum of nine competency behavior dimensions rated normatively by external raters). People Type cluster validities (uncorrected) were r=.29 for Influencing People and r=.16 for Adapting Approaches. Task Type cluster validities were .21 for Solving Problems and .16 for Delivery.

At this stage, single item ratings for People Leader, People Supporter, Task Leader and Task Supporter were gathered, which were later superseded by Influencing People, Adapting Approaches, Solving Problems and Delivering Results cluster level unit weight aggregates.

The data from the development study were used to create 108 competency potential facet equations designed to optimize the content, construct and criterion-related validity within the Wave aligned model. These equations were then applied to the standardization study data and minor adjustments were made to about 25% of the equations. Kurz et al. (2007) showed People Type cluster level validities of .38 for Influencing People and .31 for Adapting Approaches. Task Type cluster level validities were somewhat lower at .25 for Solving Problems and .22 for Achieving Objectives.

These equations were cross-validated on a sample of 308. In Project Epsom (see Validity chapter) an overall Types score (high on all clusters) Types total achieved a concurrent criterion-related validity of .27 (.48 adjusted for criterion unreliability) against a three item 'Global' rating of overall performance. With Influencing People correlating .24 (.42) and Adapting Approaches correlating .16 (.29) the Transformer total achieved a validity of .23 (.41). With Solving Problems correlating .15 (.27) and Delivering Results .21 (.37), the Transactor total achieved a validity of .22 (.39). These and other data in the Validity chapter provide empirical support for the validity of the Wave Types model, both for measuring overall job performance but also for specific behavioral competencies.

10.4 Applications

Saville Consulting Wave Types have implications for behavior in a number of areas including:

- Team Development
- Group Effectiveness
- Organizational Culture
- Individual Development
- Conflict Resolution
- Leadership Assessment
- Change Management
- Organizational Synergy & Development

Team Development

Team development is based on a team having an understanding of its strengths and limitations and how the interactions within the team can be productive or counter-productive. Whereas the Expert report provides very rich and detailed insights about people, it may be too detailed for a group context, especially if people are being introduced to the concept of individual differences. There is where the Types report can really add value. It is a simple, high-level view of the person and how they interact in their work setting, and it can help people appreciate their role and the role of others in a manner that is non-technical and easy to understand.

A common process for team development involves individual feedback of Saville Consulting Wave Types reports to members of the team followed by a group feedback, where the team, with a trained facilitator, reviews the whole team. This process highlights which issues the team needs to actively manage or develop, or even what external resources could be brought into the team to make it more effective. Types can also help individuals understand where they have synergies with others and where there is the potential for clashes.

Group Effectiveness

Understanding Wave Types is particularly useful in providing broad summaries of the key differentiators in the contribution of individuals to the performance of a group. In particular, they can help the group to see collective strengths and limitations, and see how different individuals have uniquely different valuable contributions to make.

Organizational Culture

The collective Types profile of an organization is indicative of organizational culture where departments and divisions can have their own sub-cultures. In an organizational unit where the Influencer-Thinker type is prevalent, for example, there is likely to be a high degree of intellectual debate about the direction of the unit and what it is trying to achieve. The 'creative conflict' that may ensue may need to be actively managed. Understanding the organizational culture, and how it relates to its units and their objectives, can be critical to optimizing individual, team and organizational effectiveness.

Individual Development

The Saville Consulting Wave Type reports provide a broad overview of individuals against four key performance areas which underpin superior performance at work. This helps individuals to develop a high level awareness of what they are most and least likely to have an impact on at work. It enables individuals to understand how best to fit themselves to appropriate tasks within the organization and to understand where they may have to apply greater effort or require more resources from others to support their work performance. The Wave Expert and Development Reports provide much richer and more detailed insight, but Types is often a first step in this process, particularly if there is a team or diadic interaction which needs particular attention.

Conflict Resolution

Organizations are essentially a complex network of formal and informal relationships which are more or less effective. Some of the vertical and lateral relationships are critical to the effective running of the organization so that any major conflicts that arise will need to be addressed. An understanding of the types of individuals concerned and where they are most likely to have synergies and clashes.

Leadership Assessment

Leadership can been seen as fundamentally tied to superior performance at work. One aspect of leadership is to role model effective behaviors at work. Saville Consulting Wave has been specifically designed to maximize the prediction and measurement of effective work behaviors. The Transformer-Transactor type is phenotypical of leaders being inclined to 'win the hearts and minds' and to 'get the right things done.' They are typical entrepreneurs who exemplify the 'One Person Team Concept' where one individual covers all aspects of running a business. A Transformer-Transactor is likely to provide a very rounded leadership style including personal modeling of effective leadership behaviors. However, the presence of several Transformer-Transactor individuals may lead to power struggles, e.g., in senior management teams.

Other types adopt a different approach to leadership. Thinkers lead from an intellectual base, but are likely to be somewhat less delivery-oriented. Influencers lead by pushing their arguments forward, but are likely to overlook objections from less vocal individuals.

When appointed to formal positions of authority, many individuals can be successful without necessarily personally supplying all the performance drivers themselves. They do this by harnessing the collective power of their team to make the group they are leading successful. Through discussion of their type, leaders can understand where their strengths are, and become more aware of how to effectively deploy them. Conversely they may recognize potential weaknesses and where they need to seek help from other members of the team, their peers or other leaders to maximize their effectiveness.

Change Management

The Saville Consulting Wave Types report also provides an insight into how individuals are likely to deal with and manage change. This can help provide an insight for individuals, teams and organizations on the position individuals are likely to adopt in relation to change and what might need to happen to allow them to 'buy in' to the change process.

Organizational Synergies & Development

The Types report can help an individual or indeed a team understand what is going to be the easiest and most effective contribution to an organization's functioning and success. Separate processes can be undertaken using the Saville Consulting Wave Performance Culture Framework to get a profile of the critical issues for a team, department and/or organization and this can be discussed alongside the Wave results as part of an individual, team, department or organizational feedback.

185

10.5 Interpreting the Types

The following pages provide descriptions of each of the types. Each page provides bullet points of key characteristics and benefits of that type, potential sources of friction and frustration for that type in team interactions, and interactions with other Saville Consulting Wave Types.

TRANSFORMER-TRANSACTORS

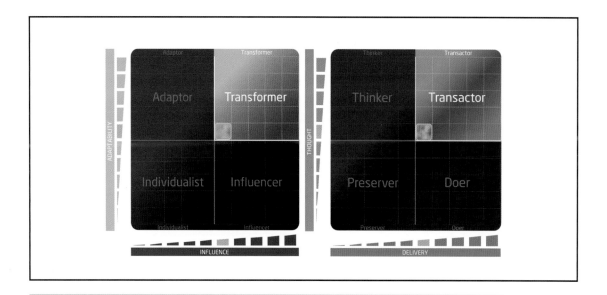

- Extremely "people" as well as "task" oriented
- Outgoing and socially skilled. Perhaps charismatic
- Provide a clear vision, sense of purpose, able to translate ideas into action
- Good coordinators. Get things done by virtue of ability to inspire and carry people with them
- Focused on excellence and delivery
- Likely to get the best from people of whatever type due to insight and understanding into what makes different people tick and ability to empathize with differing needs and viewpoints
- Will value individual qualities and skills. Should be able to relate well, and be agreeable, to most people

Potential sources of friction/frustration:

- with Influencers who launch competing initiatives – possibly in an abrasive manner due to their lower degree of social, behavioral and emotional adaptability

- with other Transformers or Transactors who are driven to take the lead and are vying for the leadership role (though less likely with the former because both sides are likely to have the social and communication skills necessary to sort out differences in a civilized manner)

- people who resist change – Individualists (especially Preservers), although are likely to recognize that even these have their place in a team carrying out routine tasks

Interactions with Other Types

Potential Synergies with:

- Adaptor-Thinkers; Adaptor-Doers; Transformer-Thinkers; Transformer-Doers

Potential Conflicts with:

- Preservers (especially Individualist-Preservers); Influencers

Transformer-Transactors combine all the characteristics of successful teams. However, they operate from one perspective only. The content of their 'vision,' the nature of the ideas they generate, their perceptions, analyses and evaluations of people and situations will be influenced by their unique personal histories. Their self-report may be overly positive (high Acquiescence) so that they may benefit from obtaining third party views to challenge their position and explore alternative perspectives. Two (or more) heads are likely to generate better solutions than one in many cases.

187

TRANSFORMER-DOERS

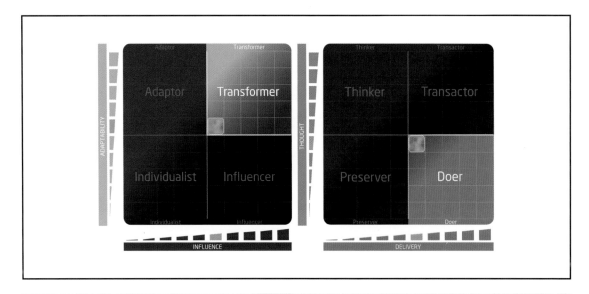

- Strong leadership orientation
- Focus on delivery
- Emphasis is operational rather than strategic
- Implement the vision, but will need someone else to provide it
- Energetic and results focused
- Set high standards
- Leadership and interpersonal skills likely to facilitate them in getting others on board, getting things done
- Good coordinators and planners, will set clear goals
- Likely to get the best from people due to insight and understanding into what makes different people tick, and ability to empathize with differing needs and viewpoints

Potential sources of friction/frustration:

- other Transformers or Transactors vying for the leadership role
- frustration with Thinkers who spend too much time on ideas and evaluation and with Preservers, who are not sufficiently focused on action
- people who resist change (Individualists, particularly Individualist-Preservers, and Individualist-Thinkers)

Interactions with Other Types

Potential Synergies with:

- Adaptor-Thinkers; Transactors

Potential Conflicts with:

- Influencers; Thinkers; Preservers; Individualists

Thinkers could provide complementary analytical and creative skills but may be seen as a challenge. Of the four Thinker types, relationships are likely to be easiest with Adaptor-Thinkers. Also likely to value Adaptor-Doers and all Transactors.

TRANSFORMER-THINKERS

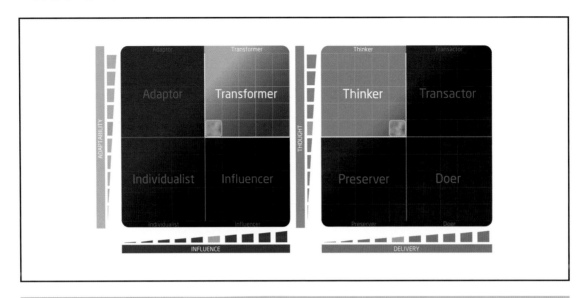

- Innovators, 'thought leaders', blue sky thinkers
- Influence via their intellects
- Thoughtful in both senses
- More people than task focused
- Supportive of others, sensitive to their differing needs and viewpoints
- Will promote team harmony
- Transformer-Thinkers are people leaders that are strategically rather than operationally inclined
- Can provide the vision but rely on others to deliver. May be disorganized
- Enjoy long periods of reflection and consultation
- Spend a lot of time deliberating but may be slow to take action

Potential sources of friction/frustration:

- may find emphasis of Doers on achieving results taxing
- may interpret behavior of Preservers and Doers as insufficiently considered or old-fashioned
- may be more comfortable with Adaptors and other Transformers than Individualists

Interactions with Other Types

Potential Synergies with:

- Doers; Adaptors

Potential Conflicts with:

- Preservers

190

Could complement or be complemented by Doers, but it could be a hard relationship to manage given the high vs. low action orientation.

TRANSFORMER-PRESERVERS

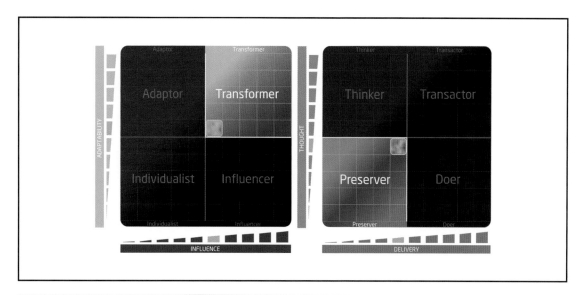

- Prominent in groups
- Emphasis on people issues rather than creation of vision and strategy or achieving results
- Good facilitators but need to be provided with vision and goals from elsewhere
- Prefer established approaches
- Focus on the concrete here and now, rather than abstract ideas and possibilities for the future
- Spontaneous rather than planned
- Leverage their influencing skills
- Network and are well-connected
- Suited to relationship management roles

Potential sources of friction/frustration:

- may find the emphasis on task at the expense of people of Individualist-Doers and Individualist-Transactors unpalatable
- may find Doers taxing
- may find Thinkers difficult to understand

Interactions with Other Types

Potential Synergies with:

- Transformer-Transactors; Doers; Thinkers

Potential Conflicts with:

- Individualist-Doers; Individualist-Transactors

Complemented by Transactors, Doers and Thinkers who focus on successful completion of the right tasks.

INFLUENCER-TRANSACTORS

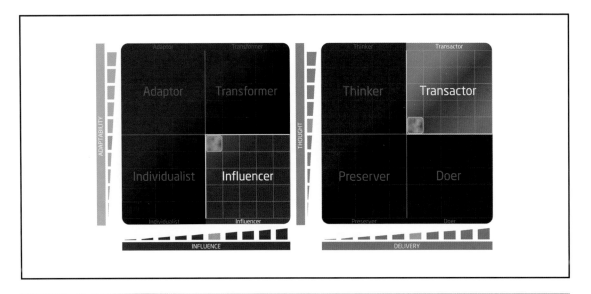

- Influencer-Transactors will provide a vision and a sense of direction
- Can translate ideas into action and will get things done
- May be prepared to upset a few people in the process
- Strong orientation towards the leadership role – likely to want to take control in any group situation
- Bring energy, drive and a clear sense of purpose to a team
- People will know what is expected of them and how it should be achieved but may not always feel that sufficient account has been taken of their varying needs and viewpoints
- May come across as tough and insensitive, but may be sensitive to criticism and react defensively
- Prepared to stick to their guns - less adaptable than most as want to push through own agenda

Potential sources of friction/frustration:

- where there are others vying for the leadership position (Transactors, Transformers and other Influencers)
- may be perceived as selfish by those who place emphasis on supporting others, teamwork, etc (Transformers, Adaptors)
- inclination to challenge and dominate may result in friction with other assertive types (Influencers and, to a lesser extent, Transformers)
- decisiveness may bring them into conflict with more consultative types (Transformer-Transactors, Transformer-Thinkers, Adaptors)

Interactions with Other Types

Potential Synergies with:

- Adaptors; Individualists (especially Individualist-Doers)

Potential Conflicts with:

- other Influencers (especially Influencer-Doers); Transformers (especially Transformer-Transactors)

Could complement or be complemented by Adaptors and Transformers although the latter may also be in competition for influence and leadership.

INFLUENCER-DOERS

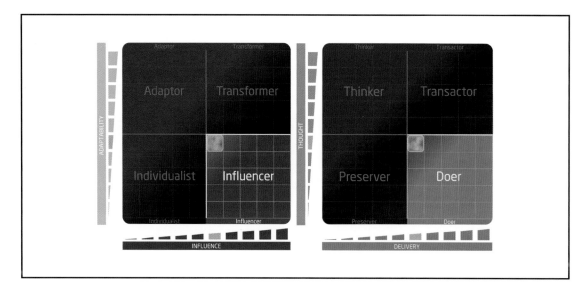

- Influencer-Doers are task-orientated and highly results focused
- Operational rather than strategic in emphasis, they will look to someone else to provide the vision but be effective in delivering
- Energetic, purposeful, directive
- Make an impact, can be relied upon to deliver, but would benefit from paying more attention to their impact on others
- Pragmatic and down to earth, focus operational rather than strategic
- Prefer stability over change
- May struggle with highly intellectual tasks and people

Potential sources of friction/frustration:

- where others are vying for leadership role (especially other Influencers)
- Thinkers may feel that their actions are autocratic, and/or that they lack imagination
- more people-orientated types (Adaptors, Transformers) may perceive them as domineering, autocratic, cold
- preference for stability may frustrate more change-oriented types (Transformer-Transactors, Transformer-Thinkers)

Interactions with Other Types

Potential Synergies with:

- Adaptor-Thinkers; Adaptor-Doers; Individualist-Thinkers

Potential Conflicts with:

- Thinkers; Transformers; other Influencers

Complemented by Adaptor-Thinkers, although may view their lack of assertive drive frustrating and slow paced.

INFLUENCER-THINKERS

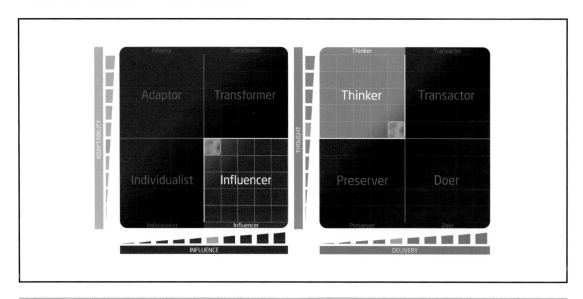

- Influence via their intellect
- Lively debaters
- Thought leaders. Visionaries
- Have very strong opinions and clear ideas about the direction things should take
- Forceful in putting their views across. Enjoy arguing
- Make an impact
- May not always give sufficient consideration to the opinions and feelings of others
- Can be sensitive to criticism and easily get defensive
- Emphasis on thought rather than action

Potential sources of friction/frustration:

- may irritate those strong on delivery (Doers, Transactors) who may perceive their inclination to analyze and argue every point as a delaying tactic
- may be perceived as aggressive by types with stronger 'soft' people skills (Adaptors, Transformers)
- preference for intellectual discussion and argument over dialogue may frustrate more consultative types (Adaptors, Transformers)

Interactions with Other Types

Potential Synergies with:

- Adaptor-Doers; Adaptor-Transactors; Individualist-Doers

Potential Conflicts with:

- Doers; Adaptors; Transformers

Complemented by Adaptor-Doers but they may not always appreciate Adaptor-Doers need for clarity and consistency to get things done.

INFLUENCER-PRESERVERS

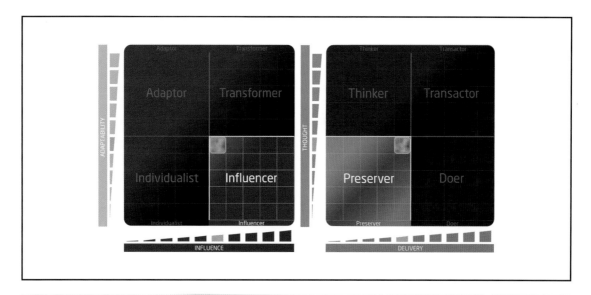

- Assertive. Like to have their opinions heard and make an impact
- Prefer to apply tried-and-tested approaches
- Prefer predictability over uncertainty
- Concrete thinkers - not into intellectual debate
- Network well, but probably prefer to maintain a degree of social distance
- Are probably more concerned with making an impact than building strong relationships
- Suited to working independently
- Interested in getting people to accept and follow their agenda
- Could be seen as manipulative by some

Potential sources of friction/frustration:

- may be perceived as cold and/or manipulative by people with more highly developed interpersonal skills (Adaptors, Transformers)
- preference for tried-and-tested approaches could frustrate more adaptable types (Adaptors, Transformers)
- may be perceived as lacking in drive by more energetic and delivery focused types (Doers, Transactors)
- may be perceived as overly domineering by some (Adaptor-Doers, Adaptor-Thinkers, Adaptor-Transactors)

Interactions with Other Types

Potential Synergies with:

- Adaptor-Doers; Adaptor-Transactors

Potential Conflicts with:

- Adaptors; Transformers; other Influencers

197

Complemented by Adaptor, Transformers and Transactors, but may have to work hard to gain influence with Thinkers and Transactors.

ADAPTOR-TRANSACTORS

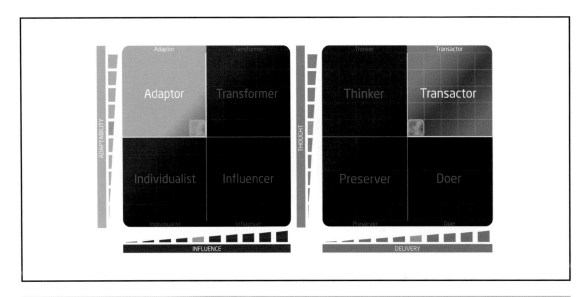

- Good team players
- Supportive, positive, flexible and adaptable
- Bring ideas and a strong task focus to the team
- Energetic and action-oriented
- Can be relied upon to deliver on time and to a high standard
- Quiet and unassertive, a force for harmony within a team
- Imaginative, potentially visionary
- May lack the assertiveness or persuasion to get ideas accepted

Potential sources of friction/frustration:

- may tend to get walked over and talked over by more assertive types (Influencers in particular)
- may be irritated by less action-orientated types (Preservers, Thinkers)
- may be frustrated by those who resist change (Individualist, Preservers)
- may find more extroverted/domineering types (Influencers, particularly Influencer-Doers, Influencer-Transactors) loud or overwhelming

Interactions with Other Types

Potential Synergies with:

- Influencers; Individualists

Potential Conflict with:

- Preservers; Thinkers

Complemented by Influencers and Transformers, may benefit from the influence and promotion brought in by these types.

ADAPTOR-DOERS

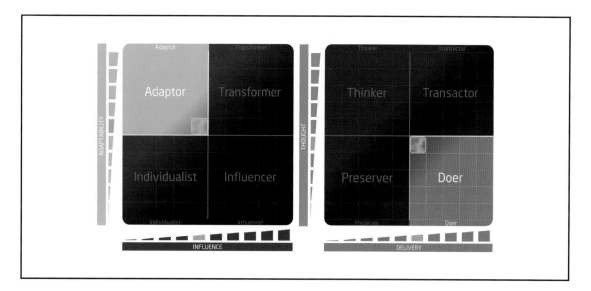

- Good team players, work collaboratively to achieve mutual goals
- Supportive, flexible, adaptable
- Good Implementers and Completer Finishers
- Likely to bring others' ideas to fruition
- Bring strong task focus to situation
- Goal-oriented but not without regard/consideration for needs of fellow team members
- Cope well with change and uncertainty

Potential sources of friction/frustration:

- thinking types may perceive them as lacking vision
- they may perceive Thinkers as overly cerebral, be frustrated by their lack of activity
- may struggle to assert their views in the presence of more dominant types (especially Influencers)

Interactions with Other Types

Potential Synergies with:

- Influencer-Thinkers; Transformer-Transactors; Transformer-Thinkers

Potential Conflicts with:

- Thinkers; Individualists

Complemented particularly by Influencer-Thinkers who can bring the ideas and the influence to get more delivered through other people.

199

ADAPTOR-THINKERS

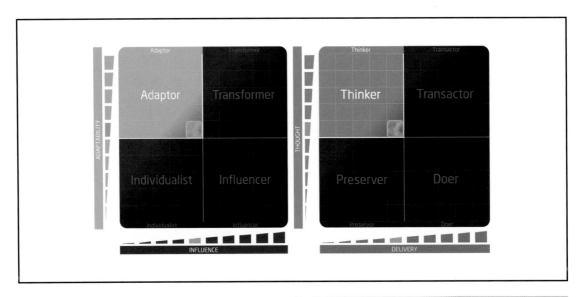

- Combine imagination, creativity and breadth of thought with analysis and logic
- Source of ideas within a team
- Sensitive and sympathetic to others' needs and viewpoints
- A force for harmony within a team
- Quiet and unassertive, may have difficulty getting ideas across and/or accepted
- Likely to spend a lot of time deliberating but be slow to take action
- Prone to be a bit disorganized

Potential sources of friction/frustration:

- may feel overwhelmed by more domineering or assertive types (particularly Influencers)
- may feel pressured by more action-orientated types (Doers and Transactors)
- will respond well to being consulted (Transformer-Transactors, Transformer-Doers)
- may be frustrated by types who are less adaptable (Individualist- Preservers)
- may irritate more action-orientated types (Doers, Transactors)

Interactions with Other Types

Potential Synergies with:

- Transformer-Transactors; Transformer-Doers; Influencer-Transactors; Influencer-Doers; Individualist-Doers

Potential Conflicts with:

- Doers; Transactors; Preservers

Complemented by Influencer-Doers who bring the necessary goal focus to achieve more and faster.

ADAPTOR-PRESERVERS

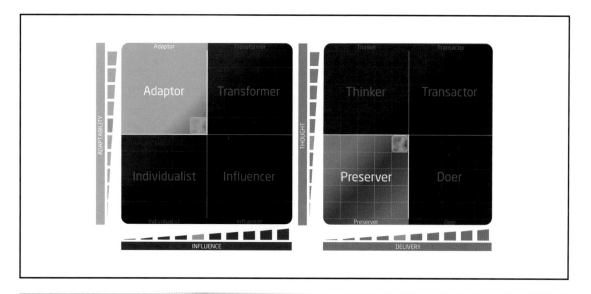

- Good team players albeit they will maintain a low profile
- Supportive, malleable, flexible, adaptable
- Considerate. Sensitive to the needs of others
- Will do what is required of them albeit at their own pace
- Cope well with change though unlikely to initiate it

Potential sources of friction/frustration:

- may feel pressured by more action-oriented types (Doers, Transactors) who, for their part, may perceive Adaptor-Preservers as lacking initiative or disinterested
- may struggle to appreciate intellectual arguments (Thinkers) and sense of urgency (Transactors, Doers)
- unlikely to assert their views in the presence of more dominant types (especially Influencers)

Interactions with Other Types

Potential Synergies with:

- Transformer-Transactors; Influencer-Transactors

Potential Conflict with:

- Doers; Transactors

Complemented by and willing to work with most other types. They often help to provide more harmony and cohesion to a team.

INDIVIDUALIST-TRANSACTORS

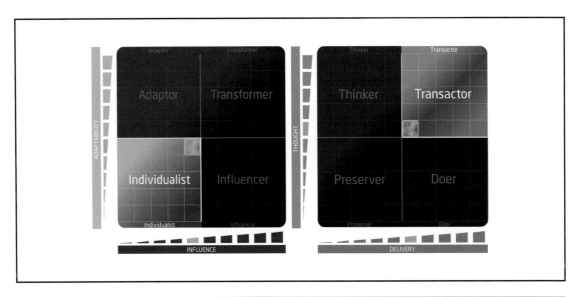

- Quiet, introverted
- Independent, self-sufficient
- Task rather than people oriented
- Combine strategic capability with a strong operational focus
- Translate ideas into action
- Pursue their goals with energy and single-minded determination
- Prefer predictability over uncertainty

Potential sources of friction/frustration:

- may not always receive the support they need from colleagues because introverted behavior means that their needs are not recognized
- may be perceived by more outgoing types (Influencers, Transformers) as unsociable, unfriendly, aloof
- may feel pressured by more communicative and sociable types (Adaptors, Transformers)
- may feel overwhelmed by more extroverted or domineering types (Influencers)

Interactions with Other Types

Potential Synergies with:

- Transformer-Transactors; Adaptor-Transactors; Influencer-Transactors; Adaptor-Doers

Potential Conflicts with:

- Influencers; Transformers; Transactors

Complemented by Transformers who can provide the people orientation to help Individualist-Transactors deliver more by involving others.

INDIVIDUALIST-DOERS

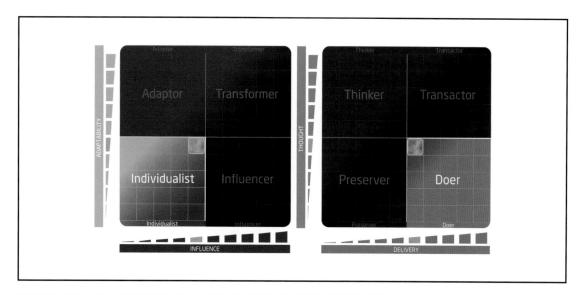

- Quiet, introverted – keep to themselves
- Independent, self-reliant
- Anxious to do well
- Possibly driven by 'fear of failure'
- Focused on delivery
- Good Implementers and Completer Finishers. Get things done
- Favor less adventurous options
- Uncomfortable with change and uncertainty

Potential sources of friction/frustration:

- may be frustrated by apparent inactivity of Thinking types
- may be seen by more extroverted types as unsociable, unfriendly, aloof
- may feel pressured by more communicative and sociable types (Influencers, Transformers)
- need for support, when it arises, may not be recognized by colleagues

Interactions with Other Types

Potential Synergies with:

- Transformer-Transactors; Transformer-Doers; Influencer-Transactors; Influencer-Doers; Thinkers

Potential Conflicts with:

- Thinkers; Influencers; Adaptors; Transformers

Complemented by Transformer-Thinkers in particular who can provide the clarity of ideas and leadership to help effective delivery. Will work best with types who provide clear direction (Transformer-Transactors, Transformer-Doers, Influencer-Transactors, Influencer-Doers).

INDIVIDUALIST-THINKERS

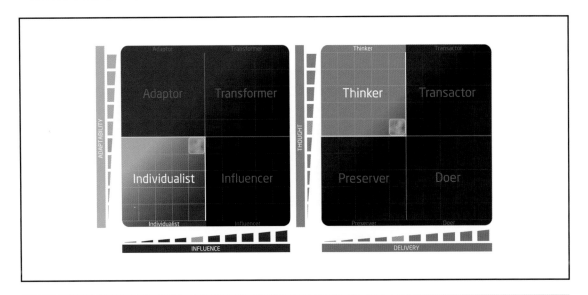

- Quiet, reserved, low profile introverts. Keep to themselves
- Intellectuals/academics
- Like research
- Focused on exploration of ideas, problem solving
- Strategically minded rather than operationally focused
- Like working on their own

Potential sources of friction/frustration:

- may have difficulty getting ideas across
- may be overlooked, walked over, talked over by more dynamic types (particularly Influencers, Doers)
- may feel overwhelmed by more communicative and sociable types (Adaptors, Transformers)
- may resist change
- may be unhappy working as part of a team and dampen rather than encourage enthusiasm in others
- may irritate more action-oriented types (especially Doers)

Interactions with Other Types

Potential Synergies with:

- Doers (especially Adaptor-Doers); Transactors (especially Transformer-Transactors)

Potential Conflicts with:

- Influencers; Adaptors; other Individualists; Transactors

204

Complemented in particular by Transformer-Doers who bring the leadership and drive to help the Individualist-Thinkers deliver their vision.

INDIVIDUALIST-PRESERVERS

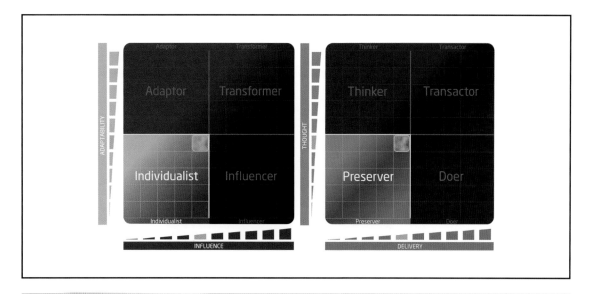

- Quiet, shy, nervous
- Low key, reserved
- Prefer working independently - comfortable working with limited social interaction
- Best suited to preserving and maintaining established systems and using tried-and-tested methods and approaches
- Can be relied upon to follow familiar routines
- Like stability, uncomfortable with change and uncertainty

Potential sources of friction/frustration:

- may be perceived by more action-oriented types (Doers, Transactors) as lacking motivation and initiative
- may perceive more extroverted types (Influencers in particular) as loud and domineering
- may irritate more communicative and sociable types (Adaptors, Transformers) and, in turn, feel pressured by them
- may not be recognized for the work they do because they often favor doing work which is low profile

Interactions with Other Types

Potential Synergies with:

- Transformer-Transactors; Adaptor-Transactors; Influencer-Transactors

Potential Conflicts with:

- Influencers; Doers; Transactors

205

Complemented by most other types who can bring in extra influence, delivery, ideas, analysis and flexibility of dealing with people.

10.6 Commonalities and Differences

This section provides descriptions of common similarities and differences that will be found within Types.

COMMONALITIES and DIFFERENCES of TRANSFORMERS

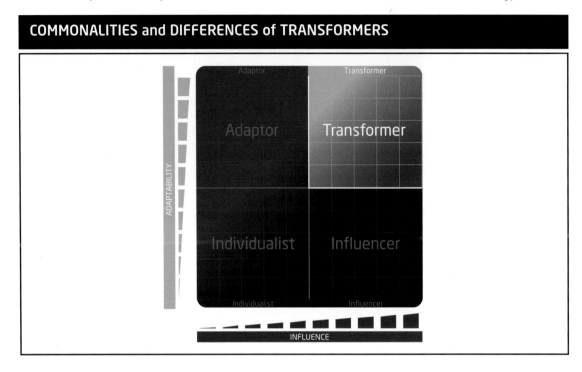

Have in common that they are:

- people-oriented
- 'natural' leaders who will provide a clear sense of direction, will inspire and motivate others
- outgoing, sociable, socially confident; good communicators, well-networked
- socially skilled, sensitive to differing needs and viewpoints, considerate
- likely to get the best from people of whatever type because of empathy and insight into what makes people tick
- emotionally resilient, calm under pressure
- flexible and adaptable
- change-oriented

Variations:

- **Transformer-Transactors** strike a balance between people and task issues, and operational and strategic focus. Visionary but also able to translate ideas into action, get things done.
- **Transformer-Doers** are people leaders that are operationally rather than strategically inclined, look to others to provide the vision but able to deliver through people.
- **Transformer-Thinkers** are people leaders that are strategically rather than operationally inclined. Can provide the vision but rely on others to deliver.
- **Transformer-Preservers** are people rather than task leaders; emphasis more on social issues. Look to others to provide the vision and also lack a strong operational focus. Less organized and results focused and probably more conventional and risk averse than other Transformer combinations.

206

COMMONALITIES and DIFFERENCES of INFLUENCERS

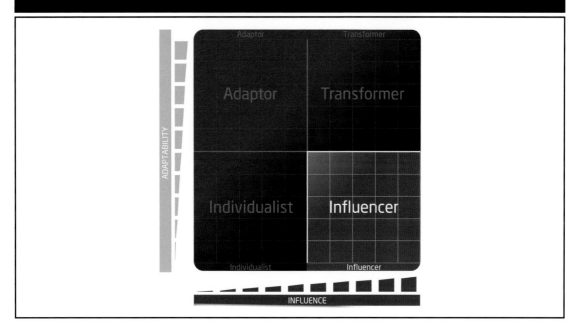

Have in common that they are:

- driven to take the lead, enjoy being in a position of power and influence
- decisive, assertive, directive
- confident communicators, prepared to voice disagreements openly, argue their case persuasively
- less team-oriented - prefer the team leader to the team member role
- potentially perceived as lacking in the 'softer' people skills (empathy, tolerance, concern for others)
- more prone to anxiety before and during important events
- more sensitive to criticism
- less likely to seek change, preferring to operate from a basis of stability

Variations:

- **Influencer-Transactors** will provide a vision and bring energy, drive and a clear sense of purpose to a team; can translate ideas into action and will get things done, although may well upset a few people in the process.
- **Influencer-Doers** are task-oriented and highly results focused. Operational rather than strategic in emphasis, they will look to someone else to provide the vision but be effective in delivering, possibly at some cost to the team harmony.
- **Influencer-Thinkers** influence via their intellects. Have strong opinions and ideas of their own about the direction things should take. Forceful in putting views across and make an impact, but less action-oriented than Influencer-Transactors and Doers.
- **Influencer-Preservers** are assertive and like to make an impact, but are less likely to introduce new ideas (are less innovative and more risk averse) than Influencer-Transactors or Thinkers and less action-oriented than Influencer-Doers and Transactors.

COMMONALITIES and DIFFERENCES of ADAPTORS

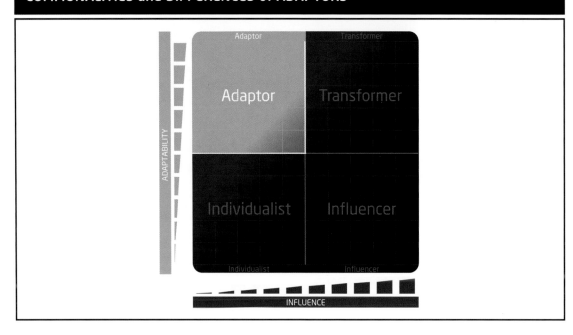

Have in common that they are:

- good team players – involving, supportive, sensitive and sympathetic to the needs and viewpoints of others
- 'agreeable' – caring, considerate, tolerant, a force for harmony and cohesion
- resilient, calm under pressure, take challenges in their stride
- less driven to take the lead, prefer to operate with clear direction from above
- quiet, less assertive, modest
- flexible and adaptable, cope well with change and uncertainty

Variations:

- **Adaptor-Transactors** are good team players who are both people and task-oriented. A source of ideas, but also bring energy and drive to a team and can be relied upon to deliver on time and to a high standard.
- **Adaptor-Doers** share with Adaptor-Transactors a strong people and task orientation but look to other people to provide the ideas which they then implement.
- **Adaptor-Thinkers** are a source of ideas but are less action-oriented than Adaptor-Doers and Transactors.
- **Adaptor-Preservers** are supportive, flexible and adaptable – good team players who will do what is required of them, albeit they will maintain a low profile.

COMMONALITIES and DIFFERENCES of INDIVIDUALISTS

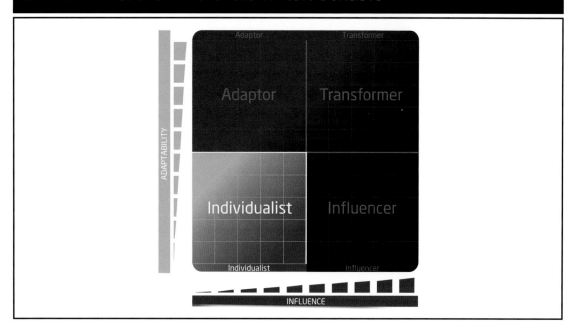

Have in common that they are:

- more introverted, quiet, less assertive
- independent and self-reliant, essentially less team-oriented, work well in isolation
- less driven to take the lead or motivated to make an impact/influence people by other means
- likely to take time to trust people
- likely to work best when not under pressure
- likely to prefer clarity and certainty

Variations:

- **Individualist-Transactors** are task rather than people-oriented, combine strategic capability with a strong operational focus, pursue goals with single-minded determination.
- **Individualist-Doers** are good implementers with a strong focus on delivery.
- **Individualist-Thinkers** are prototypical intellectuals focused on exploration of ideas and problem solving. Strategic rather than operational in emphasis and less action-oriented than Individualist-Doers or Transactors.
- **Individualist-Preservers** have less intellectual curiosity and imagination than Individualist-Thinkers and Transactors and lack the action orientation of Individualist-Doers and Transactors. Prefer to work with clear direction on tasks which are not high risk or high profile.

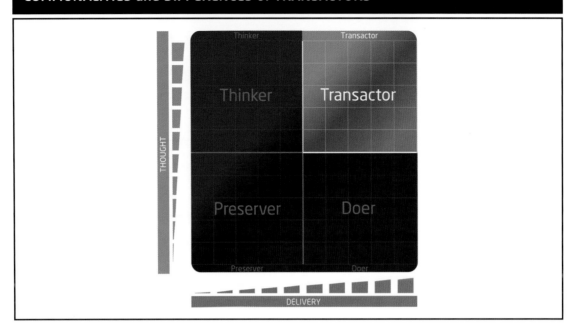

Have in common that they are:

- task-oriented
- likely to combine a capacity for breadth of vision with analytical skill
- likely to combine strategic capability with operational focus
- able to translate ideas into action
- energetic, action-oriented and results focused
- well-organized, effective planners
- reliable in delivery
- meticulous

Variations:

- **Transformer-Transactors** strike a balance between people and task issues; they will provide clear direction and be focused on achieving results, but with due consideration for the needs and viewpoints of others.
- **Influencer-Transactors** will provide a vision and bring energy, drive and a clear sense of purpose to a team; they will get things done, but may well upset a few people in the process.
- **Adaptor-Transactors** are good team players who are both people and task-oriented. Will help promote harmony within a team.
- **Individualist-Transactors** are task rather than people-oriented and will pursue goals with single minded determination.

COMMONALITIES and DIFFERENCES of DOERS

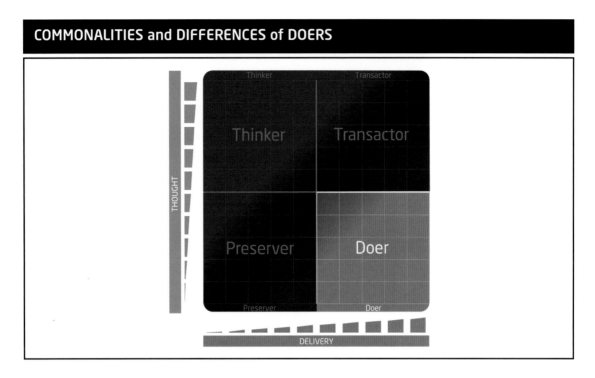

Have in common that they are:

- energetic and action-oriented
- results focused
- driven
- organized
- meticulous
- reliable
- delivery focused
- good implementers

Variations:

- **Transformer-Doers** are both task and people-oriented. Interpersonally skilled, they are able to deliver through people.
- **Influencer-Doers** are task-oriented and highly results focused. They can be relied upon to deliver but are prepared to do so in a way that may be seen as abrasive.
- **Adaptor-Doers** are good team players who are also strong implementers. They will work collaboratively with others to achieve mutual goals.
- **Individualist-Doers** are good implementers with a strong focus on delivery. They will probably work best on their own.

COMMONALITIES and DIFFERENCES of THINKERS

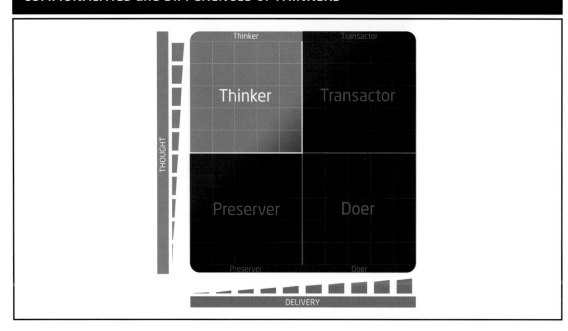

Have in common that they are:

- imaginative
- visionary
- strategic
- open minded
- logical, rational, analytical
- prone to be disorganized
- disinterested in detail
- risk takers

Variations:

- **Transformer-Thinkers** are more people than task-focused. They will provide the vision and deliver through others.
- **Influencer-Thinkers** have strong opinions and ideas of their own about the direction things should take. They are forceful in putting views across and make an impact, but may upset a few people in the process and be less effective than Transformer-Thinkers in delivering through other people.
- **Adaptor-Thinkers** are good team players, a source of ideas and force for harmony within a team.
- **Individualist-Thinkers** are prototypical intellectuals focused on exploration of ideas and problem solving.

COMMONALITIES and DIFFERENCES of PRESERVERS

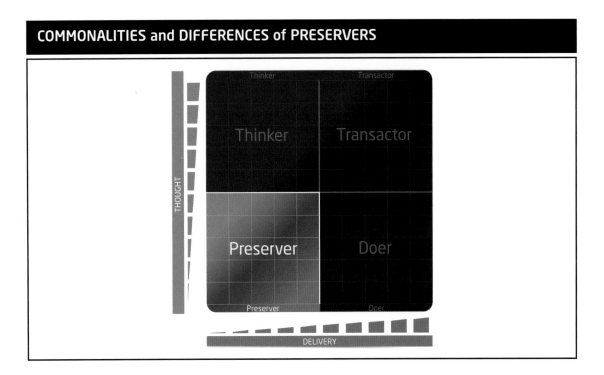

Have in common that they are:

- likely not to waste effort changing what works well already
- more conventional in their thinking and approach
- less intellectual
- less ambitious
- focused on the concrete here and now

Variations:

- **Transformer-Preservers** are social rather than task leaders; emphasis more on people issues.
- **Influencer-Preservers** are assertive and like to make an impact; they are likely to be less sensitive to the needs of others than Transformer-Preservers or Adaptor-Preservers.
- **Adaptor-Preservers** are supportive, flexible and adaptable – good team players who will do what is required of them, albeit they will maintain a low profile.
- **Individualist-Preservers** are probably the most quiet, reserved and 'low key' of all the types. They tend not to want to change things themselves, but can be encouraged to input ideas for improvement from their experience.

10.7 Using Types with Teams

'THE ONE PERSON TEAM'

Since a team is generally considered, by definition, to be a group of two or more people working together to achieve an objective, strictly speaking there can be no such thing as a one person team. However, on the face of it, Transformer-Transactors combine all the characteristics of successful teams.

They combine (among other things):

- an equally strong task and people orientation
- strong leadership qualities with a strong team orientation
- authoritativeness and 'softer' people skills
- confidence with sensitivity
- decisiveness and flexibility
- breadth of thought and vision with analytical skill
- strategic capability with operational focus
- energy with structure and focus

Limitations of the 'one person team'

They operate from one perspective only. The content of their 'vision,' the nature of the ideas they generate, their perceptions, analyses and evaluations of people and situations will be influenced by their unique personal histories. They have no third party to challenge their position or offer an alternative perspective. Therefore, if, for no other reason than this, two heads (or more) are likely to be better than one, however 'balanced.'

Synergies

Because of their well-developed interpersonal skills and insight into people's behavior, Transformer-Transactors are likely to relate well and get the best from most people.

Adaptor-Thinkers and Adaptor-Doers are likely to complement them particularly well.

Potential Conflicts/Frustrations

Of all the Types, Transformer-Transactors are most likely to become impatient/feel frustrated with Individualists and Individualist-Preservers in particular. This is because of the apparent resistance to change of these Types and a reluctance to question and take risks, coupled with an unwillingness to engage socially.

They could also find themselves in conflict for the leadership role with Influencers, particularly Influencer-Transactors whose directive stance they are unlikely to appreciate.

'TWO PEOPLE TEAMS' WITH COMPLEMENTARY CHARACTERISTICS

Influencer-Thinkers with Adaptor-Doers

Influencer-Thinkers are thought leaders who will be a source of ideas and provide a vision. They will have strong opinions about the direction things should take and put their views across forcefully. They will make an impact. They are likely to debate issues at length and may win the arguments - at an intellectual level. Where they are

likely to be less effective is in implementing the vision and getting other people to act on their ideas - not least because they may be abrasive when putting their points across and react negatively to criticism.

Adaptor-Doers are good team players who look to others to provide vision and clear direction, which Influencer-Thinkers will do. They, for their part, will bring the energy, drive and strong task focus that is lacking in Influencer-Thinkers and get things done (they are good implementers and good at completing and finishing tasks). Where other parties are involved, they will also provide the interpersonal skills and sensitivity needed to oil the social wheels. Flexible, adaptable, positive and resilient they will provide the support that Influencer-Thinkers may need to help them cope with change and other stressors.

Individualist-Transactors and Transformer-Preservers

Individualist-Transactors are quiet introverts who are task rather than people-oriented. They combine strategic capability with a strong operational focus. They have the capacity to create a vision for the future, but may need encouragement and help to communicate it. Similarly they may have difficulty getting their ideas accepted (or even recognized) because of limitations in their ability to communicate effectively. They are neither natural leaders nor team players. Energetic and driven, they pursue their goals with single-minded determination and in a planned and orderly way, but may be oblivious to the needs of others in the process and fail to get support from others when needed. They may at times get very anxious, particularly under pressure.

In contrast, Transformer-Preservers are extroverts and much more people than task focused. They are good communicators, socially adroit, and sensitive and considerate in their behavior towards others. While likely to gravitate towards the leadership role in team situations, they will look to others to provide a vision which Individualist-Transactors can do. Their focus is on the concrete here and now, rather than abstract ideas and possibilities for the future and they tend to react spontaneously to situations rather than plan ahead. They are calm and easy-going rather than highly driven and cope well with pressure.

The two types can thus be seen to have complementary skills - each fills gaps in the other's repertoire. This is not to say that they will share the same values nor even like each other; for example, Individualist-Transactors may despair of the Transformer-Preserver's relative disinterest in thoughts and ideas and apparent lack of energy and drive, while Transformer-Preservers, for their part, may deplore the Individualist-Transactor's lack of social skills and emphasis on task at the expense of people.

'TWO PEOPLE TEAMS' WITH POTENTIAL CLASHES

Influencer-Thinker with another Influencer-Thinker

Both are likely to be forceful characters with very strong opinions, ideas and agendas of their own. Problems will begin when these are out of alignment. Each will want to convince the other of the rightness of their position and be prepared to argue their case. Neither will want to back down. Moreover, any criticism of an idea is likely to be taken personally, increasing the likelihood of negative feeling (hostility even) and a further 'digging in of heels.' Adding to the difficulties will be the lack of empathy and tolerance of each party – the unwillingness to listen, to see things from the other's perspective. At worst this could be a pairing characterized by much heated debate and very little action.

'THREE, FOUR OR MORE PEOPLE TEAMS'

Most teams are composed of more than two people and they possess a mixture of complementary synergies and potential clashes. The principles of the one and two person teams can be carried over to understanding the interaction, functioning and effectiveness of these larger teams. See the following pages for a summary of potential synergies and clashes between Saville Consulting Wave Types.

215

10.8 Transformers - Potential Synergies and Conflicts

TRANSFORMER

Transformer-Transactors

Potential Synergies with:

- Adaptor-Thinkers; Adaptor-Doers; Transformer-Thinkers; Transformer-Doers

Potential Conflicts with:

- Preservers (especially Individualist-Preservers); Influencers

Transformer-Doers

Potential Synergies with:

- Adaptor-Thinkers; Transactors

Potential Conflicts with:

- Influencers; Thinkers; Preservers; Individualists

Transformer-Thinkers

Potential Synergies with:

- Doers; Adaptors

Potential Conflicts with:

- Preservers

Transformer-Preservers

Potential Synergies with:

- Transformer-Transactors; Doers; Thinkers

Potential Conflicts with:

- Individualist-Doers; Individualist-Transactors

10.9 Influencers - Potential Synergies and Conflicts

INFLUENCER

Influencer-Transactors

Potential Synergies with:

- Adaptors; Individualists (especially Individualist-Doers)

Potential Conflicts with:

- other Influencers (especially Influencer-Doers); Transformers (especially Transformer-Transactors)

Influencer-Doers

Potential Synergies with:

- Adaptor-Thinkers; Adaptor-Doers; Individualist-Thinkers

Potential Conflicts with:

- Thinkers; Transformers; other Influencers

Influencer-Thinkers

Potential Synergies with:

- Adaptor-Doers; Adaptor-Transactors; Individualist-Doers

Potential Conflicts with:

- Doers; Adaptors; Transformers

Influencer-Preservers

Potential Synergies with:

- Adaptor-Doers; Adaptor-Transactors

Potential Conflicts with:

- Adaptors; Transformers; other Influencers

10.10 Adaptors - Potential Synergies and Conflicts

ADAPTOR

Adaptor-Transactors

Potential Synergies with:

- Influencers; Individualists

Potential Conflict with:

- Preservers; Thinkers

Adaptor-Doers

Potential Synergies with:

- Influencer-Thinkers; Transformer-Transactors; Transformer-Thinkers

Potential Conflicts with:

- Thinkers; Individualists

Adaptor-Thinkers

Potential Synergies with:

- Transformer-Transactors; Transformer-Doers; Influencer-Transactors; Influencer-Doers; Individualist-Doers

Potential Conflicts with:

- Doers; Transactors; Preservers

Adaptor-Preservers

Potential Synergies with:

- Transformer-Transactors; Influencer-Transactors

Potential Conflict with:

- Doers; Transactors

10.11 Individualists - Potential Synergies and Conflicts

INDIVIDUALIST

Individualist-Transactors

Potential Synergies with:

- Transformer-Transactors; Adaptor-Transactors; Influencer-Transactors; Adaptor-Doers

Potential Conflicts with:

- Influencers; Transformers; Transactors

Individualist-Doers

Potential Synergies with:

- Transformer-Transactors; Transformer-Doers; Influencer-Transactors; Influencer-Doers; Thinkers

Potential Conflicts with:

- Thinkers; Influencers; Adaptors; Transformers

Individualist-Thinkers

Potential Synergies with:

- Doers (especially Adaptor-Doers); Transactors (especially Transformer-Transactors)

Potential Conflicts with:

- Influencers; Adaptors; other Individualists; Transactors

Individualist-Preservers

Potential Synergies with:

- Transformer-Transactors; Adaptor-Transactors; Influencer-Transactors

Potential Conflicts with:

- Influencers; Doers; Transactors

219

10.12 Further Reference Material

Further information can be found in the Case Studies and Reports chapters of this handbook.

11.0 Reports

11.1 Selection of Wave Styles Reports

This section provides a selection of Saville Consulting Wave Professional Styles Example Reports.

- ## Expert

  This is the most popular report for trained users of Saville Consulting Wave Professional Styles.

- ## Personal

  This report is provided complimentary with the Expert report and provides the assessees with a profile report summarising their results.

- ## Line Manager

  This report is designed for the other stakeholders who may or may not be trained users such as prospective line managers. The report is provided under the supervision of a trained user.

- ## Entrepreneurial

  Refer to Entrepreneurial chapter in this handbook.

- ## Types

  Refer to Types chapter in this handbook.

- ## Summary Development Report

  This report provides development advice based on the individual's competency potential. The report provided here is the Summary Development Report. A more extensive Premium Development Report is also available.

More information on reports, including Saville Consulting Wave driven interview guides, can be found at www.savilleconsulting.com.

Expert Report for
Alex Staton

Professional

Styles

Contents

About this Report

This report is based upon the Styles assessment, which explores an individual's motives, preferences, needs and talents in critical work areas.

The results are based on a comparison with a group of over 1,000 professionals and are presented on a 1 to 10 sten scale.

Since the questionnaire is a self-report measure, the results reflect the individual's self-perceptions. Nevertheless, our extensive research has shown it to be a valid measure of how people will operate in the workplace.

It should be remembered that the information contained in this report is potentially sensitive and every effort should be made to ensure that it is stored in a secure place.

The information contained within this report will provide an overview of the respondent's motives, preferences, needs and talents at work for 12 to 24 months, depending upon circumstances.

The report was produced using Saville Consulting software systems. It has been derived from the results of a questionnaire completed by the respondent, and reflects the responses they made.

This report has been generated electronically. Saville Consulting do not guarantee that it has not been changed or edited. We can accept no liability for the consequences of the use of this report, howsoever arising.

The application of this questionnaire is limited to Saville Consulting employees, agents of Saville Consulting and clients authorized by Saville Consulting.

223

Introduction to Assessment Report

This report provides information on motives, preferences, needs and talents, based on Alex Staton's responses to the Styles questionnaire.

Executive Summary Profile

The Executive Summary Profile outlines the 12 main sections of the profile, grouped under the four major cluster headings of Thought, Influence, Adaptability and Delivery. Beneath each of the 12 section headings information is given on the three underlying dimensions - 36 dimensions in total.

Full Psychometric Profile

The Full Psychometric Profile focuses on the 36 Professional Styles dimensions, which are arranged under four main cluster headings (Thought, Influence, Adaptability and Delivery), with one page devoted to each cluster. Each cluster breaks down into three sections (12 in total), each consisting of three dimensions. These 36 dimensions are each comprised of three underlying facets (108 in total), with verbal descriptions of the facet scores shown underneath the dimension title.

Summary Psychometric Profile

The Summary Psychometric Profile gives an overview of the 36 Styles dimensions of the profile on one page. It highlights where there is a facet range, and where motive or talent is higher (whichever is higher is indicated by M or T) and where Normative or Ipsative is higher (whichever is higher is indicated by an N or I).

Competency Potential Profile

The Competency Potential Report is based on links established between the 108 facets of the Styles questionnaire and a detailed, independent assessment of work performance on over 1,000 professionals. Based on real data, this gives a unique prediction of Alex Staton's likely strengths and limitations in 12 key performance areas. Underlying components of performance are reflected in the verbal descriptions and scores under each of the 12 competency headings. This prediction should be interpreted against key work requirements as established through job analysis or competency profiling methods. Highly positive profiles may reflect an unrealistically positive self-view while low scoring profiles may reflect an overly critical self-view. In such cases, it is particularly important to verify the results against other information.

Predicted Culture/Environment Fit

The Predicted Culture/Environment Fit Report gives an indication of the aspects of the culture, job and environment that are likely to enhance or inhibit a person's success. Saville Consulting's groundbreaking research suggests that people's motives and talents interact in important ways with culture, job and environment characteristics to help determine their work performance and competency.

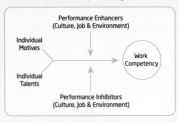

224

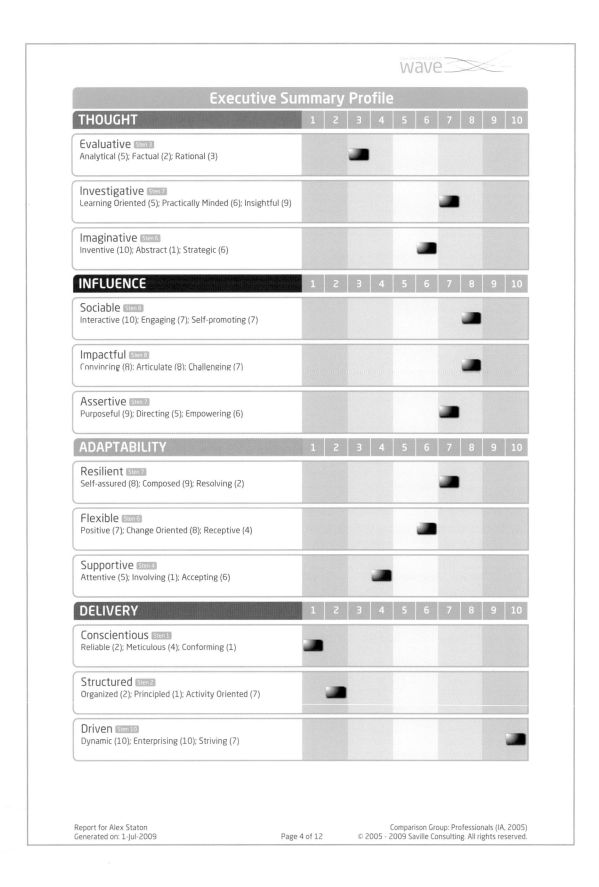

Executive Summary Profile

THOUGHT | 1 2 3 4 5 6 7 8 9 10

Evaluative Sten 3
Analytical (5); Factual (2); Rational (3)

Investigative Sten 7
Learning Oriented (5); Practically Minded (6); Insightful (9)

Imaginative Sten 6
Inventive (10); Abstract (1); Strategic (6)

INFLUENCE | 1 2 3 4 5 6 7 8 9 10

Sociable Sten 8
Interactive (10); Engaging (7); Self-promoting (7)

Impactful Sten 8
Convincing (8); Articulate (8); Challenging (7)

Assertive Sten 7
Purposeful (9); Directing (5); Empowering (6)

ADAPTABILITY | 1 2 3 4 5 6 7 8 9 10

Resilient Sten 7
Self-assured (8); Composed (9); Resolving (2)

Flexible Sten 6
Positive (7); Change Oriented (8); Receptive (4)

Supportive Sten 4
Attentive (5); Involving (1); Accepting (6)

DELIVERY | 1 2 3 4 5 6 7 8 9 10

Conscientious Sten 1
Reliable (2); Meticulous (4); Conforming (1)

Structured Sten 2
Organized (2); Principled (1); Activity Oriented (7)

Driven Sten 10
Dynamic (10); Enterprising (10); Striving (7)

Report for Alex Staton
Generated on: 1-Jul-2009

Page 4 of 12

Comparison Group: Professionals (IA, 2005)
© 2005 - 2009 Saville Consulting. All rights reserved.

Full Psychometric Profile - Overview

This full psychometric profile provides a detailed assessment of Alex Staton's responses to the Professional Styles questionnaire.

It begins with a summary of response patterns followed by an explanation of the profile structure. The next four pages report on the results of the four major clusters.

Response Summary

	1	2	3	4	5	6	7	8	9	10
Ratings Acquiescence Overall, neither overly lenient nor critical in self-ratings						■				
Consistency of Rankings Consistent in rank ordering of characteristics								■		
Normative-Ipsative Agreement Overall, there is a fairly high degree of alignment between normative and ipsative scores							■			
Motive-Talent Agreement Overall, the degree of alignment between Motive and Talent scores is slightly less than for most people				■						

Profile Breakdown

Saville Consulting's extensive research indicates the best predictor of performance at work is generally the score indicated by the sten marker (combined Normative-Ipsative). Information is also provided on subtle differences highlighted by the profile:

Facet Range. Where the range of facet scores within any dimension is of three stens or more, this is indicated both by hatching on the dimension scale and the provision of individual facet scores in parentheses alongside each verbal facet description.

Normative-Ipsative Split. Differences between Normative (rating) and Ipsative (ranking) scores of three stens or more are indicated by the markers **N** and **I**, respectively. Where Ipsative scores are higher than Normative ones, the person may have been overly self critical in their Normative self descriptions. If Normative scores are higher than Ipsative, it may mean that the person has been less self critical and has possibly exaggerated their Normative description. This provides specific areas for further verification, rather than one unspecified measure of social desirability.

Motive-Talent Split. Differences between Motive and Talent scores of three stens or more on a given dimension are indicated by the markers **M** and **T**, respectively. Such differences may suggest an incentive to develop in given areas, or indicate areas where environmental influences are having a strong impact.

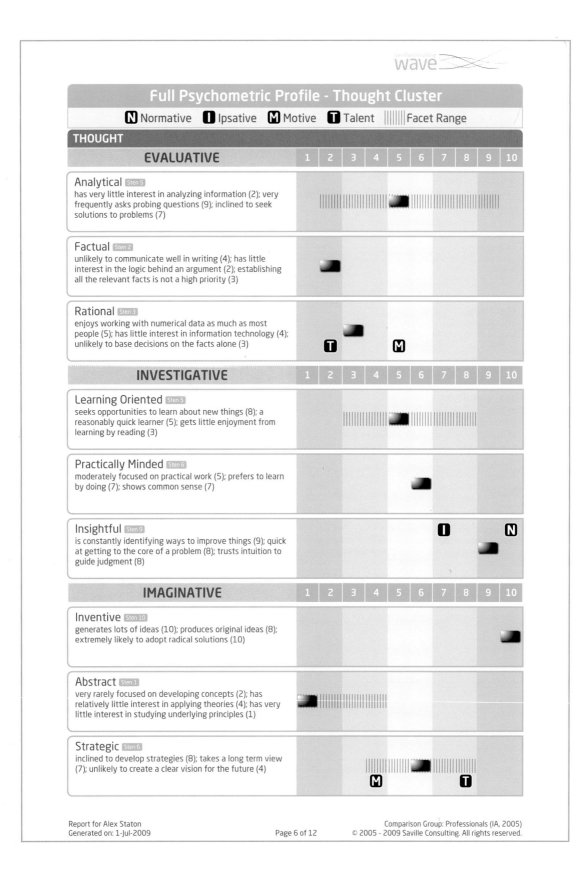

Full Psychometric Profile - Thought Cluster

N Normative   **I** Ipsative   **M** Motive   **T** Talent |||||| Facet Range

THOUGHT

EVALUATIVE	1	2	3	4	5	6	7	8	9	10

Analytical Sten 5
has very little interest in analyzing information (2); very frequently asks probing questions (9); inclined to seek solutions to problems (7)

Factual Sten 2
unlikely to communicate well in writing (4); has little interest in the logic behind an argument (2); establishing all the relevant facts is not a high priority (3)

Rational Sten 3
enjoys working with numerical data as much as most people (5); has little interest in information technology (4); unlikely to base decisions on the facts alone (3)

INVESTIGATIVE	1	2	3	4	5	6	7	8	9	10

Learning Oriented Sten 5
seeks opportunities to learn about new things (8); a reasonably quick learner (5); gets little enjoyment from learning by reading (3)

Practically Minded Sten 6
moderately focused on practical work (5); prefers to learn by doing (7); shows common sense (7)

Insightful Sten 9
is constantly identifying ways to improve things (9); quick at getting to the core of a problem (8); trusts intuition to guide judgment (8)

IMAGINATIVE	1	2	3	4	5	6	7	8	9	10

Inventive Sten 10
generates lots of ideas (10); produces original ideas (8); extremely likely to adopt radical solutions (10)

Abstract Sten 1
very rarely focused on developing concepts (2); has relatively little interest in applying theories (4); has very little interest in studying underlying principles (1)

Strategic Sten 6
inclined to develop strategies (8); takes a long term view (7); unlikely to create a clear vision for the future (4)

Report for Alex Staton
Generated on: 1-Jul-2009
Page 6 of 12

Comparison Group: Professionals (IA, 2005)
© 2005 - 2009 Saville Consulting. All rights reserved.

Full Psychometric Profile - Influence Cluster

N Normative	**I** Ipsative	**M** Motive	**T** Talent	||||||| Facet Range

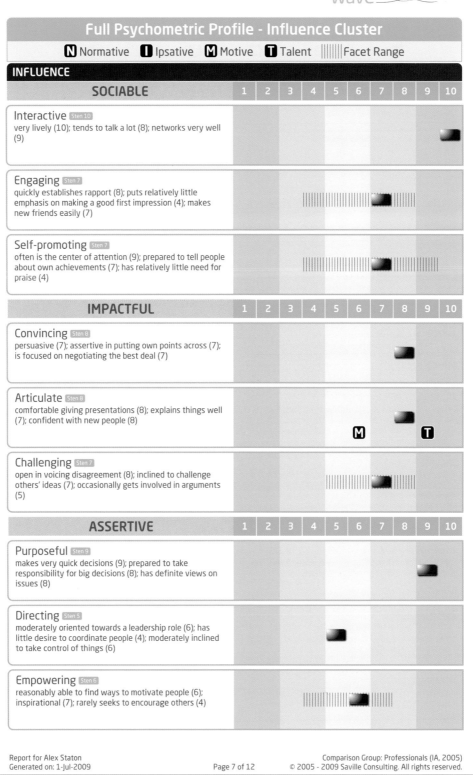

INFLUENCE

SOCIABLE	1	2	3	4	5	6	7	8	9	10

Interactive Sten 10
very lively (10); tends to talk a lot (8); networks very well (9)

Engaging Sten 7
quickly establishes rapport (8); puts relatively little emphasis on making a good first impression (4); makes new friends easily (7)

Self-promoting Sten 7
often is the center of attention (9); prepared to tell people about own achievements (7); has relatively little need for praise (4)

IMPACTFUL	1	2	3	4	5	6	7	8	9	10

Convincing Sten 8
persuasive (7); assertive in putting own points across (7); is focused on negotiating the best deal (7)

Articulate Sten 8
comfortable giving presentations (8); explains things well (7); confident with new people (8)

Challenging Sten 7
open in voicing disagreement (8); inclined to challenge others' ideas (7); occasionally gets involved in arguments (5)

ASSERTIVE	1	2	3	4	5	6	7	8	9	10

Purposeful Sten 9
makes very quick decisions (9); prepared to take responsibility for big decisions (8); has definite views on issues (8)

Directing Sten 5
moderately oriented towards a leadership role (6); has little desire to coordinate people (4); moderately inclined to take control of things (6)

Empowering Sten 6
reasonably able to find ways to motivate people (6); inspirational (7); rarely seeks to encourage others (4)

228

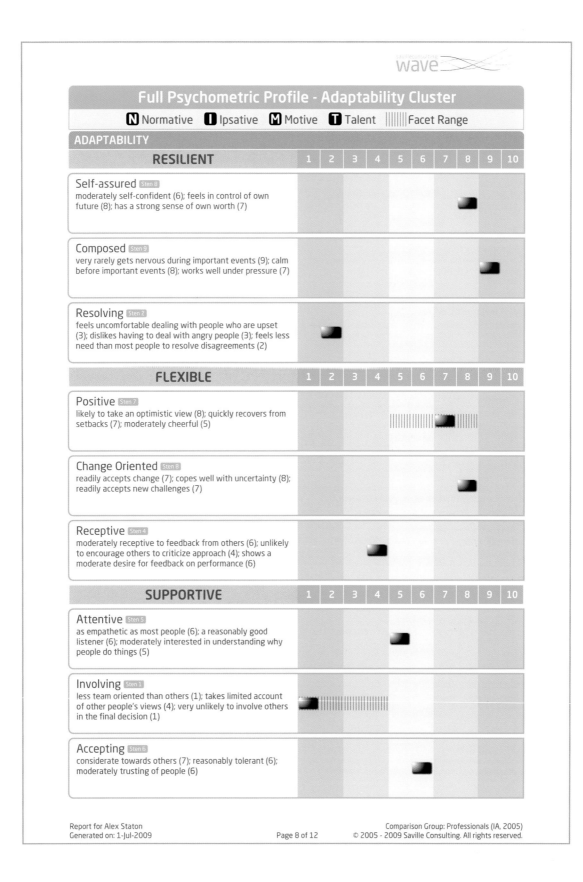

Full Psychometric Profile - Adaptability Cluster

N Normative **I** Ipsative **M** Motive **T** Talent |||||| Facet Range

ADAPTABILITY

RESILIENT — 1 2 3 4 5 6 7 8 9 10

Self-assured Sten 8
moderately self-confident (6); feels in control of own future (8); has a strong sense of own worth (7)

Composed Sten 9
very rarely gets nervous during important events (9); calm before important events (8); works well under pressure (7)

Resolving Sten 2
feels uncomfortable dealing with people who are upset (3); dislikes having to deal with angry people (3); feels less need than most people to resolve disagreements (2)

FLEXIBLE — 1 2 3 4 5 6 7 8 9 10

Positive Sten 7
likely to take an optimistic view (8); quickly recovers from setbacks (7); moderately cheerful (5)

Change Oriented Sten 8
readily accepts change (7); copes well with uncertainty (8); readily accepts new challenges (7)

Receptive Sten 4
moderately receptive to feedback from others (6); unlikely to encourage others to criticize approach (4); shows a moderate desire for feedback on performance (6)

SUPPORTIVE — 1 2 3 4 5 6 7 8 9 10

Attentive Sten 5
as empathetic as most people (6); a reasonably good listener (6); moderately interested in understanding why people do things (5)

Involving Sten 1
less team oriented than others (1); takes limited account of other people's views (4); very unlikely to involve others in the final decision (1)

Accepting Sten 6
considerate towards others (7); reasonably tolerant (6); moderately trusting of people (6)

Report for Alex Staton
Generated on: 1-Jul-2009

Page 8 of 12

Comparison Group: Professionals (IA, 2005)
© 2005 - 2009 Saville Consulting. All rights reserved.

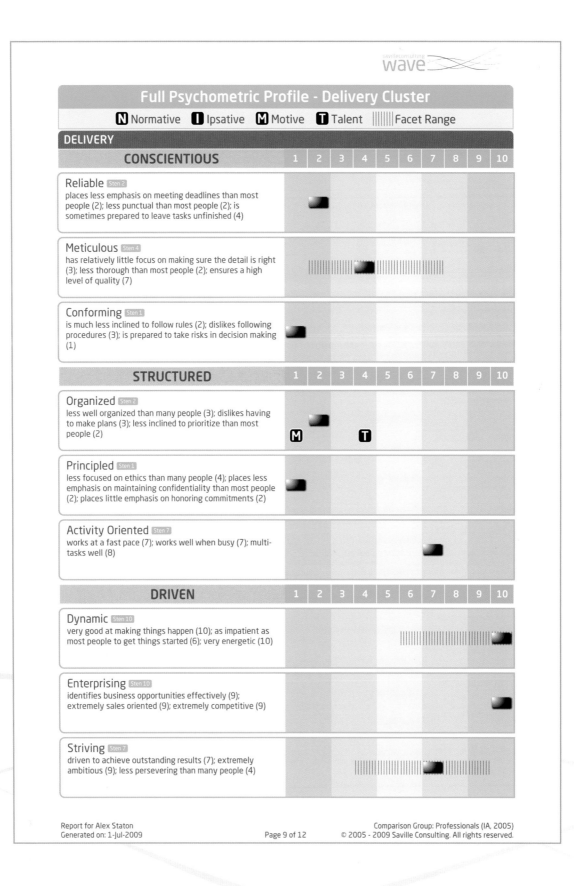

Full Psychometric Profile - Delivery Cluster

N Normative **I** Ipsative **M** Motive **T** Talent ||||||Facet Range

DELIVERY

CONSCIENTIOUS

	1	2	3	4	5	6	7	8	9	10

Reliable Sten 2
places less emphasis on meeting deadlines than most people (2); less punctual than most people (2); is sometimes prepared to leave tasks unfinished (4)

Meticulous Sten 4
has relatively little focus on making sure the detail is right (3); less thorough than most people (2); ensures a high level of quality (7)

Conforming Sten 1
is much less inclined to follow rules (2); dislikes following procedures (3); is prepared to take risks in decision making (1)

STRUCTURED

	1	2	3	4	5	6	7	8	9	10

Organized Sten 2
less well organized than many people (3); dislikes having to make plans (3); less inclined to prioritize than most people (2)

Principled Sten 1
less focused on ethics than many people (4); places less emphasis on maintaining confidentiality than most people (2); places little emphasis on honoring commitments (2)

Activity Oriented Sten 7
works at a fast pace (7); works well when busy (7); multi-tasks well (8)

DRIVEN

	1	2	3	4	5	6	7	8	9	10

Dynamic Sten 10
very good at making things happen (10); as impatient as most people to get things started (6); very energetic (10)

Enterprising Sten 10
identifies business opportunities effectively (9); extremely sales oriented (9); extremely competitive (9)

Striving Sten 7
driven to achieve outstanding results (7); extremely ambitious (9); less persevering than many people (4)

230

Summary Psychometric Profile

N Normative   **I** Ipsative   **M** Motive   **T** Talent |||||| Facet Range

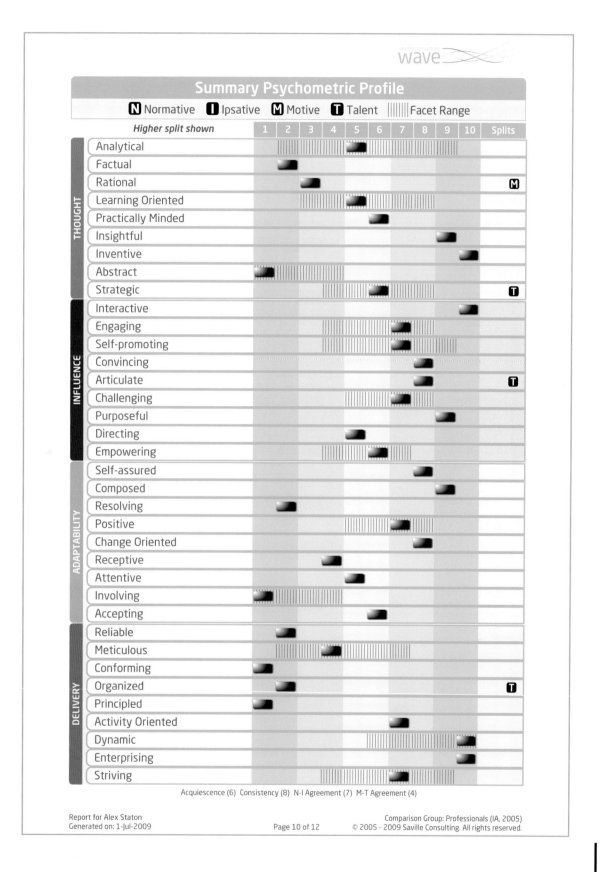

	Higher split shown	1	2	3	4	5	6	7	8	9	10	Splits
THOUGHT	Analytical											
	Factual											
	Rational											**M**
	Learning Oriented											
	Practically Minded											
	Insightful											
	Inventive											
	Abstract											
	Strategic											**T**
INFLUENCE	Interactive											
	Engaging											
	Self-promoting											
	Convincing											
	Articulate											**T**
	Challenging											
	Purposeful											
	Directing											
	Empowering											
ADAPTABILITY	Self-assured											
	Composed											
	Resolving											
	Positive											
	Change Oriented											
	Receptive											
	Attentive											
	Involving											
	Accepting											
DELIVERY	Reliable											
	Meticulous											
	Conforming											
	Organized											**T**
	Principled											
	Activity Oriented											
	Dynamic											
	Enterprising											
	Striving											

Acquiescence (6) Consistency (8) N-I Agreement (7) M-T Agreement (4)

Report for Alex Staton
Generated on: 1-Jul-2009   Page 10 of 12   Comparison Group: Professionals (IA, 2005)
© 2005 - 2009 Saville Consulting. All rights reserved.

Competency Potential Profile

This report gives Alex Staton's areas of greater and lesser predicted potential based on our extensive international database linking Saville Consulting Wave to work performance.

Competency Description	Potential	

SOLVING PROBLEMS

Evaluating Problems
Examining Information (6); Documenting Facts (2); Interpreting Data (3)
█ █ █ 3
Low
higher than about 10% of professionals

Investigating Issues
Developing Expertise (6); Adopting Practical Approaches (8); Providing Insights (9)
█ █ █ █ █ 8
High
higher than about 90% of professionals

Creating Innovation
Generating Ideas (9); Exploring Possibilities (4); Developing Strategies (8)
█ █ █ █ 7
Fairly High
higher than about 75% of professionals

INFLUENCING PEOPLE

Building Relationships
Interacting with People (9); Establishing Rapport (8); Impressing People (8)
█ █ █ █ █ 9
Very High
higher than about 95% of professionals

Communicating Information
Convincing People (7); Articulating Information (7); Challenging Ideas (7)
█ █ █ █ █ 8
High
higher than about 90% of professionals

Providing Leadership
Making Decisions (9); Directing People (6); Empowering Individuals (6)
█ █ █ █ 7
Fairly High
higher than about 75% of professionals

ADAPTING APPROACHES

Showing Resilience
Conveying Self-Confidence (8); Showing Composure (9); Resolving Conflict (2)
█ █ █ █ 7
Fairly High
higher than about 75% of professionals

Adjusting to Change
Thinking Positively (7); Embracing Change (7); Inviting Feedback (6)
█ █ █ █ 7
Fairly High
higher than about 75% of professionals

Giving Support
Understanding People (5); Team Working (2); Valuing Individuals (5)
█ █ █ 4
Fairly Low
higher than about 25% of professionals

DELIVERING RESULTS

Processing Details
Meeting Timescales (1); Checking Things (3); Following Procedures (1)
█ 1
Extremely Low
higher potential than about 1% of professionals

Structuring Tasks
Managing Tasks (2); Upholding Standards (3); Producing Output (6)
█ 2
Very Low
higher than about 5% of professionals

Driving Success
Taking Action (10); Seizing Opportunities (9); Pursuing Goals (7)
█ █ █ █ █ 9
Very High
higher than about 95% of professionals

232

Predicted Culture/Environment Fit

Based on extensive Saville Consulting people and culture audit data, this report highlights the aspects of the culture, job and environment that are likely to enhance or inhibit Alex Staton's success:

Performance Enhancers

⊕ where energy levels are high, there is a strong action orientation and people are rewarded for taking the initiative and making things happen

⊕ where commercialism and entrepreneurialism are valued, and the emphasis is on identifying business opportunities and outperforming the competition

⊕ where the ability to get rapidly to the core of issues and readily identify solutions to problems is highly valued

⊕ where there are numerous opportunities for making new contacts and developing relationships, and good networking is seen as a key to success

⊕ where value is placed on the ability to cope with pressure, emergencies and tensions

⊕ where creativity and innovation are encouraged, and radical ideas and solutions welcomed

⊕ where people are encouraged to assume responsibility for important decisions and decisiveness is a valued characteristic

⊕ where it is important to make an immediate, positive impact and be able to establish new relationships quickly

Performance Inhibitors

⊘ where energy levels are low and people show little initiative

⊘ where the culture is non-commercial, non-competitive and non-profit oriented

⊘ where little value is placed on providing new insights and identifying potential improvements

⊘ where there are few networking opportunities

⊘ where a lack of anxiety is interpreted as a lack of motivation

⊘ where conventional attitudes prevail, traditional approaches are preferred and people are discouraged from generating new ideas

⊘ where the responsibility for major decisions rests with other people and there is little opportunity to influence the outcome

⊘ where there is no requirement to make a good first impression and building relationships is not encouraged

233

Personal Report for
Alex Staton

Professional

Styles

Introduction to the Personal Report

Thank you for completing the Styles questionnaire. This report provides you with summary feedback about your motives, preferences, needs and talents in a number of work relevant areas.

When reading this report of your professional style, please remember that it is based on the information that you have provided. It describes how you perceive yourself, rather than how you might be seen by someone else. Nevertheless, research suggests that self-report can be a powerful predictor of how you will operate at work.

Information is provided on the 36 Styles dimensions, which are grouped under 12 section headings for each of the four major clusters – Thought, Influence, Adaptability and Delivery. Each dimension consists of 3 facets.

Your results combine your rating and ranking responses, and have been compared with those of a large group of professionals. For each of the dimensions your score is graphically represented on a 1-10 scale. The dimension score indicates how extreme your results are: Scores of 5 and 6 are typical of the comparison group while 1 and 10 are extreme scores achieved only by about 1% of the comparison group. Beneath each dimension name are verbal descriptions which represent the 3 facet scores that comprise the dimension score. Major variations in the verbal descriptions within a dimension are indicative of a broad range of facet scores and as such merit reflection and discussion.

On some dimensions (e.g., "Reliable") most people will rate themselves highly on the relevant questions. As a consequence, and because the results are relative, you may find that you score lower than you might have expected in such areas. It is also important to bear in mind that scores should be interpreted in terms of what is desirable for a particular job. For example, being "Compliant" may be desirable for administrative jobs that require strict adherence to rules and procedures but may be undesirable for senior roles that require some degree of risk taking and ingenuity in overcoming bureaucratic rules and procedures.

About this Report

The information contained within this report is likely to provide a valid overview of your motives, preferences, needs and talents at work (relative to others) for 12 to 24 months, depending upon your circumstances.

The report was produced using Saville Consulting software systems. It has been derived from the results of a questionnaire completed by you, the respondent, and reflects the responses made by you.

This report has been generated electronically. Saville Consulting do not guarantee that it has not been changed or edited. We can accept no liability for the consequences of the use of this report, howsoever arising.

The application of this questionnaire is limited to Saville Consulting employees, agents of Saville Consulting and clients authorized by Saville Consulting.

Report for Alex Staton
Generated on: 1-Jul-2009

Page 2 of 6

Comparison Group: Professionals (IA, 2005)
© 2005 - 2009 Saville Consulting. All rights reserved.

235

Personal Report - Thought Cluster

THOUGHT

EVALUATIVE	1	2	3	4	5	6	7	8	9	10
Analytical has very little interest in analyzing information; very frequently asks probing questions; inclined to seek solutions to problems					■					
Factual unlikely to communicate well in writing; has little interest in the logic behind an argument; establishing all the relevant facts is not a high priority		■								
Rational enjoys working with numerical data as much as most people; has little interest in information technology; unlikely to base decisions on the facts alone			■							

INVESTIGATIVE	1	2	3	4	5	6	7	8	9	10
Learning Oriented seeks opportunities to learn about new things; a reasonably quick learner; gets little enjoyment from learning by reading					■					
Practically Minded moderately focused on practical work; prefers to learn by doing; shows common sense						■				
Insightful is constantly identifying ways to improve things; quick at getting to the core of a problem; trusts intuition to guide judgment									■	

IMAGINATIVE	1	2	3	4	5	6	7	8	9	10
Inventive generates lots of ideas; produces original ideas; extremely likely to adopt radical solutions										■
Abstract very rarely focused on developing concepts; has relatively little interest in applying theories; has very little interest in studying underlying principles	■									
Strategic inclined to develop strategies; takes a long term view; unlikely to create a clear vision for the future						■				

Report for Alex Staton
Generated on: 1-Jul-2009

Page 3 of 6

Comparison Group: Professionals (IA, 2005)
© 2005 - 2009 Saville Consulting. All rights reserved.

236

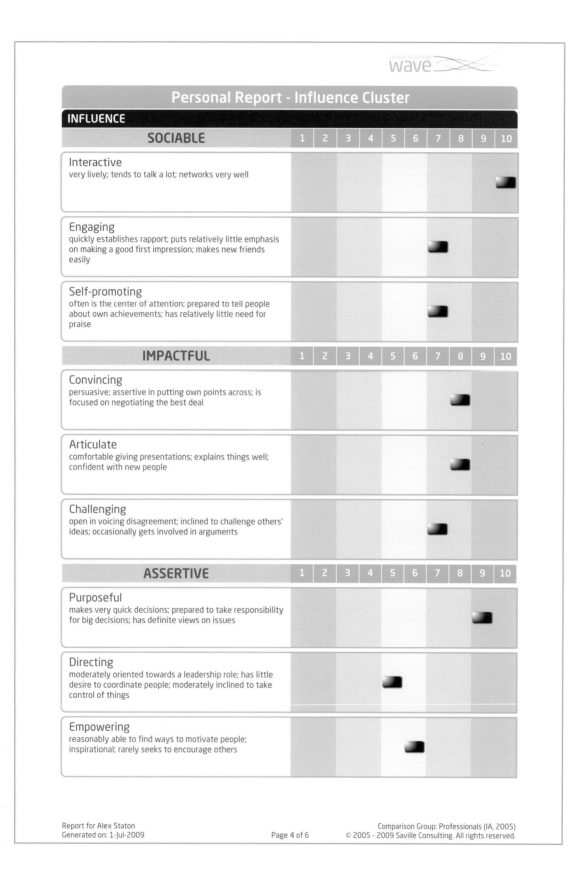

Personal Report - Influence Cluster

INFLUENCE

SOCIABLE	1	2	3	4	5	6	7	8	9	10

Interactive
very lively; tends to talk a lot; networks very well

Engaging
quickly establishes rapport; puts relatively little emphasis on making a good first impression; makes new friends easily

Self-promoting
often is the center of attention; prepared to tell people about own achievements; has relatively little need for praise

IMPACTFUL	1	2	3	4	5	6	7	8	9	10

Convincing
persuasive; assertive in putting own points across; is focused on negotiating the best deal

Articulate
comfortable giving presentations; explains things well; confident with new people

Challenging
open in voicing disagreement; inclined to challenge others' ideas; occasionally gets involved in arguments

ASSERTIVE	1	2	3	4	5	6	7	8	9	10

Purposeful
makes very quick decisions; prepared to take responsibility for big decisions; has definite views on issues

Directing
moderately oriented towards a leadership role; has little desire to coordinate people; moderately inclined to take control of things

Empowering
reasonably able to find ways to motivate people; inspirational; rarely seeks to encourage others

Report for Alex Staton
Generated on: 1-Jul-2009

Page 4 of 6

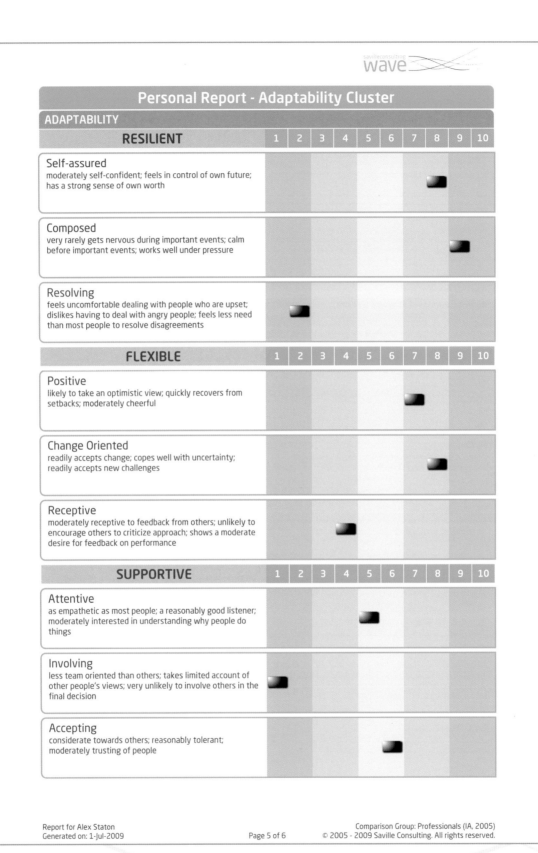

Personal Report - Adaptability Cluster

ADAPTABILITY

RESILIENT	1	2	3	4	5	6	7	8	9	10

Self-assured
moderately self-confident; feels in control of own future; has a strong sense of own worth

Composed
very rarely gets nervous during important events; calm before important events; works well under pressure

Resolving
feels uncomfortable dealing with people who are upset; dislikes having to deal with angry people; feels less need than most people to resolve disagreements

FLEXIBLE	1	2	3	4	5	6	7	8	9	10

Positive
likely to take an optimistic view; quickly recovers from setbacks; moderately cheerful

Change Oriented
readily accepts change; copes well with uncertainty; readily accepts new challenges

Receptive
moderately receptive to feedback from others; unlikely to encourage others to criticize approach; shows a moderate desire for feedback on performance

SUPPORTIVE	1	2	3	4	5	6	7	8	9	10

Attentive
as empathetic as most people; a reasonably good listener; moderately interested in understanding why people do things

Involving
less team oriented than others; takes limited account of other people's views; very unlikely to involve others in the final decision

Accepting
considerate towards others; reasonably tolerant; moderately trusting of people

238

Personal Report - Delivery Cluster

DELIVERY

CONSCIENTIOUS	1	2	3	4	5	6	7	8	9	10

Reliable
places less emphasis on meeting deadlines than most people; less punctual than most people; is sometimes prepared to leave tasks unfinished — *2*

Meticulous
has relatively little focus on making sure the detail is right; less thorough than most people; ensures a high level of quality — *4*

Conforming
is much less inclined to follow rules; dislikes following procedures; is prepared to take risks in decision making — *1*

STRUCTURED	1	2	3	4	5	6	7	8	9	10

Organized
less well organized than many people; dislikes having to make plans; less inclined to prioritize than most people — *2*

Principled
less focused on ethics than many people; places less emphasis on maintaining confidentiality than most people; places little emphasis on honoring commitments — *1*

Activity Oriented
works at a fast pace; works well when busy; multi-tasks well — *7*

DRIVEN	1	2	3	4	5	6	7	8	9	10

Dynamic
very good at making things happen; as impatient as most people to get things started; very energetic — *10*

Enterprising
identifies business opportunities effectively; extremely sales oriented; extremely competitive — *10*

Striving
driven to achieve outstanding results; extremely ambitious; less persevering than many people — *7*

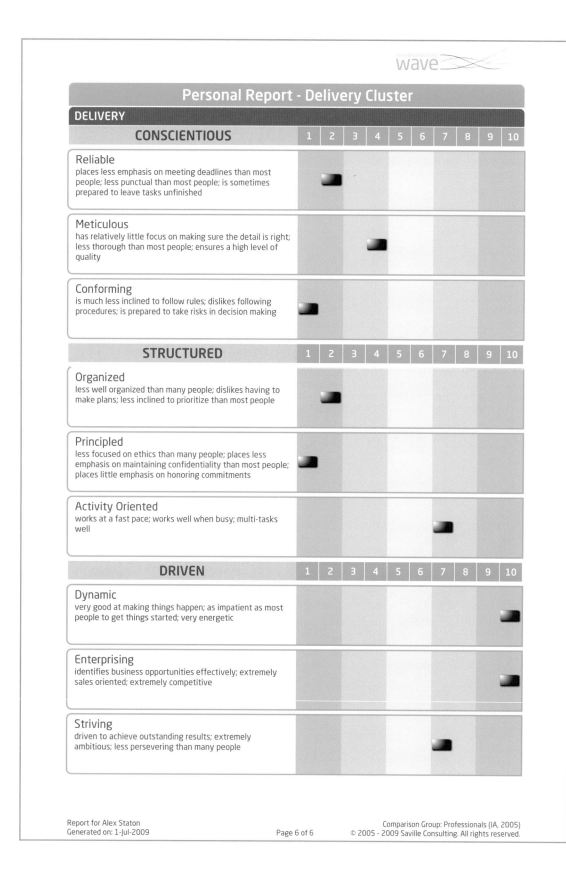

Report for Alex Staton
Generated on: 1-Jul-2009

Page 6 of 6

Comparison Group: Professionals (IA, 2005)
© 2005 - 2009 Saville Consulting. All rights reserved.

239

Line Manager Report for
Alex Staton

Professional

Styles

About this Report

This report is based upon the Saville Consulting Wave Styles assessment, which explores an individual's motives, preferences, needs and talents in critical work areas.

The results are based on a comparison with a group of over 1,000 professionals and are presented on a 1 to 10 sten scale.

Since the questionnaire is a self-report measure, the results reflect the individual's self-perceptions. Nevertheless, our extensive research has shown it to be a valid measure of how people will operate in the workplace.

It should be remembered that the information contained in this report is potentially sensitive and every effort should be made to ensure that it is stored in a secure place.

The information contained within this report is likely to remain valid for 12 to 24 months, depending upon circumstances.

The report was produced using the Saville Consulting Oasys system. It has been derived from the results of an assessment completed by the respondent, and reflects the responses they made.

This report has been generated electronically. Saville Consulting do not guarantee that it has not been changed or edited. We can accept no liability for the consequences of the use of this report, howsoever arising.

The application of this assessment is limited to Saville Consulting employees, agents of Saville Consulting and clients authorized by Saville Consulting.

Report for Alex Staton
Generated on: 2-Jul-2009

Page 2

Comparison Group: Professionals (IA, 2005)
© 2005 - 2009 Saville Consulting. All rights reserved.

241

Introduction to the Line Manager Report

This report provides information about an individual's Competency Potential and Predicted Culture/Environment fit based on Saville Consulting's extensive validation research.

Competency Potential Profile

The Competency Potential Report is based on links established between the 108 facets of the Styles questionnaire and a detailed, independent assessment of work performance on over 1,000 professionals. Based on real data, this gives a unique prediction of Alex Staton's likely strengths and limitations in 12 key performance areas. Underlying components of performance are reflected in the verbal descriptions and scores under each of the 12 competency headings. This prediction should be interpreted against key work requirements as established through job analysis or competency profiling methods. Highly positive profiles may reflect an unrealistically positive self-view whilst low scoring profiles may reflect an overly critical self-view. In such cases, it is particularly important to verify the results against other information.

Predicted Culture/Environment Fit

The Predicted Culture/Environment Fit Report gives an indication of the aspects of the culture, job and environment that are likely to enhance or inhibit a person's success. Saville Consulting's groundbreaking research suggests that people's motives and talents interact in important ways with culture, job and environment characteristics to help determine their work performance and competency.

How to use this report

The report can be used in a variety of talent management activities including personnel selection, placement, promotion and talent development. The report is designed to be interpreted by line managers, assessors, interviewers and other key stakeholders to inform their decision making without the need for specific training or expertise in the area of psychometric assessment. The competency model is designed to be universally applicable and is based on extensive research. The relative importance of each competency should be determined at the start of the assessment process. In addition, the information in this report should be used in combination with other work-relevant information about the individual when making employment related decisions.

This report should only be supplied by a specialist who is qualified to use the full range of Saville Consulting Wave tools, including the Expert Report that provides more detailed information (e.g. on an individual's underlying talents and motives).

242

Competency Potential Profile

This report gives Alex Staton's areas of greater and lesser predicted potential based on our extensive international database linking Saville Consulting Wave to work performance.

Competency Description		Potential
SOLVING PROBLEMS	**Evaluating Problems** Examining Information (6); Documenting Facts (2); Interpreting Data (3)	▮▮▮ 3	**Low** higher potential than about 10% of professionals
	Investigating Issues Developing Expertise (6); Adopting Practical Approaches (8); Providing Insights (9)	8	**High** higher potential than about 90% of professionals
	Creating Innovation Generating Ideas (9); Exploring Possibilities (4); Developing Strategies (8)	7	**Fairly High** higher potential than about 75% of professionals
INFLUENCING PEOPLE	**Building Relationships** Interacting with People (9); Establishing Rapport (0); Impressing People (9)	9	**Very High** higher potential than about 95% of professionals
	Communicating Information Convincing People (7); Articulating Information (7); Challenging Ideas (7)	8	**High** higher potential than about 90% of professionals
	Providing Leadership Making Decisions (9); Directing People (6); Empowering Individuals (6)	7	**Fairly High** higher potential than about 75% of professionals
ADAPTING APPROACHES	**Showing Resilience** Conveying Self-Confidence (8); Showing Composure (9); Resolving Conflict (2)	7	**Fairly High** higher potential than about 75% of professionals
	Adjusting to Change Thinking Positively (7); Embracing Change (7); Inviting Feedback (6)	7	**Fairly High** higher potential than about 75% of the comparison group
	Giving Support Understanding People (5); Team Working (2); Valuing Individuals (5)	4	**Fairly Low** higher potential than about 25% of professionals
DELIVERING RESULTS	**Processing Details** Meeting Timescales (1); Checking Things (3); Following Procedures (1)	1	**Extremely Low** higher potential than about 1% of the comparison group
	Structuring Tasks Managing Tasks (2); Upholding Standards (3); Producing Output (6)	2	**Very Low** higher potential than about 5% of the comparison group
	Driving Success Taking Action (10); Seizing Opportunities (9); Pursuing Goals (7)	9	**Very High** higher potential than about 95% of the comparison group

Report for Alex Staton
Generated on: 2-Jul-2009

Page 4

Comparison Group: Professionals (IA, 2005)
© 2005 - 2009 Saville Consulting. All rights reserved.

Predicted Culture/Environment Fit

Based on extensive Saville Consulting research linking the styles of individuals to culture at work, this report highlights the aspects of the culture, job and environment that are likely to enhance or inhibit Alex Staton's success:

Performance Enhancers

⊕ where energy levels are high, there is a strong action orientation and people are rewarded for taking the initiative and making things happen

⊕ where commercialism and entrepreneurialism are valued and the emphasis is on identifying business opportunities and outperforming the competition

⊕ where the ability to get rapidly to the core of issues and readily identify solutions to problems is highly valued

⊕ where there are numerous opportunities for making new contacts and developing relationships, and good networking is seen as a key to success

⊕ where value is placed on the ability to cope with pressure, emergencies and tensions

⊕ where creativity and innovation are encouraged and radical ideas and solutions welcomed

⊕ where people are encouraged to assume responsibility for important decisions and decisiveness is a valued characteristic

⊕ where it is important to make an immediate, positive impact and be able to establish new relationships quickly

Performance Inhibitors

⊘ where energy levels are low and people show little initiative

⊘ where the culture is non-commercial, non-competitive and non-profit oriented

⊘ where little value is placed on providing new insights and identifying potential improvements

⊘ where there are few networking opportunities

⊘ where a lack of anxiety is interpreted as a lack of motivation

⊘ where conventional attitudes prevail, traditional approaches are preferred and people are discouraged from generating new ideas

⊘ where the responsibility for major decisions rests with other people and there is little opportunity to influence the outcome

⊘ where there is no requirement to make a good first impression and building relationships is not encouraged

244

Entrepreneurial Potential Report for Alex Staton

powered by Entrecode®

Professional

Styles

Contents

About this Report

This report is based upon the Styles assessment which explores an individual's approach to work in a number of relevant areas. It indicates an individual's entrepreneurial potential based on the Entrecode® model of successful entrepreneurs.

The results are based on a comparison with a group of over 1,000 professionals and are presented on a 1 to 10 sten scale. A score of 1 indicates low potential and a score of 10 indicates high potential.

Since the questionnaire is a self-report measure, the results reflect the individual's self-perceptions. Nevertheless, our research has shown it to be a valid predictor of how people will operate in the workplace.

It should be remembered that the information contained in this report is potentially sensitive and every effort should be made to ensure that it is stored in a secure place.

The information contained within this report is likely to provide a valid overview of the respondent's approach to work for 12 to 24 months, depending upon circumstances.

The report was produced using the Saville Consulting software systems. It has been derived from the results of a questionnaire completed by the respondent, and reflects the responses made by them.

246

Introduction to the Entrepreneurial Potential Report

This report provides information on the entrepreneurial potential of Alex Staton based on responses to the Styles questionnaire.

The Entrecode® Research Model

The basis of this entrepreneurial potential report is the Entrecode® model (www.entrecode.co.uk) of successful entrepreneurs who have created and led high value businesses, often starting with virtually nothing. The Entrecode® model was derived from more than fifteen years of research undertaken by Professor David Hall and his associates.

This report predicts potential for each of the 6 core areas outlined in the Entrecode® model, from 'Getting in the Zone' through to 'Building Capability':

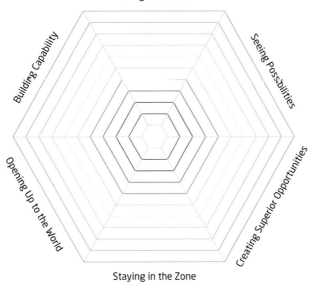

Entrepreneurial Potential Summary

The Entrepreneurial Potential Summary provides information on the 6 core areas of the Entrecode® model, followed by a brief description of each area.

Entrepreneurial Potential Profile

The Entrepreneurial Potential Profile provides greater detail by breaking the 6 core areas down into 21 aspects of entrepreneurial potential. For each of the 21 areas a description is provided which varies according to Alex Staton's score.

247

Entrepreneurial Potential Summary

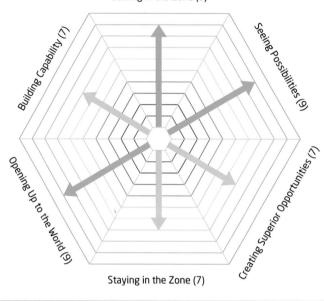

Getting in the Zone
the optimal state of mind to create success

Seeing Possibilities
the unique ways in which entrepreneurs view the world, take in information and create insights

Creating Superior Opportunities
identifying client problems that need to be solved and leveraging solutions to transform business results

Staying in the Zone
prioritizing, sequencing and focusing energy on a very specific target

Opening Up to the World
building networks, and forming relationships to enable the business to develop

Building Capability
focusing efforts on building the capacity of the business

248

Entrepreneurial Potential Profile

GETTING IN THE ZONE

Achievement Drive	8	shows determination and purpose to succeed and achieve results
Compelling Vision	7	builds a compelling vision of what the endgame will look like
Energy	10	consistently puts lots of energy into making things happen
Action Oriented	8	does not hold back from taking the initiative, preferring to take action quickly and decisively

SEEING POSSIBILITIES

Big Picture	8	focused on the big picture and likely to be less interested in low-level issues
Options Thinking	8	explores a wider range of alternative approaches to issues than most
Savvy	8	relies on own intuition and experience to make judgments

CREATING SUPERIOR OPPORTUNITIES

Problem Seeking	10	puts significant effort into finding out which problems customers really want to address
Synthesis	4	may be less inclined than others to make the connection between insights gained from different sources
Problem Solving	8	produces strong commercial solutions to customer problems that often lead to new business opportunities
Customer Delivery	3	may sometimes be less focused than others on delivering a high quality service to customers

Entrepreneurial Potential Profile

STAYING IN THE ZONE

Focus	**5**	generally stays focused on priorities, not easily distracted
Positive Mindset	**8**	maintains an optimistic outlook, responding positively to new challenges
Self-determining	**8**	comfortable making decisions that will shape own destiny
Persistence	**5**	reasonably persistent in seeing things through to the end, recovering from setbacks as quickly as most people

OPENING UP TO THE WORLD

Expressing Passion	**8**	talks enthusiastically and persuasively, may be seen by many as inspirational
Purposeful Networking	**9**	shows great flair in building and maintaining appropriate networks to establish useful business relationships
Creating Partnerships	**9**	highly skilled at negotiating, generating sales and building strong commercial partnerships

BUILDING CAPABILITY

Building Up the Team	**5**	reasonably focused on building and motivating the team
Experiential Learning	**8**	ready to try things out and to learn from pragmatic experimentation and experience
Staying on Track	**7**	invests effort into maintaining performance and seeking continuous improvement

250

Entrepreneurial Potential Scale

The results are based on a comparison with a group of over 1,000 professionals and are presented on a 1 to 10 sten scale.

1 = higher potential than about 1% of professionals

2 = higher potential than about 5% of professionals

3 = higher potential than about 10% of professionals

4 = higher potential than about 25% of professionals

5 = higher potential than about 40% of professionals

6 = higher potential than about 60% of professionals

7 = higher potential than about 75% of professionals

8 = higher potential than about 90% of professionals

9 = higher potential than about 95% of professionals

10 = higher potential than about 99% of professionals

Report for Alex Staton
Generated on: 1-Jul-2009

Page 7 of 7

Comparison Group: Professionals (IA, 2005)
© 2005 - 2009 Saville Consulting. All rights reserved.

251

saville consulting
wave

Types Report for
Alex Staton

Professional

Styles

Contents

About this Report

This report is based upon the Styles assessment that explores an individual's behavioral tendencies in a number of work relevant areas.

The results are based on a comparison with a group of over 1,000 professionals and are presented on a 1 to 10 sten scale.

Since the questionnaire is a self-report measure, the results reflect the individual's self-perceptions. Nevertheless, our extensive research has shown it to be a valid measure of how people will operate in the workplace.

It should be remembered that the information contained in this report is potentially sensitive and every effort should be made to ensure that it is stored in a secure place.

The information contained within this report is likely to provide a valid overview of the respondent's behavioral tendencies at work for 12 to 24 months, depending upon circumstances.

The report was produced using Saville Consulting software systems. It has been derived from the results of a questionnaire completed by the respondent and reflects the responses they made.

This report has been generated electronically. Saville Consulting do not guarantee that it has not been changed or edited. We can accept no liability for the consequences of the use of this report.

The application of this questionnaire is limited to Saville Consulting employees, agents of Saville Consulting and clients authorized by Saville Consulting.

253

Introduction to the Types Report

This report outlines the typical approach of Alex Staton at work based on responses to the Saville Consulting Wave Styles questionnaire.

Saville Consulting Wave™ Types

Research has shown that the Saville Consulting Wave™ Types are powerful predictors of performance in a range of key areas.

Note: Typologies are useful generalizations about people. However, generalizations by their nature make it inevitable that respondents will identify more closely with some aspects of the description of their type than others.

Styles Assessment

The report draws on the four Clusters in the Styles assessment that cover three Sections each:

Thought
Evaluative, Investigative, Imaginative

Influence
Sociable, Impactful, Assertive

Adaptability
Resilient, Flexible, Supportive

Delivery
Conscientious, Structured, Driven

People & Task Types

This report integrates results in the 'People' Clusters (Influencing People and Adapting Approaches) into four People Types, and results on the 'Task' Clusters (Solving Problems and Delivering Results) into four Task Types.

The People Type for Alex Staton is shown on the following page followed by the Task Type.

On the Type chart the distance from each axis indicates how clear or differentiated the type is. Scores close to the corners of the chart indicate that the type is very clear and that the type description will apply very consistently. Scores next to an axis suggest that the individual may adopt the behaviors associated with either side of the axis.

Saville Consulting Wave™ Types Implications

Saville Consulting Wave™ Types have implications for behavior in leadership roles, team/peer interaction, change management and synergies with various organizational cultures.

254

People Type

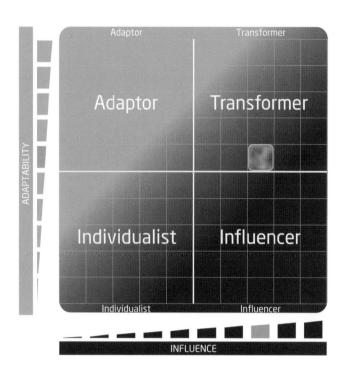

Transformer

Transformers combine interpersonal sensitivity with powerful social networks and definite leadership impact. As the results are not strongly differentiated, Alex Staton is most likely to adopt this type, but may often adopt other types.

255

Task Type

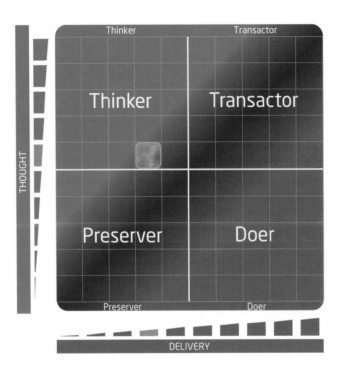

Thinker

Thinkers get straight to the core of a problem to find solutions. They may pursue ideas at the expense of accomplishing results. As the results are not strongly differentiated, Alex Staton is most likely to adopt this type, but may often adopt other types.

256

Transformer-Thinker

Transformer-Thinkers show great flexibility and a thirst for change. They have an enquiring and challenging approach which is balanced by supportiveness for their colleagues and teams.

Leadership Style

- Transformer-Thinkers provide a very flexible and accommodating approach to leading teams.
- They are persuasive individuals capable of inspiring others to give their best.
- Their thoughtful analysis and insights often leads others to seek their views.
- Leaders of this type are often visionaries rather than implementers and may at times struggle to deliver.

Team & Peer Interaction

- They enjoy team work and harmonious relationships, and influencing others to their point of view.
- People with this approach are likely to be supportive and positive in team or peer processes.
- Transformer-Thinkers are likely to be enthusiastic about new projects and ideas. They are eager to discuss things but less likely to put ideas into action.

Managing Change

- Transformer-Thinkers present a very powerful profile for leading and facilitating change.
- Their resilience, flexibility and communicative style, coupled with sound judgment of situations, are powerful assets to any organizational change initiative.
- They can be exceptional sponsors of change, who think ahead and inspire people with their enthusiasm.
- Their caring and insightful approach to people can make it difficult for them to take tough action that hurts the feelings of others.

Cultural Synergies & Maximizing Potential

- Transformer-Thinkers like to discuss their many plans and ideas but their enthusiasm may not be matched by their meticulousness in finishing tasks.
- They require stimulating work that provides scope for innovation and time for discussion – pressure to get results may reduce motivation.
- Transformer-Thinkers prefer environments where a clear vision for the future and sound judgment are valued.
- They are best suited to more fluid cultures where people are generally supportive of each other.

Saville Consulting Wave™ Types Model

People Types

Adaptor Adaptors are supportive, resilient and flexible in response to change. They are quiet and accommodating.	**Transformer** Transformers combine interpersonal sensitivity with powerful social networks and definite leadership impact.
Individualist Individualists are task rather than people-focused. They prefer environments where their specialist expertise is valued.	**Influencer** Influencers excel at communicating their message. They enjoy using power and single-mindedly pursue their goals.

Task Types

Thinker Thinkers get straight to the core of a problem to find solutions. They may pursue ideas at the expense of accomplishing results.	**Transactor** Transactors combine thoughtful analysis with the driven pursuit of goals. They enjoy challenges and can be relied upon to deliver results.
Preserver Preservers adopt conventional approaches to their work and prefer a steady work pace.	**Doer** Doers approach their work with dynamism and conscientiousness. They prefer action over intellectualized debate.

258

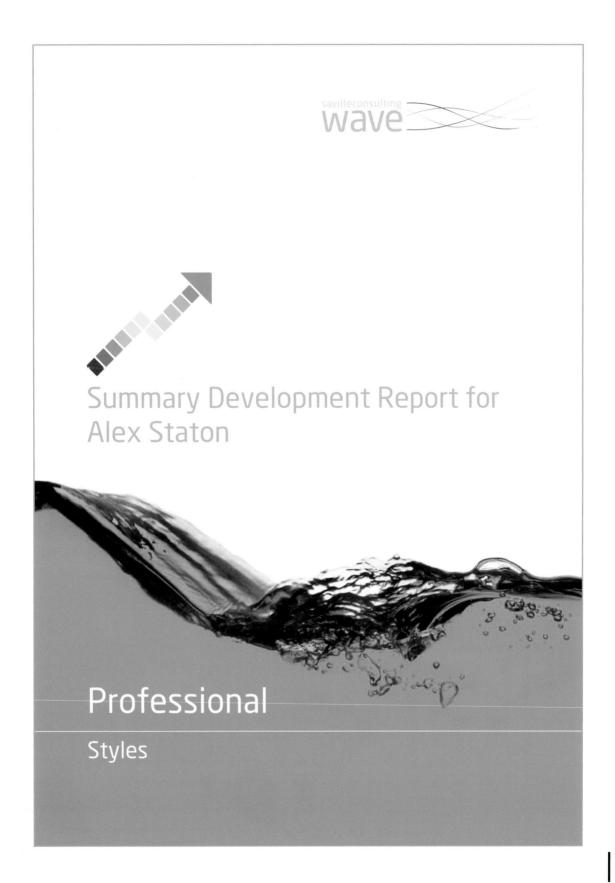

Summary Development Report for
Alex Staton

Professional

Styles

Contents

About this Report

This report is based upon the Styles assessment, which explores an individual's motives, preferences, needs and talents in critical work areas.

The results are based on a comparison with a group of over 1,000 professionals and are presented on a 1 to 10 sten scale.

Since the questionnaire is a self-report measure, the results reflect the individual's self-perceptions. Nevertheless, our extensive research has shown it to be a valid measure of how people will operate in the workplace.

It should be remembered that the information contained in this report is potentially sensitive and every effort should be made to ensure that it is stored in a secure place.

The information contained within this report will provide an overview of the respondent's motives, preferences, needs and talents at work for 12 to 24 months, depending upon circumstances.

The report was produced using Saville Consulting software systems. It has been derived from the results of a questionnaire completed by the respondent, and reflects the responses they made.

This report has been generated electronically. Saville Consulting do not guarantee that it has not been changed or edited. We can accept no liability for the consequences of the use of this report, howsoever arising.

The application of this questionnaire is limited to Saville Consulting employees, agents of Saville Consulting and clients authorized by Saville Consulting.

260

Introduction to Assessment Report

This development report summarizes the actions that could be taken to develop Alex Staton. Based on the results of the assessment it outlines what actions could be considered to improve performance at work. The appropriateness of each piece of advice will differ for each individual and will to some extent depend on the job role and the opportunities and resources available. The report is divided into two sections. These sections are composed of the following four types of development advice.

Building Strengths

Successful people tend to know what they are good at and play to these strengths. Before trying to make up for, or develop limitations, it may be worth considering how to make the most of these strengths. This summary report shows Building Strengths for the eight highest competency dimensions.

Possible Overplayed Strengths - 'Watch Fors'

Clear areas of strength are most likely to contribute to effectiveness at and enjoyment of work. They may, however, lead to unwanted or undesirable consequences. For each of the areas of particular strength, the potential pitfalls are highlighted together with actions to reduce or avoid their negative impact. This summary report shows Possible Overplayed Strengths for the four highest competency dimensions.

Development Tips

While building strengths is likely to be a more rewarding way to develop, it may be that there is a requirement to develop in areas that are less strong. For these areas development tips are provided on how to improve performance. This summary report shows Development Tips for the eight lowest competency dimensions.

Managing Limitations

Areas of limitation are unlikely to be areas where there is a strong desire or capability to easily change. It may be better to be realistic about these areas and rather than attempt to change them, be clear on how best to manage them. If there are no clear areas of limitation, this section will be blank. This summary report shows Managing Limitations for the four lowest competency dimensions.

261

Building Strengths

Taking Action		Extremely High
Investing Energy; Using Initiative; Making Things Happen	 **10**	performed better than 99% of comparison group

- Make sure others are also on board before diving into something new.

- Consider special projects that involve troubleshooting, crisis management, or consulting.

- Gain experience through short term contracts, secondments or temporary assignments.

- Use this high energy to inject a renewed enthusiasm into projects where people are uninspired or demotivated.

- Take something that is important but has stalled due to lack of commitment or motivation, and get it moving along.

- Develop a reputation for taking the initiative and resolving issues before they escalate.

- Seek opportunities to start new initiatives, practice areas, lines of business, or turning poorly performing areas around.

- Look for things that really need to be done, but there is inertia of indecision. Make a commitment to yourself to move them on.

262

Possible Overplayed Strengths

Taking Action		Extremely High
Investing Energy; Using Initiative; Making Things Happen	 **10**	performed better than 99% of comparison group

- Does the excitement of starting something new come at the expense of doing more routine work? ACTION: Schedule time for routine maintenance activities or to check ongoing tasks so they are not left undone.

- Is the thrill of crisis management overshadowing planning and problem prevention? ACTION: Implement systems and processes that will reduce the likelihood of problems or crises recurring.

- Is your energy being channeled as appropriately as possible? ACTION: Before rushing on to the next activity take time out to stop and think "is this the best use of time and energy?"

- Is there a danger of overstepping the mark and doing things that have been ruled out by others? ACTION: Be careful not to do something that is not wanted or needed and that no-one will be thankful for. Be selective and use your initiative wisely.

- Is there a readiness to embark on new work where there is a low degree of knowledge and understanding? ACTION: Consult experts before taking the initiative in a new work area.

- Does a desire to make things happen tend to throw existing projects into disarray? ACTION: Be careful that in making things happen this does not require resources that are already fully committed to existing projects. Avoid taking on too much and fulfill

263

Building Strengths

Generating Ideas		Very High
Producing Ideas; Inventing Approaches; Adopting Radical Solutions	 **9**	performed better than 95% of comparison group

- Ensure that ideas are supported by a rational argument and a strong business case.

- Be aware of who the key stakeholders and decision makers are. These are the people to sell ideas to.

- Ask for feedback on the quality of ideas and how they are presented.

- Look at the best ideas that have previously been rejected and see if they could be revived.

- Get involved in the early stages of projects. This is where suggestions will be welcomed.

- Investigate techniques to improve creativity.

- Put together a creative group of experts from different areas to solve intractable problems. Apply "work-out" or six-sigma principles.

- Present a range of ideas, offering varying degrees of change from where things are now.

264

Possible Overplayed Strengths

Generating Ideas Producing Ideas; Inventing Approaches; Adopting Radical Solutions	 9	Very High performed better than 95% of comparison group

- Is there a strong focus on generating ideas at the expense of delivery? ACTION: Be careful not to get spread too thinly - try out the best formed ideas, not all of the ideas.

- Is a passion for producing ideas creating difficulties when listening to others' ideas and accepting alternative views? ACTION: Treat other people's ideas with respect and review their merit alongside own ideas.

- Is continuously pursuing ideas after they have been rejected having an impact on own reputation? ACTION: Be clear about which ideas will always be rejected. Look to avoid these same pitfalls when putting forward new or revised ideas.

- With so many ideas, it may be difficult to prioritize and progress the key ones. ACTION: identify the ideas that matter. Promote these and avoid presenting lots of ideas at once.

- Are there so many ideas that it is difficult to identify the really good ones? ACTION: Aim for fewer, well argued propositions.

- Is a quest for creativity at the expense of considering essential parameters and requirements? ACTION: Understand and adhere to the requirements of the brief.

- Does too radical an approach risk a loss of credibility with some key stakeholders? ACTION: Always seek feedback from stakeholders and be aware of what they are looking for.

- Is the focus on doing things differently so great that it risks losing what works well now? ACTION: Be clear on the reasons things shouldn't change and be prepared to have changes as additions or new services rather than simply scrapping what went before.

265

Building Strengths

Making Decisions Assuming Responsibility; Deciding on Action; Standing by Decisions		Very High performed better than 95% of comparison group

- Inject pace and decisiveness into project groups and make things happen.

- In meetings always look for decisions and action points.

- Make sure your approach to risk is calculated. Assume the worst will happen and build in contingencies.

- Honestly review the quality of the decisions made and identify why they were the right or wrong decision. Think what it would have taken for the right decision to be made. Learn from this.

- Invest energy on the tasks that have the most impact and benefit.

- Volunteer to lead projects and take on new tasks. Take the opportunities to work outside your comfort zone.

- Facilitate the decision making process. Outline the key options/risks for everyone.

- Encourage people to make decisions and commit to action. Move debate on towards a conclusion.

- Grasp opportunities and make things happen.

- Identify the experts and key opinion leaders who can be consulted and ask for advice before committing to important decisions.

- Look for agreement and support from others before concluding on important decisions.

- Ensure that a decision is well implemented. A common reason for having to change a decision is ineffective implementation.

- Put a sign off process in place for key decisions.

266

Possible Overplayed Strengths

Making Decisions Assuming Responsibility; Deciding on Action; Standing by Decisions	 **9**	Very High performed better than 95% of comparison group

- Is there a danger of being seen as too dominant in group or team settings? ACTION: Appoint other people to chair some meetings and establish actions.

- Is there a danger of being ready to make the decision but not ensuring the decision is effectively implemented? ACTION: Be sure to stay involved to help translate a decision into practical actions.

- Do you sometimes step on other people's toes? Avoid encroaching on other people's areas of responsibility. ACTION: Respect the boundaries of other people's roles and concentrate on your own responsibilities.

- Look out for over-commitment and unnecessarily increasing workload and responsibilities leading to poorer delivery. ACTION: Discuss shifting responsibilities with line manager and be wary of adding responsibilities.

- When there is an important but non-urgent decision to be made, is there a tendency make a quick decision without appropriate deliberation? ACTION: Identify decisions that are important to get right but are non-urgent and consider how the decision would be best made.

- Do you find yourself making (or imposing) decisions without much consultation or collaboration with others? ACTION: Think how to build in time to consult and consider alternative views. Consider the risks of not getting other people's buy-in.

- Is there a risk of making decisions before colleagues are ready to implement them? ACTION: Give colleagues time to work through the implications of implementing a decision, and give them time to work out how to make the decision work.

- Is there a greater determination to follow a particular course of action because there is strong opposing advice? ACTION: Don't try to prove a point by making a decision that you may later regret.

- Be aware that people who are seen as fixed in their view or opinionated can also be seen as lacking objectivity. ACTION: Step back and consider whether there is a danger that personal opinions or attitudes are driving decisions rather than relevant criteria.

Building Strengths

Providing Insights		Very High
Identifying Key Issues; Making Intuitive Judgments; Continuously Improving Things		performed better than 95% of comparison group

- Identify areas where the capacity to improve things will have the most benefit.

- Identify an area which is in need of change. For each of the problems identified, suggest solutions and provide them to key staff.

- Help others by showing them how you go about identifying what the key issues are. Get them to consider the key objectives, the dependencies in projects and evaluate the key risks.

- Learn to understand your intuition. Reflect on when your intuition has been right and wrong. Use this information to guide when to rely on intuition in the future and where one should place greater weight on other information available.

- Offer suggestions on potential enhancements and improvements to managers/team leaders. Sell the benefits of making the changes.

- Look for areas of rapid change and "quick wins". Seek out managers who are appreciative of your ideas and will use your suggestions constructively.

268

Possible Overplayed Strengths

Providing Insights Identifying Key Issues; Making Intuitive Judgments; Continuously Improving Things		Very High performed better than 95% of comparison group

- Might providing new insights and re-visiting work be causing problems for others because things keep changing? ACTION: Try to create a more structured improvement process where changes are made in a coordinated way and are clearly communicated.

- Do very insightful people sometimes risk jumping to conclusions on the basis of very little data or analysis? ACTION: Build some review time into your thinking and consider how you manage risk.

- Could recommendations feel as if they have been imposed upon others? Might this lessen the impact with very analytical colleagues? ACTION: Ensure that all members of the team are aware of all the issues, before making decisions.

- Could less insightful colleagues feel left behind as they haven't pulled out the key issues as quickly? ACTION: Make the key points of an argument clear. Be prepared to justify the thinking behind an argument.

- Is there a danger that a personal analysis of the key issues could be out of line with what matters to the key stakeholders? ACTION: Make sure to discuss personal analyses of key issues with relevant stakeholders.

- Could people who are quick to get to the core of a problem sometimes not spend sufficient time explaining their thinking to others? ACTION: Make sufficient time to justify and explain own recommendations and conclusions to colleagues.

- Is there a danger of being too quick to make assumptions and reaching own conclusions? ACTION: Challenge and evaluate own assumptions before reaching conclusions.

- Could there be an over-willingness to make decisions on the basis of intuition in the absence of substantive data? ACTION: Identify key data sources to support own intuition.

- Is there a readiness to make decisions in areas where own expertise is limited? ACTION: Be honest about your strengths. Seek advice from experts when needed?

- Is the change really worth the disruption it will cause? ACTION: Ensure that improvements will demonstrate a return on investment and are worth doing.

- Could the suggested improvements be too difficult for people to implement easily? ACTION: Think about the practicalities of implementing ideas cost effectively - are simpler changes possible?

- Could seeking to improve things constantly mean that existing processes are not sufficiently embedded and used? ACTION: Ensure that improvements will demonstrate a return on investment and are worth doing.

- Might others view instigating improvements as change for change's sake? ACTION: Ensure that suggestions for change are well thought through and well argued.

Building Strengths

Developing Relationships		Very High
Making Contact; Strengthening Relationships; Networking	 9	performed better than 95% of comparison group

- Look to involve the quieter members of the team and access all their available talent.

- Think who it is important to develop a better relationship with. Invest time in improving these relationships.

- Get in contact with all new stakeholders who interface with the role/department.

- Think through ways to make contact which could improve a relationship, e.g., inviting to a particular event, going for lunch, etc.

- Engage others and generate enthusiasm for achievement within the team.

- Use enthusiasm to inject energy into projects and inspire others to achieve.

- Enthusiasm can be infectious. Spend time sharing with colleagues why their ideas/new services are good.

- Improve the dynamics in slow or confrontational meetings. Inject a positive outlook and energy in these interactive forums.

- Offer to introduce contacts to people who may be helpful to each other.

- Make the most of own network - ask good personal contacts to facilitate introductions with their useful contacts.

- Be sure to devote some time to networking over the phone and to use the skills even when very busy.

- Make sure to network with purpose and spend time with people where there is potentially a mutual benefit.

Building Strengths

Coping with Pressure		Very High
Tolerating Stress; Coping with Important Events; Remaining Calm	 9	performed better than 95% of comparison group

- Lead by example and show others how to be calm in a crisis.

- Observe potential problems developing and intervene calmly before things escalate.

- Test the relationship between pressure and performance. Find the optimum level of pressure to put yourself under to drive personal performance.

- Know your own stress limits. Over confidence in this area can result in own stress levels increasing fast which could impact your job performance and health.

- Look for roles where composure is an asset.

- Demonstrate the capacity to cope with pressure in a fast paced environment.

- Seek work in more multifaceted roles with complex demands to build your capacity to handle pressure.

270

Building Strengths

Tackling Business Challenges		Very High
Identifying Business Opportunities; Outperforming Competitors; Generating Sales	 **9**	performed better than 95% of comparison group

- Show others how to seize new opportunities through professional/industry groups (e.g., present, contribute to newsletters or journal articles, write a blog).

- Develop a reputation for being responsive by being quick to respond to others.

- Study the market trends and suggest potential product/service development opportunities.

- Explore how customers commission suppliers and seek constant feedback about what they like and dislike about all their suppliers.

- Consider documenting competitor intelligence for colleagues. Share tips for beating the competition.

- Learn from the competitive bids that were lost. Undertake a complete review and seek full feedback from the customer.

- Look for opportunities to support or manage larger/global/strategic customer accounts.

- Ask for referrals and recommendations and build up a list of testimonials.

- Improve your knowledge of a product and of the customers so that both are outstanding and customers look to you for your advice and expertise.

Building Strengths

Impressing People		High
Attracting Attention; Promoting Personal Achievements; Gaining Recognition	 **8**	performed better than 90% of comparison group

- Volunteer for roles to represent the team to others.

- Volunteer to present and undertake activities that increase personal exposure.

- Volunteer to be the representative for your own team. Be the spokesperson.

- Seek roles that encourage selling ideas and influencing others.

- Promote the good work of the team and colleagues when appropriate.

- Think of different media to promote achievements (e.g., internal newsletters, professional bodies or trade press, etc).

- Be factual in self promotion. Use quantifiable data and qualitative comments of clients and stakeholders.

- Identify managers and colleagues who are happy to give support and praise when needed.

- Who has formed a less positive impression of you? Work hard at changing his or her impression.

Report for Alex Staton
Generated on: 1-Jul-2009

Page 13 of 21

Comparison Group: Professionals (IA, 2005)
© 2005 - 2009 Saville Consulting. All rights reserved.

271

Development Tips

Meeting Timescales Keeping to Schedule; Meeting Deadlines; Finishing Tasks		Extremely Low performed better than only 1% of comparison group

- List the activities required to complete the project. Keep a record of tasks completed.

- Be realistic about how long things take. Seek advice on areas that are less familiar.

- Start seeing deadlines as fixed and important.

- Create a clear schedule indicating "who, when and where" for each activity; make regular adjustments to the schedule.

- Address the reasons that contribute to tardiness, such as distractions, over committing, placing less value on other participants' time, poor planning.

- Allow time for contingency and review.

- Create a discipline for finishing and tying up all the loose ends. Celebrate when you are finished to reward yourself.

- Failure to finish tasks can really detract from the quality of the work. Delegate the final touches if necessary to deliver on time.

Managing Limitations

Meeting Timescales Keeping to Schedule; Meeting Deadlines; Finishing Tasks		Extremely Low performed better than only 1% of comparison group

- Ask for help splitting the overall project up into more manageable component tasks and work streams.

- Remove distractions when working to a deadline and defer less urgent tasks until after the deadline.

- Avoid committing to a task or project that is impossible, given other commitments, to deliver on time. Ask what is required (i.e., time, skills, resources) and, if necessary, escalate resourcing of the task or project upwards to resolve these issues.

- Review each activity on the schedule including how long each lasts, people involved and sequencing. Review progress at regular intervals or critical points.

- Clarify the start time and precise location of meetings or events. Get clear directions. Allow time for traffic or other delays.

- Seek advice about breaking the overall project timelines down into smaller units, perhaps setting daily or even hourly milestones.

- Appreciate that any delays will put pressure on colleagues responsible for the next stage of the process.

- Agree on a precise specification of any deliverables required by the deadline to avoid surprises later on.

272

Development Tips

Following Procedures		Extremely Low
Adhering to Rules; Following Instructions; Minimizing Risks	**1** ▢▢▢▢▢▢▢▢	performed better than only 1% of comparison group

- Have company policy and procedure manuals at hand. Refer to them before completing new tasks.

- Learn how following the key business processes benefit the department, organization, customers, shareholders and community.

- Break the overall project timelines down into shorter intervals for more regular progress and process checks.

- Only argue for "exceptions" to the rule in truly exceptional cases.

- Don't assume that more work can be done by simply flexing other deadlines without checking with the other project managers/resources first.

- Be careful to follow the full set of instructions to avoid any costly missed steps and re-work.

- Start big tasks early. Don't delay the start and leave things until the last minute.

- Check if there is an established list of known risks for your organization's industry sector. Identify which resources are at risk in your organization and consider what you can do to minimize those risks and their potential consequences.

- Learn more about legal obligations and commit to discharging these effectively to minimize risk.

Managing Limitations

Following Procedures		Extremely Low
Adhering to Rules; Following Instructions; Minimizing Risks	**1** ▢▢▢▢▢▢▢▢	performed better than only 1% of comparison group

- Review key company/departmental policies and procedures to make sure you are in compliance with them.

- Seek an explanation of which key business processes must be followed and the consequences of not doing so.

- Be aware of industry rules and regulations e.g., health and safety and professional best practices, and follow them appropriately.

- Write down key instructions and refer to them regularly.

- Ask an experienced colleague to help you list the sources of risk and their probability of occurrence and constraints. Weight these up before committing to a course of action.

- Find out from others about legal obligations that need to be followed and commit to discharging these effectively to minimize risk.

273

Development Tips

Team Working		Very Low
Joining Team Activities; Encouraging Team Contributions; Involving Others in Decisions		performed better than only 5% of comparison group

- Spend time getting to know team members, their roles and contribution.

- Discuss how to work together to ensure mutual benefit.

- Make sure that all the relevant people who may interface with the product/service are included.

- See the benefit in more than one view and think about how the suggestions of others provide a meaningful contribution.

- It may be better to talk to some people one-on-one before a meeting to get their views.

- Make sure that all relevant parties have been given the opportunity to make their views known.

- Set clear timescales for consultation and decision making.

- Ensure that everyone knows who is responsible for the overall decision.

Managing Limitations

Team Working		Very Low
Joining Team Activities; Encouraging Team Contributions; Involving Others in Decisions		performed better than only 5% of comparison group

- Seek opportunities to work independently, particularly following times when you have been working closely with others.

- Think through who has a complementary style at work and who is enjoyable to work with.

- Be clear about what needs to be done with others and what can be done alone.

- Consider when it is important for you to seek others contributions. Also consider how best to do this, e.g., via e-mail, team meetings, etc.

- Work out who are the stakeholders impacted by a decision and use others to facilitate their input.

274

Development Tips

Resolving Conflict		Very Low
Calming Upset People; Handling Angry Individuals; Resolving Arguments		performed better than only 5% of comparison group

- Listen actively and attentively. Suspend judgment.

- Focus on facts and data. Try not to be overly influenced by people's emotions and dominance.

- Spot potential problems early and step in quickly before the conflict escalates and people get angry.

- Allow people to have their say. Try not to cut them short or interrupt. Take a deep breath to keep calm, then maintain an objective approach to control the emotion of the situation. Speaking softly can help calm others.

- Find areas where there is common agreement.

- Empathize with people and help them to see that they are being listened to and understood.

- Understand the context for the argument and then hear both sides.

- Remain objective and dispassionate. Resist any temptation to be personally involved or take sides.

Managing Limitations

Resolving Conflict		Very Low
Calming Upset People; Handling Angry Individuals; Resolving Arguments		performed better than only 5% of comparison group

- Avoid front line roles where the potential for conflict is high.

- Refer problems on to others if it is clear that intervening may exacerbate the situation.

- If you have little patience for upset people, perhaps it is better for someone else to deal with them. Tell the upset person that you are getting them help while you find someone better suited than yourself.

- If you dislike confrontation, perhaps you should let other people handle angry individuals. If you anger easily, resist the temptation to argue.

- Think carefully before trying to resolve a disagreement as you may become involved in the disagreement rather than helping to resolve it.

275

Development Tips

Organizing Resources Planning Activities; Setting Priorities; Managing Projects		Very Low performed better than only 5% of comparison group

- Perform or allocate tasks in line with capabilities and interests. Use more appealing tasks as rewards and give people assignments to stretch them.

- Keep "live" files requiring action close at hand. Delegate filing or dedicate a set time each week for this activity.

- Anticipate likely project derailers and build contingencies for them into your plans. Communicate promptly with team members as plans change.

- Review plans with a colleague to ensure they are clear and aligned with objectives.

- Build contingency into all stages of planning.

- Highlight the inter-dependencies in the plan. Ensure everyone understands the implications of their contribution to this.

- Try to balance both the urgency and importance of tasks when establishing their priority.

- Be clear about immediate priorities as well as those for the next 30 and 90 days. Review and revise them regularly.

- Complete one work step before progressing to the next. When forced to change track, be sure to return to the earlier work step.

- When doing something for the first time, take a note of each step. Have the notes ready for review before doing the task for a second time.

276

Development Tips

Documenting Facts Finding Facts; Understanding Logical Arguments; Writing Fluently	■ 2 □□□□□□□□	Very Low performed better than only 5% of comparison group

- Start by creating a clear, simple structure of key headers which represent the topics to be covered in the written document.

- Question from the reader's viewpoint whether there is sufficient information to fully understand what is being documented.

- Get examples of gifted writers and look at how they structure their approach and consider what can be used from their work.

- Seek information from as many different sources as possible as information is often not in the first place it is sought.

- List all the information that is relevant before starting to look for it.

- Take a point of view which is opposite to your own and rehearse the arguments against it.

- Take time to check the accuracy and completeness of information rather than accepting it at face value.

- Review own documents and try to rewrite with the fewest possible words, while maintaining the key meaning and messages.

- Before starting to write say out loud what needs to be expressed and pull the points/arguments together verbally.

Development Tips

Checking Details Spotting Errors; Ensuring Accuracy; Producing High Quality Work	■■ 3 □□□□□□□	Low performed better than only 10% of comparison group

- Take responsibility for own work and learn from past mistakes - don't expect others always to check and correct details.

- Use spell check, excel and other software tools to spot spelling and grammatical errors, mathematical errors, formatting problems, etc.

- Be disciplined about thoroughly checking the accuracy of facts and figures.

- Aim to get it right first time. Monitor the level and amount of modifications and corrections spotted by others and reduce this over time.

- Allow time to apply the final "polish" to a key deliverable in order to create added value.

277

Development Tips

Upholding Standards Acting with Integrity; Maintaining Confidentiality; Behaving Ethically		Low performed better than only 10% of comparison group

- Look for opportunities to consistently exhibit company values in your work.

- Don't break commitments unless it is really unavoidable - even then have a back up plan.

- Show integrity by acting in line with what is expected from others (i.e., "walk the talk"). Avoid dealing with people or situations inconsistently.

- If in any doubt, ask whether information is confidential.

- Always play by company rules when it comes to managing finances/equipment, sharing information and interactions with others.

278

Comments/Actions

PART 4

TECHNICAL

12.0 Construction

This chapter describes the development process used to construct Wave Professional Styles assessments. A general background to Wave Professional Styles can be found in the Introduction chapter. Validation was fundamental to the development of the Wave Professional Styles questionnaires, and users can find further details about the unique approach used to validate the questionnaires in the Validity chapter.

12.1 Development Background

Development Goal

The primary assessment goal of Saville Consulting Wave® Styles is to accurately forecast people's performance at work. This is accomplished by maximizing the criterion-related validity with job performance and other work related effectiveness outcomes. In addition to validity, the Wave Styles questionnaires are designed to be fair in application and applicable internationally.

By achieving these goals, the Wave Styles questionnaires are designed to provide real value to organizations through improved workforce productivity and performance and lead to a strong return on initial investment.

The quest for enhanced validity should be the core mission of the test or questionnaire developer. We also believe it is a priority for assessment and test users. Users have the potential to maximize the benefit they provide in practice by using tools where criterion-related validity is higher.

An assessment tool must be easy to use, acceptable to participants, attractive, and be applicable to today's modern workplace. Saville Consulting Wave questionnaire administration, scoring, and reports are designed to ensure that this validity is easily accessible and understood by the user. We do this by providing the user with clear, well-researched links between Saville Consulting Wave Styles scales and measures of workplace competencies. This enables Wave to give a better, more valid indication of overall effectiveness in terms of proficiency and potential for future success than other conventionally developed personality assessments.

Validation is fundamental to the development of the Wave Professional Styles questionnaires, and users can find further details about the unique approach used to validate the questionnaires in the Validity chapter.

Saville Consulting Integrated Development

Three approaches to questionnaire design were used in the development of Wave Professional Styles. The first two we refer to as "deductive" and "inductive" approaches and they are commonly used to create conventional multi-scale personality questionnaires. The latter approach we refer to as "validation-centric" and it is one of the fundamental design features that makes the Wave Professional Styles questionnaires different.

Conceptual Overview of Wave Integrated Development

Figure 12.1 Conceptual Overview of Wave Integrated Development

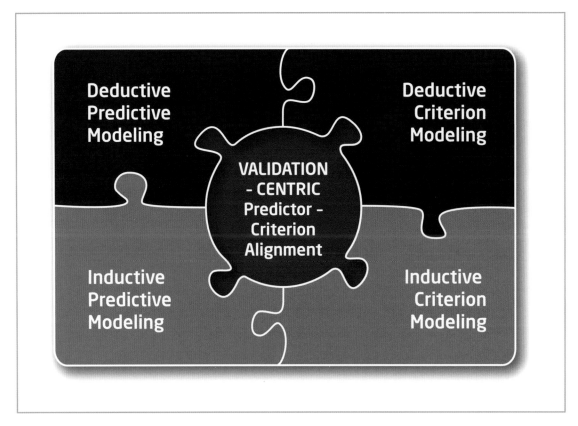

Saville Consulting Wave Professional Styles was based on both inductive and deductive modeling at both the predictor and criterion ends of assessment. These predictors and criteria were aligned and the validity maximized by performance driven, validation-centric item/scale choice. Criterion related validity was central to item choice in the development phase of the questionnaire. This is the essence of the validation-centric approach to creating performance driven assessment and maximizing validity.

Inductive Approach to Questionnaire Development

Questionnaires that are inductively developed are based on a process that focuses primarily on its internal structure and not on criterion-related validity. A statistical approach such as factor analysis is commonly used to create personality scales by identifying items that group together (i.e., factors). This approach tends to produce questionnaires that have low correlations between the scales within the questionnaire. Items (and scales) are typically removed that sit between these factors. A concept like Self Assurance, for example, might be removed from a Five Factor Model (FFM) questionnaire measure because it sits between the factors of Emotional Stability and Extraversion – it is related to both factors. The rationale for including an item (or scale), according to this approach, is not based fundamentally on an item's relevance to an external criterion but rather on how it relates to other items in the questionnaire (that is, the questionnaire's internal structure). The principle objective of the inductive approach is parsimony (as in the FFM) and not improved criterion-related validity. The examination of validity typically is undertaken after the questionnaire is built.

Deductive Approach to Questionnaire Development

Questionnaires that are deductively developed focus on measuring concepts that are deemed relevant to the developer. The developer writes questions to measure a particular concept or trait of interest to them. Developers using a deductive approach do not ignore the internal structure of their questionnaire, however. Typically, the developer writes more items for the trial form of the questionnaire than will be included in the final version of questionnaire (e.g., a third more items than are needed in the final version). The degree to which the items correlate with other items in the same scale is often an important criterion for item selection. Unlike the inductive approach, scales that sit between "factors" will not necessarily be removed from the questionnaire if the developer deems them useful. Questionnaires designed using this approach tend to have scales that correlate more highly with each other when compared to scales developed using an inductive approach. Scales developed using a deductive approach often have high internal consistency reliability, and often upon close inspection, the items in the scale can be found to be repetitive and the concept measured by the scale relatively narrow. As with the inductive approach, an examination of validity typically comes sometime after the questionnaire is built.

Neither the inductive nor deductive method of questionnaire development focuses on empirical validity until late in the development process (or more usually until after the development approach is complete). Both approaches assume that the items written for the questionnaire are good and reliable (i.e., they measure a concept reliably). With both approaches, items are removed that do not correlate with the other items in the questionnaire. But what if those "maverick" items are good predictors of a critical workplace behavior? There is no way of knowing that without external validity data.

Validation-Centric Approach to Questionnaire Development

The validation-centric approach to questionnaire development differs from the inductive and deductive approaches. Item selection begins by looking for items or item groupings (facets) that have the best criterion-related validity rather than selecting items based on how they correlate with other items or how they contribute to a scale's internal structure, such as the item's impact on a scale's mean, standard deviation, or other psychometric characteristics.

An advantage of this approach is the ability to create short and concise but highly valid scales. For instance, Burisch (1997) created short scales by selecting the most valid items from longer scales. Using a double cross-validated research design, he then found that these short scales were capable of greater validity than the conventionally developed scales eight times longer!

Methodological Pitfalls of Validation-Centric Development

A list of methodological pitfalls of a validation-centric approach is presented below along with means of addressing them.

Sample sizes need to be relatively large – recommend in excess of 300 people – to reduce Type I and Type II errors in item selection and to detect differences in validity coefficients. Validation samples of this size are rare as they are typically not easy to achieve early in questionnaire development.

Bizarre items and the black box approach. There is a danger that if item writing and reviewing is not against a clear *a priori*, deductive model that "bizarre" items can be found to correlate with an external criterion. Type I errors can mean that spurious correlations with external criteria can lead to inappropriate items being selected. Items must be written and reviewed against a clear model and principles. A deductive approach to item writing and the use of an *a priori* model can prevent an item intended to measure one concept being used to measure a different concept, e.g., can prevent items about Creativity being used to measure Extraversion. Hence, it is important to make *a priori* hypotheses regarding which items should correlate with which work behaviors and not to rely on a "dust bowl" or "black box" approach to empirical validity.

285

One validity study does not a questionnaire make. The first draft of a validation-centric developed questionnaire uses the results of an initial development trial to select items with the best validity. However, the results of this initial trial need to be cross-validated at the standardization stage of development as the validation results from the initial sample could be partially inflated by capitalizing on sample specific error variance. Cross-validation ensures the item validities with their aligned criterion are strong and stable across samples of participants.

Performance criteria are inherently unreliable, so it is important that the measures are of clear observable aspects of work performance that can be accurately rated by a boss or co-worker. Single item descriptions of work behaviors or competencies provide the opportunity to break jobs down into their behavioral elements (although these do have limited reliability as job performance criteria).

See the Validity chapter for a discussion on the criterion problem.

While there are pitfalls in using validity data to develop personality questionnaires, they can be overcome yielding benefits for questionnaire users. More work is required at the early stages of questionnaire development, but with large sample sizes, good item writing and review procedures, a large item pool and a clear *a priori* model of work traits and behaviors, questionnaire developers can improve their forecasting accuracy by using validation data early in the development process.

Validity and Scale Development

Burisch (1984) points out that mixed approaches, which include validity data as part of scale development, are surprisingly rare in questionnaire development.

"Actually this is rarely done, particularly the combination of deductive scale writing and external information for item analysis."

In developing the Saville Consulting Wave Styles questionnaires, a mixed approach was used that included deductive, inductive and validation-centric methodologies.

Validity and Expert Judgment

The superiority of validation data in driving expert decision making is a well established finding across different disciplines. The correlation with previous objective criterion/outcome data provides a superior approach to decision making, when compared to the subjective judgment of "experts". This finding is replicated across many different fields of application and is supported by a meta-analytic study by Grove et al (2000).

What is surprising is that the use of criterion-related validity data is so rarely used for item selection and scale development. Most developers develop scales using only internal item parameters. Validation is often an afterthought in questionnaire development - rather than something that drives scale development for the purpose of improving criterion related validity through selecting the most valid items to create more valid scales. Using validity as a rationale for item selection helps to create shorter, more efficient scales with better overall validity.

12.2 Wave Professionals Styles Development

The development of the Wave Professional Styles questionnaires took place in two major phases: the construction phase and the standardization phase. These two phases can be broken down into a number of individual steps as shown in Figure 12.2.

Fig 12.2 Overview of Key Steps in Wave Professional Styles Development

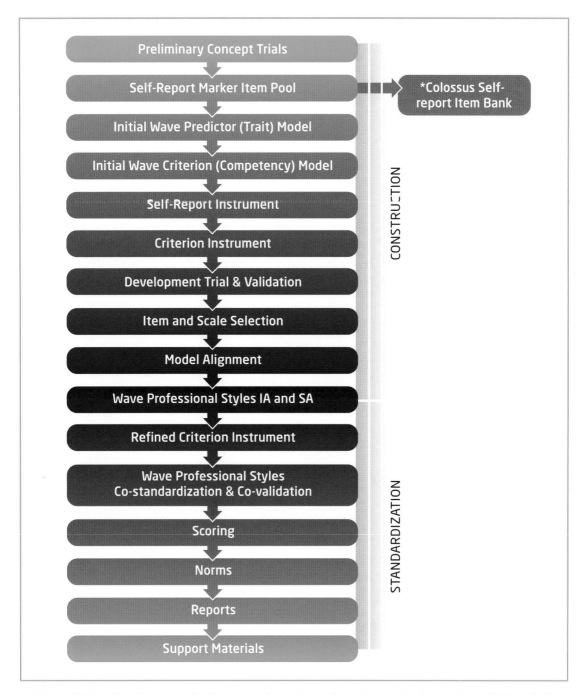

Colossus Self-Report Item Bank was developed but not used for item/facet scale selection in the Development Trial, the Self-Report Marker Item Pool was used. Parallel items were drawn from Colossus for the Co-Standardization Trial.

Preliminary Concept Trials

In essence, these were "proof of concept and method trials" before investing in the full development and standardization trials of Wave. The content never led to the development of a questionnaire directly from this trial. However, these trials helped to identify the most promising content which was then refined for use in the main development trial.

These preliminary trials were conducted to investigate the properties of different item types; specifically, "effectiveness" items (measuring talent) and "need" items (measuring motive). These trials also pilot tested psychometric properties of a series of short scales (facets) that were designed as part of a model hierarchy to increase the fidelity of assessment by measuring very specific facets of behavior.

A total of over 500 items were trialed on 205 participants from a mixed occupational group. These items were rated against a ten point true/false anchored Likert-type scale. The items were designed to measure 50 different traits. For each of these traits, motive and talent items were written. Items were both positively and negatively keyed. Three alternate forms of the questionnaire were created. Measures of response style and social desirability were included in this trial.

Exemplars of Items included in preliminary trials:

> I **enjoy** generating lots of ideas (motive or need item)
> I **produce** lots of ideas (talent or effectiveness item)

Prior to the study, *a priori* hypotheses were made regarding the structure of the items and scales. These hypotheses were confirmed based on the results of the trials. Specifically, the factor structure and scale intercorrelation matrix reflected the deductive model structure and indicated that it was possible to have a large number of short scales that were internally reliable and that showed good construct independence. A subset of the items was also subject to a retest to check for stability.

The trials confirmed the authors' previous findings that the negatively worded and keyed items, with words such as "not," had less reliability and a less complex factor structure than positively keyed items without negation.

The preliminary trial also provided the necessary information on the scaling properties of the items to begin development of a new dynamic response format. This dynamic response format, designed for use on the Internet, calculates ipsative scores from the rank order of items based on normative ratings, and if certain tied ratings are encountered, will adaptively represent tied items for ranking. The true-false rating scale was amended following this trial to a nine-point Likert-type agreement scale following some small within subject comparative trials of different rating scales.

Self-Report Marker Item Pool

The original Wave development project created 214 self-report concepts or behavioral facets to be used in the development trial (plus measures of impression management and social desirability). These 214 facets were identified through an iterative process of delineation and refinement by a team of six experienced individual difference psychologists. Each of the 214 concepts was composed of a motive and a talent component making 428 concepts in total (plus social desirability and impression management). In other words, each facet is comprised of two items, one measuring motive and other measuring talent.

An initial draft model was developed by taking the Big Five personality factors and splitting one of the factors, Extraversion, into an interpersonal and achievement-oriented component which is also sometimes considered as part of Conscientiousness. This achievement component differentially predicts important work outcomes which was the reason for separating this out. The resulting six broad general factors were then divided to create twelve categories based on being high or low on each of the six factors.

These twelve categories were further developed to create sub-areas. This was accomplished by examining:

- Criterion frameworks and competency models used by private and public organizations
- Review of existing personality and occupational questionnaires and competency assessment tools
- Validation review of scales from existing assessment tools
- Rational process of splitting scales into meaningful subcomponents
- Identification of new measures, behaviors and performance criteria

Perhaps the most under-rated skill of all in questionnaire development is that of the item writer and reviewer. It is fundamental to Wave Styles' development philosophy that the quality of items is central to the validity of the questionnaire. Over two working person years was taken up with item writing and review by a team of highly experienced individual difference Psychologists.

A set of item writing guidelines and review criteria were created for item writers and reviewers. These are summarized below.

Item Writing Guidelines and Review Criteria

- Targeted
- Simple
- Short
- Unitary
- Unique
- Comprehensible
- Avoiding Idioms and Metaphors
- Non-Opaque
- Self Referent
- Behavioral
- Positively Phrased
- Avoiding Stereotypical, Biased Content
- Non Bizarre
- Non Clinical
- Motive or Talent

Targeted – a clear objective in the development of Wave was to write items based on a clear understanding of what "good looks like." Items were designed to be unipolar with higher scores indicating more effective performance. Exemplars of individuals with particular traits were used as part of this process to identify whether each item was worded effectively. For example, one of the facets is labeled "discreet" and its items deal with "maintaining confidentiality." The item writers sought individuals whom they had observed behaviorally to be lower on this trait to check that they would not positively endorse the statement as written. Care was also taken to avoid focusing on concepts that were likely to have negative correlations with overall job performance and potential ratings. Aspects of adapting approaches associated with emotional resilience and agreeableness were, for example, amended to reflect more proactive, pro-social behaviors.

Simple – the items were written and reviewed to be as simple a construction as possible to measure the trait being targeted. Frequently used words were preferred over less frequently used ones. One concept only is measured by an item, and conjunctions such as "and", "or" or "but" are avoided.

289

Short – long items tend to have lower reliability which will impact on their validity. Wherever possible Wave Styles items were written short and then shortened. However, extremely short or one word items, e.g., an adjective like Sociable, can fail to convey subtlety and precision of meaning when targeting a narrow trait. The longest item in the Wave Styles questionnaires has eleven words and the shortest item has three words. The mean number of words in an item is 6.7.

Comprehensible – an important feature of any item is that reviewers and respondents understand and agree upon its meaning.

Direct – there is no attempt in Wave Styles items to conceal the meaning of any item or make them indirect or opaque. Indeed, they are deliberately written with a high degree of "directness" or transparency so that the respondents are clear what they are being asked and are not surprised later by their results. Opaque or indirect items can lack face validity for the respondent and require many more items in a scale to measure the concept reliably and validly.

Avoiding Idioms and Metaphors – items such as "I like to beat others" can have more than one interpretation. Few idioms or metaphors translate successfully across language and cultures and can lead to the gross misinterpretation of an item. They are best avoided.

Positively Phrased – items that employ negation by using words such as "not" typically have lower reliability and are prone to respondent response error due to misreading. Negative items can help in controlling acquiescence responding, but this can result in lower reliability.

Self-Referent – items ask respondents to rate and rank their own motives and talents. Items that ask for opinions or attitudes such as, "I think a team needs a leader" were avoided.

Behavioral – the items focus on behaviors that are more or less observable. Talent items look for direct expression of these behaviors in terms of action, and motive items focus on the individual's needs and preferences which make particular behaviors more likely. This behavioral approach makes responses more verifiable as the traits should correlate with effective expression of these behaviors which can be observed and rated by others.

Avoiding Stereotypical or Biased content – care was taken by reviewers and item writers to avoid items that might focus on specific knowledge or experience which a particular protected group may have less or limited access to. As a matter of course opinions and attitudes on specifics of the real world (such as particular people or events) have been avoided. Items were specifically reviewed by international reviewers with consideration to culture, country of origin, ethnicity, age, gender, sexual orientation, and religious belief. (See Fairness chapter for information about group differences.)

Non-bizarre – item content was not designed to be strange or sensational, or present hypothetical scenarios whether likely or unlikely to be faced by the respondents in their working life.

Non-clinical – items that refer to mental or physical disorders or that describe mental or physical symptoms that may indicate a clinical abnormality were avoided. The items were designed to be relevant and acceptable to typical working adults. Items that could be perceived as an invasion of privacy with regards to mental health issues were also avoided.

Work Relevant - the items in Saville Consulting Wave Styles predictor (trait) model and criterion (competency) model were written and reviewed to be work relevant and positive with regards to achieving overall effectiveness at work.

Internationally Relevant - the items chosen were reviewed to be in simple business English and easy to translate. Individuals from over 50 countries were involved in the item trialing and review process. Words with a common spelling in US and UK English were used whenever possible, but separate versions were created due to a few items containing spelling differences that were not possible to change.

Readability Statistics

Counts		
	Words	1458
	Characters	6550
	Sentences	216
Averages	Words per Sentence	6.7
	Characters per Word	4.3
Averages	Flesch Reading Ease	70.1
	Flesch-Kincaid Grade Level	5.1

Readability Scores

Each readability test bases its rating on the average number of syllables per word and words per sentence. The following sections explain how each test scores your file's readability.

Flesch Reading Ease test

This test rates text on a 100-point scale. The higher the score, the easier it is to understand the document. For most standard files, you want the score to be between 60 and 70.

The formula for the Flesch Reading Ease score is: 206.835 - (1.015 x ASL) - (84.6 x ASW)

where:

ASL = average sentence length (the number of words divided by the number of sentences)
ASW = average number of syllables per word (the number of syllables divided by the number of words)

Flesch-Kincaid Grade Level test

This test rates text on a U.S. school grade level. For example, a score of 8.0 means that an eighth grader can understand the document. For most documents, aim for a score of approximately 7.0 to 8.0.

The formula for the Flesch-Kincaid Grade Level score is: (.39 x ASL) + (11.8 x ASW) - 15.59

where:

ASL = average sentence length (the number of words divided by the number of sentences)
ASW = average number of syllables per word (the number of syllables divided by the number of words)

Initial Wave Predictor (Trait) Model

A deductive approach to item development was used at this early stage to sort the 214 facets (428 items – a facet is a two-item scale) into the initial model. This was an iterative process that resulted in the framework shown in Figure 12.3.

Figure 12.3 Deductive Facet Styles Bank Structure prior to Item Selection on Development Trial

Solving Problems	Influencing People	Adapting Approaches	Delivery Results
Abstract	Articulate	Accepting	Action Orientation
Analytical	Challenging	Attentive	Commercial
Change	Communicative	Caring	Compliant
Conceptual	Convincing	Calm	Dependable
Creativity	Directing	Customer	Dutiful
Factual	Empowering	Decisions	Energetic
Feedback Criticism	Engaging	Dutiful	Enterprising
Intellectual	Enthusiastic	Ethics	Getting Things Done
Inventive	Gregarious	Facilitating	Insight and Awareness
Learning	Leading	Flexible	Meticulous
Motivating Self	Motivating Others	Insight and Awareness	Organized
Pragmatic	Outspoken	Involving	Planning
Rational	Personal Confidence	Motivating Self	Productive
Thoughtful	Purposeful	Participative	Quality
Visionary	Self-promoting	Positive	Reliable
	Showing Emotion	Receptive	Striving
		Resilience	
		Resolving	
		Self-assured	

Two further scales were developed to measure social desirability and impression management.

Colossus Self-Report Item Bank

Once the initial 428 "marker" items were created, additional parallel items were written to match the original marker items. The result was an item bank of over 4,280 items called Colossus. This item bank was created to allow for the future development of parallel versions of Wave and to be available for custom questionnaire development.

Initial Wave Criterion (Competency) Model

Based on the literature review of common behavioral criteria and popular competency models as well as the latest research in normal personality theory and the validity of these different measures, the same deductive approach was used to create the Wave criterion model. The goal was to use the model to create items that would be used to gather performance ratings for validation purposes. This would enable the use of the validation-centric approach to select the most valid predictor items and to ensure alignment and validity between the predictor and criterion models.

The criterion model was written in parallel to the predictor model by four psychologists to produce 44 behavioral competency dimensions. These were aligned to the Wave Professional Styles item bank and grouped into a hierarchical structure that included four clusters and 12 sections.

The criterion rating items had a two word title in bold followed by a list of three subcomponents. The 132 competency facet subcomponents in the initial trial were aligned to the deductive Wave predictor model.

Figure 12.4 shows the original criterion model with the clusters and sections. For more information on the underpinning of the structure of the Wave model, see the section later in this chapter on Important Perspectives Related to Wave Model Development.

Figure 12.4 The Initial Deductive Wave Criterion Model - Included Competency Dimensions before development trial

Competency Dimension	Cluster	Section *
Generating Ideas - e.g., producing ideas; making inventions; adopting radical solutions	Solving Problems	Creating Innovation
Exploring Possibilities - e.g., Identifying underlying principles; applying theories; developing concepts	Solving Problems	Creating Innovation
Developing Strategies - e.g., anticipating trends; forming strategies; vision for the future	Solving Problems	Creating Innovation
Providing Insights - e.g., resolving problems; using intuition; making incisive judgments	Solving Problems	Judging Situations
Implementing Practical Solutions - e.g., applying practical skills; utilizing common sense; testing ideas	Solving Problems	Judging Situations
Developing Expertise - e.g., taking up learning opportunities; acquiring knowledge and skills; exploring specialist issues	Solving Problems	Judging Situations
Documenting Facts - e.g., finding facts; probing arguments; writing fluently	Solving Problems	Evaluating Information
Analyzing Situations - e.g., anticipating problems; analyzing information; producing solutions	Solving Problems	Evaluating Information
Interpreting Data - e.g., quantifying issues; evaluating data objectively; utilizing technology	Solving Problems	Evaluating Information
Making Decisions - e.g., assuming responsibility; deciding course of action; standing by decisions	Influencing People	Providing Direction
Leading People - e.g., coordinating groups; providing leadership; controlling things	Influencing People	Providing Direction
Providing Inspiration - e.g., motivating individuals; inspiring people; giving encouragement	Influencing People	Providing Direction
Convincing People - e.g., persuading others; negotiating; shaping opinions	Influencing People	Asserting Views
Challenging Ideas - e.g., questioning assumptions; arguing own perspective; willing to disagree	Influencing People	Asserting Views
Articulating Information - e.g., giving presentations; explaining things; projecting social confidence	Influencing People	Asserting Views
Impressing People - e.g., attracting attention; promoting personal achievement; getting recognition	Influencing People	Communicating with People
Developing Relationships - e.g., making contact; strengthening relationships; networking	Influencing People	Communicating with People
Establishing Rapport - e.g., welcoming people; putting people at ease; making friends	Influencing People	Communicating with People

294

Competency Dimension	Cluster	Section *
Team Working - e.g., joining team activities; encouraging team contributions; involving others in decisions	Adapting Approaches	Helping People
Understanding People - e.g., listening to people; appreciating others' feelings; understanding motivation	Adapting Approaches	Helping People
Valuing Individuals - e.g., tolerating individual differences; trusting people; showing consideration	Adapting Approaches	Helping People
Resolving Conflict - e.g., calming upset people; handling angry individuals; resolving arguments	Adapting Approaches	Coping with Stress
Conveying Self-Confidence - e.g., valuing own contributions; projecting inner confidence; determining own future	Adapting Approaches	Coping with Stress
Coping with Pressure - e.g., tolerating stress; coping with important events; appearing calm under pressure	Adapting Approaches	Coping with Stress
Thinking Positively - e.g., projecting cheerfulness; being optimistic; recovering from setbacks	Adapting Approaches	Adapting to Change
Inviting Feedback - e.g., encouraging critical thinking; encouraging feedback; acknowledging criticism	Adapting Approaches	Adapting to Change
Embracing Change - e.g., tolerating uncertainty; coping with change; adapting to new circumstances	Adapting Approaches	Adapting to Change
Checking Details - e.g., identifying errors; ensuring accuracy; ensuring high quality	Delivering Results	Driving Results
Meeting Timescales - e.g., keeping to schedules; meeting deadlines; finishing tasks	Delivering Results	Driving Results
Following Procedures - e.g., adhering to rules; following instructions; minimizing risks	Delivering Results	Driving Results
Organizing Resources - e.g., identifying requirements; planning activities; managing projects	Delivering Results	Structuring Tasks
Upholding Standards - e.g., acting with integrity; maintaining confidentiality; behaving ethically	Delivering Results	Structuring Tasks
Completing Tasks - e.g., working efficiently; utilizing time effectively; multi-tasking	Delivering Results	Structuring Tasks
Taking Action - e.g., investing energy; using initiative; sustaining physical activity	Delivering Results	Striving for Success
Pursuing Goals - e.g., acting with determination; persisting through difficulties; achieving results	Delivering Results	Striving for Success
Tackling Challenges - e.g., identifying business opportunities; outperforming competitors; generating profit	Delivering Results	Striving for Success

Figure 12.5 The Deductive Wave Criterion Model - Deleted Competency Dimensions

Competency Dimension	Cluster	Section *
Investing Trust - e.g., believing in people; giving autonomy; trusting others' intentions	Adapting Approaches	Facilitating Work
Conveying Enthusiasm - e.g., being positive; generating excitement; creating enthusiasm	Influencing People	Building Relationships
Accepting Responsibility - e.g., acting with integrity; admitting mistakes; honoring commitments	Delivering Results	Executing Assignments
Fulfilling Obligations - e.g., being reliable; conforming to organizational values; showing loyalty	Delivering Results	Executing Assignments
Outperforming Competitors - e.g., being competitive; grasping opportunities; winning business	Delivering Results	Delivering Results
Developing Others - e.g., giving encouragement; motivating people; enabling development	Influencing People	Asserting Views
Pioneering New Methods - e.g., challenging convention; improving work methods; designing new approaches	Solving Problems	Developing Concepts
Developing Self-Insight - e.g., developing self-awareness; reflecting on experience; learning from experience	Solving Problems	Developing Concepts

Note. Names used here may be unfamiliar to current users as they were draft names used at this stage in the Development of Wave Professional Styles and were later finalized.

Self-Report Instrument

The 428 marker items were placed in an online questionnaire which was used on a Nine-point Likert-type agreement scale (see Administration chapter for further details). The impression management and social desirability items were also included in this trial instrument. The item order was also reviewed to prevent repeats of items from similar constructs presented in a block of items presented at the same time on the computer screen.

Criterion Instrument

A work effectiveness inventory was created using the behavioral items in Figure 12.4 and two items of job proficiency and potential for progression. Ratings were made using a seven-point Likert-type scale ranging from Extremely Ineffective (1) to Extremely Effective (7). There was also a "no evidence" option for each rating. The work effectiveness inventories were administered online to a manager, colleague, friend or partner of the Wave Style questionnaire respondent.

Development Trial & Validation

1,011 respondents from over 50 countries completed the Wave Styles Development Trial Self-Report Questionnaire. Between 386 and 394 of these respondents also had external ratings of performance from the work effectiveness inventory (the criterion instrument). This number varied due to the "no evidence" option on the criterion rating instrument.

Item and Scale Selection

The primary objective of this stage was to select the most valid facets (predictors) and criteria. This process aligned the Wave predictors and criteria and thereby created a model that would maximize criterion-related validity. Each criterion dimension was reviewed in turn to examine how the *a priori* matched facets correlated with ratings of overall proficiency and potential. The correlation between the facet and its matched criterion was also examined. Facets that correlated best with the overall proficiency and potential and with their matched criterion were selected for inclusion. Refer to Figure 12.6 which provides a simplified overview of the item selection process.

Figure 12.6 Model Creation

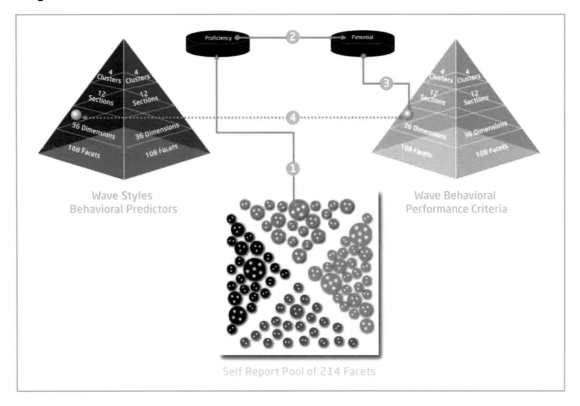

1. For each criterion dimension, the facets in the self-report (predictor) model that were aligned to it were examined. For instance, for the criterion dimension of Generating Ideas, the matched self report facet/items in the area of Creativity and Inventive were examined. The first step was to check that the facets/items correlated with the rater's external view of the individual's overall job proficiency.

2. Next the facet was considered for selection if it correlated strongly with the future progression criteria (potential).

3. Then the facet's correlation with its matched criterion was examined, e.g., Creative items with Generating Ideas competency.

4. After passing these steps the most valid facets were placed into the Wave predictor model and selected for the Wave Professional Styles questionnaire. For the Generating Ideas criterion this first facet was called Creative.

5. The process continued by selecting the next most valid facet. For the Generating Ideas competency, this second facet selected was called Original. The next most valid facet for the Generating Ideas competency was called Radical. For each Wave competency, the three facets that correlated highest with overall performance and proficiency as well as its aligned competency were selected to form the Wave Styles dimension.

6   The new dimension was named based on the content that was selected for inclusion (i.e., the three facets). For instance, the Wave Professional Styles dimension that has been selected to best predict the competency Generating Ideas was named Inventive.

This process continued until all the competencies were examined and all the Wave Styles (trait) dimensions created. In practice, eight of forty-four competency criteria were dropped based on their overlap with other competency dimensions and their weaker correlations with overall performance and potential. This led to an aligned predictor and competency model with four clusters, 12 sections, 36 dimensions and 108 facets. This meant that of the original 214 facets only 108 of the most valid facets were selected into the Professional Styles questionnaire. As a reminder, each of the Wave Styles facets is composed of one motive item and one talent item. With 108 facets, this resulted in a 216 item questionnaire.

It should be noted that the ratio of deselected to selected items is much higher than with most self-report questionnaire development. The ratio of deselected to selected Wave items was 1:1 rather than 1:3 which is more typical. This oversupply of high quality items was purposely designed to create the mechanism where validity would be maximized.

There can be a problem with this approach due to the ratio of the number of variables being selected from versus the number of subjects in the study. This problem, can lead to results which do not cross validate as the initial selection capitalizes on error variance or chance outcomes. This was controlled by *a priori* limiting the number of variables that were available to be selected for criteria.

It was interesting to note during item selection that items and facets that correlated strongly with each other in the trials often had far from identical patterns of correlation with the criteria. This is a finding that was also observed in our co-validation research of different instruments, Project Epsom, where scores from assessment instruments that correlate strongly with each other had markedly different correlations with the criteria (see Validity chapter for more information about Project Epsom).

Additional Item Selection Criteria

While the choice of items was based primarily on the validity of the criteria against overall proficiency and potential and of the predictors' validity in relation to the aligned behavioral criterion, other considerations were important in the selection of items into the Wave Professional Styles model.

Again, the first concern was for enhanced validity and not for an optimal factor structure of the predictors and the criteria. Wave Styles was not designed to have a "pure" factor structure. However, there was a need to create predictor measures that could be organized into a hierarchy with a good degree of construct independence while demonstrating acceptable degrees of internal consistency reliability (although alternate form reliability in the subsequent standardization trial provided a more critical test of precision of measurement).

Therefore, once the Wave dimensions had been created using the validation-centric method described, an examination of the internal consistency reliability was undertaken. The goal at the Wave dimension level was to create dimensions with an internal consistency between .60 and .90 (using Cronbach's Alpha). With regards to our goals for test-retest and alternate form reliabilities, our aim was for the Wave dimensions to have the highest possible reliabilities.

Intercorrelation matrices of the Wave facets were run on the 1,011 respondents in the development sample. These were supplemented by a number of factor analyses. These included exploratory factor analysis with a relatively high number of factors. For example, a Principal Components Analysis with Varimax rotation to create 50 factors. This helped to provide an insight of how the facets grouped.

12.3 Model Alignment - The final model of predictor and criterion

Figure 12.7 The Final Matched Model - the top three levels of Wave Professional Styles

Predictor Cluster	▶	Criterion Cluster
Thought	▶	Solving Problems
Influence	▶	Influencing People
Adaptability	▶	Adapting Approaches
Delivery	▶	Delivering Results

Predictor Section		Criterion Section
Evaluative Investigative Imaginative	▶	Evaluating Problems Investigating Issues Creating Innovation
Sociable Impactful Assertive	▶	Building Relationships Communicating Information Providing Leadership
Resilient Flexible Supportive	▶	Showing Resilience Adjusting to Change Giving Support
Conscientious Structured Driven	▶	Processing Details Structuring Tasks Driving Success

Predictor Dimension		Criterion Dimension
Analytical Factual Rational		Examining Information Documenting Facts Interpreting Data
Learning Oriented Practically Minded Insightful Inventive Abstract Strategic	▶	Developing Expertise Adopting Practical Approaches Providing Insights Generating Ideas Exploring Possibilities Developing Strategies

299

Predictor Dimension	Criterion Dimension
Interactive	Interacting with People
Engaging	Establishing Rapport
Self-promoting	Impressing People
Convincing	Convincing People
Articulate	Articulating Information
Challenging	Challenging Ideas
Purposeful	Making Decisions
Directing	Directing People
Empowering	Empowering Individuals
Self-assured	Conveying Self-Confidence
Composed	Showing Composure
Resolving	Resolving Conflict
Positive	Thinking Positively
Change Oriented	Embracing Change
Receptive	Inviting Feedback
Attentive	Understanding People
Involving	Team Working
Accepting	Valuing Individuals
Reliable	Meeting Timescales
Meticulous	Checking Things
Conforming	Following Procedures
Organized	Managing Tasks
Principled	Upholding Standards
Activity Oriented	Producing Output
Dynamic	Taking Action
Enterprising	Seizing Opportunities
Striving	Pursuing Goals

Response Style Scale Development

The social desirability and impression management items were dropped following the development trial. There were three primary reasons for the removal of these scales:

1 Social desirability and impression management factored cleanly with a high factor loading on specific personality based factors indicating that they were measuring specific personality variance rather than any broad response style. (For example, Impression Management Positive and Negative scales and the Social Desirability Positive scale factored cleanly with high factor loadings into a factor with other facets about personal organization. Social desirability negatively factored into a factor about openness to change). Even if high scores could be shown to correlate with response distortion on these scales, it would not be possible to separate out which was personality variance and which reflected distortion, i.e., the large degree of construct irrelevant variance severely limited these scales' effective applicability.

2 Overall measures such as acquiescence and consistency from averaging and aggregating differences across similar items gave broader information on response style.

3 Individual information from the difference between ipsative and normative scores at the dimension level in the standardization trial provide more specific information on where social desirable or undesirable responding within a profile is occurring. That is, rather than having a general social desirability scale, it was possible to tap into desirability in responding by comparing ipsative and normative dimension scores and therefore identify specific scales where over and under-rating may be occurring.

Wave Professional Styles - Standardization Trial

The standardization trial was designed to operationalize the Professional Styles model using a new dynamic response format. This involved asking respondents to first rate each item in a block of six items using a free choice, Likert rating scale. Certain tied items are then represented to the respondents and they are asked to use a forced choice response format to select which of the tied items are Most and on some occasions also Least like them. We refer to this dynamic rating-ranking process as the "Ra-Ra" response format. This format allows for both a normative and ipsative score for each Wave dimension. (More information is given on the Response Format chapter.)

In the standardization trial, the 216 items selected from the development trial were used with the new Ra-Ra response format. The items were arranged in blocks of six. In all the 216 items were covered in 36 blocks of six items

A number of design constraints were used for assigning the items into blocks.

1 Blocks of six were arranged to be composed of entirely motive items or entirely talent items.

2 The structure of the blocks was developed to balance the number of comparisons across the model, e.g., if two dimensions are regularly paired together due to an uneven model then it can create an unrealistically negative correlation between these two scales. It was not possible to accomplish perfect balance in the design using 36 scales, but never the less it was important to ensure a well balanced solution.

3 Four of the items were from different clusters in the model (Wave has four clusters)

4 Where clusters overlap in one block the items come from a different sections within the cluster

5 Assign items with similar mean endorsement values (from the development trial) in each block to control for item attractiveness, which is important when items are being ranked. The first constraints still allowed freedom to balance items with similar endorsement values.

301

Next, 216 parallel items were drawn from the Colossus Bank that provided for an alternate form version of the Wave Professional Styles questionnaire[1]. This resulted in two alternative form questionnaires being co-standardized with a total of 432 items in 72 blocks. One questionnaire is Professional Styles - Invited Access (IA) and the second questionnaire is Professional Styles - Supervised Access (SA). This allowed for alternate form reliabilities to be calculated.

Respondents were first asked to rate each set of six items online in a block on a nine-point Likert-type rating scale ranging from Very Strongly Disagree (1) to Very Strongly Agree (9). The scoring software immediately calculates the rankings from these rating responses, and presents back to the respondent the items which were tied.

There are some exceptions to this tiebreaking step when the software allows for a small number of ties. This was based on experience that some ties can be tolerated without reducing the reliability of the ipsative scores (similarly other questionnaires such as OPQ32i which is fully ipsative do not require full ranking of scores within a block of items).

The respondent then selects the item which is Most like them and the item which is Least like them. This process continues, if necessary, until the ties are removed. However, if there are no ties then the respondent simply progresses to the next block of six items without the need for a ranking task. (See Response Format chapter for more information.)

Refined Criterion Instrument

An update of the original work effectiveness survey was designed for collecting criterion ratings only on the 36 behavioral work effectiveness areas selected following the standardization trial. The instrument also asked raters to provide ratings of overall effectiveness in terms of job proficiency and potential for future progression. This instrument forms the basis of the Saville Consulting Wave Performance 360 multi-rater assessment.

Wave Professional Styles Co-standardization and Validation

The questionnaire was standardized on a total of 1,153 individuals. Independent external criterion ratings were available on between 556 and 658 of these depending on the criterion dimension (a no evidence option led to the variation in the matched validation sample size). As this was an *a priori* model it allowed for cross-validation into a new sample of respondents. Also, having the two questionnaires provided an opportunity to examine alternate form reliabilities. Details of the results of this study can be found in various chapters of the handbook. Details of the sample can be found in the Appendices.

Scoring

At the final stages of development different scoring regimes were investigated. These included the use of matrix algebra to recreate full sets of rankings from an incomplete matrix of rankings. The ipsative score and normative scores were also looked at in different combinations before arriving at a final process for scoring the questionnaires to ensure both high reliability and validity.

The normative score is based on converting the nine-points on the agreement scale to ranking scores. The rankings are initially determined by examining the rating value assigned to each of the six items. The highest rated item is assigned the highest rank and so forth. Ties are broken by the subsequent force choice ranking task so that each of the six items receives a rank score. Each item therefore receives a normative rating score ranging from one to nine and an ipsative ranking score ranging from one to six. The final overall Wave Styles trait score for any scale at any level in the Wave model is based on both the normative and ipsative scores.

1 As each item in Wave has a specific unique measurement purpose, item level equivalence is something that we are working towards from the design stage.

Development of Competency Potential Equations

A final stage was to develop the Competency Potential equations that are designed to maximize the validity of Wave Professional Styles in predicting the competencies in the Wave Competency model.

At each level in the Wave model hierarchy there is one predictor component from Professional Styles questionnaire that is aligned to a specific competency (the Wave Style scale and Wave Competency scale are matched *a priori* and validated empirically). The styles scale (and any subcomponents) were selected on the basis of validity to be the highest individual predictor (or predictors), but secondary predictors (other facets from across the model) do provide incremental validity when predicting competency potential.

The development of the competency potential scales identified these additional predictor elements and gave them prediction weights (lower weights than the matched component which account for the majority of the predicted variance).

These equations were subsequently cross-validated to ensure that the equations are robust and can be generalized to new populations of respondents.

Example of Competency Potential Facet Equation

Identifying Business Opportunities (Competency Potential Facet) =	
Business Opportunity Oriented (Styles Facet) x 21	+
Leadership Oriented (Styles Facet) x 4	+
Deciding on Action (Styles Facet) x 3	+
Action Oriented (Styles Facet) x 2	+
Visionary (Styles Facet) x 1	

Preferred Culture

In addition, a series of culture assessments was developed and co-standardized with the Wave Professional Styles questionnaires. This allowed for the modeling and validation of the preferred work culture and environment that individuals would like to work in. This provides the basis of the section in the report on predicted culture/environment fit.

Norms

The initial norms were then created based on the initial standardization sample. Further discussion about norms can be found in the Norms chapter.

Reports

Reports were then built to be straightforward, clear, attractive, and easy to understand. The Expert Bundle was designed to have Line Manager and Personal Reports and provide the expert Wave user with information on the individual's style, motive-talent splits, ipsative-normative splits, facet ranges, predicted culture/environment fit and competency potential.

303

See Introduction and Reports chapters for further information.

Support Materials

Following the completion of the standardization trial, the internet assessment platform called Saville Consulting Oasys – the Online Assessment System, was finalized and launched. Documentation was made available in the form of training slides and technical documentation on Wave Professional Styles for users.

A Preparation Guide was also developed that could be provided to respondents prior to the administration of Wave. The preparation guide is available as a pdf document free of charge. It can be emailed to candidates in advance of completion of Wave Professional Styles. This can be downloaded from www.savilleconsulting.com.

Since its development for gathering validation evidence, the criterion model and surveys have formed the basis of a variety of new tools that are designed to help Wave Professional Styles be applied more innovatively and effectively. These include:

The Saville Consulting Wave:

- Performance Culture Framework Card Deck
- Job Profiler
- Performance 360

12.4 Important Perspectives Related to Wave Aligned Model Development

The Five Factor Model (FFM) or the "Big Five" Personality Factors

The broad factors known as Openness to Experience, Conscientiousness, Extraversion, Agreeableness and Neuroticism form the FFM. Barrick & Mount (1991) outlined the research base for these broad trait factors, and traced back their origins to the work of Norman (1963). Over the years different names have been used for what is now understood to be essentially the same construct set. Neuroticism is increasingly referred to in the wake of Positive Psychology as Emotional Stability or Confidence, while Agreeableness and Openness to Experience are sometimes measured through their opposite pole, e.g., Independence and Conventionality, respectively. The NEO questionnaire (Costa & McCrae, 1992) is perhaps the most commonly used FFM questionnaire.

The "Great Eight" Competencies

Kurz & Bartram (2002) expanded the FFM by adding three new categories (Intelligence, Need for Power and Need for Achievement) into the Great Eight (G8) competencies. The G8 are designed to account for individual differences in work performance rather than measure personality traits per se. The authors defined competencies in relation to their significance for performance at work as "sets of behaviors that are instrumental in the achievement of desired results or outcomes."

This definition of competencies has important implications for the development of the Wave Performance model as it indicates that there should be a positive association between competencies and achievement of desired results and outcomes. For this to be the case competencies should correlate with overall measures of performance.

The origins of the model can be traced back to the meta-analysis work of Robertson & Kinder (1993) who created a criterion taxonomy to classify various "local" performance criteria. This led to the development of a range of competency inventories enabling large scale validation work like the international validation study by Nyfield et al. (1995).

Amendments were made to the Saville Consulting Wave criterion model and predictor facets based on an understanding of how the different Great Eight constructs relate to, and fail to relate to, overall performance positively (see Bartram 2005 for example). In particular, Supporting and Cooperating and Adapting and Coping were amended to focus on behavioral aspects that were hypothesized to better underpin overall measures of performance.

Alpha and Beta

Digman (1997) investigated the higher-order factor structure of the FFM and found that Agreeableness and Conscientiousness (usually together with Emotional Stability) formed a higher-order factor he called "Alpha" while Extraversion and Openness to Experience formed a "Beta" factor. The sections on the left of the Wave Wheel, figure 12.8, from Structured to Evaluative broadly cover the Alpha supra-factor, and the sections on the right from Investigative to Driven broadly cover the Beta supra-factor.

305

Figure 12.8 The Wave Wheel

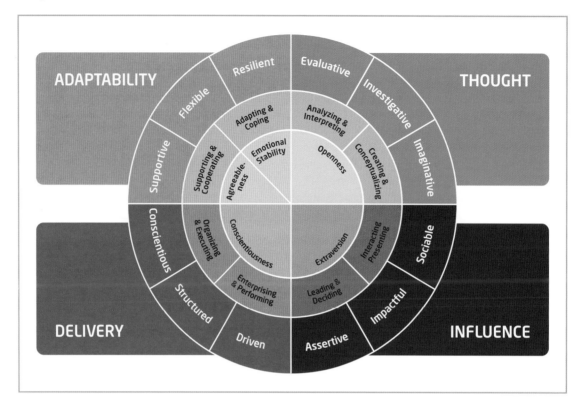

The Big One

Since the original development of Wave, Musek (2007) has published a paper which aligns to Wave's construction approach in identifying a "Big One" of personality which is super-ordinate to Alpha and Beta. This is an extremely broad overall factor of personality, and it would be unusual to find someone to be high on every aspect of it. Some people will be high on both Alpha and Beta, or at the next subordinate level (e.g., FFM), some people profile as Extrovert, Agreeable, Emotionally Stable, Conscientious and Open to Experience.

The Four Clusters of Performance and Potential

The clusters bring together the diverse range of theories and assessment approaches from the predictor and criterion domain into one model which is designed to underpin performance and potential at work.

Bartram, Baron & Kurz (2003) outlined four Leadership Functions that could be viewed as a higher-order structure of the Great Eight. Kurz (2005) measured the Leadership Functions by aggregating relevant competency ratings and identified what ability, interest, motivation and styles variables underpin them. He challenged the distinction of Transformational and Transactional components in the SHL Corporate Leadership Model (Bartram, 2002) as factor analysis results showed that a better account of the data was provided by a top level distinction akin to Digman's Alpha vs. Beta factors in conjunction with the classic People vs. Task orientation well known from leadership research.

The Four clusters of Saville Consulting Wave effectively parallel the four Leadership Functions, but serve as a generic model of work performance across all levels of work complexity and job level.

The clusters are utilized in the Types Report where Influence and Adaptability combine to define four People Types, and Thought and Delivery to define four Task Types. In combination, they define sixteen types that chart transformational and transactional aspects of performance. The Transformer-Transactor type is the most prevalent and effective type in managerial and leadership roles with high staff and resource responsibilities. The Transformer-Transactor aligns with Musek's Big One Factor.

In Saville Consulting Wave there is also matched predictor-criterion alignment and this then forms not only a Big One of personality but also of trait measures that are effective indicators of overall performance or effectiveness at work. The weighting of the factors is based on predictor-criterion associations rather than factor loadings.

Twelve Behavior Sections of Performance and Potential

The Wave model is hierarchical and the four behavioral clusters are each broken down into three sections for a total of twelve sections. The sections in Saville Consulting Wave are transparently mapped to the Big Five and Great Eight constructs yet are designed to provide wider and more detailed coverage that better reflects complexity of people and jobs.

13.0 Response Format

The Dynamic Online "Ra-Ra" Response Format

Saville Consulting Wave® Styles use a new dynamic online response format developed and designed specifically for these assessments. The format is neither ipsative nor normative, but a new method which starts with rating and adaptively moves onto ranking when there is insufficient information to differentiate the rated scores into rankings. We call this dynamic rating-ranking process the "Ra-Ra" response format.

The new format is designed to give the benefits of both ipsative and normative formats, while reducing some of the negative consequences of each. We acknowledge that some users may prefer one format over another, and for those that prefer ipsative scoring, they can focus on this score component while those that prefer normative can focus on the normative component.

Before discussing the new format in more detail, a brief overview of some of the properties of ipsative and normative formats are given for reference.

Normative Scores

Normative questionnaires have no inter-relationship between the items; each item stands alone and the response to an item only changes the scores on one primary scale of the questionnaire that the item is a part of.

Simple normative formats include:

Adjective Checklist

Mark all the statements that apply to you by ticking the box next to each statement

- Creative ✔
- Reliable ☐
- Organized ✔
- Adaptable ✔
- Talkative ☐

Two Answer Option (or dichotomous)

Unipolar - Yes/No or True/False

e.g., I am full of new ideas - True/False?

Bipolar e.g., either/or

Which one of the following best describes you:

Theoretical
Observant

More than Two Answer Options (or polychotomous)

Bipolar

Which of the following best describes you:

> I would like to live in the city
> In between
> I would like to live in the countryside

Unipolar - Agreement Scale

I am creative

| Strongly Disagree | Disagree | Unsure | Agree | Strongly Agree |

Unipolar - Behavioral Frequency Scales

I have ideas

| Never | Sometimes | Frequently | Often | Always |

Unipolar - Behavioral Intensity Scales

My creativity is:

| Low | Moderate | High |

Unipolar- Behavioral Effectiveness Scales

Generating Ideas

| Highly Ineffective | Ineffective | Fairly Ineffective | Unsure | Fairly Effective | Effective | Highly Effective |

N.B. While some of these items above are forced-choice they all can be scored normatively as opposed to ipsatively. The answer options chosen in an item will only impact on the scores on one primary scale of the inventory.

310

Normative scores have the advantage that an individuals are free to be where they want on each and every scale. They could get a maximum score on all the scales (i.e., get a sten score of 10 on each scale) or a minimum score on every scale.

They do, however, suffer from some potential disadvantages:

1. **Halo and Horns**

   As well as raters operating a halo when they rate other people - individuals can view themselves more positively or negatively and self-rate accordingly. This can falsely overinflate or under-estimate an individual's scores on scales of a self-report assessment. This can also falsely lift the intercorrelations in a normative questionnaire where the average intercorrelation across the scales does not reflect the intercorrelations of the true scores. Note. this should be distinguished from an overall true positive intercorrelation that may exist between behaviors (normative scores are likely to provide an overestimate of the true positive relationship between scales on a self report assessment).

2. **Central Tendency/Extremity**

   Individual respondents often differ in the degree to which they use the extremes of polychotomous normative items. This variation in how extreme the responses and hence the profiles are, may be manifest in behavior and be construct relevant. However, it may not be reflected in behavior and be construct irrelevant and thereby misleading to the interpreter of the profile.

3. **Acquiescence**

   Not everyone agrees to statements to an equal extent, and some people are more likely to acquiesce than others. This response pattern could be manifest in an individual's behavior, e.g., being more 'accommodating.' But the response pattern is also likely to impact across the whole profile and it is unlikely a person is 'high' or 'low' across all constructs measured. One approach to reduce the impact of acquiescence is to reverse the polarity of a proportion of the items. However, this may lead to a number of negative consequences such as erroneously bipolar scales, fewer scales created, and use of items with negation (such as 'not'). All of these can serve to reduce fidelity and/or reliability of the assessment.

4. **Social Desirability**

   Social desirability responding can be related to a number of features of individuals, including high self esteem, an eagerness to please, a concern to conform with social norms, etc. The impact of socially desirable responding on a profile can potentially be quite complex. It could have the effect, for example, of the respondent not being prepared to disclose weaknesses which are not considered to be socially desirable, such as 'being inattentive.' Alternatively, it could manifest in a more profound lifting of the scores on 'positive' characteristics across the profile or parts of the profile. Also, the opposite impact on the profile can occur with low social desirability responding.

5. **Cognitive Complexity in Self Concept**

   An associated issue, related to halo and social desirability, is an individual's capacity to differentiate many characteristics within themselves. This capacity can be viewed as an individual difference in itself. Some people may articulate their self concept quite simply and not differentiate the type of extrovert they are in great detail, whereas another individual may have a very detailed, well differentiated, hi-fidelity concept of their extrovert behavior that they can articulate. A normative questionnaire may result in a flat profile for individuals who cannot distinguish characteristics within themselves with great complexity.

311

6. Faking

Respondents can make a conscious effort to distort the results in, for example, a high stakes selection situation (normally favorably). They also may semi-consciously be trying to create a favorable impression. This can be seen by individuals making the best of what they have rather than being highly critical (analogous in an application form to making the career highlights sound best and minimizing or omitting the negative outcomes, without committing the act of giving inaccurate facts). Such impression management, conscious faking and social desirability are often difficult to differentiate in practice.

Despite all these problems normative questionnaires do work and are valid. However, in high stakes situations there are greater concerns about faking and response distortion. Faking, response distortion and social desirability can reduce opportunities to see the more self-critical responses in many normative profiles.

Ipsative Scoring

With ipsative scoring, the scores have a degree of dependency on each other. Different responses to an item will impact scores on more than one primary scale of the questionnaire. In essence, by giving the scores on an item to one primary scale you take it away from another (or others).

Fully ipsative questionnaires have a fixed total score. If all the scale scores are added together it will always result, by definition, in one fixed value. Therefore, what ipsative scoring is doing is apportioning the scores across the scales.

Ipsative item formats include:

Dichotomous Either/Or

Which one of the following best represents you:

    Influential
    Organized

Polychotomous Rank

Rank the following statement 1,2,3 and 4, where 1 is most like you and 4 is least like you

    Persuades others
    Analyzes information
    Ignores insults
    Organizes work

Polychotomous Most/Least

Simpler designs just ask Most (2 points) Least (0 points)

    Persuades others
    Analyzes information
    Ignores insults
    Organizes work

The important characteristic of ipsative scoring methods is that they create scores between scales that are interdependent. When scales are interdependent, it means that it is impossible to be high (or low) on every scale of the questionnaire. Also, the fewer primary scales assessed in the ipsative measure the greater the impact of the interdependency of the full scales themselves. This is shown in Graph 16.1.

Graph 16.1 The impact of the number of ipsative scales on the average intercorrelation among the scales.

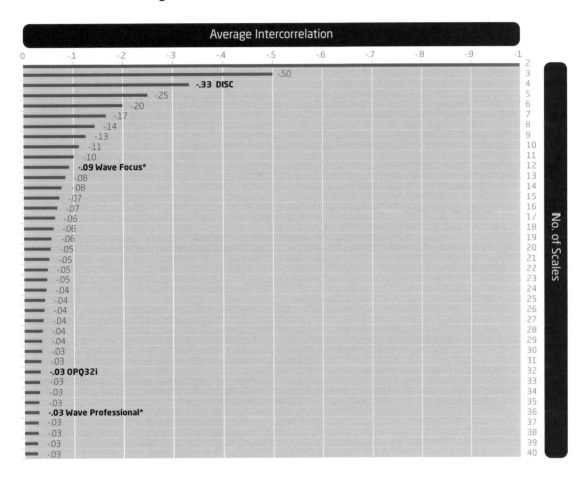

DISC- Thomas International DISC – 4 scales- average intercorrelation of -.33

OPQ32 – Occupational Personality Questionnaire 32i – 32 scales – average intercorrelation of scales of - .03

Wave Professional has 36 scales in ipsative design giving average for the ipsative score component of – .03 and Wave Focus has 12 scales – giving average for this score component of - .09.

N.B. Wave Professional and Focus have a normative component so the actual average intercorrelations of combined scores are slightly positive rather than negative.

Ipsative questionnaires have the advantage that it is not possible to be high on every scale and with a higher number of scales, they present the relative preferences of the individual. By asking an individual to choose between different statements, we can measure that individual's relative preferences compared to simply asking the individual to describe him or herself (normative responses). A person may claim to enjoy all flavors of ice cream, but we can learn which flavor the person likes best by seeing which flavor they choose most often. Life in critical moments can be about making choices between a number of different options and ipsative scores are designed to better reflect these choices.

However, ipsative questionnaires also have limitations:

1. **Potential for Increasing Error**

   One potential problem for ipsative scoring is that the questionnaire could present false or unrealistic choices to an individual. The individual in this case, could essentially be answering randomly without the responses being a representation of their underlying trait score. To reduce this it is important that the design of the ipsative questionnaire avoids presenting individuals with choices which are highly correlated while at the same time have similar mean endorsement values. This can also be a problem on normative forced-choice formats.

2. **Limits Freedom/Acceptability**

   This is a property of forced-choice items in general that is not restricted solely to ipsatively scored items. The choice given may be restrictive and this may be irritating to the respondents where they feel that they are having to make a choice that does not adequately represent them. This may have the advantage of 'forcing out' some less socially desirable limitations or development needs, but at the cost of lowering the acceptability of the questionnaire to some users.

3. **Interdependency**

   Digman (1997) provides evidence in favor of higher order factors of personality, where Alpha is Conscientiousness, Agreeableness and Emotional Stability and Beta is made up of Extraversion and Openness to Experience. Furthermore, Musek (2007) argues that Alpha and Beta are correlated, underpinning the 'Big One' factor of personality. If personality related characteristics are being measured, then the Big Five should be expected to show an overall small positive intercorrelation. Ipsative measures may therefore force the intercorrelations down unrealistically. The problem with interdependency is an increasing problem for questionnaires with few scales and where the true score intercorrelations are likely to be more strongly positive.

4. **Norming and intra-individual vs. inter-individual comparisons**

   There is an argument which can be made that ipsative scores present a comparison within an individual, not between individuals, which makes standardizing against a comparison group inappropriate. The argument runs that a comparison of individual scores across individuals is not meaningful. The argument clearly holds more true where there are a smaller number of scales. However, as the number of scales increases and the degree of interdependency decreases (as shown in Graph 16.1), this issue diminishes until scale intercorrelations drop to near zero, and it is increasingly unlikely and unusual to find people who might be high on all the scales (particularly if there are relatively low intercorrelations between the scales).

5. **Loss of a Degree of Freedom**

   If you have information on all but one of the scales, the final scale is just a linear composite of the other scales. The interdependency and this loss of a degree of freedom can affect some assumptions, some statistical analyses and critically, some applications of the tool. To give an example of how this can become an issue, imagine that a user decides to use a tool with 16 ipsative scales designed to measure

personality characteristics. Through job analysis 12 of these scales are identified to be job-related, and a linear composite is made by unit weighting and summing these 12 scales. This composite score, however, is also the negative or inverse composite of the four remaining scales (this creates an argument to also check that the four remaining scales not included in the equations are negative indicators of success!).

6.   Problems with Statistical Procedures

Some have argued that the problems of ipsative scoring are such that it is impossible to analyze or interpret using standard procedures (Hicks, 1970; Johnson, Wood & Blinkhorn, 1988) or that such scores can only be used in restricted contexts (Closs, 1996; Cornwell & Dunlap, 1994). However, others have argued that ipsative data is amenable to analysis using standard techniques and that its other properties often make it at least as useful as normative data (Gordon 1976; Saville & Wilson, 1991). Great care certainly needs to be taken with certain statistical procedures in interpreting the results. For example, there is no literature that the authors are aware of that canonical analysis is appropriate for ipsative data. Care also needs to be taken with factor analysis of ipsative only data. Bipolar factors often result in practice with one of the factors, for example, breaking across the opposite poles of the other factors making the results more difficult to interpret.

Despite these limitations, ipsative questionnaires can give a meaningful picture of the validity and utility with external criteria (that are not part of the score dependency). That is not to say that ipsative scoring cannot positively or negatively impact criterion validity, it can. For example, a scale like Agreeableness, when scored normatively, can have a positive correlation with an externally rated criterion such as overall performance, but when ipsatively scored can have a negative correlation depending upon the number of other scales and the intercorrelation among scales.

Ipsative and Normative Scoring

From a practical standpoint, it is useful to know both how positive someone is about themselves in general across the entire questionnaire (normative profile), and the relative emphasis they place on different behaviors (ipsative profile). However, asking for ipsative and normative scores on the same item is clearly lengthy, inefficient and potentially frustrating for respondents. The Ra-Ra (Rating-Ranking) method was developed to address this problem.

Saville Consulting Wave Dynamic Online Format

Saville Consulting Wave's dynamic online format is designed to be a more efficient method of creating a combined score with ipsative and normatively scored subcomponents. The Wave Styles questionnaire presents a page with six statements and a normative, free choice rating scale.

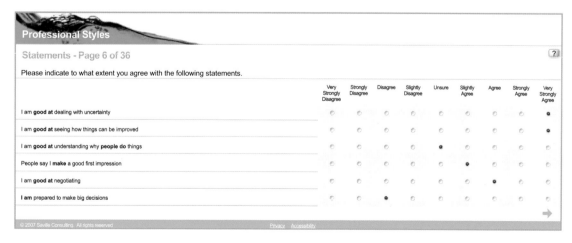

315

Once the ratings on the page are complete, normative ratings are saved and then ipsative ranks are calculated by the Oasys™ online assessment system. In this instance, it is easy to assign an ipsative score to most of the statements. Statements are rank ordered according to their normative ratings and an ipsative score is assigned. In the example, the ipsative score can be determined with the lowest ranked item of 'Disagree' being ranked last, 6th (and assigned an ipsative score of 1), the 'Unsure' rating being ranked 5th (and will receive an ipsative score of 2), 'Slightly Agree' will receive an ipsative score of '3', and 'Agree' and ipsative score of '4'. The two Very Strongly Agree statements are not possible to rank as they have equal ratings, so no ipsative score is assigned at this stage. If certain ranks cannot be determined from the normative ratings alone, a new page is created (see below). This page displays the tied items and asks the respondent to review the tied statements and use a forced-choice response format to determine which statement should be ranked higher.

The item being assigned 'most' now results in a top ipsative score of '6' and the remaining item is assigned an ipsative score of '5'.

When more than two choices are ranked a most and least task is displayed. Where all the six statements have tied ratings, two 'most and least tasks' will be displayed one after another, assigning the most (6) and least (1) extreme rankings on the first ranking screen. On the subsequent screen the remaining four statements are displayed with the most receiving an ipsative score of five and the least receiving a score of two. Finally, the remaining two statements each receive a score of three and a half (there is no discernable increment in validity or reliability from seeking to differentiate the middle two statements). The questionnaire then presents a new page with six new statements.

By this mechanism, both ipsative and normative scores are computed efficiently and the two scores are also summed to create a combined score.

Benefits of the Dynamic Format:

1. High Validity

In Project Epsom, the nine-item global Overall Performance scale had raw uncorrected validities of .32 normative, .34 ipsative and .36 for the Wave Professional Styles combined competency potential measures (N=280). This pattern replicates earlier criterion-related validity work on a sample of over 500 participants (MacIver et al, 2008). For Wave Focus, the pattern on Project Epsom is .24 ipsative, .27 normative and .29 combined (N=280). The effect sizes and sample size are insufficient to confirm the finding that one method is higher than the other at present, but the findings are consistent with the notion that the new format has at least equivalent (if not higher) validity than normative or ipsative counterpart scores alone. As further samples continue to build, this will be the subject of meta-analytic analyses.

We typically look to see if a questionnaire measures what it is designed to measure, but we can also look at the discriminant validity to see if it also measures competencies that it was not designed to measure. The average correlation with the 35 off-diagonals for the 36 Normative Competency Potential Wave Professional dimensions is .06 for normative, .02 for ipsative, and .03 for the combined score. The combined score having better (lower) discriminant validity than normative and practically on a par with ipsative discriminant validity. These differences are particularly important where differential prediction is needed across different possible outcomes, such as prioritizing individual development actions or career guidance.

316

2. **High Reliability**

Support for the use of the new combined method with alternate forms for normative, ipsative and combined styles scores all averaging in the .80's. Refer to the Reliability chapter for further information.

3. **High Variance**

The method allows for the creation of normed scores at the facet level. The ipsative and normative scores are combined, and the use of the nine-point agreement scale with blocks of six statements significantly increases the number of raw score points available per item. This ensures sufficient variance at the facet level thereby allowing for shorter scales to be scored and profiled.

4. **Stronger Intra-individual Differentiation**

Another consideration is whether the profile of scores provided by a Wave Styles questionnaire gives better intra-individual variation. This, in combination with good convergent and discriminant validity, will lead to better validity in making differential selection decisions (between different jobs), or career planning and identifying individual development actions.

To investigate this an analysis was conducted. For each respondent in the Wave standardization sample a standard deviation was calculated across the twelve competency potential section scores generated using each of the different scoring methods. This provided an SD for each individual based on how differentiated the respondent's score was for each of the scoring methods. The average of this SD was calculated across the 1,153 participants in the study.

The differentiation across the twelve sections for the Wave Competency Potential scores for normative is 1.26, for ipsative 1.93, and for the combined score is 1.81.

The results indicate that ipsative has the greatest intra-individual differentiation, but that the combined score was very close to this.

5. **Candidate Acceptability**

Using a combined method results in a lower proportion of forced-choice questions being asked than with a forced-choice fully ipsative design (such as Thomas International DISC or OPQ32i). This has the benefit of increasing the acceptability of the user experience. The dynamic format of Wave combines the candidate-friendly free choice rating format with the more discerning ranking format in order to maximize usability and efficiency for the respondent.

6. **Making Faking More Complex**

No questionnaire is unfakable, but the addition of the ranking component increases the complexity that would be required in the process of faking. An individual has to try to control a greater number of variables when doing the rating and ranking tasks.

7. **Making Distortion Easier to Detect**

A combined score is always plotted, but when a difference of three or more stens between the ipsative score and the normative score exists this difference is plotted on the profile chart. The user can see which response format resulted in the higher score and by how much. The reliability and validity indicate that the normative, ipsative and combined scores are all valid, so it provides an opportunity for the individual interpreter to find out where distortion may be taking place and find out the reasons for the difference between the two scores. It could be that the ipsative score on a scale is a better representation of behavior than the normative, or vice versa.

317

Limitations of the Dynamic Format

No format results in a perfect, error free representation of trait scores. While the new format conveys clear advantages by dynamically presenting ratings and rankings, not all of the limitations present in normative and ipsative scores are eradicated. For instance, the interactive nature may result in people altering their rating responses to avoid ties as this will reduce the number of ranking tasks they complete to break the ties (and finish the questionnaire sooner). This is something to be aware of when interpreting the profile, particularly with respondents who were not very motivated to complete the questionnaire (see Feedback chapter). Despite this, the results discussed above indicate that the dynamic online format has advantages over ipsative and normative scores alone.

Response Format Summary

The new response format of Saville Consulting Wave provides an efficient mechanism that increases the fidelity of measurement, allowing more information to be measured in less time. The validity and reliability is equal to if not better than either the normative and ipsative components in the score (and time will tell if the combination has better convergent validity still than either of the individual components). This is accomplished while reducing the positive intercorrelation present within normative only scores of the Wave Professional Styles intercorrelation matrix and allowing ipsative and normative differences within the profile to pinpoint potential areas of distortion.

14.0 Professional Styles Norms

14.1 About Norms

When interpreting the results of an assessment it is often useful to know how each individual score compares to scores achieved by others. Knowing whether a score is high, low or average compared to others requires that we have a norm group. Norms allow for comparison of an individual's score on an assessment to a relevant comparison group. The use of norms ensures that, when comparing the scores of different individuals, you can be sure you are comparing like with like.

There are various standard scales that could be used to assess individuals on aptitude and behavioral styles assessments. Often different scales are used for aptitude and behavioral assessments. To allow for a common simple language on both behavioral style and aptitude tests, 'Sten' scores are available. 'Sten' stands for 'Standard to ten' and Stens provide a score which ranges from 1 to 10 with 5 and 6 straddling the average (mean) score. While this provides a simple scale for users, it is also useful to understand how these scores relate to percentiles in the normal distribution. See Figure 14.1. below.

Figure 14.1 Stens 1 - 10 and their relation to percentiles in the normal distribution

1 - Extremely Low	- performed better than only 1% of comparison group
2 - Very Low	- performed better than only 5% of comparison group
3 - Low	- performed better than only 10% of comparison group
4 - Fairly Low	- performed better than only 25% of comparison group
5 - Average	- performed better than only 40% of comparison group
6 - Average	- performed better than 60% of comparison group
7 - Fairly High	- performed better than 75% of comparison group
8 - High	- performed better than 90% of comparison group
9 - Very High	- performed better than 95% of comparison group
10 - Extremely High	- performed better than 99% of comparison group

For simplicity for users these figures are rounded to give whole number percentiles (positive integers) where possible as a multiple of 5 or 10 which are near the centre of each Sten score. This avoids creating the perception of over accuracy in the score particularly as stens are bands of scores which are subject to a degree of error.

Calculating Sten Scores

When using Wave Professional Styles the user does not need to calculate Sten scores manually as the Oasys online assessment system does this. However, for those who are interested or would like a reminder, the formulas for calculating Sten scores are presented for reference below.

Sten scores are calculated from a person's raw scores on an aptitude or behavioral styles assessment.

To work out a person's Sten score, you first need to calculate the Z-score. A Z-score represents how far away a person's score is from the group mean in standard deviation units. The formula to calculate a person's Z-score is as follows:

$$Z\text{-score} = \frac{\text{Individual's raw score} - \text{Mean of the group}}{\text{Standard Deviation}}$$

319

$$\text{Z-score} = \frac{X - \bar{X}}{SD}$$

From this, you can work out a person's Sten score. The formula for calculating Sten scores is given below:

$$\text{Sten score} = (\text{Z-score} \times 2) + 5.5$$

A Sten score gives a rounded representation of a person's score against a benchmark comparison group. One sten score covers half of a standard deviation from the bottom of the score to the top of the Sten score.

SEm – Standard Error of the Mean

Standard Error of the Mean (SE_{mean}) is a measure of how accurate a representation your sample mean is of the 'true' population mean. The larger your sample size, the more accurate it is at representing the true population mean. Table 14.1 demonstrates how SE_{mean} is related to sample size.

There is always a quest within psychometric assessment to have the largest possible numbers for the analysis and interpretation of data. While this is essential for reliability and validity analysis, when considering Standard Error of the Mean, it can be seen that this is not always so necessary. As can be seen in Table 14.1, after a sample size of around 500, the impact of increasing sample size upon Standard Error of the Mean only serves to make an already small error even smaller.

So although in general the larger sample size the better, in terms of normative data collection, collecting very large samples numbers is often less important than other considerations. The most important consideration in collecting normative data in practice when samples get bigger is often how representative the sample is of the population.

Table 14.1. Standard error of the Mean at different sample sizes

Sample Size	SE_{mean} (stens)
50	.29
100	.20
250	.13
500	.09
1,000	.06
10,000	.02

A note on the importance of normative information and validity

If a test has a wide range of different norm groups with thousands of people in each but has no evidence of validity, then norms in and of themselves are of no value for the purpose of predicting job performance or potential.

Available Norm Groups

Saville Consulting's development program is producing versions of Wave Styles in over 25 languages. Please contact your local Saville Consulting office for further information.

14.2 Professional Styles Standardization Norm Group Description

Norm Group Name: Professionals (2005)

This sample consisted of 1,153 participants, approximately 96% of whom were currently employed in a range of job functions across a wide range of industry sectors. Of these, approximately 75% worked in the following industry sectors: banking, financial services, oil/gas & utilities, hospitality, recruitment, and insurance. The remaining 25% worked in other industry sectors including consulting services, manufacturing & production, healthcare, engineering, education & training and HR.

The breakdown of the standardization sample is provided below (with response rates for each biographical section given in the foot notes):

Gender[1]

53% of the sample were female and 47% were male.

Figure 14.2 Gender breakdown for Standardization sample (N−1,153)

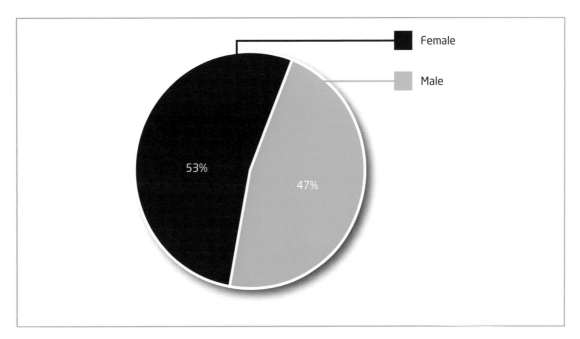

Age[2]

The age of the group ranged from 17 to 65 years, with a mean age of 36 years.

Cultural Background[3]

83% of the sample described themselves as white British, 12% as other white backgrounds (including Irish, European, American, Canadian, New Zealander and white Caribbean) with the remaining 5% of the sample describing themselves as either Indian, Pakistani, Chinese, Asian Other, Black Caribbean, Black African, or as mixed

321

[1] Based on 100% sample response
[2] Based on 94% sample response
[3] Based on 90% sample response

origin (e.g., White and Black Caribbean). 98% of the group described their understanding of written English either 'as a first language speaker' or 'fluently'[4].

Figure 14.3 Cultural background breakdown for Standardization sample *(N=1,153)*

Education (highest UK qualification)[5]

12% of the group had a postgraduate degree as their highest qualification, 25% of the group had a degree, 15% had a professional qualification (e.g. Chartership), 35% had school level qualifications (including A Level, GCSE or equivalent), 7% had an HNC, HND or equivalent, with 4% having 'other' qualifications (e.g. NVQ) with the remaining 2% of the group having no formal qualifications.

Figure 14.4 Education level (highest UK qualification) of Standardization sample *(N=1,153)*

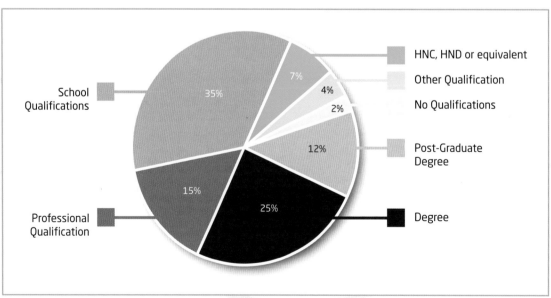

---

[4] Based on 88% sample response.
[5] Based on 86% sample response.

Work Function[6]

The participants worked in a range of job functions and areas. 77% of the group worked in the following functions/areas: HR, Customer Service, Accounts and Finance, Sales and Administration. The remaining 23% worked in a range of other functions/areas including Engineering, IT, Marketing, Executive, Office Management, Production, R&D and Catering.

Work Experience[7]

36% of the group had more than 20 years' work experience, 33% had between 10 and 20 years, 13% between 6 and 9 years, 11% between 3 and 5 years, 5% between 6 months' and 3 years and 1% had less than 6 months work experience.

Figure 14.5 Work experience level of Standardization sample *(N=1,153)*

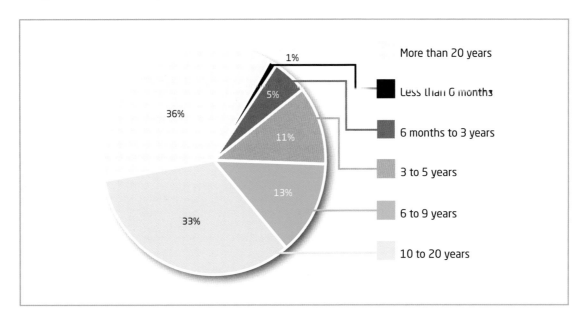

[6] Based on 86% sample response
[7] Based on 94% sample response

14.3 Professional Styles Standardization Norm Tables

Table 14.2 Professional Styles Standardization Group Norm Table, Invited Access (IA).
(N=1,153)

Dimension	IA Mean	IA SD
Analytical	62.87	9.78
Factual	65.89	8.86
Rational	53.82	13.09
Learning Oriented	62.43	11.93
Practically Minded	67.38	9.68
Insightful	65.42	8.73
Inventive	52.83	13.41
Abstract	58.21	11.41
Strategic	56.13	11.20
Interactive	53.75	13.63
Engaging	67.11	10.88
Self-promoting	45.80	12.32
Convincing	55.80	10.31
Articulate	57.59	12.25
Challenging	51.39	11.72
Purposeful	54.60	10.96
Directing	58.81	12.86
Empowering	59.44	12.67
Self-assured	59.70	11.06
Composed	53.40	13.50
Resolving	58.65	11.90
Positive	65.93	10.92
Change Oriented	61.75	11.34
Receptive	60.20	9.76
Attentive	65.43	11.08
Involving	65.55	9.10
Accepting	63.60	12.01
Reliable	64.95	13.41
Meticulous	64.48	13.69
Conforming	53.48	14.52
Organized	64.94	11.40
Principled	71.84	9.66
Activity Oriented	65.35	10.63
Dynamic	57.83	10.53
Enterprising	53.24	15.15
Striving	61.82	10.50

Reference: Appendix B

Table 14.3 *Professional Styles Standardization Group Norm Table, Supervised Access (SA).* *(N=1,153)*

Dimension	SA Mean	SA SD
Analytical	62.82	9.95
Factual	64.93	9.56
Rational	52.80	13.55
Learning Oriented	64.42	10.99
Practically Minded	67.57	9.49
Insightful	66.00	8.87
Inventive	52.36	13.32
Abstract	55.69	12.04
Strategic	53.61	12.08
Interactive	52.31	12.50
Engaging	67.07	11.49
Self-promoting	43.85	12.34
Convincing	51.20	10.63
Articulate	56.56	11.89
Challenging	49.96	12.09
Purposeful	54.91	11.03
Directing	56.22	12.65
Empowering	59.31	13.17
Self-assured	61.62	12.28
Composed	52.16	14.09
Resolving	55.50	13.05
Positive	64.91	10.17
Change Oriented	61.49	11.59
Receptive	58.63	9.50
Attentive	63.77	11.68
Involving	63.02	9.51
Accepting	65.51	10.84
Reliable	66.00	12.47
Meticulous	64.65	13.04
Conforming	54.12	14.65
Organized	65.44	11.43
Principled	74.38	9.77
Activity Oriented	64.47	11.07
Dynamic	57.09	10.92
Enterprising	52.80	15.00
Striving	62.10	10.63

Reference: Appendix B

14.4 Professional Styles Regional Norm Tables

Table 14.4 Professional Styles UK Senior Managers & Executives Group Norm Table, Invited Access (IA). (N=4,276)

Dimension	IA Mean	IA SD
Analytical	67.06	8.31
Factual	66.12	8.27
Rational	54.16	11.83
Learning Oriented	63.42	9.68
Practically Minded	65.13	9.47
Insightful	70.50	7.71
Inventive	61.10	12.15
Abstract	59.29	10.43
Strategic	68.46	10.70
Interactive	53.07	11.53
Engaging	63.96	9.60
Self-promoting	41.65	10.22
Convincing	59.72	9.19
Articulate	63.51	9.73
Challenging	50.94	9.92
Purposeful	60.66	9.52
Directing	69.13	9.30
Empowering	70.56	10.15
Self-assured	61.52	9.18
Composed	57.80	11.53
Resolving	59.34	9.98
Positive	66.56	9.95
Change Oriented	69.21	10.00
Receptive	61.92	9.17
Attentive	64.15	10.27
Involving	66.50	9.34
Accepting	61.47	10.48
Reliable	64.82	11.71
Meticulous	62.48	12.45
Conforming	44.49	12.74
Organized	67.72	10.30
Principled	74.92	8.48
Activity Oriented	66.25	9.08
Dynamic	66.28	9.19
Enterprising	59.24	13.31
Striving	69.67	9.07

Reference: Appendix D

Table 14.5 Professional Styles UK Professionals & Managers Group Norm Table, Invited Access (IA). *(N=9,884)*

Dimension	IA Mean	IA SD
Analytical	67.07	8.35
Factual	66.59	8.26
Rational	55.11	12.18
Learning Oriented	64.13	9.87
Practically Minded	66.45	9.42
Insightful	69.65	7.75
Inventive	59.88	12.25
Abstract	59.69	10.43
Strategic	66.11	11.02
Interactive	53.01	11.62
Engaging	64.32	9.82
Self-promoting	41.94	10.40
Convincing	58.84	9.40
Articulate	62.96	10.08
Challenging	50.81	10.06
Purposeful	59.19	9.92
Directing	67.58	10.28
Empowering	68.39	10.86
Self-assured	61.79	9.32
Composed	56.68	11.48
Resolving	59.08	10.56
Positive	66.27	9.92
Change Oriented	67.63	10.11
Receptive	62.36	9.38
Attentive	64.13	10.45
Involving	66.84	9.42
Accepting	62.01	10.52
Reliable	66.20	11.78
Meticulous	64.07	12.28
Conforming	47.48	13.47
Organized	68.59	10.30
Principled	74.73	8.61
Activity Oriented	65.80	9.50
Dynamic	64.63	9.38
Enterprising	57.63	13.78
Striving	68.74	9.37

Reference: Appendix E

327

Table 14.6 Professional Styles UK Mixed Occupational Group Norm Table, Invited Access (IA). (N=10,953)

Dimension	IA Mean	IA SD
Analytical	67.05	8.38
Factual	66.71	8.24
Rational	55.27	12.22
Learning Oriented	64.49	9.90
Practically Minded	66.81	9.43
Insightful	69.40	7.81
Inventive	59.58	12.27
Abstract	59.83	10.41
Strategic	65.67	11.05
Interactive	53.21	11.70
Engaging	64.60	9.90
Self-promoting	41.97	10.40
Convincing	58.56	9.47
Articulate	62.83	10.15
Challenging	50.68	10.16
Purposeful	58.75	10.03
Directing	66.95	10.61
Empowering	67.83	11.05
Self-assured	62.07	9.36
Composed	56.50	11.49
Resolving	59.18	10.63
Positive	66.30	9.89
Change Oriented	67.38	10.12
Receptive	62.54	9.36
Attentive	64.30	10.47
Involving	67.00	9.42
Accepting	62.24	10.49
Reliable	66.66	11.75
Meticulous	64.49	12.23
Conforming	48.32	13.60
Organized	68.83	10.24
Principled	74.81	8.57
Activity Oriented	65.90	9.61
Dynamic	64.24	9.50
Enterprising	57.36	13.88
Striving	68.71	9.45

Reference: Appendix F

Table 14.7 Professional Styles UK Graduates Group Norm Table, Invited Access (IA).
(N=4,021)

Dimension	IA Mean	IA SD
Analytical	67.66	8.54
Factual	67.54	8.31
Rational	55.91	12.40
Learning Oriented	66.70	9.48
Practically Minded	67.10	9.43
Insightful	68.80	7.98
Inventive	58.89	12.47
Abstract	61.18	10.60
Strategic	64.92	10.90
Interactive	54.06	12.02
Engaging	65.87	10.15
Self-promoting	43.71	10.80
Convincing	57.95	9.78
Articulate	63.14	10.31
Challenging	51.88	10.78
Purposeful	57.72	10.33
Directing	65.54	11.14
Empowering	65.31	11.32
Self-assured	62.89	9.55
Composed	55.31	11.62
Resolving	58.46	10.67
Positive	65.61	10.09
Change Oriented	66.41	10.21
Receptive	64.33	9.21
Attentive	64.24	10.86
Involving	66.52	9.72
Accepting	62.16	10.48
Reliable	66.43	11.87
Meticulous	65.21	12.19
Conforming	49.37	13.61
Organized	68.76	10.56
Principled	73.41	9.07
Activity Oriented	66.17	9.86
Dynamic	63.71	9.64
Enterprising	57.54	14.11
Striving	69.44	9.44

Reference: Appendix G

Table 14.8 Professional Styles US Senior Managers & Executives Group Norm Table, Invited Access (IA). *(N=597)*

Dimension	IA Mean	IA SD
Analytical	68.79	8.17
Factual	67.46	8.74
Rational	55.65	11.57
Learning Oriented	66.14	9.79
Practically Minded	66.96	8.68
Insightful	70.76	7.36
Inventive	59.75	10.81
Abstract	61.72	10.51
Strategic	68.48	9.88
Interactive	52.07	11.53
Engaging	63.80	9.91
Self-promoting	41.78	10.98
Convincing	57.67	9.65
Articulate	64.80	10.02
Challenging	51.13	10.83
Purposeful	61.19	9.89
Directing	68.93	9.48
Empowering	67.09	11.00
Self-assured	64.47	8.78
Composed	57.45	11.47
Resolving	57.83	10.83
Positive	65.79	9.63
Change Oriented	67.71	9.99
Receptive	61.40	8.96
Attentive	63.16	11.26
Involving	65.09	10.41
Accepting	62.74	11.17
Reliable	64.94	11.82
Meticulous	63.40	12.63
Conforming	46.79	12.88
Organized	66.65	10.88
Principled	78.69	7.24
Activity Oriented	66.39	9.81
Dynamic	66.63	9.15
Enterprising	62.24	13.48
Striving	72.73	8.66

Reference: Appendix H

Table 14.9 Professional Styles US Professionals & Managers Group Norm Table, Invited Access (IA). *(N=1,849)*

Dimension	IA Mean	IA SD
Analytical	68.54	8.36
Factual	67.01	8.54
Rational	56.21	11.61
Learning Oriented	66.66	9.99
Practically Minded	68.05	8.36
Insightful	69.96	7.53
Inventive	57.97	11.30
Abstract	60.96	10.29
Strategic	66.20	10.13
Interactive	52.83	11.85
Engaging	64.91	10.27
Self-promoting	41.69	10.95
Convincing	56.48	9.67
Articulate	64.38	10.35
Challenging	49.35	10.96
Purposeful	59.27	9.95
Directing	67.53	10.02
Empowering	66.14	10.93
Self-assured	64.92	8.57
Composed	56.42	11.75
Resolving	57.61	10.60
Positive	66.10	9.50
Change Oriented	66.51	10.30
Receptive	62.51	9.23
Attentive	63.72	10.67
Involving	65.92	9.90
Accepting	64.28	10.33
Reliable	66.29	11.77
Meticulous	64.86	11.94
Conforming	49.90	13.13
Organized	67.63	10.44
Principled	78.34	7.36
Activity Oriented	66.30	9.95
Dynamic	64.94	9.71
Enterprising	60.30	14.13
Striving	71.95	8.66

Reference: Appendix I

331

Table 14.10 *Professional Styles US Mixed Occupational Group Norm Table, Invited Access (IA).* *(N=2,143)*

Dimension	IA Mean	IA SD
Analytical	68.28	8.44
Factual	66.86	8.57
Rational	55.90	11.63
Learning Oriented	66.66	10.00
Practically Minded	68.15	8.37
Insightful	69.59	7.69
Inventive	57.46	11.48
Abstract	60.64	10.48
Strategic	65.74	10.22
Interactive	53.14	11.99
Engaging	65.52	10.47
Self-promoting	41.94	11.29
Convincing	56.40	9.75
Articulate	64.46	10.54
Challenging	48.90	11.12
Purposeful	58.71	10.09
Directing	66.88	10.44
Empowering	65.54	11.23
Self-assured	65.20	8.71
Composed	56.02	11.80
Resolving	57.47	10.77
Positive	66.26	9.65
Change Oriented	65.91	10.51
Receptive	62.69	9.32
Attentive	64.01	10.65
Involving	65.75	9.93
Accepting	64.40	10.22
Reliable	66.58	11.78
Meticulous	65.13	11.86
Conforming	50.62	13.31
Organized	67.74	10.45
Principled	78.29	7.55
Activity Oriented	66.25	10.05
Dynamic	64.51	9.85
Enterprising	60.49	14.69
Striving	71.93	8.83

Reference: Appendix J

Table 14.11 Professional Styles US Graduates Group Norm Table, Invited Access (IA).
(N=685)

Dimension	IA Mean	IA SD
Analytical	67.92	8.81
Factual	66.80	8.54
Rational	55.88	12.28
Learning Oriented	66.94	10.35
Practically Minded	68.55	8.26
Insightful	69.53	8.08
Inventive	57.06	12.15
Abstract	60.66	10.90
Strategic	64.55	10.45
Interactive	53.84	12.77
Engaging	65.97	10.63
Self-promoting	44.06	12.16
Convincing	56.20	9.88
Articulate	63.70	10.04
Challenging	50.82	11.48
Purposeful	58.14	10.21
Directing	66.09	10.78
Empowering	63.01	11.18
Self-assured	65.09	9.28
Composed	54.99	11.97
Resolving	56.94	10.76
Positive	65.22	10.08
Change Oriented	65.66	10.67
Receptive	64.80	9.32
Attentive	63.74	11.10
Involving	65.55	9.50
Accepting	63.81	10.16
Reliable	65.53	12.05
Meticulous	64.70	11.78
Conforming	51.10	13.95
Organized	66.49	11.08
Principled	76.72	8.00
Activity Oriented	66.20	10.12
Dynamic	63.79	9.95
Enterprising	59.89	14.58
Striving	72.04	8.65

Reference: Appendix K

Table 14.12 *Professional Styles International Senior Managers & Executives Group Norm Table, Invited Access (IA).* (N=953)

Dimension	IA Mean	IA SD
Analytical	67.84	8.45
Factual	66.97	8.29
Rational	56.24	12.13
Learning Oriented	65.63	9.93
Practically Minded	66.59	9.02
Insightful	71.36	7.97
Inventive	60.93	11.87
Abstract	60.65	10.61
Strategic	67.95	10.32
Interactive	53.50	11.50
Engaging	63.73	9.84
Self-promoting	42.61	10.92
Convincing	60.64	9.67
Articulate	63.79	9.57
Challenging	53.72	11.21
Purposeful	62.77	9.86
Directing	69.27	9.96
Empowering	68.19	10.74
Self-assured	65.02	9.20
Composed	57.89	11.10
Resolving	57.49	10.61
Positive	66.34	9.24
Change Oriented	68.09	9.76
Receptive	61.01	9.03
Attentive	63.25	11.01
Involving	64.65	9.98
Accepting	61.49	10.59
Reliable	65.71	11.76
Meticulous	63.33	12.33
Conforming	46.83	13.25
Organized	67.10	11.14
Principled	77.39	8.08
Activity Oriented	66.19	9.82
Dynamic	67.54	9.23
Enterprising	62.54	12.95
Striving	71.58	8.69

Reference: Appendix L

Table 14.13 Professional Styles International Professionals & Managers Group Norm Table, Invited Access (IA). *(N=2,600)*

Dimension	IA Mean	IA SD
Analytical	68.12	8.30
Factual	67.17	8.17
Rational	57.79	12.43
Learning Oriented	66.48	9.76
Practically Minded	67.60	8.69
Insightful	70.34	7.68
Inventive	59.30	11.81
Abstract	60.51	10.23
Strategic	65.48	10.46
Interactive	53.77	11.73
Engaging	63.93	9.99
Self-promoting	42.75	10.73
Convincing	59.90	9.85
Articulate	63.33	10.03
Challenging	53.85	11.32
Purposeful	61.15	10.32
Directing	67.86	10.52
Empowering	66.62	10.88
Self-assured	65.06	9.27
Composed	57.02	11.38
Resolving	56.90	10.61
Positive	66.03	9.62
Change Oriented	66.89	10.15
Receptive	62.30	9.26
Attentive	63.54	10.70
Involving	65.93	9.71
Accepting	62.58	10.40
Reliable	67.23	11.62
Meticulous	64.97	11.78
Conforming	50.67	13.63
Organized	68.48	10.44
Principled	77.46	7.73
Activity Oriented	65.71	10.20
Dynamic	65.76	9.59
Enterprising	59.99	14.06
Striving	70.90	8.99

Reference: Appendix M

Table 14.14 *Professional Styles International Mixed Occupational Group Norm Table, Invited Access (IA).* *(N=3,095)*

Dimension	IA Mean	IA SD
Analytical	68.00	8.31
Factual	67.18	8.13
Rational	58.06	12.42
Learning Oriented	66.98	9.77
Practically Minded	68.14	8.71
Insightful	69.64	7.93
Inventive	58.92	11.95
Abstract	60.51	10.21
Strategic	64.78	10.69
Interactive	54.07	11.87
Engaging	64.38	10.03
Self-promoting	42.99	11.06
Convincing	59.49	10.00
Articulate	62.95	10.29
Challenging	53.41	11.42
Purposeful	60.19	10.47
Directing	66.55	11.37
Empowering	65.69	11.08
Self-assured	65.29	9.49
Composed	56.74	11.42
Resolving	56.73	10.82
Positive	66.03	9.61
Change Oriented	66.44	10.21
Receptive	62.81	9.32
Attentive	63.78	10.51
Involving	66.07	9.63
Accepting	62.93	10.30
Reliable	68.11	11.67
Meticulous	65.54	11.55
Conforming	52.32	13.86
Organized	68.98	10.32
Principled	77.26	7.88
Activity Oriented	65.63	10.23
Dynamic	64.95	9.71
Enterprising	59.61	14.17
Striving	70.77	9.13

Reference: Appendix N

Table 14.15 *Professional Styles International Graduates Group Norm Table, Invited Access (IA).* (N=1,423)

Dimension	IA Mean	IA SD
Analytical	68.04	8.45
Factual	67.46	7.93
Rational	58.01	13.04
Learning Oriented	68.29	9.71
Practically Minded	68.62	8.83
Insightful	69.02	7.95
Inventive	58.70	12.08
Abstract	60.87	10.20
Strategic	64.39	10.51
Interactive	56.14	12.14
Engaging	65.65	10.45
Self-promoting	44.32	11.64
Convincing	59.88	10.05
Articulate	64.08	10.26
Challenging	53.97	11.27
Purposeful	59.77	10.12
Directing	66.87	10.88
Empowering	65.14	11.15
Self-assured	65.81	9.83
Composed	56.04	11.60
Resolving	56.65	10.79
Positive	65.97	9.85
Change Oriented	66.27	10.04
Receptive	64.77	9.25
Attentive	64.36	10.68
Involving	66.54	9.69
Accepting	62.94	9.88
Reliable	68.00	11.97
Meticulous	65.57	11.76
Conforming	53.23	13.90
Organized	69.20	10.46
Principled	76.66	8.18
Activity Oriented	66.01	10.06
Dynamic	64.64	9.68
Enterprising	59.95	14.27
Striving	71.20	9.18

Reference: Appendix O

337

Table 14.16 Professional Styles Australian Professionals & Managers Group Norm Table, Invited Access (IA). *(N=474)*

Dimension	IA Mean	IA SD
Analytical	67.41	8.28
Factual	69.53	7.72
Rational	54.08	11.87
Learning Oriented	66.62	9.33
Practically Minded	69.15	8.32
Insightful	68.17	8.86
Inventive	55.24	11.63
Abstract	61.60	9.74
Strategic	64.44	10.07
Interactive	53.03	11.08
Engaging	64.32	9.44
Self-promoting	40.18	10.36
Convincing	55.17	9.42
Articulate	62.84	9.38
Challenging	49.11	10.84
Purposeful	57.19	10.57
Directing	66.43	10.71
Empowering	65.33	10.73
Self-assured	62.06	8.65
Composed	55.07	11.26
Resolving	60.69	10.93
Positive	64.76	9.28
Change Oriented	65.05	9.63
Receptive	62.63	8.79
Attentive	66.19	10.36
Involving	69.18	9.88
Accepting	64.87	9.97
Reliable	67.28	11.88
Meticulous	67.26	11.91
Conforming	54.35	12.06
Organized	69.93	10.53
Principled	77.43	7.52
Activity Oriented	66.20	10.23
Dynamic	60.47	10.13
Enterprising	52.91	13.53
Striving	65.69	9.73

Reference: Appendix P

14.5 Further Reference Material

Further information can be found in the Fairness chapter and appendices of this handbook.

15.0 Reliability

When people are tested on different occasions or on different versions of the same test why do they get different scores? Because we cannot measure people's traits with perfect reliability.

Reliability of any test or assessment is concerned with how precisely the instrument measures particular characteristics or traits.

Reliability estimates provide an index of how precise and error free a tool is in measuring the desired constructs. The reliability of a test or assessment is an important prerequisite to allowing the test user to draw accurate inferences from assessment scores. The observed scores on the assessment are intended to provide an approximation of the individual's true scores. If test or profile scores are unreliable then they provide a less precise and less accurate reflection of the individual's true scores. The higher the reliability, the less the error and the more likely the observed scores are an accurate reflection of the individual's true scores.

Reliability is merely a stepping stone or prerequisite of test or questionnaire validity. If a test user is to draw a correct and meaningful inference from assessment scores, then the assessment must first be reliable. But that is not enough because the assessment should also be supported by appropriate validity data. In essence, a questionnaire must be measuring a construct reliably for it to go on to be a valid indicator from which a test user can then draw appropriate inferences and make accurate decisions. The greater the reliability, the greater the chance of high validity.

There are several methods of estimating test reliability. Three common approaches are detailed below:

Test-Retest Reliability

One estimate of reliability is to look at the stability of test scores over time. This can be accomplished by a group of individuals completing the test or assessment on one occasion and then sitting a test or assessment again on another occasion.

The (Pearson Product-Moment) correlation coefficient between how the group scores on a scale on one occasion and then on the second occasion provides this estimate of reliability.

A development aim of Wave Styles was that this form of reliability should be as high as possible.

Alternate Form Reliability

Where two or more versions of the test or assessment have been developed by the same developers, it is possible to estimate the reliability between the versions.

A group of people complete both versions of the test or assessment and a correlation coefficient (Pearson Product Moment) is calculated. This correlation provides an index of alternate form reliability. In other words, people who score high on one version also score high on the alternate version, and low scorers score low on both. When an assessment has high alternate form reliability, it means we can be confident that a person would achieve a similar score irrespective of which version of the assessment was used.

A development aim of Wave Styles was that this form of reliability should be as high as possible.

Internal Consistency Reliability

This form of reliability is an index of how the items in a test (or a personality scale) relate to one another. It carries the practical advantage that it can be computed without the need for a retest or an alternative form, but there are some drawbacks.

341

For self-report questionnaires it is important that internal consistency reliability is satisfactorily high without being artificially inflated. For instance, a personality scale with repetitive item content will have high internal consistency reliability estimates, but lack breadth of measurement. This narrowness of coverage of the content domain in a questionnaire may fall well short of what scales should be measuring and is likely to impact on the empirical validity of the test in forecasting effectiveness on independently assessed criteria. In the development of Wave Styles this problem of 'Bloated Specifics' was avoided by drawing on three distinct facet constructs for each Wave dimension. The selection of these facets was primarily based on their concurrent validity with internal consistency reliability being of secondary concern. This approach also ensured good construct separation between the dimensions measured by the Wave Styles questionnaires.

A development aim of Wave Styles was to have internal consistency reliability estimates of the Wave dimensions between .60 and .90. In essence, this form of reliability was seen by the authors as a measure of the breadth or narrowness of the scale. The results for alternate form and test-retest give a better indication of the reliability of Wave Styles questionnaires.

Sources of Error affecting Reliability

Assessment scores can contain errors of measurement from a number of sources, for example:

- Questionnaire Design – questions with negative phrasing or asking more than one question in an item tend to increase measurement error
- Individual - mood, temperament, motivation, well-being
- Environment - noise, temperature, presence of others
- Administration - degree and consistency of standardization
- Scoring – the accuracy of the scoring key and scoring process

Maximizing Reliability

The primary development aim of Wave was to develop a high validity instrument to predict performance outcomes at work. For an instrument to be highly valid it also needs to be reliable. To achieve this aim, specific steps were taken to ensure high reliability:

1. Negative phrased and keyed items were avoided. Negative items had less reliability in early trials
2. Questionnaire Instructions were standardized
3. A Normative Development Trial preceded the Full Standardization Trial that used the new Ra-Ra (Rate-Rank) response format
4. Questions were balanced in blocks of six to standardize the number of comparisons across different dimensions
5. Items were selected for blocks based on their mean endorsement value from the normative trial to ensure the items within a block were equally attractive to respondents
6. Items were written and reviewed against clear criteria (see Construction chapter)
7. Items were not included if they had low reliability as well as validity

Standard Error of Measurement

When test or assessment users receive a test score they make inferences, communicate and/or make decisions based on the test score. However, the observed score is subject to error and so to be in a better position to use the test score, it is important for a test user to have an appreciation of the band of error around the score and know how likely it is to contain the individual's true score. To do this the Standard Error of Measurement is computed (SEm).

Formula

The Standard Error of Measurement (SEm) equals the Standard Deviation of a group multiplied by the square root of one minus the reliability coefficient.

$$SEm = SD \sqrt{(1 - r_t)}$$

Where:

SEm = Standard Error of Measurement

SD = Standard Deviation of the sample that the reliability coefficient was calculated from

r_t = the reliability coefficient (test-retest, alternate form, internal consistency)

If we take the average alternate reliability of the Wave Styles scales, which was r= .86 in the standardization trials, and want to calculate the Standard Error of Measurement for a sten score, then:

SD Sten Score = 2
Alternate Form Reliability = .86

$$SEm = 2 \sqrt{(1 - 0.86)}$$
$$= 2 \times .37$$
$$= .74$$

A band of 1 SEm (i.e., .74 stens) either side of an individual's score results in a 68% probability that this band contains the true score for the individual. For instance, with a sten score of 6, we are confident that 68% of the time the person's true score will be between 5.26 and 6.78 - or 1 SEm to either side of the observed score.

By placing a band of 2 SEms (i.e., 2 x .74 stens or 1.48 stens) either side of the observed score gives a 96% probability that this band contains the true score for this individual.

+/- 1SEm – 68% Probability
+/- 2SEm – 96% Probability

In practice, stens are rounded to the nearest whole number between 1 and 10.

15.1 Reliability Overview

Alternate Form Reliability

The alternate form reliability of Saville Consulting Wave Professional Styles is based on two versions of Professional Styles; Invited Access (IA) and Supervised Access (SA). Table 15.1 shows the means and standard deviations for both versions of the Professional Styles questionnaire, along with their Normative, Ipsative and Total Score alternate form reliability coefficients (r_t).

Alternate form reliabilities of .70 and above are regarded by the authors as acceptable levels of reliability for a trait measure although higher levels than this are desirable. The median reliability of the Total Score (combined Normative and Ipsative) scales was .87 and the minimum reliability estimate for any dimension was .78.

Normative and Ipsative scores of the questionnaire also had good alternate form reliabilities, with a median reliability of .86 for Normative and .83 for Ipsative, and minimum reliability estimates of .78 for Normative and .72 for Ipsative.

Construct independence between the scales is demonstrated by the 'Other Highest Correlation' and 'Other Dimension' columns which show the highest correlation (other than with the parallel version of the dimension of the same name) of one dimension in one version with the dimension in another (the off diagonals in a correlation matrix).

As can be seen from Table 15.1, these correlations are substantially lower than the Alternate Form correlations between same scales, demonstrating good construct independence of the dimensions at the individual dimension level. The highest correlation between different dimensions across the two versions is between Organized (SA) and Reliable (IA) with a correlation between the scales of .60. However, the respective alternate form reliability estimates of the two dimensions are .88 for Organized and .91 for Reliable.

Internal Consistency Reliability

Tables 15.2 & 15.3 provide the internal consistency (Cronbach's Alpha) of the 36 dimensions of Professional Styles for Invited Access (IA) (Table 15.2) and Supervised Access (SA) (Table 15.3). The dimensions of Wave Professional Styles were designed to have internal consistency estimates ranging from .60 to a maximum of .90. The median internal consistency (across the 72 dimensions across the two versions) is in the center of this desired range. Only one scale fell outside this – Insightful on Invited Access with an internal consistency of .58. However, Insightful has highly acceptable alternate form reliability and test-retest reliability estimates which are the fundamental reliability measures for Wave Styles.

Test-Retest Reliability

Table 15.4 provides the test-retest reliability of Saville Consulting Wave Professional Styles administered at a one month interval. Test-retest reliabilities of .70 and above are acceptable levels of reliability. The 36 dimensions of Wave Professional Styles demonstrate high test-retest reliabilities with coefficients ranging from .71 (Purposeful and Attentive) to .91 (Enterprising) and a median reliability coefficient of .80.

15.2 Reliability Tables

Table 15.1 Professional Styles Alternate Form Reliability - Invited Access (IA) vs. Supervised Access (SA) - Normative, Ipsative and 36 combined Normative-Ipsative dimensions. *(N=1,153)*

Dimension	(IA) Mean	(IA) SD	(SA) Mean	(SA) SD	Norms. r_t	Ips. r_t	Total Score SEm (stens)	Total Score r_t	Other Highest Correlation	Other Dimension
Analytical	62.87	9.78	62.82	9.95	.85	.79	.80	.84	.50	Abstract
Factual	65.89	8.86	64.93	9.56	.79	.79	.87	.81	.38	Analytical
Rational	53.82	13.09	52.80	13.55	.91	.88	.57	.92	.49	Analytical
Learning Oriented	62.43	11.93	64.42	10.99	.86	.84	.72	.87	.51	Abstract
Practically Minded	67.38	9.68	67.57	9.49	.85	.83	.75	.86	.26	Rational
Insightful	65.42	8.73	66.00	8.87	.82	.72	.92	.79	.45	Strategic
Inventive	52.83	13.41	52.36	13.32	.91	.87	.60	.91	.54	Strategic
Abstract	58.21	11.41	55.69	12.04	.85	.77	.82	.83	.51	Learning Oriented
Strategic	56.13	11.20	53.61	12.08	.84	.79	.80	.84	.54	Inventive
Interactive	53.75	13.63	52.31	12.50	.90	.85	.63	.90	.58	Engaging
Engaging	67.11	10.88	67.07	11.49	.87	.83	.72	.87	.58	Interactive
Self-promoting	45.80	12.32	43.85	12.34	.89	.84	.66	.89	.42	Interactive
Convincing	55.80	10.31	51.20	10.63	.85	.78	.80	.84	.54	Challenging
Articulate	57.59	12.25	56.56	11.89	.91	.86	.60	.91	.39	Interactive
Challenging	51.39	11.72	49.96	12.09	.86	.81	.75	.86	.54	Convincing
Purposeful	54.60	10.96	54.91	11.03	.87	.80	.72	.87	.53	Directing
Directing	58.81	12.86	56.22	12.65	.89	.84	.66	.89	.54	Empowering
Empowering	59.44	12.67	59.31	13.17	.90	.85	.66	.89	.54	Directing
Self-assured	59.70	11.06	61.62	12.28	.86	.78	.77	.85	.37	Positive
Composed	53.40	13.50	52.16	14.09	.90	.84	.66	.89	.48	Change Oriented
Resolving	58.65	11.90	55.50	13.05	.88	.84	.69	.88	.47	Attentive
Positive	65.93	10.92	64.91	10.17	.85	.81	.77	.85	.38	Change Oriented
Change Oriented	61.75	11.34	61.49	11.59	.85	.82	.75	.86	.48	Composed
Receptive	60.20	9.76	58.63	9.50	.81	.73	.94	.78	.24	Involving
Attentive	65.43	11.08	63.77	11.68	.83	.85	.75	.86	.52	Accepting
Involving	65.55	9.10	63.02	9.51	.79	.81	.87	.81	.51	Accepting
Accepting	63.60	12.01	65.51	10.84	.78	.82	.87	.81	.52	Attentive
Reliable	64.95	13.41	66	12.47	.89	.89	.60	.91	.60	Organized
Meticulous	64.48	13.69	64.65	13.04	.87	.87	.66	.89	.50	Organized
Conforming	53.48	14.52	54.12	14.65	.89	.90	.60	.91	.48	Reliable
Organized	64.94	11.40	65.44	11.43	.86	.88	.69	.88	.60	Reliable
Principled	71.84	9.66	74.38	9.77	.81	.77	.87	.81	.34	Accepting
Activity Oriented	65.35	10.63	64.47	11.07	.90	.86	.66	.89	.30	Reliable
Dynamic	57.83	10.53	57.09	10.92	.87	.81	.72	.87	.48	Directing
Enterprising	53.24	15.15	52.8	15.00	.93	.89	.53	.93	.53	Striving
Striving	61.82	10.50	62.10	10.63	.86	.79	.77	.85	.53	Enterprising
Mean	60.04	11.55	59.42	11.65	.86	.83	.73	.86	.48	
Median	59.95	11.37	60.40	11.64	.86	.83	.72	.87	.51	
Min.	45.80	8.73	43.85	8.87	.78	.72	.53	.78	.24	
Max.	71.84	15.15	74.38	15.00	.93	.90	.94	.93	.60	

Table 15.2 Internal Consistency Reliability of Professional Styles - Invited Access.
(N=1,153)

Dimension	Mean	SD	SEm (sten)	r_t
Analytical	62.87	9.78	1.23	.62
Factual	65.89	8.86	1.27	.60
Rational	53.82	13.09	1.04	.73
Learning Oriented	62.43	11.93	1.01	.75
Practically Minded	67.38	9.68	1.12	.68
Insightful	65.42	8.73	1.29	.58
Inventive	52.83	13.41	.75	.86
Abstract	58.21	11.41	.99	.76
Strategic	56.13	11.20	1.03	.74
Interactive	53.75	13.63	.96	.77
Engaging	67.11	10.88	1.02	.74
Self-promoting	45.80	12.32	.94	.78
Convincing	55.80	10.31	1.11	.69
Articulate	57.59	12.25	1.03	.74
Challenging	51.39	11.72	1.01	.75
Purposeful	54.60	10.96	1.23	.62
Directing	58.81	12.86	.89	.80
Empowering	59.44	12.67	.79	.84
Self-assured	59.70	11.06	1.17	.66
Composed	53.40	13.50	.93	.79
Resolving	58.65	11.90	.98	.76
Positive	65.93	10.92	.97	.76
Change Oriented	61.75	11.34	.93	.78
Receptive	60.20	9.76	1.22	.63
Attentive	65.43	11.08	.96	.77
Involving	65.55	9.10	1.10	.70
Accepting	63.60	12.01	.91	.79
Reliable	64.95	13.41	.88	.81
Meticulous	64.48	13.69	.74	.86
Conforming	53.48	14.52	.78	.85
Organized	64.94	11.40	.97	.70
Principled	71.84	9.66	1.12	.69
Activity Oriented	65.35	10.63	.98	.76
Dynamic	57.83	10.53	1.14	.67
Enterprising	53.24	15.15	.85	.82
Striving	61.82	10.50	1.18	.65
Mean	60.04	11.55	1.01	.74
Median	59.95	11.37	1.00	.76
Min	45.80	8.73	.74	.58
Max	71.84	15.15	1.29	.86

Table 15.3 Internal Consistency Reliability of Professional Styles - Supervised Access.
(N=1,153)

Dimension	Mean	SD	SEm (sten)	r_t
Analytical	62.82	9.95	1.17	.66
Factual	64.93	9.56	1.15	.67
Rational	52.80	13.55	.97	.76
Learning Oriented	64.42	10.99	1.04	.73
Practically Minded	67.57	9.49	1.08	.71
Insightful	66.00	8.87	1.13	.68
Inventive	52.36	13.32	.74	.86
Abstract	55.69	12.04	.90	.80
Strategic	53.61	12.08	.86	.82
Interactive	52.31	12.50	1.00	.75
Engaging	67.07	11.49	.87	.81
Self-promoting	43.85	12.34	.90	.80
Convincing	51.20	10.63	1.07	.71
Articulate	56.56	11.89	1.05	.72
Challenging	49.96	12.09	.94	.78
Purposeful	54.91	11.03	1.19	.65
Directing	56.22	12.65	.89	.80
Empowering	59.31	13.17	.74	.86
Self-assured	61.62	12.28	.96	.77
Composed	52.16	14.09	.83	.83
Resolving	55.50	13.05	.81	.84
Positive	64.91	10.17	1.06	.72
Change Oriented	61.49	11.59	.83	.83
Receptive	58.63	9.50	1.17	.66
Attentive	63.77	11.68	.82	.83
Involving	63.02	9.51	1.04	.73
Accepting	65.51	10.84	1.02	.74
Reliable	66.00	12.47	.89	.80
Meticulous	64.65	13.04	.71	.87
Conforming	54.12	14.65	.71	.87
Organized	65.44	11.43	.90	.80
Principled	74.38	9.77	.92	.79
Activity Oriented	64.47	11.07	.86	.82
Dynamic	57.09	10.92	1.07	.71
Enterprising	52.80	15.00	.83	.83
Striving	62.10	10.63	1.14	.67
Mean	60.04	11.55	1.01	.74
Median	59.95	11.37	1.00	.76
Min	45.80	8.73	.74	.58
Max	71.84	15.15	1.29	.86

347

Table 15.4 Test-Retest Reliability of Professional Styles Normative Invited Access.
(N=112)

Dimension	Mean$_{t1}$	SD$_{t1}$	Mean$_{t2}$	SD$_{t2}$	SEm (Sten)	r$_t$
Analytical	40.91	5.57	41.99	4.55	1.04	.73
Factual	42.64	5.04	42.85	4.62	.96	.77
Rational	33.68	8.08	35.25	8.05	.85	.82
Learning Oriented	41.70	5.74	42.47	5.33	.94	.78
Practically Minded	42.31	5.45	41.99	6.10	.87	.81
Insightful	39.62	5.33	39.73	4.54	.98	.76
Inventive	36.36	7.70	36.96	6.89	.69	.88
Abstract	39.31	6.51	40.45	5.43	.98	.76
Strategic	38.54	6.44	39.30	5.45	1.04	.73
Interactive	36.66	7.99	37.45	7.47	.66	.89
Engaging	41.39	5.73	41.29	5.42	.92	.79
Self-promoting	31.89	7.11	33.59	6.86	.89	.80
Convincing	38.05	6.07	38.54	5.72	1.02	.74
Articulate	37.90	7.48	38.28	7.20	.75	.86
Challenging	34.35	7.04	35.47	7.25	.75	.86
Purposeful	34.88	6.70	34.88	6.30	1.08	.71
Directing	37.53	7.28	37.68	6.95	.82	.83
Empowering	39.30	6.56	39.56	5.81	.89	.80
Self-assured	39.57	6.13	40.41	5.27	.98	.76
Composed	31.74	8.19	37.48	6.23	1.06	.72
Resolving	36.99	7.13	37.71	6.68	.89	.80
Positive	40.66	6.48	40.60	6.76	.85	.82
Change Oriented	38.03	6.60	38.33	5.58	.98	.76
Receptive	38.95	5.68	39.50	6.07	.89	.80
Attentive	42.18	5.71	43.17	4.96	1.08	.71
Involving	41.46	5.31	41.72	5.01	1.02	.74
Accepting	40.76	5.73	41.18	5.19	1.00	.75
Reliable	41.39	7.20	43.06	6.22	.82	.83
Meticulous	40.37	6.80	41.75	5.88	.89	.80
Conforming	33.33	7.58	35.08	6.98	.82	.83
Organized	40.34	5.98	40.89	5.64	.96	.77
Principled	43.91	5.47	43.31	5.66	.89	.80
Activity Oriented	40.62	6.19	41.21	5.80	.94	.78
Dynamic	39.53	6.02	39.70	5.66	.94	.78
Enterprising	34.21	8.71	34.71	7.88	.60	.91
Striving	40.18	6.37	41.55	5.99	.89	.80
Mean	38.65	6.53	39.42	6.04	.91	.79
Median	39.42	6.46	39.72	5.85	.91	.80
Min	31.74	5.04	33.59	4.54	.60	.71
Max	43.91	8.71	43.31	8.05	1.08	.91

Note. Subjects completed Wave twice at a 1 month interval.

Table 15.5 Internal Consistency Reliability of Professional Styles with a US sample.
(N=2,102)

Dimension	Mean	SD	SEm (sten)	r_t
Analytical	67.46	8.70	1.28	.59
Factual	66.91	8.52	1.28	.59
Rational	55.44	11.88	1.09	.71
Learning Oriented	66.26	9.90	1.07	.71
Practically Minded	68.52	8.21	1.21	.63
Insightful	69.04	7.72	1.39	.52
Inventive	57.02	11.37	.89	.80
Abstract	59.97	10.48	.99	.75
Strategic	65.23	10.25	1.05	.72
Interactive	53.88	12.08	.99	.76
Engaging	66.89	10.53	.94	.78
Self-promoting	41.66	11.17	.94	.78
Convincing	56.05	9.74	1.19	.65
Articulate	64.56	10.84	1.05	.73
Challenging	47.60	11.03	1.03	.73
Purposeful	57.92	10.33	1.20	.64
Directing	66.70	10.66	1.02	.74
Empowering	65.54	11.31	.84	.82
Self-assured	65.58	8.75	1.33	.56
Composed	55.32	11.96	1.04	.73
Resolving	57.52	10.82	.97	.76
Positive	66.86	9.73	1.03	.74
Change Oriented	64.58	10.59	1.01	.74
Receptive	61.85	9.20	1.26	.60
Attentive	64.23	10.27	1.00	.75
Involving	65.88	9.81	.99	.75
Accepting	64.71	9.97	1.06	.72
Reliable	67.63	11.41	.93	.78
Meticulous	66.08	11.49	.90	.80
Conforming	52.37	13.14	.86	.81
Organized	68.61	10.36	1.00	.75
Principled	78.54	7.45	1.10	.70
Activity Oriented	66.55	9.99	.95	.77
Dynamic	64.31	9.61	1.22	.63
Enterprising	59.80	15.53	.79	.84
Striving	71.64	8.97	1.24	.62
Mean	62.74	10.38	1.06	.71
Median	64.97	10.34	1.03	.74
Min	41.66	7.45	.79	.52
Max	78.54	15.53	1.39	.84

Graph 15.1 Internal Consistency Reliability of Professional Styles (Invited Access) for 13 norm groups across UK, US, International and Australia

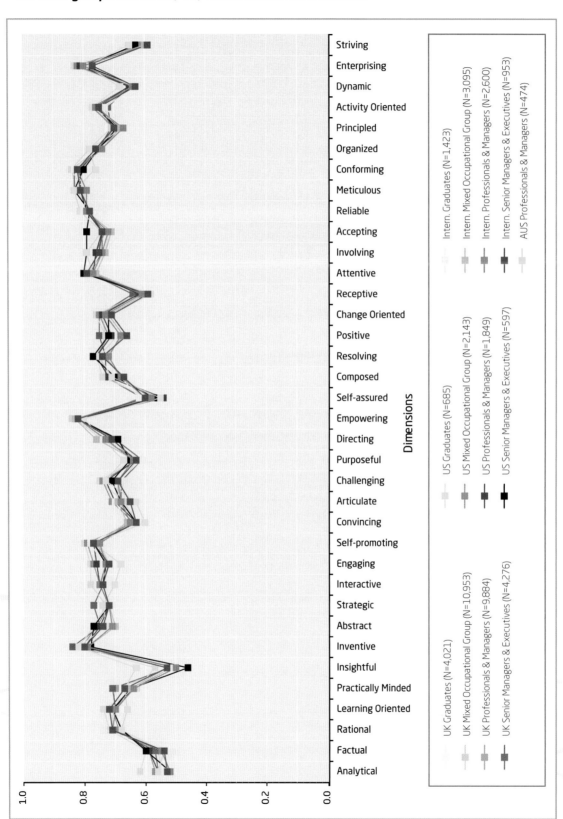

15.3 Reliability of Facet Scales

Wave Professional Styles is composed of 108 different two item facet scales. While the individual 108 facet scales are not individually plotted on a profile, a Wave user's attention is drawn to facet ranges, where there is a difference of three of more sten scores between the three facet scales within each dimension. Internal Consistency is not an ideal method of reliability estimation for the facet scales of Wave Professional Styles as the two items of each facet are designed to measure different content (i.e. one motive and one talent item). Alternate Form Reliabilities range from .50 to .90 for two item facet scales (Ra-Ra) with median of .78 (n=1153). This compares with Alternate Form Reliabilities of Wave Professional Styles six item dimension scales of r=.86 (composed of three facet scales – six items).

36 of the facet concepts of Wave Professional Styles have also been subject to test-retest in two item facet scales in Wave Focus Styles for over six months and the figures ranged from .58 to .84 for two item facet scales with median of .72 (n=214).

15.4 Summary of Reliability

No measure of human traits has perfect reliability, yet good reliability of measurement is an important property of any assessment. This chapter highlights in particular, given the design of Wave Professional Styles, the importance of alternate form reliability as an appropriate method for the estimation of reliability.

The method of development of Wave Professional Styles targeted scales to have internal consistencies (Cronbach's Alpha) between .60 and .90. The reason for targeting this level of internal consistency is that internal consistency provides a measure of scales' breadth of content measurement.

Wave Professional Styles was designed by selecting facets/items with varied content within each of the dimensions. The internal consistency of the dimensions (Cronbach's alpha) ranged at standardization from .58 to .86. Subsequent analysis of usage data since standardization shown in Graph 15.1 indicates that the scales of Analytical, Factual, Insightful, Convincing, Self-assured, Receptive and Striving have reliabilities in one or more subgroups of less than .60. Despite the breadth of these scales they have good Alternate Forms/Test-Retests: Analytical .84/.73; Factual .81/.77; Insightful .79/.76; Convincing .84/.74; Self-assured .85/.76; Receptive .78/.80; Striving .85/.80. This indicates that despite their breadth of measurement these dimensions are reliable, stable and reproducible. Information on the validity of these dimensions can be found in the Validity chapter.

Alternate form median at standardization was .87 (no corrections applied) for the dimensions and the reliabilities ranged from .78 to .93. A Test-Retest was conducted with a month's interval between original test and retest during development and achieved a median of .80 for the dimensions.

Alternate form also provides a method of investigating construct separation and the Wave Professional Styles dimensions provide clear evidence supporting this separation.

15.5 Further Reference Material

Further information can be found in the Norms, Fairness chapters and appendices of this handbook.

16.0 Validity

If making better decisions about people is important, then it is essential for an assessment instrument to provide evidence of its validity.

This chapter is divided into two parts. The first part focuses on construct-related validity evidence and the second part focuses specifically on criterion-related validity evidence. Because validity is fundamental and central to effective test application, this chapter begins with a general discussion of validity. It continues by offering perspectives upon validity which are important underpinnings for the user in understanding what makes the Wave Styles questionnaires different from traditional personality questionnaires.

How do we know that a test or an assessment works and actually does what it claims to do? How do we know if the inferences and decisions made using one assessment are any better than another? How can we know which assessment tools are most accurate and will maximize the amount of benefit derived from the information provided? Which tool is the best investment for our organization?

These and other related questions are fundamental to the development and continuous improvement of assessment practices and tools in the workplace. These questions directly relate to the validity of a test or assessment.

What is Validity?

Wave Styles assessments have been designed to maximize validity in forecasting overall effectiveness at work and key workplace competencies.

> Validity is a unitary concept. It is the degree to which all the accumulated evidence supports the intended interpretation of the test scores for the proposed purpose.
>
> *Standards for Educational and Psychological Measurement, American Psychological Association 1999*

Accumulated evidence can come from many places. Today's understanding of validity evolved from the notion that there are different types of validity evidence, and it is important to understand these aspects of validity evidence and how they relate to Wave Styles assessments. These aspects of validity evidence help to support different inferences that can be made from test scores.

Predictive – Predictive Validity – a type of criterion-related validity evidence. This type of evidence is particularly applicable when one wishes to make an inference from a test or assessment score about the test taker's position on another independently evaluated criterion variable at a later date.

An example of a predictive validation study would be to investigate if an assessment designed to forecast sales potential correlated with future sales performance. Such a validation study might be based on the identification of critical sales behaviors through a job analysis study. This leads to an assessment being selected that purports to measure the sales behaviors in question. This measure is then administered to applicants for a sales job – but the assessment scores are not used to decide which sales applicants are actually hired. The job analysis and the selection of the test lead directly to an *a priori* hypothesis that higher test scores will be related to better sales performance (which could be measured, for example, by sales revenue generated in a quarter). Time goes by and the newly selected sales staff get on with their jobs. A year later (or at an appropriate time to judge) sales performance is collated and analyzed to see if higher test scores do generate more sales revenue. The presence of an association or correlation between assessment results and later how the sales staff perform can then be evaluated. Typically, the organizer of the study may consider how likely the correlation is to assume a different range of values including whether it is not likely to be a zero correlation (statistical significance). This also might be followed by an examination of aspects of the study that might have an effect on the size of the association (e.g., restriction of range, inter-rater reliability being less than perfect).

353

Note that often a 'hard' criterion such as sales performance is not practically achievable in many jobs. And even 'hard' job performance criteria can have systematic biases, e.g., being given a geographical region that has historically poor sales.

Supervisor ratings are an alternative method of job assessment which are often collected (see the Criterion Problem Revisited in this chapter).

Sometimes predictive validation studies are run on a well-established test being actively used by an organization. Under these circumstances, the organization's selection process may have removed low scorers based on the results of the assessment, and it is therefore not possible to later assess how these low scorers on the test or assessment might subsequently perform in the job. This restriction of range will reduce the size of the association seen between the assessment and the job performance measure and consequently underestimate the usefulness of the test.

Concurrent – another type of criterion-related validity evidence. It is similar to a predictive validation design in that a predictor assessment is correlated with a criterion outcome of performance in the job. The difference is that there is not a time lag between the initial assessment and the independent evaluation of performance on the job (the assessment score and job performance measure are collected concurrently).

One advantage of a concurrent validation study is that users don't have to administer a test at time one and then wait until time two before examining the relationship between the test and job performance. If a relationship is found between the test scores and current levels of performance, then concurrent validation evidence provides support for the test to be used with job applicants to identify those who are more likely to perform better. For practical reasons, organizations rarely want to have a substantial delay before seeing if a test works for them.

As with a predictive design, a potential difficulty in running this type of study is the need for a sufficiently large sample of participants to make the interpretation of the association between the predictor and criteria statistically meaningful.

Another problem is poor performers (or indeed good performers) may have already left the organization or have been promoted (leading to potential restriction of range).

One common confusion is the use of benchmarking studies as a means to validate a test. Benchmarking is a useful exercise where, for example, the characteristics of top performers are identified. The objective is typically to identify what top performers have in common (e.g., which personality traits) so that future hires can be selected using this "top performer" scoring template.

The problem with this approach is that, while it tells us what top performers have in common, it fails to tell us what makes them different from average or poor performers. A benchmarking study is useful in identifying the characteristics that top performers have in common, but it does not tell us which characteristics are unique to top performers only. An associated problem is that it may just be a matter of luck that the top performers tend to be high on certain characteristics and not related to their superior performance. Such benchmarking studies used in isolation (without being used alongside a concurrent or predictive design and job analysis) carry particular dangers for organizations as they may lead to the organization using a spurious "scoring key" which is not associated with superior performance (lacks criterion-related validity). The result could not only be that the organization selects many poor performers, but it is likely to lay itself open to an increased risk of litigation if the assessment process is perceived as unfair.

Content – a type of validity evidence related to the appropriateness of the content of the assessment. It seems obvious that a typing test is a "valid" test for a typist job because the content of the test matches closely the content of the job. Giving a typing test to a CEO candidate might appear odd, however, because the content of the test does not seem appropriate given the content of a typical CEO position.

354

Unlike the types of criterion-related validity described above, a content validation study does not rely upon a statistical analysis. Rather, it uses a rationale approach to linking job content to test content. A job analysis study is required to identify and document the critical work behaviors and competencies tied to job success. Once identified, assessment tools that measure that same domain of content (i.e., tasks, behaviors, skills, knowledge) are identified. Job simulation exercises or situational judgment tests are often considered job relevant and content valid when the exercises or situations presented resemble the same as those found on the job.

Likewise, a job analysis may identify certain behaviors such as Team Working or Empowering Others to be critical to job success, and Wave competencies can be identified that are similar to the "behavioral domain" identified in the job analysis. In this way, the Wave dimensions can be mapped to a job for the purposes of predicting Person-Job Fit. The Wave competencies can also be mapped to client competency models to enable the use of the Wave Styles questionnaire to measure the client's own competencies.

One way to identify and document critical workplace competencies, behaviors and aptitudes is to use the Wave Job Profiler or the Wave Performance Culture Framework Cards. Job experts make ratings online or sort competency cards to specify which competencies are important. This semi-structured approach is a valuable addition to any job analysis study.

Content validity evidence by itself is sufficient to justify an assessment program even for high stakes situations like pre-employment selection and is an accepted validation strategy by regulatory commissions (i.e., Uniform Guidelines on Employee Selection Procedures published by Equal Employment Opportunity Commission of the US Government). However, it is but one type of validity evidence and we recommend the collection of empirical data using criterion-related validation studies in addition to content validation studies.

Construct Validity is a type of validity evidence that shows that a test or questionnaire measures the psychological construct that it purports to measure. It is important because it impacts how a test score is interpreted. If a questionnaire claims to measure extroversion, how do we know it actually measures extroversion and not emotional stability? If an assessment claims to measure extroversion but does not, then any interpretation of that score would be wrong and could cause harm to the respondent and to the organization.

An assessment instrument, its items, internal structure and design, and the responses test takers give all lead to scores to be interpreted as representations of underlying psychological constructs. Inferences made on these scores are based on the proposed psychological construct and its relationship with other constructs, both theoretically and empirically. In essence, all validity evidence contributes to an understanding of an assessment instrument's construct validity. Evidence of criterion-related and content validity are therefore subordinate to construct validity – all forms of validity contribute to construct validity. Construct validity is therefore a continuing scientific pursuit to build up a body of evidence about how an assessment instrument works rather than simply something that a test possesses or does not possess (see for example, Landy, 1985).

Wave Professional Styles and Validity

Wave Professional Styles questionnaires are unique in that validity was specifically examined early in the development phase to maximize their opportunity to demonstrate superior criterion-related validity when applied in the workplace. This was done by selecting the most valid items for inclusion in the questionnaires from a very large item and facet scale pool.

Saville Consulting run an extensive validation program in addition to the individual studies commissioned by our clients. Our program includes the co-validation of Wave Styles questionnaires with other personality assessments against a wide range of work criteria across mixed occupational groups. These and other studies provide evidence that supports the inferences made on Wave Styles reports and provide evidence to support the appropriate use of the Wave Professional Styles questionnaires.

355

We believe that validation should start by being clear on the inferences that are to be drawn from the assessment and using those to guide the strategy for collecting validation evidence. This helps create a well directed program that includes specifying who should be included in a study, what performance variables (criteria) should be collected, and which evaluation approaches and statistical methods are appropriate.

The modern conception of test validity has at its heart the notion that we are validating the inferences that are made from test scores. Therefore, the first step is to be clear about the nature of these inferences.

Inferences from Test or Assessment Scores

An inference from a test score or set of questionnaire scores can be general or local. For example, "High scorers on this scale will demonstrate more creativity" is a general inference. A criterion-related validation design might be an appropriate starting point to examine the validity of this inference. A statistically significant positive correlation with a moderate effect size between the scale score and a measure of creativity would provide clear evidence that supports this general inference. Such evidence provides us with confidence that the scale is meaningful and the inference or interpretation we then draw about one person's creativity using the scale score is appropriate. General inferences such as these can be explicitly stated as hypotheses and tested empirically.

If a test or assessment score is shown to be a valid measure of a psychological construct like creativity, and if we learn from a job analysis study that a construct like creativity is important to successful job performance, then we may want to use the test or assessment score to identify which people are more creative than others. In other words, if creativity is an important component of a job (content domain of a job), then we can use a test to measure that specific job component.

When we explicitly state the relationship between the assessment tools and the components of a job, this is referred to as evidence of **job component validity** and can allow for an assessment of synthetic validity. The inferences made from the test are interpreted in light of those specific job components. **Synthetic validity** is a logical process of inferring validity on the basis of the relationships between components of a job and tests of the attributes that are needed to perform the job components. Note in synthetic validity the relationships between the job components and the tests are typically established in one validation study of workers, and then a job analysis only is conducted on the new job to identify job components. The similarity or equivalence between the new job analysis and the previous validation study allows the validity to be estimated in the new job. It is synthetic because the validity has not been directly calculated based on a criterion validation study on the new job.

If all of the scores (predictors) in a questionnaire correlate positively with the performance criterion each is designed to measure, we refer to this as **saturated validity**. Saturated validity is where all the predictor scales of a questionnaire correlate with all the *a priori* hypothesized criteria. Clearly, there is the issue of levels of saturation/levels of validity on each scale of a model – but if *all* the scales in an assessment show meaningful correlations with *a priori* specified independently assessed criteria (i.e. from independent raters of performance) we refer to this as saturation of the model or assessment. Another related issue is the overall level of validity against each criterion.

Thus far we have discussed general inferences that apply across a group of test takers. With any probabilistic approach such as personnel selection, no inference or decision is perfectly accurate. However, across a large group of test takers, valid scores will improve the accuracy of the inferences overall compared to the accuracy of inferences when the valid test is not used. Again, the test may not be perfect, but may nevertheless add significant value and productivity benefits to an organization compared to not using the test or assessment.

Eventually every test user uses a test or assessment score to make inferences and important decisions about an individual. Should this applicant be hired? Is this employee a good candidate for a leadership development program? Which position is this candidate best suited for? Which competencies should a person develop to improve performance at work? Is this person ready for a bigger job assignment? These are examples of individual local inferences made based at least partly on a test score.

356

It follows that, (a) if critical job components are identified and explicitly mapped to scores from an assessment tool, and (b) if the assessment tool has empirical evidence of saturated validity, then local inferences and test score interpretation will be more accurate as the validity of the assessment tool increases (MacIver et al., 2008).

This concept is especially important for multi-scale personality or styles questionnaires that require a user to interpret a profile of scores rather than a single test score. Making local inferences based on profile pattern interpretation can be a difficult and complex undertaking. Even though local inferences made using profile interpretation often may not be made explicitly regarding how the pattern of test scores relate to the local decision, it is still important to investigate the accuracy/validity of these local inferences and their impact on independent evaluations of work performance.

The bottom line – the accuracy and validity of both general and local inferences will improve when an assessment process has evidence of criterion-related validity across the full range of job components.

With regards to making inferences about behavioral competencies specifically, the Wave Professional Styles scales demonstrate both strong criterion-related validity across a range of behavioral competencies, and the range of behavioral competencies have been shown to be important to overall job proficiency. This increases the confidence that the inferences made using Wave Professional Styles, whether general or local, will be more accurate and valid than inferences made using methods or tools that have no validity evidence or tools that have lesser validity.

Inferences in Practice - Selection

In a practical sense, multi-scale assessment tools can contribute to personnel selection decisions in two ways:

1. using a subset of job-relevant scales, explicit prediction equations are created for each performance competency (based on empirical evidence and/or expert judgment) and applied to each job applicant in a consistent and objective manner (general inferences explicitly used to inform local inferences). An example of this is the Competency Potential scores provided in the Wave reports. A logical extension is the creation of one overall fit score for a particular job by creating a weighted composite of the assessment scores.

2. a trained/qualified professional reviews the pattern of scores on a profile chart and makes an interpretation of the pattern of scores relative to important job competencies which is then used to make inferences about the suitability of the applicant for the job (local inferences)

In both these instances, criterion-related validity (i.e., giving a valid estimation of likely performance levels) is critical. In the first instance, it is critical that the assessment tool provides criterion-related validity and that this has been cross-validated to ensure that the prediction equations will generalize to new situations, industries and workforces.

In the second case, it is the user who is doing the profile interpretation and integrating the results to make a local inference without local validation to explicitly guide the interpretation. Instead, users will need to rely on their understanding of the job and the evidence of test validity provided by the test publisher and other published research about the assessment tool.

We believe that test users benefit from the creation of a clear and straightforward approach that makes clear to the user the links between the predictors and criteria. The Wave Professional Styles scales are explicitly linked to specific behavioral competencies, thereby making the link between specific predictors and criteria clear and straightforward. Figure 16.1 shows the Saville Consulting Wave Aligned Criterion and Predictor Model. This aligned or matched model helps users to understand how each scale in the Wave Styles model (predictors) relates to the Wave model of behavioral competencies (performance criteria).

Figure 16.1. The Saville Consulting Wave Aligned Criterion and Predictor Model

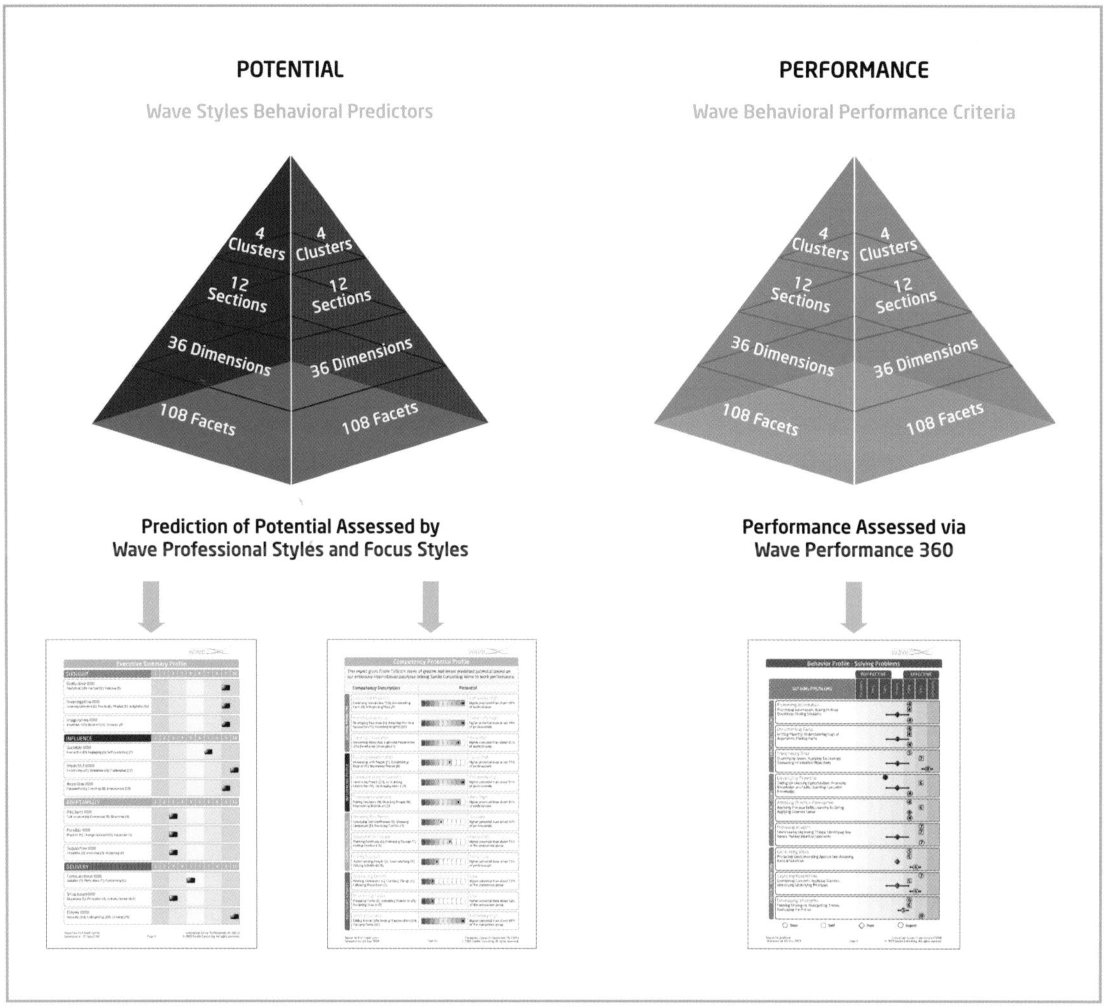

The Importance of Validity Data in Practice - Two Examples

Wave Professional Styles is designed to offer users a job relevant, saturated, validation centric model that clearly links Wave Styles scales (predictors) to Wave competencies (performance criteria). These are important features that provide practical advantages to end users allowing them to make better, more informed local or global inferences about people at work. The advantages of this approach are highlighted in the two examples that follow.

Personnel Selection

In personnel selection, how can validity data be used to ensure that a test is used appropriately?

1. **Job analysis** – a job analysis study provides the justification (i.e., content and job component validity) for using an assessment. The Saville Consulting Wave Job Profiler and Saville Consulting Wave Performance Culture Framework provide a simple process for job experts to identify critical job competencies and components using the Wave competency model. Once the critical competencies are known, it is an easy step to select the appropriate/valid Wave Styles scales for making more accurate global or local inferences. Moreover, an index of Person-Job Fit can be calculated and reported based on the identification and assessment of the critical job components.

2. **Mapping to competency model** – detailed job descriptions already exist for many jobs so instead of conducting a job profiling study, the 147 components of the Saville Consulting criterion model (that includes aptitudes, behavioral and global outcomes) can be mapped to an organization's existing competency model. Once links between a client model and the Wave competency model are made, Wave Styles scales can be used for making selection decisions with reports using the organization's own competency model rather than the Wave competency model, which provides the underlying framework for the selection process.

3. **Local validation study** – without prior evidence of empirical validity, neither of the first two approaches is justified. Where no validation evidence exists, it is possible to conduct a local validation study. However, this is not feasible for many jobs or organizations due to an insufficient sample size which results in low statistical power and inconclusive results.

4. **Validity generalization** – this is generalizing the results from existing validation studies to new situations. This is especially useful when it is not feasible to conduct local validation studies. There are different ways to generalize validity, but three typical ways include: (a) transportability, (b) synthetic or job component validity, and (c) meta-analysis. Each is discussed below.

Perhaps a Sales Manager is interested in using an assessment tool to hire better sales staff. Unfortunately, the organization does not employ enough sales staff to conduct a local validation study. However, the test may have been previously validated for the selection of sales staff in a different organization. If the original validation study is sound, and its relevance to the new job is clear and sufficient, then the validity of the test can be "transported" from the previous job to the new situation. The Sales Manager now can use the assessment with confidence because of the transportability study. There are also some potential difficulties with this approach:

- Job analysis information must be available to compare the marker job with the target job. The job analyses must be sufficiently detailed to ensure the jobs are indeed compatible.

- The original study may be flawed. If so, the flaws are also transported to the target job.

- Unique local contextual conditions impact validity that are different in the new job, e.g., the applicant pool may have very different qualities.

- Jobs are dynamic and jobs that were once compatible may not stay that way.

An alternative approach is to rely on job component validity. This approach was introduced earlier in this chapter (see Inferences from Test or Assessment Scores). Basically, this approach starts with a job profiling study to identify critical job components. Once the critical components are known, an assessment is identified that purports to be a valid measure of that critical job component, and a score for the assessment is used to make inferences about that job component. If the relationship between the assessment and the job components is established, then the assessment can be generalized to other jobs having the same job components.

Wave Professional Styles has been designed to make this simpler to accomplish for users. Through the validation-centric process and the subsequent cross validation and criterion-related validation studies, the relationship is well-established between the Wave Professional Styles scales and the Wave behavioral competencies. The Wave Job Profiler and/or the Wave Performance Culture Framework cards make the identification of critical job components an easy and efficient undertaking. A user can move quickly from the job analysis study to organizing the assessment process, perhaps using Wave reports to match people to jobs or simply prioritizing the competency potential scores according to relevance or importance.

This also allows for approaches to estimate synthetic validity, i.e., the validity that should be expected from the target job given the job component validity. However, in addition to synthetic validity it is important to look for criterion-related validity with overall proficiency measures to verify that the assessment tools help drive superior performance at work (see the section that follows on the Criterion Problem Revisited comparing individual behavioral criteria versus overall performance criteria).

359

Meta-analysis is another common way to generalize validity. Meta-analysis requires the accumulation of findings from a number of validity studies to determine the best estimates of the predictor-criterion relationship for the kinds of work domains and settings included in the studies. Unlike transportability or job component validity, studies that rely on content validity approaches to understand the predictor-criterion relationship, meta-analyses rely exclusively on criterion-related validation studies. This approach has the benefit of reducing problems often associated with local validation studies. These include sampling error and other statistical artifacts. However, expert judgment is still required in interpreting and applying the results of meta-analytic studies. This includes closely examining the underlying assumptions, the tenability of the assumptions, how the artifacts may influence results, and finally the impact of potential moderator variables. As more and more empirical studies are conducted using Wave Professional Styles, this will enable a meta-analytic study to be conducted to summarize the accumulated findings from these individual studies. However, it should also be noted that large mixed occupational samples already conducted (such as the original validation as part of the standardization and Project Epsom), have certain advantages over meta-analyses as they can for example avoid file drawer effects that can inflate estimates of validity.

Development

Validity evidence provides similar benefits for those using Wave Professional Styles in a development context. Assessment for development often addresses two key things: (a) self-awareness – are the participants aware of their areas of strength and weakness? Do they have hidden potential or perhaps an Achilles' heel that may result in a career derailment if left unchecked?, and (b) job relevance - how do the participants' profiles relate to critical job requirements?

Various assessment tools have been created from the Wave Styles Aligned Model. Of course the Wave Styles questionnaires were developed to measure the Wave Styles scales, but the Wave competency model was also used to measure current job behaviors using the Wave Performance 360 questionnaire and the Wave Job Profiler was created to identify critical job or role competencies. The application of all of these tools provides a powerful combination for development by enabling various comparisons to be made to identify "development gaps," for instance:

1. By comparing the Wave Performance 360 Report with a Wave Job Profiler Report, you can see how a participant is performing on critical job components as part of a training needs analysis.

2. By comparing a Wave Professional Styles Expert Report with a Wave Job Profiler Report, you can see if a person has the competency potential (motive and talent) to move into a new role while identifying gaps where a coaching intervention may help smooth the transition process.

3. By comparing a Wave Professional Styles Expert Report with a Wave Performance 360 Report, you can compare competency potential with current performance on the competency for purposes of determining readiness to advance as part of a succession planning exercise, or to spot gaps between current performance and competency potential that could be due to lack of training or motivation to perform.

Development professionals and executive coaches address these and related issues with a multitude of clients in their daily work. They often rely on their intuition and experience to gain insights into the individual and the challenges and opportunities that person faces. Competency-based tools to assess role requirements and work behaviors can add structure and rigor to this process. The Wave Professional Styles questionnaires can help to "explain" poor or outstanding work behaviors and enable users to gauge how easy it will be for them to develop a certain competency.

To illustrate this, take an example of a performance-potential gap analysis. According to the Wave model, a person who scores high on a Wave Styles dimension (e.g., Empowering) would be expected to receive high ratings from others in the Wave Performance 360 assessment on the matched Wave competency (e.g., Empowering Individuals), assuming the constructs are properly aligned in the model and their relationship has been empirically

validated. A high score on the Empowering dimension indicates the person has indicated that they are both talented and motivated when it comes to empowering others, and this behavior is expected to be observed by others in the workplace – most likely their subordinates.

If the data from the Wave self-assessment and the Wave Performance 360 are aligned, then there is no great surprise, but if the results of the 360 indicate lower performance on Empowering Individuals than would be expected from the self-assessment, then this can be further examined. In this case the person appears to have the potential to be an effective performer based upon the information provided by Wave Professional Styles, but for some reason is not seen by others as performing up to their potential. A development intervention may help this person reach their full potential in this area, perhaps by clarifying roles and responsibilities, improving time management, gaining confidence in the ability of team members to take on additional responsibilities, etc. Note that the assessments did not solve the development issue, but it did draw attention to it so that appropriate inferences and actions could be taken. Validation evidence is important in this case because we expected to see a relationship between the Wave Professional Styles report assessment and the Wave Performance 360 report because the relationship between them has been validated.

Criterion-Centric Approaches to Validation

The starting point for the development of an assessment is a clear measure of the criterion it is designed to predict. Models and classifications of physical illness have been available for centuries. Models of mental disorders have also been available to practitioners of medicine, psychology and psychiatry for well over half a century (the Diagnostic and Statistical Manual of Mental Disorders or DSM for example was first published in 1952). The presence of such models has allowed for an evaluation of the efficacy of different diagnostic, screening and treatment protocols enabling a continuous process of improvement in these fields.

By contrast, assessment in the workplace has been more concerned about the characteristics and psychometric properties of tests and other predictors than the workplace criterion they attempt to measure (Landy, 2007). Many HR professionals and testing experts believed that a high degree of situational specificity existed requiring a local validation study as the only reliable way to examine the predictor-criterion relationship. In addition, organizations preferred to develop their own models of values and competencies (criterion models) to capture their unique character. The result has been a lack of interest in looking for the common threads across jobs and industries, geographies, and cultures.

The work of Hunter and Schmidt on meta-analysis in 1984 laid waste to situational specificity as the predominant working hypothesis in assessment by demonstrating that cognitive tests' validity generalize with overall measures of job performance across jobs. In more recent meta-analyses, moderators of cognitive validity have been identified, i.e., as job level or complexity increases, so does the validity of cognitive tests (Anderson and Salgado, 2002) against the backdrop of validity generalization. An important lesson to be drawn from research on cognitive abilities is that firstly it is important to be clear on how validity generalizes to establish a baseline understanding, and then secondly it is important to look at moderating variables to explain inconsistent results.

Unlike in the area of cognitive ability assessment, validity generalization of personality assessment is the exception rather than the rule, and local validation of the organization's own criteria remains the preferred approach. One reason for this has been the lack of consistent frameworks that classify and codify work competencies and criteria. Local studies do have their advantages, but they also have their drawbacks – most notably small sample sizes and a lack of statistical power. We believe that to progress we need to establish comprehensive behavioral criterion models that are linked to common measures of work effectiveness and outcomes that generalize across different jobs, industries and cultures. That is, we need to become criterion-centric rather than predictor-centric in our research.

Some advances have been made, however. Attempts have been made to group work criteria into meaningful classifications to allow for research to be conducted to evaluate the effectiveness of different measures in different criterion classifications (Campbell et al., 1993, Robertson and Kinder, 1993, Bartram, 2005, MacIver et al,. 2006, Hogan et al., 2007).

361

The Criterion Problem Revisited

In the criterion domain, Saville Consulting Wave was designed to provide measures of work effectiveness against two types of criteria:

- Specific behavioral competencies (behavior effectiveness criteria).

- Overall performance effectiveness that includes: job proficiency, potential, and the application of expertise in the workplace (global performance criteria).

Which criteria matters more – general global performance measures or specific behavioral competencies and their subcomponents? That behavioral competencies link to personality and styles measures is not controversial and has been extensively reported elsewhere (Robertson & Kinder, 1993; Kurz & Bartram, 2002). Robertson, Callinan and Bartram (2003) stated that, "We define competencies as sets of behaviors that are instrumental in the delivery of desired results or outcomes." Competencies are important to success at work and as a result should show clear links to global measures of performance effectiveness.

In practice, many organizations define competencies/criteria through job analysis, but some also rely upon common sense methods for identifying job competencies. While these approaches often appear logical and job relevant, there is no guarantee they will show a positive correlation with overall performance measures. Consider these examples provided by Schultz (1998). Would you have second thoughts about evaluating tests for the following roles against the suggested criteria?

Job Role	Criteria
Toll collector	Accuracy of Making Change
Tax collector	Amount of Delinquent Taxes Collected

At first these criteria appear almost self-evident. Yet, years ago when the Port Authority of New York and New Jersey implemented "accuracy" as a selection criterion for toll collectors, the result was traffic being backed up for miles. Speed of making change was more important to overall job performance, even at the expense of some minor errors. Likewise, the best tax collectors often have very good rapport with taxpayers, and so have fewer delinquencies to collect.

We believe that a competency should be positively associated with improved overall performance and potential. That is, competencies/criterion models should be developed based on their relationship to global measures of performance and potential. The choice, then, is not between overall global effectiveness measures and specific behavioral measures, but rather modeling and researching links between these two types of competencies to better understand their relationship. That said, there may be some competencies that are important but that do not directly contribute to overall performance effectiveness. These may be competencies that impact job satisfaction, team cohesion, or corporate values – and these may be important criteria in their own right even though they may not underpin more effective individual job performance. Still these links to other important criteria should be empirically tested.

The aim of Wave Styles was to create assessments that have been designed to not only be the most effective indicators of individual behavioral effectiveness, but also be indicators that will generalize to forecast overall measures of effectiveness at work when scales are combined. In fact, the authors argue that the competency predictions should be built to maximize the forecasting of overall effectiveness first and their matched behavioral competencies second. For these reasons the criterion-related validation evidence in this chapter is presented using both types of criteria – overall performance effectiveness and individual behavioral competencies.

Magic Bullets in Validation

The statistical argument

A related issue to the foregoing is that validity may not come from one scale that is highly valid, but from many scales that each account for a unique bit of the variance in the criterion. However, validation studies are often conducted in an attempt to find a magic bullet, i.e., the most effective individual scale (or a composite of two or three scales) that accounts for the majority of the criterion variance. These approaches often suffer from statistical artifacts such as sampling effects where the highest correlation for one sample of participants will tend to regress towards the mean when cross validated using a new sample of participants. These dangers are amplified when a large number of scales are being considered without *a priori* hypotheses indicating how each scale is expected to relate to performance criteria.

A key drawback of this approach is that if many of the correlations with overall performance measures have small true effective sizes, then "statistical fishing" and *post hoc* analysis lead to Type II errors due to the lack of statistical power. So that a number of scales which have small correlations with criteria may not be included yet they could contribute to the overall prediction. Examining how a large number of individual scales correlates with performance is an exploratory approach which can lead to incorrect findings and confirmatory bias.

Rather than scanning many individual predictor correlations with the risk of making Type I and Type II errors, the approach to validation argued for here is to create predictions across the scales of the predictor assessments.

This is accomplished by creating one broad composite predictor score or job fit index using the relevant prioritized predictor scores. This overall composite fit index is correlated with overall job effectiveness to establish the validity (this would be done in addition to correlation individual behavioral prediction scores with individual behavioral criteria).

The philosophical argument

Assume the validity of a magic bullet assessment and the validity of a composite Person-Job Fit index are the same when validated against a measure of overall job effectiveness. Does it matter which approach is used? We believe the broader composite Person-Job Fit index is still superior. The reason for this is the following. The composite predictor score is comprised of multiple measures of different individual competencies while the magic bullet measures a much more limited set of work behaviors. Having a wider array of competencies from which to draw may help to stabilize validity when the demands of the job are variable and prone to change rapidly, requiring workers to rely on multiple competencies to meet the demands of the job, particularly if these competencies, as we believe they should, show positive associations with overall performance.

Wave Professional Styles and Improved Validity

Wave Professional Styles is expected to have higher criterion-related validity than personality questionnaires developed using conventional approaches. Maximizing validity was central to the development strategy. While there are great advantages in terms of efficiency of the rate-rank format and in depth interpretation from the motive-talent concept, it is focusing on clear work related outcomes (see Morgeson et al (2007) which comments on this topic) in this instance in terms of behavioral competencies as well as overall effectiveness at work that is a central, if not the sole contributor, to this increase in criterion related validity.

A clear focus and model of what is to be predicted was the start point and then extensive item writing and review to create items underpinning effectiveness at work. This was followed by a selection of items from a large item pool creating the basis for improved validity. The fact that validation-centric item selection and competency potential equation building should subsequently lead to more accurate forecasting of work outcomes perhaps should not be surprising: the superiority has been previously been demonstrated of methods

363

that have been built using the statistical relationship between predictor and outcome (so called actuarial or mechanical methods) over methods which lack this information (see Grove et al., 2000 for meta-analysis comparing actuarial and non actuarial prediction across different fields. Note. This finding holds true in fields with a clear history of theory and research).

Wave Professional Styles is a valid measure of important workplace behaviors and competencies. What may be more surprising is the improved validity for measuring overall job performance and effectiveness compared to traditional personality questionnaires. This is because, while the Wave Styles model was not designed to be structurally aligned with overall performance, its items were selected because they correlated well with measures of overall performance in addition to their *a priori* matched competency.

Some may argue that Wave Professional Styles shows higher validity coefficients because it uses its own aligned competency model, and that using a structurally aligned predictor-criterion inflates its validity compared to criteria that are structurally independent of the Wave Styles model. In the section that follows, we show results comparing Wave Professional Styles to the Great Eight performance competencies to show that Wave's improved criterion-related validity will generalize to an independently developed performance criterion model and is not an artifact of the aligned Wave predictor-criterion model. Results against overall effectiveness are of fundamental importance and are not structurally aligned in content to the Wave behavioral model. The cross validated results of overall effectiveness in mixed occupational groups then give an indication of the criterion related validity of Wave Professional Styles without the concern that the content alignment could be partially inflating these results.

16.1 Validity Research

Project Epsom 397

Concurrent Validity: Wave and other Personality Assessments 402

Measuring Work Performance Competencies – The Great Eight 406

16.2 Construct Validity

Construct Validity: Wave Styles and other Personality Assessments

A large-scale co-validation study ("Project Epsom") was carried out as part of the Wave Research and Development program. This study was designed to establish and compare the validity of a number of commonly used personality measures. Participants (N = 308) from a diverse range of job sectors completed an assortment of personality measures. This section looks at the construct validity of Wave Professional Styles with these other personality assessments.

The tables over page (Tables 16.1 – 16.36) relate to this co-validation study. Each table below covers one of the 36 Wave dimensions (i.e., from 'Analytical' to 'Striving'). Individuals' scores on these 36 dimensions were compared to their scores on the scales of eight other well-known personality measures. The personality measures included here from this co-validation study are: Wave Professional Styles, OPQ32i, NEO-PI-R, 16PF-5, Firo B, Hogan Personality Inventory (HPI), Thomas International Personal Profile Analysis (DISC), Hogan Development Survey (HDS) and the Myers-Briggs Type Indicator (MBTI). This study enabled in-depth comparison of individuals' scores across these nine measures in order to examine the construct validity of Wave Professional Styles.

For more information on Project Epsom, refer to the Criterion-related Validity section in this chapter.

Tables 16.1 – 16.36 show how each dimension of Wave Professional Styles correlates with scales from the other personality assessments. The tables are useful for users of other tools to understand the constructs measured by each Wave dimension. They are also useful for users of other tests to see where Wave Styles measures constructs, not directly assessed by other personality questionnaires.

Where the strongest correlation or correlations reach or exceed .40 or meet or are lower (more negative) than -.40 the correlations are shown in bold in the tables. Where all the correlations with a particular questionnaire are weaker (closer to zero) than .40 or -.40 the strongest correlation is shown, but not in bold type.

All correlations on the matrices can be found in the appendix and are highlighted with green if the correlation is greater than or equal to .40 or in orange if the correlation is less than or equal to -.40.

Note: Firo B and 16PF-5 scales are shown at two levels on the appendices as space allowed.

Table 16.1 Wave Dimension ANALYTICAL

WAVE DIMENSION: ANALYTICAL		
Correlations with Other Assessments: Those high on Wave Styles Analytical are...		

Likely to be high on...			Likely to be low on...		
OPQ	**Evaluative**	**r= .42**	OPQ	Affiliative	r= -.29
	Data Rational	**r= .40**			
NEO	**O5 Ideas**	**r= .42**	NEO	E1 Warmth	r= -.21
16PF	Reasoning	r= .33	16PF	Warmth	r= -.28
FiroB	Scale E "I control people"	r= .27	FiroB	Scale I "I am open with people"	r= -.16
				Scale K "People are open with me"	
					r= -.16
HPI	**Curiosity**	**r= .41**	HPI	Likes People	r= -.26
DISC	Dominance	r= .22	DISC	Influence	r= -.22
HDS	Reserved	r= .23	HDS	Dutiful	r= -.23
MBTI	**Thinking**	**r= .41**	MBTI	**Feeling**	**r= -.41**

Table 16.2 Wave Dimension FACTUAL

WAVE DIMENSION: FACTUAL		
Correlations with Other Assessments: Those high on Wave Styles Factual are...		

Likely to be high on...			Likely to be low on...		
OPQ	Evaluative	r= .39	OPQ	Optimistic	r= -.22
NEO	O6 Values	r= .19	NEO	Extraversion (Global factor)	r= -.11
	Openness (Global factor)	r= .19			
16PF	Reasoning	r= .29	16PF	Warmth	r= -.13
FiroB	Scale L "I want people to be open with me"	r= .16	FiroB	Scale J "I want to be open with people"	r= -.04
HPI	Education	r= .28	HPI	Likes People	r= -.20
DISC	Compliance	r= .13	DISC	Influence	r= -.15
HDS	Reserved	r= .09	HDS	Colorful	r= -.16
MBTI	Intuition	r= .15	MBTI	Sensing	r= -.15

370

Table 16.3 Wave Dimension RATIONAL

WAVE DIMENSION: RATIONAL

Correlations with Other Assessments: Those high on Wave Styles Rational are...

Likely to be high on...			Likely to be low on...		
OPQ	**Data-rational**	**r= .61**	OPQ	Affiliative	r= -.28
NEO	C2 Order	r= .21	NEO	O3 Feelings	r= -.36
	C6 Deliberation	r= .21			
16PF	Privateness	r= .20	16PF	**Sensitivity**	**r= -.50**
				Warmth	**r= -.40**
FiroB	Scale F		FiroB	Scale K	
	"I want to control people"	r= .18		"People are open with me"	r= -.16
HPI	**Math Ability**	**r= .44**	HPI	Likes People	r= -.23
	Curiosity	**r= .41**			
DISC	Dominance	r= .09	DISC	Influence	r= -.17
HDS	Reserved	r= .22	HDS	Excitable	r= -.14
MBTI	Thinking	r= .38	MBTI	Feeling	r= -.38

Table 16.4 Wave Dimension LEARNING ORIENTED

WAVE DIMENSION: LEARNING ORIENTED

Correlations with Other Assessments: Those high on Wave Styles Learning Oriented are...

Likely to be high on...			Likely to be low on...		
OPQ	Conceptual	r= .38	OPQ	Caring	r= -.18
NEO	O5 Ideas	r= .34	NEO	A3 Altruism	r= -.17
16PF	Openness to Change	r= .25	16PF	Warmth	r= -.20
FiroB	Scale A "I include people"	r= .10	FiroB	Scale I	
	Scale E "I control people"	r= .10		"I am open with people"	r= -.12
HPI	**Reading**	**r= .45**	HPI	Caring	r= -.23
DISC	Dominance	r= .12	DISC	Steadiness	r= -.09
HDS	Imaginative	r= .13	HDS	Dutiful	r= -.21
	Reserved	r= .13			
MBTI	Intuition	r= .21	MBTI	Sensing	r= -.21

© 2009 Saville Consulting. All rights reserved. Version 1.0.

Table 16.5 Wave Dimension PRACTICALLY MINDED

WAVE DIMENSION: PRACTICALLY MINDED

Correlations with Other Assessments: Those high on Wave Styles Practically Minded are...

Likely to be high on...			Likely to be low on...		
OPQ	Detail Conscious	r= .25	OPQ	Behavioral	r= -.21
NEO	C1 Competence	r= .17	NEO	O1 Fantasy	r= -.20
16PF	Perfectionism	r= .11	16PF	Abstractedness	r= -.29
FiroB	Scale C "Others include me"	r= .07	FiroB	Need for Control	r= -.11
HPI	Calmness	r= .16	HPI	Education	r= -.19
	Curiosity	r= .16			
DISC	Steadiness	r= .09	DISC	Influence	r= -.12
HDS	Diligent	r= .16	HDS	Colorful	r= -.16
MBTI	Sensing	r= .24	MBTI	Intuition	r= -.24

Table 16.6 Wave Dimension INSIGHTFUL

WAVE DIMENSION: INSIGHTFUL

Correlations with Other Assessments: Those high on Wave Styles Insightful are...

Likely to be high on...			Likely to be low on...		
OPQ	Evaluative	r= .28	OPQ	Affiliative	r= -.34
NEO	C1 Competence	r= .27	NEO	N6 Vulnerability	r= -.25
16PF	Self-reliance	r= .27	16PF	Warmth	r= -.29
FiroB	Scale F "I want to control people"	r= .34	FiroB	Scale G "People control me"	r= -.13
HPI	Curiosity	r= .28	HPI	Impulse Control	r= -.20
DISC	Dominance	r= .37	DISC	Steadiness	r= -.29
HDS	Bold	r= .26	HDS	Dutiful	r= -.31
	Mischievous	r= .26			
MBTI	Thinking	r= .29	MBTI	Feeling	r= -.29

Table 16.7 Wave Dimension INVENTIVE

WAVE DIMENSION: INVENTIVE
Correlations with Other Assessments: Those high on Wave Styles Inventive are...

Likely to be high on...

OPQ	**Innovative**	**r= .76**
NEO	Openness (Global factor)	r= .39
16PF	**Abstractedness**	**r= .45**
	Openness to Change	**r= .45**
FiroB	Scale E "I control people"	r= .39
HPI	**Generates Ideas**	**r= .52**
DISC	**Dominance**	**r= .43**
HDS	**Imaginative**	**r= .48**
MBTI	**Intuition**	**r= .51**

Likely to be low on...

OPQ	**Rule Following**	**r= -.49**
	Conventional	**r= -.46**
NEO	C6 Deliberation	r= -.24
16PF	Rule Conscious	r= -.26
FiroB	Scale J "I want to be open with people"	r= -.12
HPI	**Impulse Control**	**r= -.43**
DISC	Steadiness	r= -.37
HDS	Dutiful	r= -.27
MBTI	**Sensing**	**r= -.51**

Table 16.8 Wave Dimension ABSTRACT

WAVE DIMENSION: ABSTRACT
Correlations with Other Assessments: Those high on Wave Styles Abstract are...

Likely to be high on...

OPQ	**Conceptual**	**r= .61**
NEO	**O5 Ideas**	**r= .48**
	Openness (Global factor)	**r= .40**
16PF	Openness to Change	r= .37
FiroB	Scale E "I control people"	r= .23
	Need for Control	r= .23
HPI	Science Ability	r= .39
DISC	Dominance	r= .17
HDS	Imaginative	r= .27
MBTI	Intuition	r= .35

Likely to be low on...

OPQ	Trusting	r= -.25
NEO	E1 Warmth	r= -.21
	Extraversion (Global factor)	r= -.21
16PF	Warmth	r= -.26
FiroB	Scale J "I want to be open with people"	r= -.14
HPI	Likes People	r= -.21
	Not Spontaneous	r= -.21
DISC	Influence	r= -.25
HDS	Dutiful	r= -.15
MBTI	Sensing	r= -.35

Table 16.9 Wave Dimension STRATEGIC

WAVE DIMENSION: STRATEGIC

Correlations with Other Assessments: Those high on Wave Styles Strategic are...

Likely to be high on...

OPQ	**Forward Thinking**	r= .47
NEO	C4 Achievement Striving	r= .34
16PF	Openness to Change	r= .35
FiroB	Scale E "I control people"	r= .37
HPI	Competitive	r= .37
DISC	Dominance	r= .37
HDS	Bold	r= .31
MBTI	Intuition	r= .25

Likely to be low on...

OPQ	Conventional	r= -.36
NEO	Agreeableness (Global factor)	r= -.28
16PF	Rule Consciousness	r= -.16
FiroB	Scale J "I want to be open with people"	r= -.06
HPI	Impulse Control	r= -.20
DISC	Steadiness	r= -.34
HDS	Dutiful	r= -.19
MBTI	Sensing	r= -.25

Table 16.10 Wave Dimension INTERACTIVE

WAVE DIMENSION: INTERACTIVE

Correlations with Other Assessments: Those high on Wave Styles Interactive are...

Likely to be high on...

OPQ	**Outgoing**	r= .73
	Socially Confident	r= .47
	Affiliative	r= .41
NEO	**Extraversion (Global factor)**	r= .54
	E2 Gregariousness	r= .52
	E1 Warmth	r= .46
16PF	**Social Boldness**	r= .57
	Liveliness	r= .50
	Warmth	r= .45
FiroB	Scale A "I include people"	r= .33
HPI	**Likes People**	r= .51
	Exhibitionistic	r= .41
DISC	**Influence**	r= .58
HDS	**Colorful**	r= .44
MBTI	**Extraversion**	r= .71

Likely to be low on...

OPQ	Emotionally Controlled	r= -.37
NEO	C6 Deliberation	r= -.26
16PF	**Privateness**	r= -.42
	Self-Reliance	r= -.41
FiroB	n/a	
HPI	Impulse Control	r= -.16
DISC	Compliance	r= -.32
HDS	**Reserved**	r= -.43
MBTI	**Introversion**	r= -.71

Table 16.11 Wave Dimension ENGAGING

WAVE DIMENSION: ENGAGING

Correlations with Other Assessments: Those high on Wave Styles Engaging are...

Likely to be high on...			Likely to be low on...		
OPQ	**Socially Confident**	**r= .55**	OPQ	Emotionally Controlled	r= -.32
	Outgoing	**r= .48**			
	Affiliative	**r= .41**			
NEO	**E1 Warmth**	**r= .62**	NEO	N4 Self-consciousness	r= -.23
	Extraversion (Global factor)	**r= .59**			
	E2 Gregariousness	**r= .54**			
16PF	**Social Boldness**	**r= .52**	16PF	**Self-reliance**	**r= -.42**
	Warmth	**r= .48**			
	Liveliness	**r= .48**			
FiroB	Scale A "I include people"	r= .38	FiroB	Need for Control	r= -.08
HPI	**Likes People**	**r= .58**	HPI	Science Ability	r= -.13
DISC	**Influence**	**r= .56**	DISC	Dominance	r= -.27
HDS	Colorful	r= .32	HDS	**Reserved**	**r= -.61**
MBTI	**Extraversion**	**r= .65**	MBTI	**Introversion**	**r= -.65**

Table 16.12 Wave Dimension SELF-PROMOTING

WAVE DIMENSION: SELF-PROMOTING

Correlations with Other Assessments: Those high on Wave Styles Self-promoting are...

Likely to be high on...			Likely to be low on...		
OPQ	**Outgoing**	**r= .45**	OPQ	**Modest**	**r= -.49**
NEO	E2 Gregariousness	r= .30	NEO	**A5 Modesty**	**r= -.51**
16PF	Social Boldness	r= .35	16PF	Privateness	r= -.28
FiroB	Need for Control	r= .37	FiroB	n/a	
HPI	**Exhibitionistic**	**r= .57**	HPI	Impression Management	r= -.26
	Entertaining	**r= .40**			
DISC	Influence	r= .28	DISC	Steadiness	r= -.23
HDS	**Colorful**	**r= .51**	HDS	Reserved	r= -.18
MBTI	Extraversion	r= .36	MBTI	Introversion	r= -.36

375

Table 16.13 Wave Dimension CONVINCING

WAVE DIMENSION: CONVINCING

Correlations with Other Assessments: Those high on Wave Styles Convincing are...

Likely to be high on...				Likely to be low on...		
OPQ	Outspoken	r= .49		OPQ	Trusting	r= -.37
	Persuasive	r= .43				
	Controlling	r= .43				
NEO	E3 Assertiveness	r= .47		NEO	**Agreeableness (Global factor)**	**r= -.53**
					A4 Compliance	**r= -.48**
					A2 Straightforwardness	**r= -.40**
16PF	**Dominance**	r= .50		16PF	Impression Management	r= -.16
FiroB	**Scale E "I control people"**	r= .58		FiroB	Scale J "I want to be open with people"	r= -.04
	Scale F "I want to control people"	r= .46				
	Need for Control (Global scale)	r= .42				
HPI	**Leadership**	r= .46		HPI	Avoids Trouble	r= -.32
DISC	**Dominance**	r= .43		DISC	Steadiness	r= -.37
HDS	Bold	r= .38		HDS	Cautious	r= -.30
	Colorful	r= .38			Dutiful	r= -.30
MBTI	Thinking	r= .29		MBTI	Feeling	r= -.29

Table 16.14 Wave Dimension ARTICULATE

WAVE DIMENSION: ARTICULATE

Correlations with Other Assessments: Those high on Wave Styles Articulate are...

Likely to be high on...				Likely to be low on...		
OPQ	**Socially Confident**	r= .59		OPQ	**Worrying**	r= -.43
	Outgoing	r= .40				
NEO	**E3 Assertiveness**	r= .45		NEO	N4 Self-consciousness	r= -.39
16PF	**Social Boldness**	r= .65		16PF	Self-reliance	r= -.27
FiroB	Scale E "I control people"	r= .35		FiroB	Scale G "People control me"	r= -.06
HPI	**No Social Anxiety**	r= .63		HPI	Impulse Control	r= -.09
	Self-Confidence	r= .41				
DISC	**Influence**	r= .41		DISC	Compliance	r= -.23
					Steadiness	r= -.23
HDS	**Colorful**	r= .46		HDS	**Cautious**	**r= -.44**
MBTI	**Extraversion**	r= .47		MBTI	**Introversion**	**r= -.47**

Table 16.15 Wave Dimension CHALLENGING

WAVE DIMENSION: CHALLENGING

Correlations with Other Assessments: Those high on Wave Styles Challenging are...

Likely to be high on...			Likely to be low on...		
OPQ	**Outspoken**	**r= .56**	OPQ	Trusting	r= -.34
NEO	N2 Angry Hostility	r= .34	NEO	**A4 Compliance**	**r= -.52**
				Agreeableness (Global factor)	**r= -.51**
				A2 Straightforwardness	**r= -.41**
16PF	**Dominance**	**r= .45**	16PF	Impression Management	r= -.24
FiroB	**Scale E "I control people"**	**r= .44**	FiroB	Scale K "People are open with me"	r= -.13
HPI	**Leadership**	**r= .40**	HPI	No Hostility	r= -.36
DISC	**Dominance**	**r= .50**	DISC	Steadiness	r= -.37
HDS	Imaginative	r= .39	HDS	Dutiful	r= -.30
MBTI	Thinking	r= .34	MBTI	Feeling	r= -.34

Table 16.16 Wave Dimension PURPOSEFUL

WAVE DIMENSION: PURPOSEFUL

Correlations with Other Assessments: Those high on Wave Styles Purposeful are...

Likely to be high on...			Likely to be low on...		
OPQ	**Decisive**	**r= .54**	OPQ	Caring	r= -.39
	Controlling	**r= .43**			
NEO	**E3 Assertiveness**	**r= .48**	NEO	Agreeableness (Global factor)	r= -.36
16PF	Dominance	r= .39	16PF	Apprehension	r= -.26
FiroB	**Scale E - "I control people"**	**r= .44**	FiroB	Scale G "People control me"	r= -.20
HPI	**Leadership**	**r= .48**	HPI	Impulse Control	r= -.29
DISC	**Dominance**	**r= .46**	DISC	Steadiness	r= -.37
HDS	Mischievous	r= .36	HDS	**Dutiful**	**r= -.40**
MBTI	Thinking	r= .32	MBTI	Feeling	r= -.32

Table 16.17 Wave Dimension DIRECTING

WAVE DIMENSION: DIRECTING

Correlations with Other Assessments: Those high on Wave Styles Directing are...

Likely to be high on...			Likely to be low on...		
OPQ	**Controlling**	**r= .78**	OPQ	Conventional	r= -.31
				Worrying	r= -.31
NEO	**E3 Assertiveness**	**r= .68**	NEO	Agreeableness (Global factor)	r= -.33
16PF	**Dominance**	**r= .46**	16PF	Sensitivity	r= -.18
	Social Boldness	**r= .44**			
FiroB	**Scale E "I control people"**	**r= .61**	FiroB	Scale G "People control me"	r= -.18
	Scale F "I want to control people"	**r= .42**			
HPI	**Leadership**	**r= .73**	HPI	Impulse Control	r= -.17
	No Social Anxiety	**r= .40**			
DISC	Dominance	r= .33	DISC	Steadiness	r= -.32
HDS	**Bold**	**r= .43**	HDS	**Cautious**	**r= -.41**
MBTI	Extraversion	r= .26	MBTI	Introversion	r= -.26

Table 16.18 Wave Dimension EMPOWERING

WAVE DIMENSION: EMPOWERING

Correlations with Other Assessments: Those high on Wave Styles Empowering are...

Likely to be high on...			Likely to be low on...		
OPQ	Controlling	r= .30	OPQ	Conventional	r= -.35
NEO	E3 Assertiveness	r= .35	NEO	C6 Deliberation	r= -.21
16PF	Social Boldness	r= .30	16PF	Tension	r= -.14
FiroB	Scale E "I control people"	r= .34	FiroB	Scale J "I want to be open with people"	r= -.03
HPI	Leadership	r= .30	HPI	Impulse Control	r= -.19
DISC	Influence	r= .18	DISC	Compliance	r= -.18
HDS	Colorful	r= .37	HDS	Reserved	r= -.20
MBTI	Extraversion	r= .26	MBTI	Introversion	r= -.26

378

Table 16.19 Wave Dimension SELF-ASSURED

WAVE DIMENSION: SELF-ASSURED

Correlations with Other Assessments: Those high on Wave Styles Self-assured are...

Likely to be high on...			Likely to be low on...		
OPQ	**Optimistic**	**r= .43**	OPQ	Democratic	r= -.23
				Modest	r= -.23
NEO	E6 Positive Emotions	r= .29	NEO	N3 Depression	r= -.38
16PF	Emotional Stability	r= .27	16PF	Apprehension	r= -.25
FiroB	Scale E "I control people"	r= .22	FiroB	Scale G "People control me"	r= -.06
	Scale F "I want to control people"	r= .22			
HPI	Self-Confidence	r= .36	HPI	Reading	r= -.16
				Impulse Control	r= -.16
DISC	Influence	r= .29	DISC	Steadiness	r= -.31
HDS	Bold	r= .34	HDS	Cautious	r= -.26
MBTI	Extraversion	r= .15	MBTI	Introversion	r= -.15

Table 16.20 Wave Dimension COMPOSED

WAVE DIMENSION: COMPOSED

Correlations with Other Assessments: Those high on Wave Styles Composed are...

Likely to be high on...			Likely to be low on...		
OPQ	**Relaxed**	**r= .44**	OPQ	**Worrying**	**r= -.65**
NEO	E3 Assertiveness	r= .31	NEO	**N1 Anxiety**	**r= -.54**
				Neuroticism (Global factor)	**r= -.47**
				N4 Self-Consciousness	**r= -.40**
				N6 Vulnerability	**r= -.40**
16PF	Social Boldness	r= .30	16PF	Apprehension	r= -.38
FiroB	Scale E "I control people"	r= .27	FiroB	Scale G "People control me"	r= -.14
HPI	**No Social Anxiety**	**r= .45**	HPI	Not Spontaneous	r= -.23
	Not Anxious	**r= .44**			
DISC	Dominance	r= .25	DISC	Compliance	r= -.29
HDS	Mischievous	r= .31	HDS	**Cautious**	**r= -.48**
MBTI	Perceiving	r= .25	MBTI	Judging	r= -.25

Table 16.21 Wave Dimension RESOLVING

WAVE DIMENSION: RESOLVING		
Correlations with Other Assessments: Those high on Wave Styles Resolving are...		

Likely to be high on...

OPQ	Caring	r= .37
NEO	Extraversion (Global factor)	r= .20
16PF	Warmth	r= .32
FiroB	Scale K "People are open with me"	r= .17
HPI	Caring	r= .21
DISC	Steadiness	r= .14
HDS	Colorful	r= .15
MBTI	Feeling	r= .17

Likely to be low on...

OPQ	Competitive	r= -.21
NEO	N4 Self-consciousness	r= -.11
16PF	Tension	r= -.28
FiroB	Scale D "I want others to include me"	r= -.01
HPI	Math Ability	r= -.08
DISC	Dominance	r= -.13
HDS	Reserved	r= -.21
MBTI	Thinking	r= -.17

Table 16.22 Wave Dimension POSITIVE

WAVE DIMENSION: POSITIVE		
Correlations with Other Assessments: Those high on Wave Styles Positive are...		

Likely to be high on...

OPQ	**Optimistic**	**r= .57**
NEO	**E6 Positive Emotions**	**r= .44**
16PF	**Emotional Stability**	**r= .48**
FiroB	Scale A "I include people"	r= .18
HPI	**Empathy**	**r= .48**
	No Depression	**r= .40**
DISC	**Influence**	**r= .45**
HDS	Colorful	r= .19
MBTI	Extraversion	r= .28

Likely to be low on...

OPQ	Evaluative	r= -.33
NEO	**N3 Depression**	**r= -.51**
	Neuroticism (Global factor)	**r= -.49**
	N2 Angry Hostility	**r= -.43**
	N1 Anxiety	**r= -.42**
	N6 Vulnerability	**r= -.40**
16PF	Tension	r= -.37
FiroB	Scale G "People control me"	r= -.20
HPI	Self Focus	r= -.21
DISC	Compliance	r= -.23
HDS	**Excitable**	**r= -.49**
MBTI	Introversion	r= -.28

Table 16.23 Wave Dimension CHANGE ORIENTED

WAVE DIMENSION: CHANGE ORIENTED					
Correlations with Other Assessments: Those high on Wave Styles Change Oriented are...					
Likely to be high on...			**Likely to be low on...**		
OPQ	Variety Seeking	r= .31	OPQ	Rule Following	r= -.39
NEO	**O4 Actions**	**r= .40**	NEO	**Neuroticism (Global factor)**	**r= -.44**
				N1 Anxiety	**r= -.43**
				N6 Vulnerability	**r= -.40**
16PF	Openness to Change	r= .35	16PF	Apprehension	r= -.30
FiroB	Scale E "I control people"	r= .14	FiroB	Scale G "People control me"	r= -.17
HPI	Experience Seeking	r= .35	HPI	Not Spontaneous	r= -.34
DISC	Dominance	r= .25	DISC	Compliance	r= -.25
HDS	Mischievous	r= .36	HDS	Cautious	r= -.37
MBTI	Perceiving	r= .33	MBTI	Judging	r= -.33

Table 16.24 Wave Dimension RECEPTIVE

WAVE DIMENSION: RECEPTIVE					
Correlations with Other Assessments: Those high on Wave Styles Receptive are...					
Likely to be high on...			**Likely to be low on...**		
OPQ	Democratic	r= .26	OPQ	Decisive	r= -.20
NEO	O3 Feelings	r= .14	NEO	C1 Competence	r= -.07
	N1 Anxiety	r= .14			
16PF	Warmth	r= .21	16PF	Self-Reliance	r= -.14
				Privateness	r= -.14
FiroB	Scale B "I want to include people"	r= .18	FiroB	n/a	
HPI	Self Focus	r= .25	HPI	Not Anxious	r= -.14
DISC	Compliance	r= .03	DISC	Influence	r= -.07
HDS	Unlikeness	r= .18	HDS	Reserved	r= -.12
MBTI	Feeling	r= .14	MBTI	Thinking	r= -.14

Table 16.25 Wave Dimension ATTENTIVE

WAVE DIMENSION: ATTENTIVE

Correlations with Other Assessments: Those high on Wave Styles Attentive are...

Likely to be high on...			Likely to be low on...		
OPQ	**Behavioral**	**r= .66**	OPQ	Competitive	r= -.32
	Caring	**r= .58**			
	Democratic	**r= .41**			
NEO	**O3 Feelings**	**r= .42**	NEO	E3 Assertiveness	r= -.25
16PF	**Warmth**	**r= .43**	16PF	Dominance	r= -.22
FiroB	Scale B "I want to include people"	r= .25	FiroB	Scale E "I control people"	r= -.28
HPI	Sensitive	r= .35	HPI	Leadership	r= -.24
DISC	Steadiness	r= .27	DISC	Dominance	r= -.36
HDS	Dutiful	r= .26	HDS	Reserved	r= -.25
MBTI	**Feeling**	**r= .47**	MBTI	**Thinking**	**r= -.47**

Table 16.26 Wave Dimension INVOLVING

WAVE DIMENSION: INVOLVING

Correlations with Other Assessments: Those high on Wave Styles Involving are...

Likely to be high on...			Likely to be low on...		
OPQ	**Democratic**	**r= .53**	OPQ	**Independent-minded**	**r= -.43**
	Caring	**r= .46**			
NEO	**Agreeableness (Global factor)**	**r= .44**	NEO	E4 Activity	r= -.18
				N2 Angry Hostility	r= -.18
16PF	Warmth	r= .27	16PF	Self-Reliance	r= -.35
FiroB	Scale I "I am open with people"	r= .17	FiroB	Scale E "I control people"	r= -.26
HPI	No Hostility	r= .28	HPI	Leadership	r= -.27
DISC	**Steadiness**	**r= .44**	DISC	**Dominance**	**r= -.41**
HDS	Dutiful	r= .32	HDS	Reserved	r= -.28
				Mischievous	r= -.28
MBTI	Feeling	r= .33	MBTI	Thinking	r= -.33

Table 16.27 Wave Dimension ACCEPTING

WAVE DIMENSION: ACCEPTING			
Correlations with Other Assessments: Those high on Wave Styles Accepting are...			

Likely to be high on...			Likely to be low on...		
OPQ	**Trusting**	**r= .54**	OPQ	Independent-minded	r= -.37
	Caring	**r= .50**			
NEO	**Agreeableness (Global factor)**	**r= .62**	NEO	N2 Angry Hostility	r= -.34
	A1 Trust	**r= .56**			
	A4 Compliance	**r= .44**			
	A6 Tender-Mindedness	**r= .40**			
16PF	Warmth	r= .29	16PF	Vigilance	r= -.39
				Tension	r= -.39
FiroB	Scale G "People control me"	r= .17	FiroB	Scale E "I control people"	r= -.34
HPI	**Trusting**	**r= .40**	HPI	Leadership	r= -.33
DISC	**Steadiness**	**r= .43**	DISC	**Dominance**	**r= -.49**
HDS	Dutiful	r= .36	HDS	**Skeptical**	**r= -.40**
MBTI	Feeling	r= .37	MBTI	Thinking	r= -.37

Table 16.28 Wave Dimension RELIABLE

WAVE DIMENSION: RELIABLE			
Correlations with Other Assessments: Those high on Wave Styles Reliable are...			

Likely to be high on...			Likely to be low on...		
OPQ	**Conscientious**	**r= .61**	OPQ	Independent-minded	r= -.31
	Detail Conscious	**r= .46**			
NEO	**C5 Self-Discipline**	**r= .56**	NEO	O1 Fantasy	r= -.32
	Conscientious (Global factor)	**r= .49**			
	C2 Order	**r= .46**			
	C3 Dutifulness	**r= .43**			
16PF	**Perfectionism**	**r= .49**	16PF	**Abstractedness**	**r= -.44**
FiroB	Scale K "People are open with me"	r= .14	FiroB	Scale E "I control people"	r= -.20
HPI	Mastery	r= .39	HPI	Exhibitionistic	r= -.25
DISC	Steadiness	r= .32	DISC	Dominance	r= -.28
HDS	**Diligent**	**r= .46**	HDS	Imaginative	r= -.27
MBTI	**Judging**	**r= .48**	MBTI	**Perceiving**	**r= -.48**

383

Table 16.29 Wave Dimension METICULOUS

WAVE DIMENSION: METICULOUS

Correlations with Other Assessments: Those high on Wave Styles Meticulous are...

Likely to be high on...			Likely to be low on...		
OPQ	Detail Conscious	r= .60	OPQ	Variety Seeking	r= -.30
	Conscientious	r= .44			
	Rule Following	r= .40			
NEO	Conscientious (Global factor)	r= .49	NEO	Openness (Global factor)	r= -.24
	C2 Order	r= .46			
16PF	Perfectionism	r= .58	16PF	Abstractedness	r= -.32
FiroB	Scale K "People are open with me"	r= .18	FiroB	Scale E "I control people"	r= -.08
	Need for Openness	r= .18		Scale A "I include people"	r= -.08
HPI	Mastery	r= .41	HPI	No Social Anxiety	r= -.24
DISC	Compliance	r= .32	DISC	Influence	r= -.24
HDS	Diligent	r= .62	HDS	Colorful	r= -.32
MBTI	Judging	r= .35	MBTI	Perceiving	r= -.35

Table 16.30 Wave Dimension CONFORMING

WAVE DIMENSION: CONFORMING

Correlations with Other Assessments: Those high on Wave Styles Conforming are...

Likely to be high on...			Likely to be low on...		
OPQ	Rule Following	r= .75	OPQ	Variety Seeking	r= -.47
	Conventional	r= .61		Innovative	r= -.46
	Detail Conscious	r= .53			
NEO	C6 Deliberation	r= .39	NEO	O4 Actions	r= -.46
				Openness (Global factor)	r= -.45
16PF	Rule Consciousness	r= .47	16PF	Openness to Change	r= -.55
	Perfectionism	r= .42		Abstractedness	r= -.41
FiroB	Scale G "People control me"	r= .23	FiroB	Scale E "I control people"	r= -.35
HPI	Impulse Control	r= .45	HPI	Experience Seeking	r= -.46
				Leadership	r= -.42
				Generates Ideas	r= -.40
DISC	Compliance	r= .51	DISC	Dominance	r= -.51
	Steadiness	r= .46			
HDS	Dutiful	r= .49	HDS	Mischievous	r= -.48
	Cautious	r= .40		Imaginative	r= -.40
MBTI	Sensing	r= .49	MBTI	Intuition	r= -.49
	Judging	r= .48		Perceiving	r= -.48

Table 16.31 Wave Dimension ORGANIZED

WAVE DIMENSION: ORGANIZED
Correlations with Other Assessments: Those high on Wave Styles Organized are...

Likely to be high on...			Likely to be low on...		
OPQ	**Detail Conscious**	**r= .61**	OPQ	Variety Seeking	r= -.28
	Conscientious	**r= .54**			
NEO	**C2 Order**	**r= .63**	NEO	O1 Fantasy	r= -.33
	Conscientious (Global factor)	**r= .61**			
	C5 Self-Discipline	**r= .53**			
	C6 Deliberation	**r= .41**			
16PF	**Perfectionism**	**r= .61**	16PF	**Abstractedness**	**r= -.41**
FiroB	Scale K "People are open with me"	r= .12	FiroB	Scale D "Others want to include me"	r= -.05
HPI	**Mastery**	**r= .40**	HPI	Thrill Seeking	r= -.24
DISC	Compliance	r= .21	DISC	Dominance	r= -.15
HDS	**Diligent**	**r= .55**	HDS	Imaginative	r= -.31
MBTI	**Judging**	**r= .64**	MBTI	**Perceiving**	**r= -.64**

Table 16.32 Wave Dimension PRINCIPLED

WAVE DIMENSION: PRINCIPLED
Correlations with Other Assessments: Those high on Wave Styles Principled are...

Likely to be high on...			Likely to be low on...		
OPQ	Conscientious	r= .30	OPQ	Outgoing	r= -.25
NEO	C3 Dutifulness	r= .38	NEO	O1 Fantasy	r= -.15
16PF	Rule Consciousness	r= .34	16PF	Abstractedness	r= -.22
FiroB	Scale K "People are open with me"	r= .15	FiroB	Need for Control	r= -.17
HPI	Impulse Control	r= .19	HPI	Exhibitionistic	r= -.22
	Mastery	r= .19			
DISC	Compliance	r= .27	DISC	Dominance	r= -.22
HDS	Diligent	r= .19	HDS	Mischievous	r= -.30
MBTI	Judging	r= .18	MBTI	Perceiving	r= -.18

Table 16.33 Wave Dimension ACTIVITY ORIENTED

WAVE DIMENSION: ACTIVITY ORIENTED

Correlations with Other Assessments: Those high on Wave Styles Activity Oriented are...

Likely to be high on...

OPQ	**Vigorous**	**r= .51**
NEO	E4 Activity	r= .25
16PF	Perfectionism	r= .16
FiroB	Scale K "People are open with me"	r= .13
HPI	Reading	r= .19
DISC	Dominance	r= .09
HDS	Diligent	r= .21
MBTI	Sensing	r= .10

Likely to be low on...

OPQ	Conceptual	r= -.16
	Democratic	r= -.16
NEO	N6 Vulnerability	r= -.19
16PF	Abstractedness	r= -.19
FiroB	Need for Control	r= -.08
	Scale G "People control me"	r= -.08
HPI	Entertaining	r= -.20
DISC	Compliance	r= -.10
HDS	Reserved	r= -.12
	Excitable	r= -.12
MBTI	Intuition	r= -.10

Table 16.34 Wave Dimension DYNAMIC

WAVE DIMENSION: DYNAMIC

Correlations with Other Assessments: Those high on Wave Styles Dynamic are...

Likely to be high on...

OPQ	Controlling	r= .39
NEO	**E4 Activity**	**r= .54**
	E3 Assertiveness	**r= .45**
16PF	Openness to Change	r= .35
	Dominance	r= .35
FiroB	**Scale E "I control people"**	**r= .47**
HPI	**Leadership**	**r= .51**
	Competitive	**r= .43**
DISC	**Dominance**	**r= .52**
HDS	Mischievous	r= .39
MBTI	Extraversion	r= .23

Likely to be low on...

OPQ	**Conventional**	**r= -.44**
NEO	Agreeableness (Global factor)	r= -.35
16PF	Rule Conscious	r= -.19
FiroB	Scale G "People control me"	r= -.12
HPI	Impulse Control	r= -.38
DISC	**Steadiness**	**r= -.50**
	Compliance	**r= -.44**
HDS	Cautious	r= -.29
MBTI	Introversion	r= -.23

Table 16.35 Wave Dimension ENTERPRISING

WAVE DIMENSION: ENTERPRISING

Correlations with Other Assessments: Those high on Wave Styles Enterprising are...

Likely to be high on...			Likely to be low on...		
OPQ	**Competitive**	**r= .54**	OPQ	Caring	r= -.38
	Persuasive	**r= .53**			
NEO	E3 Assertiveness	r= .37	NEO	**Agreeableness (Global factor) r= -.42**	
16PF	**Dominance**	**r= .40**	16PF	Sensitivity	r= -.21
FiroB	**Scale E "I control people"**	**r= .47**	FiroB	Scale G "People control me"	r= -.11
	Scale F "I want to control people"	**r= .41**			
HPI	**Competitive**	**r= .44**	HPI	Impulse Control	r= -.25
DISC	**Dominance**	**r= .47**	DISC	**Steadiness**	**r= -.51**
				Compliance	**r= -.41**
HDS	**Colorful**	**r= .49**	HDS	Cautious	r= -.34
MBTI	Thinking	r= .18	MBTI	Feeling	r= -.18

Table 16.36 Wave Dimension STRIVING

WAVE DIMENSION: STRIVING

Correlations with Other Assessments: Those high on Wave Styles Striving are...

Likely to be high on...			Likely to be low on...		
OPQ	**Achieving**	**r= .59**	OPQ	Caring	r= -.30
NEO	**C4 Achievement Striving**	**r= .48**	NEO	Agreeableness (Global factor)	r= -.33
16PF	Dominance	r= .24	16PF	Sensitivity	r= -.13
				Apprehension	r= -.13
FiroB	Scale E "I control people "	r= .36	FiroB	Scale G "People control me"	r= -.13
HPI	**Competitive**	**r= .55**	HPI	Impulse Control	r= -.17
DISC	Dominance	r= .38	DISC	Steadiness	r= -.38
HDS	Bold	r= .36	HDS	Cautious	r= -.22
MBTI	Thinking	r= .16	MBTI	Feeling	r= -.16

Construct Validity: Factor Analysis

An eight factor solution was specified to investigate how the Wave Professional Styles dimension related to the Great Eight competencies. Despite Wave Professional Styles being a self-report assessment, it is criterion centric - and therefore it is of interest to see how the structure of its scales align to an external criterion model.

The 36 Wave dimension scales were entered into a Principal Components Factor Analysis followed by Varimax rotation. Eight factors were specified. These eight factors accounted for 60.1% of the variance. The Rotated Component Matrix (see Table 16.37 on the next page) shows the dimensions loading on to the eight factors. We have postulated names for these eight factors, aligning to the 'Great Eight' competencies. It can be seen from the dimensions loading on these factors that the factors specified in the Factor Analysis are relatively well aligned to the constructs measured by the 'Great Eight.'

Table 16.37 Wave Professional Styles' 36 dimensions Factor Analysis.

	ROTATED COMPONENT MATRIX							
	Component							
	1	2	3	4	5	6	7	8
Postulated Names for Interpretation of the Factors:	Enterprising & Performing	Leading & Deciding	Organizing & Executing	Interacting & Presenting	Supporting & Cooperating	Adapting & Coping	Creating & Conceptualizing	Analyzing & Interpreting
WAVE DIMENSIONS								
Analytical							.51	.49
Factual							**.77**	
Rational								**.78**
Learning Oriented							**.77**	
Practically Minded								**.56**
Insightful	.49							
Inventive	.47							
Abstract							.52	
Strategic	**.71**							
Interactive				**.72**				
Engaging				**.77**				
Self-promoting				.50				
Convincing		**.78**						
Articulate				**.64**				
Challenging		**.72**						
Purposeful		**.60**				.44		
Directing		**.58**						
Empowering					.45			
Self-assured	**.63**							
Composed						**.72**		
Resolving					**.58**			
Positive						.44		
Change Oriented						**.65**		
Receptive								
Attentive					**.76**			
Involving					**.70**			
Accepting					**.65**			
Reliable			**.77**					
Meticulous			**.73**					
Conforming			.51					
Organized			**.80**					
Principled			.48					
Activity Oriented						.53		
Dynamic	**.64**							
Enterprising	**.57**							
Striving	**.70**							

Loadings >.55 in bold | Loadings <.40 omitted. N=308.

Construct Validity: Wave Professional Styles

This study compared two versions of Wave Styles - Wave Professional Styles and Wave Focus Styles. The 36 dimensions of Wave Professional Styles were correlated with the 36 facets of Wave Focus Styles. Table 16.38 shows the mean and standard deviation for both versions of the Wave questionnaire, along with their construct validity coefficient (r). The median correlation of the Wave Professional Styles dimensions was .71, with a minimum correlation of .50 for Learning Oriented and a maximum of .84 for Conforming. These are not adjusted for any statistical artifacts such as the reliability of the two measures.

Table 16.39 shows the construct correlations for the Wave Professional Styles' Competency Potential scales. As can be seen from the table, these coefficients are slightly larger than for Styles dimensions, consistent with their greater average criterion-related validity. The median coefficient for Wave Competency Potential scales between the two measures was .76, with a minimum correlation of .42 for Adopting Practical Approaches and a maximum of .89 for Following Procedures. This lower correlation for Adopting Practical Approaches is related to the fact that no facet was included in Focus Styles measuring this construct.

Details of the Project Epsom sample can be found in the Appendices.

Table 16.38 36 Wave Professional Styles Dimensions against 36 Wave Focus Styles Facets. *(N=308)*

Professional Styles Dimension	Focus Styles Facet	Professional Styles Dimension		Focus Styles Facet		r
		Mean	SD	Mean	SD	
Analytical	Focused on Information Analysis	61.12	8.94	17.95	5.62	.67
Factual	Focused on Written Communication	64.69	8.92	18.82	6.44	.62
Rational	Data Oriented	50.31	13.37	14.97	6.57	.72
Learning Oriented	Open to Learning	63.73	10.10	22.50	4.24	.51
Learning Oriented*	Quick Learning	68.35	10.55	22.39	4.17	.50
Insightful	Focused on Improving Things	64.38	8.58	22.53	3.65	.56
Inventive	Creative	53.17	13.00	18.68	4.86	.76
Abstract	Conceptual	56.07	10.95	18.30	4.70	.55
Strategic	Strategic	55.56	10.58	17.55	4.84	.56
Interactive	Lively	56.43	12.64	21.02	5.23	.66
Engaging	Rapport Focused	67.12	11.02	22.77	4.61	.75
Self-promoting	Attention Seeking	46.67	12.41	11.44	5.64	.70
Convincing	Persuasive	53.77	10.44	16.24	4.48	.72
Articulate	Presentation Oriented	57.35	12.03	14.76	6.97	.76
Challenging	Prepared to Disagree	48.07	12.40	15.86	5.28	.66
Purposeful	Responsibility Seeking	52.37	11.79	17.94	5.13	.71
Directing	Leadership Oriented	57.93	13.55	18.34	4.91	.75
Empowering	Motivating	58.74	10.49	20.64	4.43	.72
Self-assured	Self-confident	62.70	10.61	20.18	5.68	.61
Composed	Relaxed at Events	52.21	12.79	13.65	6.19	.76
Resolving	Comfortable with Upset People	58.76	11.38	19.00	5.73	.78
Positive	Optimistic	65.34	10.58	22.91	4.68	.69
Change Oriented	Change Oriented	58.96	11.05	20.63	4.62	.71
Receptive	Responsive to Feedback	59.81	9.99	20.19	4.13	.70
Attentive	Empathic	64.76	11.02	23.29	4.67	.71
Involving	Team Oriented	64.12	9.95	23.39	4.50	.65
Accepting	Considerate	63.71	10.27	24.06	4.17	.60
Reliable	Deadline Focused	66.71	12.50	23.06	4.74	.74
Meticulous	Detail Focused	64.74	12.13	22.07	5.23	.78
Conforming	Rule Focused	56.14	13.89	19.66	5.69	.84
Organized	Methodical	67.29	10.08	22.49	5.09	.79
Organized*	Focused on Planning	70.26	9.66	22.16	3.91	.71
Activity Oriented	Quick Working	66.49	10.84	22.25	4.74	.71
Dynamic	Action Oriented	59.05	10.01	21.88	4.00	.64
Enterprising	Business Opportunity Oriented	50.83	14.97	17.53	5.15	.74
Striving	Results Oriented	62.12	10.91	21.00	4.60	.66
	Mean	59.72	11.23	19.78	4.98	.69
	Median	59.43	10.93	20.41	4.79	.71
	Min	46.67	8.58	11.44	3.65	.50
	Max	70.26	14.97	24.06	6.97	.84

*This Professional Styles dimension is repeated as facets which were part of 'Practically Minded' and 'Principled' in Wave Professional Styles were not included in Focus Styles.

Note: Any raw correlation higher than .12 is statistically significant at the p<.05 level (two tailed) and any raw correlation higher than .10 is statistically significant at the p<.05 level (one tailed). N=308.

Table 16.39 36 Wave Professional Styles derived Competency Potential scores against 36 Wave Focus Styles derived Competency Potential scores. (N=308)

Professional Styles Competency Potential	Focus Styles Competency Potential	Professional Styles Mean	SD	Focus Styles Mean	SD	r
Examining Information	Examining Information	2815.36	434.10	2465.95	458.05	.76
Documenting Facts	Documenting Facts	2957.67	398.84	2631.59	540.11	.74
Interpreting Data	Interpreting Data	2488.13	587.18	2555.79	641.79	.77
Developing Expertise	Developing Expertise	2942.61	431.44	3036.47	413.55	.67
Adopting Practical Approaches	Adopting Practical Approaches	3098.66	445.05	1517.03	266.13	.42
Providing Insights	Providing Insights	2983.51	423.07	2441.96	352.48	.75
Generating Ideas	Generating Ideas	2514.69	606.19	2382.12	458.18	.83
Exploring Possibilities	Exploring Possibilities	2693.75	506.33	2293.43	403.19	.69
Developing Strategies	Developing Strategies	2699.42	465.46	2379.81	429.73	.65
Interacting with People	Interacting with People	2726.13	543.42	2806.19	491.60	.76
Establishing Rapport	Establishing Rapport	3117.21	576.85	2562.31	453.76	.82
Impressing People	Impressing People	2279.98	544.41	1489.39	396.23	.71
Convincing People	Convincing People	2489.16	514.22	2402.95	439.75	.81
Articulating Information	Articulating Information	2663.79	550.48	2808.19	568.46	.85
Challenging Ideas	Challenging Ideas	2455.96	510.67	2291.55	513.99	.70
Making Decisions	Making Decisions	2487.05	581.63	2082.69	435.06	.80
Directing People	Directing People	2855.53	581.75	3376.32	626.22	.77
Empowering Individuals	Empowering Individuals	2888.98	464.76	3434.35	508.02	.72
Conveying Self-Confidence	Conveying Self-Confidence	2838.22	504.23	3064.75	572.61	.69
Showing Composure	Showing Composure	2622.70	526.69	2432.67	512.20	.74
Resolving Conflict	Resolving Conflict	2944.61	475.39	2918.69	516.06	.77
Thinking Positively	Thinking Positively	3096.61	472.93	2771.29	440.39	.76
Embracing Change	Embracing Change	2782.38	503.20	3192.65	485.81	.77
Inviting Feedback	Inviting Feedback	2845.55	423.25	3214.79	409.63	.72
Understanding People	Understanding People	3099.69	571.97	2955.43	544.10	.80
Team Working	Team Working	3035.04	452.79	2910.16	419.63	.76
Valuing Individuals	Valuing Individuals	3074.57	511.43	2805.76	466.22	.74
Meeting Timescales	Meeting Timescales	3226.18	601.06	2993.80	515.82	.82
Checking Things	Checking Things	3137.37	576.93	2444.37	461.35	.84
Following Procedures	Following Procedures	2966.34	658.37	2516.28	525.16	.89
Managing Tasks	Managing Tasks	3136.40	437.91	2430.92	358.87	.79
Upholding Standards	Upholding Standards	3348.29	472.80	2577.20	365.21	.58
Producing Output	Producing Output	3212.51	493.67	2648.63	416.44	.75
Taking Action	Taking Action	2750.55	489.80	2795.91	414.88	.75
Seizing Opportunities	Seizing Opportunities	2490.41	673.00	2728.73	521.82	.80
Pursuing Goals	Pursuing Goals	2833.80	545.64	2553.72	456.52	.75
	Mean	2849.97	515.47	2636.50	466.64	.75
	Median	2850.54	508.50	2604.40	458.12	.76
	Min	2279.98	398.84	1489.39	266.13	.42
	Max	3348.29	673.00	3434.35	641.79	.89

Note: Any raw correlation higher than .12 is statistically significant at the p<.05 level (two tailed) and any raw correlation higher than .10 is statistically significant at the p<.05 level (one tailed). N=308

Intercorrelation - Construct Separation

The 36 dimensions of Wave Professional Styles show clear construct separation from each other with every single dimension in the Invited Access form having the highest correlation with its respective scale in the Supervised Access form. As an example, the Inventive dimension in the Invited Access form correlates most strongly with Inventive in the Supervised Access form, not with Abstract nor any other scale. The highest non-matched correlation is .60 between Reliable (SA) and Organized (IA) with their respective alternate form reliabilities being .91 and .88 (N=1,153) (See Reliability chapter). The average intercorrelation of the normative questionnaires is only .26 and on the combined ipsative and normative scores the average intercorrelation of the 36 dimensions is .06.

For more details on intercorrelations between Wave dimensions, please see Appendices.

Construct Validity of Facet Scales

One method for understanding the separation of constructs is that individual facet scales have unique variance which is not individually captured by another scale. The alternate form matrix of the two forms of Wave Professional Styles facet scales provides a method of understanding the construct separation of 108 two item facet scales. The main diagonal of 108 correlations of this matrix provides the alternate form reliabilities of the facet scales (alternate form reliabilities range from .50 to .90 for two item facet scales (ra-ra) with median of .78 (n=1153)). Construct separation is indicated with the off diagonal correlations being of lower value than this main diagonal. In total there are 11,556 off-diagonals. The main diagonal was higher than the off diagonals in all but two cases, demonstrating strong construct separation. The two cases of facet construct overlap occurred in each case with facets from the main and off diagonal coming from within the same dimension.

16.3 Criterion-related Validity

Concurrent Validity: Wave Professional Styles and Job Performance

Standardization Data

For more details on the Standardization sample refer to the Norm and Construction chapters.

Table 16.40 Concurrent Validity of Wave Professional Styles against independent criteria (external ratings of work performance competencies), both unadjusted and adjusted for criterion unreliability. (N=556-658)*

Professional Styles Dimension	Criterion	Criterion Mean	Criterion SD	r	r_c
Analytical	Examining Information	5.08	1.01	.13	.26
Factual	Documenting Facts	5.14	1.02	.17	.29
Rational	Interpreting Data	5.11	1.00	.24	.46
Learning Oriented	Developing Expertise	5.23	1.11	.11	.19
Practically Minded	Adopting Practical Approaches	5.45	.92	-.02	-.04
Insightful	Providing Insights	5.09	1.02	.07	.14
Inventive	Generating Ideas	4.87	1.06	.28	.42
Abstract	Exploring Possibilities	4.92	1.03	.13	.21
Strategic	Developing Strategies	4.58	1.09	.27	.54
Interactive	Interacting with People	5.03	1.16	.21	.42
Engaging	Establishing Rapport	5.39	1.14	.32	.63
Self-promoting	Impressing People	4.61	1.15	.17	.32
Convincing	Convincing People	4.78	1.01	.13	.26
Articulate	Articulating Information	4.90	1.17	.33	.66
Challenging	Challenging Ideas	5.11	1.06	.29	.47
Purposeful	Making Decisions	5.06	1.04	.24	.48
Directing	Directing People	4.77	1.20	.34	.68
Empowering	Empowering Individuals	4.73	1.20	.31	.62
Self-assured	Conveying Self-Confidence	4.88	1.11	.20	.40
Composed	Showing Composure	4.97	1.11	.18	.36
Resolving	Resolving Conflict	4.88	1.06	.19	.38
Positive	Thinking Positively	5.10	1.11	.20	.40
Change Oriented	Embracing Change	5.18	1.08	.21	.42
Receptive	Inviting Feedback	4.76	1.11	.13	.26
Attentive	Understanding People	5.10	1.12	.19	.35
Involving	Team Working	5.20	1.12	.16	.32
Accepting	Valuing Individuals	5.21	1.12	.17	.34
Reliable	Meeting Timescales	5.27	1.18	.34	.45
Meticulous	Checking Things	5.26	1.08	.24	.39
Conforming	Following Procedures	5.46	.95	.17	.26
Organized	Managing Tasks	5.11	1.07	.20	.32
Principled	Upholding Standards	5.89	.96	.13	.21
Activity Oriented	Producing Output	5.33	1.11	.18	.26
Dynamic	Taking Action	5.15	1.06	.27	.54
Enterprising	Seizing Opportunities	4.72	1.15	.26	.42
Striving	Pursuing Goals	5.28	1.03	.14	.28
	Mean	5.07	1.08	.20	.37
	Median	5.10	1.09	.20	.37
	Min	4.58	.92	-.02	-.04
	Max	5.89	1.20	.34	.68

*Sample size varied due to no evidence option on criterion ratings. r is the unadjusted validity coefficient. r_c validities have been adjusted for attenuation based on the reliability of the criteria (based on 236 pairs of criterion ratings).

Note: Any raw correlation higher than .09 is statistically significant at the p<.05 level (two tailed) and any raw correlation higher than .07 is statistically significant at the p<.05 level (one tailed). This is based on statistical significance values for the lowest sample size of N=556 to give a conservative estimate of significance.

395

Table 16.41 Concurrent Validity of Wave Professional Styles Competency Potential Dimensions against independent criteria (external ratings of work performance competencies), both unadjusted and adjusted for criterion unreliability. (N=500-632)*

Professional Styles Dimension	Criterion	Criterion Mean	Criterion SD	r	r_c
Examining Information	Examining Information	5.08	1.01	.19	.38
Documenting Facts	Documenting Facts	5.14	1.02	.24	.41
Interpreting Data	Interpreting Data	5.11	1.00	.27	.52
Developing Expertise	Developing Expertise	5.23	1.11	.11	.19
Adopting Practical Approaches	Adopting Practical Approaches	5.45	.92	.10	.18
Providing Insights	Providing Insights	5.09	1.02	.17	.34
Generating Ideas	Generating Ideas	4.87	1.06	.32	.48
Exploring Possibilities	Exploring Possibilities	4.92	1.03	.19	.31
Developing Strategies	Developing Strategies	4.58	1.09	.28	.56
Interacting with People	Interacting with People	5.03	1.16	.27	.54
Establishing Rapport	Establishing Rapport	5.39	1.14	.34	.67
Impressing People	Impressing People	4.61	1.15	.25	.46
Convincing People	Convincing People	4.78	1.01	.21	.42
Articulating Information	Articulating Information	4.90	1.17	.40	.80
Challenging Ideas	Challenging Ideas	5.11	1.06	.31	.50
Making Decisions	Making Decisions	5.06	1.04	.31	.62
Directing People	Directing People	4.77	1.20	.36	.72
Empowering Individuals	Empowering Individuals	4.73	1.20	.33	.66
Conveying Self-Confidence	Conveying Self-Confidence	4.88	1.11	.37	.74
Showing Composure	Showing Composure	4.97	1.11	.22	.44
Resolving Conflict	Resolving Conflict	4.88	1.06	.22	.44
Thinking Positively	Thinking Positively	5.10	1.11	.27	.54
Embracing Change	Embracing Change	5.18	1.08	.27	.54
Inviting Feedback	Inviting Feedback	4.76	1.11	.19	.38
Understanding People	Understanding People	5.10	1.12	.22	.40
Team Working	Team Working	5.20	1.12	.23	.46
Valuing Individuals	Valuing Individuals	5.21	1.12	.19	.38
Meeting Timescales	Meeting Timescales	5.27	1.18	.36	.48
Checking Things	Checking Things	5.26	1.08	.24	.39
Following Procedures	Following Procedures	5.46	.95	.22	.33
Managing Tasks	Managing Tasks	5.11	1.07	.27	.43
Upholding Standards	Upholding Standards	5.89	.96	.12	.20
Producing Output	Producing Output	5.33	1.11	.25	.36
Taking Action	Taking Action	5.15	1.06	.28	.56
Seizing Opportunities	Seizing Opportunities	4.72	1.15	.33	.53
Pursuing Goals	Pursuing Goals	5.28	1.03	.21	.42
	Mean	5.07	1.08	.25	.47
	Median	5.10	1.09	.25	.45
	Min	4.58	.92	.10	.18
	Max	5.89	1.20	.40	.80

*Sample size varied due to no evidence option on criterion ratings. r is the unadjusted validity coefficient. r_c validities have been adjusted for attenuation based on the reliability of the criteria (based on 236 pairs of criterion ratings). As single item criteria were used - items with inter-rater reliabilities of .25 or less were set to .25 to limit the degree of adjustment. No further corrections were applied (e.g., restriction of range, predictor unreliability).

Note: Any raw correlation higher than .09 is statistically significant at the p<.05 level (two tailed) and any raw correlation higher than .08 is statistically significant at the p<.05 level (one tailed). This is based on statistical significance values for the lowest sample size of N=500 to give a conservative estimate of significance. Criterion Mean and SD taken from (identical to) Table 16.40.

Project Epsom

Project Epsom is a major research initiative, initiated by the Research and Development team of Saville Consulting. The aim of Project Epsom was to compare the validities of a range of the most popular personality questionnaires currently on the market while attending to some of the problems of current research in this field. One important problem of validity research is that it is difficult to integrate validity data and compare tests on their validity when each study inevitably uses different methodologies, measures against different criteria and uses different samples. In choosing a test to use, practitioners are faced with a vast array of information on the validity of different tests, but how can you compare the usefulness of tests if they are all compared against different criteria? Project Epsom was set up to address these very issues.

All the personality questionnaires used in Project Epsom were validated using the same sample and the same work performance measures. The criteria used to measure the validity of the tools was the externally-developed SHL Great Eight competency framework (Kurz & Bartram, 2002) along with a global performance measure, in order to ensure fairness of comparison and to avoid content bias towards the Saville Consulting questionnaires. The content of the global performance measure originates with the work of Nyfield et al. (1995) and covers three key areas: Applying Specialist Expertise, Accomplishing Objectives and Demonstrating Potential.

Co-validation, such as that carried out in this project, allows for a more meaningful comparison of the validity of different tests on the same criteria and sample.

More information on Project Epsom can be found in:

Saville, P. (2008). *Personality Questionnaires – Valid Inferences, False Prophecies. Presented at the Division of Occupational Psychology of the British Psychological Society Annual Conference, UK, January 2008.*

Saville, P, MacIver, R., Kurz, R. & Hopton, T. (2008). *Project Epsom: How Valid Is Your Questionnaire? Phase 1: A New Comparative Study of the Major Personality Questionnaires in Predicting Job Performance. Saville Consulting Group: Jersey.*

Saville, P, MacIver, R., Kurz, R. & Hopton, T. (2008). *Project Epsom: How Valid Is Your Questionnaire? Management Summary: A New Comparative Study of the Major Personality Questionnaires in Predicting Job Performance. Saville Consulting Group: Jersey.*

Saville, P., MacIver, R., Kurz, R., Staddon, H., Hopton, T., Oxley, H., Mitchener, A., Tonks, K., Schmidt, G., Schmidt, S. & Saville, J. (2009). *A Step Towards Validity Generalization across Self-Report Personality Questionnaires: A Co-Validation of Saville Consulting Wave Professional Styles, Wave Focus Styles, Saville PP, OPQ32i, NEO-PI-R, Hogan Personality Inventory and 16PF5. Paper Presented at the British Psychological Society, Division of Occupational Psychology, Blackpool, UK.*

MacIver, R., Saville, P., Kurz, R., Oxley, H., Feindt, S., Beaujouan, Y-M., McDowall, A. (2009) *Effectiveness at Work: Investigating the Structure and Prediction of Performance Based on a Co-validation of Seven Personality and Three Aptitude Assessments. Symposium presented at European Association of Work and Organizational Psychology Conference, Santiago, Spain.*

Method

A total of 308 participants completed a range of different tests including the Professional Styles and Focus Styles versions of the Saville Consulting Wave® questionnaire, Saville Personality Profile, OPQ®, Hogan Personality Inventory, 16PF5 and NEO-PI-R. The majority also completed a larger range of questionnaires including the Hogan Development Survey, Thomas International DISC, DISCUS, and MBTI assessments. The presentation order of these questionnaires was counterbalanced across participants in order to prevent fatigue and drop out effects. Each participant was asked to nominate two other people who would act as independent "raters" and who evaluated their performance at work.

397

Saville Personality Profile is a questionnaire developed for Project Epsom. The approach to development was primarily deductive (as was for example the development of OPQ®). It uses the same rate-rank dynamic format as developed for Wave Professional Styles and is composed of motive and talent items, has 36 primary facet scales, but takes less than 15 minutes to complete.

The following section provides information on some of the key findings in Project Epsom related to Wave Professional Styles.

Note: For the sake of simplicity, the decision was taken not to include statistical significance within each table. For the Epsom sample (N=308), any raw correlation higher than .12 is statistically significant at the p<.05 level (two tailed) and any raw correlation higher than .10 is statistically significant at the p<.05 level (one tailed).

Project Epsom Data

A sample of employees from a range of business sectors completed Wave Professional Styles and were simultaneously rated by external raters on their job performance. External raters completed a questionnaire asking them to rate the participant on several Work Performance Competencies.

The concurrent validity of the 36 dimensions of Wave Professional Styles against their related job performance criteria can be found in Table 16.42.

Wave's derived Competency Potential 36 scales were also compared to job performance in order to see whether they provide incremental validity on top of the validity of the original 36 Wave Styles scales. These validity coefficients can be found in Table 16.43.

The concurrent validity of the 12 sections of Wave Professional Styles against their related job performance criteria can be found in Table 16.44. Wave's Competency Potential 12 sections were also compared to their related job performance criteria. The validity of the 12 sections of Wave's Competency Potentials scores can be found in Table 16.45.

Raters in Project Epsom

It should be noted that Project Epsom was designed to validate a large number of different assessment instruments in one study. Both the main participants in the study and the raters were paid. Most of the raters were the majority of these being peers.

Do the results differ here from the results achieved for Wave Professional Styles with solely managerial ratings of performance? To investigate this in the standardization study of Wave Professional Styles, 338 managers rated the performance of individuals against a two item composite of performance and potential (which later formed the global effectiveness scales of the BAG model - see Introduction chapter). The same methodology of computing the Great Eight was conducted as with Project Epsom. As with Project Epsom an overall unit weighted composite of the Great Eight scores for Wave Professional Styles was created and correlated with managerial ratings of overall effectiveness based on the performance and potential criterion items. The overall validity of the Wave Styles Competency Potential scores in this solely managerial rating sample is .33 uncorrected which is in line with the Project Epsom overall uncorrected validity in a mixed rater sample. This cross validation provides further support for the enhanced validity of Wave Professional Styles Competency Potential scores in managerial as well as mixed rater samples.

Table 16.42 Concurrent Validity of Wave Professional Styles against independent criteria (external ratings of work performance competencies), both unadjusted and adjusted for criterion unreliability. (N=308)

Wave Professional Styles Dimension (Predictor)	Work Performance Competency (Criterion)	Criterion Mean	Criterion SD	r	r_c*
Analytical	Examining Information	5.77	.88	.11	.23
Factual	Documenting Facts	5.57	1.06	.12	.23
Rational	Interpreting Data	5.48	1.04	.10	.20
Learning Oriented	Developing Expertise	5.69	1.04	.12	.24
Practically Minded	Adopting Practical Approaches	5.86	1.00	.18	.36
Insightful	Providing Insights	5.62	1.01	.12	.24
Inventive	Generating Ideas	5.33	1.02	.21	.43
Abstract	Exploring Possibilities	5.15	1.07	.06	.12
Strategic	Developing Strategies	5.06	1.14	.21	.43
Interactive	Interacting with People	5.94	1.11	.27	.48
Engaging	Establishing Rapport	6.03	1.09	.30	.52
Self-promoting	Impressing People	5.26	1.36	.17	.34
Convincing	Convincing People	5.32	1.03	.17	.34
Articulate	Articulating Information	5.32	1.24	.34	.59
Challenging	Challenging Ideas	5.46	1.11	.24	.49
Purposeful	Making Decisions	5.55	1.05	.21	.41
Directing	Directing People	5.25	1.22	.29	.52
Empowering	Empowering Individuals	5.40	1.20	.22	.40
Self-assured	Conveying Self-Confidence	5.30	1.22	.25	.49
Composed	Showing Composure	5.19	1.41	.14	.27
Resolving	Resolving Conflict	5.27	1.20	.16	.31
Positive	Thinking Positively	5.48	1.17	.19	.33
Change Oriented	Embracing Change	5.42	1.06	.22	.43
Receptive	Inviting Feedback	5.11	1.25	.06	.11
Attentive	Understanding People	5.72	1.16	.24	.49
Involving	Team Working	5.69	1.09	.12	.23
Accepting	Valuing Individuals	5.71	1.03	.15	.27
Reliable	Meeting Timescales	5.81	1.19	.26	.49
Meticulous	Checking Things	5.76	1.01	.20	.37
Conforming	Following Procedures	5.62	1.15	.30	.59
Organized	Managing Tasks	5.73	1.03	.19	.38
Principled	Upholding Standards	6.05	.94	.16	.32
Activity Oriented	Producing Output	5.92	.98	.33	.66
Dynamic	Taking Action	5.63	1.00	.23	.45
Enterprising	Seizing Opportunities	4.91	1.29	.31	.62
Striving	Pursuing Goals	5.63	1.02	.26	.51
	Mean	5.53	1.11	.20	.38
	Median	5.55	1.09	.20	.38
	Min	4.91	.88	.06	.11
	Max	6.05	1.41	.34	.66

*r is the unadjusted validity coefficient. r_c validities have been corrected for attenuation based on the reliability of the criteria (based on 263 pairs of criterion ratings). As single item criteria were used - items with inter-rater reliabilities of .25 or less were set to .25 to limit the degree of adjustment. No further corrections were applied (e.g., restriction of range, predictor unreliability).

Note: Any raw correlation higher than .12 is statistically significant at the p<.05 level (two tailed) and any raw correlation higher than .10 is statistically significant at the p<.05 level (one tailed). N=308

399

Table 16.43 Concurrent Validity of Wave derived Competency Potential scores
(36 Dimension level) against independent criteria (external ratings of work performance
competencies), both unadjusted and adjusted for criterion unreliability. (N=308)

Wave Competency Potential (Predictor)	Work Performance Competency (Criterion)	Criterion Mean	Criterion SD	r	rc*
Examining Information	Examining Information	5.77	.88	.17	.34
Documenting Facts	Documenting Facts	5.57	1.06	.19	.38
Interpreting Data	Interpreting Data	5.48	1.04	.13	.26
Developing Expertise	Developing Expertise	5.69	1.04	.08	.15
Adopting Practical Approaches	Adopting Practical Approaches	5.86	1.00	.23	.45
Providing Insights	Providing Insights	5.62	1.01	.22	.44
Generating Ideas	Generating Ideas	5.33	1.02	.21	.43
Exploring Possibilities	Exploring Possibilities	5.15	1.07	.08	.16
Developing Strategies	Developing Strategies	5.06	1.14	.22	.44
Interacting with People	Interacting with People	5.94	1.11	.30	.53
Establishing Rapport	Establishing Rapport	6.03	1.09	.28	.49
Impressing People	Impressing People	5.26	1.36	.21	.41
Convincing People	Convincing People	5.32	1.03	.22	.44
Articulating Information	Articulating Information	5.32	1.24	.38	.67
Challenging Ideas	Challenging Ideas	5.46	1.11	.26	.52
Making Decisions	Making Decisions	5.55	1.05	.23	.46
Directing People	Directing People	5.25	1.22	.31	.56
Empowering Individuals	Empowering Individuals	5.40	1.20	.24	.43
Conveying Self-Confidence	Conveying Self-Confidence	5.30	1.22	.27	.55
Showing Composure	Showing Composure	5.19	1.41	.17	.33
Resolving Conflict	Resolving Conflict	5.27	1.20	.20	.39
Thinking Positively	Thinking Positively	5.48	1.17	.21	.38
Embracing Change	Embracing Change	5.42	1.06	.25	.51
Inviting Feedback	Inviting Feedback	5.11	1.25	.09	.17
Understanding People	Understanding People	5.72	1.16	.27	.53
Team Working	Team Working	5.69	1.09	.15	.31
Valuing Individuals	Valuing Individuals	5.71	1.03	.15	.28
Meeting Timescales	Meeting Timescales	5.81	1.19	.27	.52
Checking Things	Checking Things	5.76	1.01	.19	.34
Following Procedures	Following Procedures	5.62	1.15	.30	.61
Managing Tasks	Managing Tasks	5.73	1.03	.23	.46
Upholding Standards	Upholding Standards	6.05	.94	.16	.32
Producing Output	Producing Output	5.92	.98	.35	.70
Taking Action	Taking Action	5.63	1.00	.27	.54
Seizing Opportunities	Seizing Opportunities	4.91	1.29	.32	.64
Pursuing Goals	Pursuing Goals	5.63	1.02	.27	.53
	Mean	5.53	1.11	.22	.43
	Median	5.55	1.09	.22	.44
	Min	4.91	.88	.08	.15
	Max	6.05	1.41	.38	.70

*r is the uncorrected validity coefficient. rc validities have been corrected for attenuation based on the reliability of the criteria (based on 263 pairs of criterion ratings). As single item criteria were used - items with inter-rater reliabilities of .25 or less were set to .25 to limit the degree of adjustment. No further corrections were applied (e.g., restriction of range, predictor unreliability).

Note: Any raw correlation higher than .12 is statistically significant at the p<.05 level (two tailed) and any raw correlation higher than .10 is statistically significant at the p<.05 level (one tailed). N = 308.

Please note: Names for both criterion and predictor scales are the same as they reflect the Saville Consulting aligned model of Work Performance. Work Performance Competencies (criteria) are external ratings of an individual's performance on the competencies listed. Wave Competency Potentials (predictors) are self-report measures of a person's potential on that competency. Competency Potential scores are generated from participants' self-report scores on Wave Styles questionnaires.

Table 16.44 Concurrent Validity of Wave Professional Styles 12 Sections against independent criteria (external ratings of work performance competencies), both unadjusted and adjusted for criterion unreliability. (N=308)

Wave Professional Styles Section (Predictor)	Work Performance Competency (Criterion)	Criterion Mean	Criterion SD	r	r_c*
Evaluative	Evaluating Problems	16.82	2.49	.06	.13
Investigative	Investigating Issues	17.18	2.45	.15	.32
Imaginative	Creating Innovation	15.54	2.64	.19	.43
Sociable	Building Relationships	17.24	2.92	.26	.46
Impactful	Communicating Information	16.10	2.63	.32	.61
Assertive	Providing Leadership	16.20	2.80	.28	.49
Resilient	Showing Resilience	15.76	2.93	.17	.31
Flexible	Adjusting to Change	16.01	2.81	.16	.34
Supportive	Giving Support	17.12	2.78	.20	.37
Conscientious	Processing Details	17.19	2.74	.27	.48
Structured	Structuring Tasks	17.69	2.31	.30	.70
Driven	Driving Success	16.17	2.71	.32	.60
	Mean	16.59	2.68	.22	.44
	Median	16.51	2.73	.23	.45
	Min	15.54	2.31	.06	.13
	Max	17.69	2.93	.32	.70

*r is the unadjusted validity coefficient. r_c validities have been adjusted for attenuation based on the reliability of the criteria (based on 263 pairs of criterion ratings). No further corrections were applied (e.g., restriction of range, predictor unreliability).

Note: Any raw correlation higher than .12 is statistically significant at the p<.05 level (two tailed) and any raw correlation higher than .10 is statistically significant at the p<.05 level (one tailed). N=308.

Table 16.45 Concurrent Validity of Wave derived Competency Potential scores (12 Section level) against independent criteria (external ratings of work performance competencies), both unadjusted and adjusted for criterion unreliability. (N=308)

Professional Styles Competency Potential (Predictor)	Work Performance Competency (Criterion)	Criterion Mean	Criterion SD	r	r_c*
Evaluating Problems	Evaluating Problems	16.82	2.49	.12	.26
Investigating Issues	Investigating Issues	17.18	2.45	.20	.42
Creating Innovation	Creating Innovation	15.54	2.64	.20	.46
Building Relationships	Building Relationships	17.24	2.92	.29	.51
Communicating Information	Communicating Information	16.10	2.63	.35	.67
Providing Leadership	Providing Leadership	16.20	2.80	.30	.53
Showing Resilience	Showing Resilience	15.76	2.93	.20	.37
Adjusting to Change	Adjusting to Change	16.01	2.81	.22	.46
Giving Support	Giving Support	17.12	2.78	.21	.38
Processing Details	Processing Details	17.19	2.74	.26	.47
Structuring Tasks	Structuring Tasks	17.69	2.31	.32	.74
Driving Success	Driving Success	16.17	2.71	.35	.65
	Mean	16.59	2.68	.25	.49
	Median	16.51	2.73	.24	.47
	Min	15.54	2.31	.12	.26
	Max	17.69	2.93	.35	.74

*r is the uncorrected validity coefficient. r_c validities have been adjusted for attenuation based on the reliability of the criteria (based on 263 pairs of criterion ratings). No further corrections were applied (e.g., restriction of range, predictor unreliability).

Note: Any raw correlation higher than .12 is statistically significant at the p<.05 level (two tailed) and any raw correlation higher than .10 is statistically significant at the p<.05 level (one tailed). N=308.

Project Epsom Data

The major co-validation study carried out by Saville Consulting ("Project Epsom") measured participants on a range of personality assessments, as well as collecting independent ratings of these individuals' job performance. This section is concerned with the concurrent, criterion-related validity of a number of these personality tools – looking at how well they relate to independent criterion measures of job performance.

As a primary development goal of Wave Professional Styles was to maximize validity in order to better forecast performance at work, the outcome of this study was of fundamental importance to Wave achieving its design goals.

The seven personality assessments used in this study were; Wave Professional Styles, Wave Focus Styles, Saville Personality Profile, OPQ32i, NEO-PI-R, Hogan Personality Inventory (HPI) and 16PF-5.

The tables below show the comparative validities of the seven personality assessments across a number of different criterion measures.

Measuring Global Overall Work Performance

Saville Consulting's Wave Performance Culture Framework consists of the BAG – Behavior, Ability and Global. Global Overall Effectiveness at work is measured by three sub-components: 'Applying Specialist Expertise,' 'Accomplishing Objectives' and 'Demonstrating Potential.' 'Overall Total Performance' consists of the sum of the three sub-components.

Individuals in this study were rated on the Overall Performance measures by external raters. The raw validity coefficients for each of the seven measures included in the study are shown in Table 16.47. To allow for the unreliability of criterion ratings, validity coefficients can be adjusted for 'criterion unreliability.' The adjusted validity coefficients are shown in Table 16.48. Both the raw and adjusted validity co-efficients are included here for comparison.

Creation of Overall Score from Each Personality Assessment

The 'Great Eight' model is a criterion-centric model of work performance developed by Kurz and Bartram (Kurz and Bartram, 2002). The 'Great Eight' are eight broad competency factors which reflect psychological constructs relating to effective work performance. The eight competencies are:

- Analyzing & Interpreting
- Creating & Conceptualizing
- Interacting & Presenting
- Leading & Deciding
- Supporting & Cooperating
- Adapting & Coping
- Organizing & Executing
- Enterprising & Performing

In order to compare personality assessments on the Great Eight competencies, composite 'Great Eight Predictor' scales were created. These were aggregated with unit weights to provide an overall score from each personality assessment.

Table 16.46 shows the *a priori* conceptual mapping of the personality assessments to the 'Great Eight' work performance competencies by subject matter experts.

Table 16.46 Conceptual Mapping of the 'Great Eight' Competencies against Wave Professional Styles' and other assessments' scales.

Great 8 Criteria	Wave Competency Potential (CP) Dimensions	Wave Professional Styles (S) Dimensions	Wave Focus Styles (S) Facets	Saville PP	OPQ32i	NEO - PI-R	HPI (HICS)	16PF5
Analyzing & Interpreting	• Examining Information • Exploring Possibilities • Interpreting Data	• Analytical • Abstract • Rational	• Information Analysis • Conceptual • Data Oriented	• Analytical • Theoretical • Data-Driven	• Evaluative • Conceptual • Data Rational	• Openness to Ideas • Compliance • Openness to Feelings (-)	• Math Ability • Education • Science Ability	• B (Intellect) • M (Abstractedness) • Q2 (Self-Reliance)
Creating & Conceptualizing	• Generating Ideas • Developing Strategies • Providing Insights	• Inventive • Strategic • Insightful	• Creative • Strategic • Focused on Improving Things	• Creative • Unconventional • Independent	• Innovative • Conventional (-) • Independent Minded	• Openness to Actions • Openness to Aesthetics • Openness to Values	• Experience Seeking • Culture • Generating Ideas	• Q1 (Openness to Change) • M (Abstractedness) • G (Rule Consciousness) (-)
Interacting & Presenting	• Articulating Information • Interacting with People • Impressing People	• Articulate • Interactive • Self-promoting	• Presentation Oriented • Lively • Attention Seeking	• Assured • Extrovert • Unreserved	• Socially Confident • Outgoing • Modest (-)	• Gregariousness • Warmth • Positive Emotions	• Like Parties • Entertaining • Exhibitionist	• H (Social Boldness) • F (Liveliness) • N (Privateness) (-)
Leading & Deciding	• Directing People • Empowering Individuals • Making Decisions	• Directing • Empowering • Purposeful	• Leadership Oriented • Motivating • Responsibility Seeking	• Leading • Sales-Oriented • Decisive	• Controlling • Persuasive • Decisive	• Assertiveness • Modesty (-) • Competence	• Leadership • No Social Anxiety • Even Tempered	• E (Dominance) • H (Social Boldness) • O (Apprehension) (-)
Supporting & Cooperating	• Understanding People • Team Working • Establishing Rapport	• Attentive • Involving • Engaging	• Empathic • Team Oriented • Rapport Focused	• Considerate • Consultative • Friendship Oriented	• Caring • Democratic • Affiliative	• Altruism • Tender-Mindedness • Trust	• Sensitive • Trusting • Virtuous	• A (Warmth) • L (Vigilance) (-) • Q2 (Self-Reliance) (-)
Adapting & Coping	• Showing Composure • Conveying Self-Confidence • Thinking Positively	• Composed • Self-assured • Positive	• Relaxed at Events • Self-Confidence • Optimistic	• Tough Minded • Laid-back • Optimistic	• Tough Minded • Relaxed • Optimistic	• Vulnerability (-) • Anxiety (-) • Depression (-)	• Not Anxious • Empathy • Identity	• O (Apprehension) (-) • C (Emotional Stability) • Q4 (Tension) (-)
Organizing & Executing	• Checking Things • Meeting Time scales • Taking Action	• Meticulous • Reliable • Dynamic	• Detail Focused • Deadline Focused • Action Oriented	• Completion Oriented • Detailed • Planful	• Conscientious • Detail Conscious • Forward Thinking	• Order • Deliberation • Dutifulness	• Impulse Control • Avoids Trouble • Mastery	• G (Rule-consciousness) • Q3 (Perfectionism) • M (Abstractedness) (-)
Enterprising & Performing	• Pursuing Goals • Producing Output • Seizing Opportunities	• Striving • Activity Oriented • Enterprising	• Results Oriented • Quick Working • Business Opportunity Oriented	• Ambitious • Vigorous • Competitive	• Achieving • Vigorous • Competitive	• Achievement Striving • Self-Discipline • Activity	• Self Confidence • Competitive • Curiosity	• Q3 (Perfectionism) • E (Dominance) • I (Sensitivity) (-)

More information on the process for creating these overall scores can be found in Saville 2009.

403

Table 16.47 *Concurrent validity of seven personality assessments against ratings of Global Overall Performance, unadjusted for criterion unreliability.* (N=308)

Personality Assessment	Applying Specialist Expertise	Accomplishing Objectives	Demonstrating Potential	Overall Total Performance	Overall Total Performance (Excl. Expertise)
Wave Professional Styles Competency Potentials	.15	.24	.34	.32	.34
Wave Professional Styles	.12	.21	.30	.28	.30
Wave Focus Styles Competency Potentials	.15	.15	.26	.25	.25
Wave Focus Styles	.13	.11	.24	.21	.22
Saville PP	.06	.12	.23	.19	.21
OPQ32i	.08	.11	.19	.17	.18
NEO-PI-R	.13	.16	.17	.20	.20
Hogan Personality Inventory (HPI)	.13	.11	.17	.18	.17
16PF-5	.04	.19	.18	.18	.21

These validities are unadjusted for any statistical artifacts.

Note: Any raw correlation higher than .12 is statistically significant at the p<.05 level (two tailed) and any raw correlation higher than .10 is statistically significant at the p<.05 level (one tailed). N=308.

Table 16.48 *Concurrent validity of seven personality assessments against ratings of Global Overall Performance, adjusted for criterion unreliability.* (N=308)

Personality Assessment	Applying Specialist Expertise	Accomplishing Objectives	Demonstrating Potential	Overall Total Performance	Overall Total Performance (Excl. Expertise)
Wave Professional Styles Competency Potentials	.33	.50	.54	.57	.58
Wave Professional Styles	.25	.46	.48	.49	.52
Wave Focus Styles Competency Potentials	.33	.32	.42	.44	.42
Wave Focus Styles	.28	.24	.38	.38	.37
Saville Personality Profile	.14	.26	.36	.33	.36
OPQ32i	.17	.24	.31	.31	.31
NEO-PI-R	.29	.34	.28	.36	.33
Hogan Personality Inventory (HPI)	.29	.23	.27	.32	.28
16PF-5	.10	.40	.29	.32	.36

Validities have been adjusted for attenuation based on the reliability of the criteria (based on 263 pairs of criterion ratings). No further corrections were applied (e.g., restriction of range, predictor unreliability).

Graph 16.1 Average (mean) validity of personality assessments against independent ratings of Overall Total Performance, adjusted for criterion unreliability. *(N=308)*

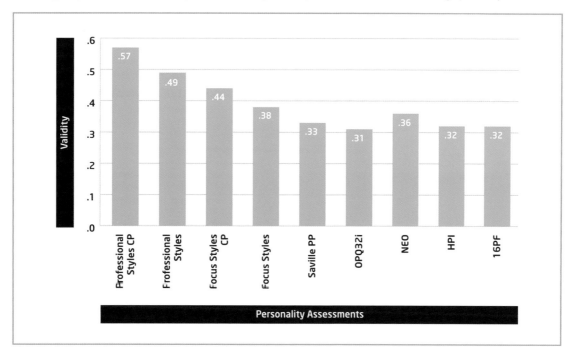

CP stands for Competency Potential, N=308.

Graph 16.2 Average Power of personality assessments against independent ratings of Overall Total Performance, adjusted for criterion unreliability. *(N=308)*

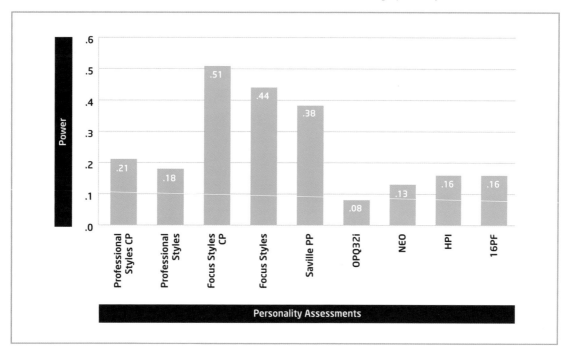

Power is calculated as validity per 15 minutes.
CP stands for Competency Potential, N=308.

405

The personality assessments included in this validation study were; Wave Professional Styles, Wave Focus Styles, OPQ32i, NEO-PI-R, Hogan Personality Inventory (HPI) and 16PF-5. Individuals were rated on the 'Great Eight' competencies by external raters.

Table 16.49 Concurrent validity of personality assessments against ratings on the 'Great Eight' work performance competencies, unadjusted for criterion unreliability.
(N=308)

	Work Performance Competency (Criterion) 'Great Eight' Criteria											
	Analyzing & Interpreting	Creating & Conceptualizing	Interacting & Presenting	Leading & Deciding	Supporting & Cooperating	Adapting & Coping	Organizing & Executing	Enterprising & Performing	Mean	Median	Min	Max
Wave Professional Styles Competency Potentials	.09	.20	.33	.30	.09	.22	.22	.34	**.22**	.22	.09	.34
Wave Professional Styles	.06	.18	.28	.29	.10	.18	.21	.31	**.20**	.20	.06	.31
Wave Focus Styles Competency Potentials	.10	.18	.31	.25	.12	.19	.18	.28	**.20**	.19	.10	.31
Wave Focus Styles	.06	.16	.26	.24	.15	.15	.16	.24	**.18**	.16	.06	.26
Saville PP	.06	.11	.25	.31	.14	.12	.15	.30	**.18**	.15	.06	.31
OPQ32i	.10	.12	.18	.28	.13	.12	.16	.23	**.17**	.15	.10	.28
NEO	.06	.03	.22	.33	.14	.20	.16	.26	**.18**	.18	.03	.33
HPI	.16	.10	.16	.28	.06	.12	.09	.20	**.15**	.14	.06	.28
16PF	.10	.04	.22	.27	.08	.14	.09	.13	**.13**	.12	.04	.27

These validities are unadjusted for any statistical artifacts.

Note: Any raw correlation higher than .12 is statistically significant at the p<.05 level (two tailed) and any raw correlation higher than .10 is statistically significant at the p<.05 level (one tailed). N=308.

Table 16.50 Concurrent validity of personality assessments against ratings on the 'Great Eight' work performance competencies, adjusted for criterion unreliability.
(N=308)

	Work Performance Competency (Criterion) 'Great Eight' Criteria											
	Analyzing & Interpreting	Creating & Conceptualizing	Interacting & Presenting	Leading & Deciding	Supporting & Cooperating	Adapting & Coping	Organizing & Executing	Enterprising & Performing	Mean	Median	Min	Max
Wave Professional Styles Competency Potentials	.20	.61	.69	.55	.21	.46	.51	.76	**.50**	.53	.20	.76
Wave Professional Styles	.13	.55	.59	.54	.22	.39	.49	.69	**.45**	.52	.13	.69
Wave Focus Styles Competency Potentials	.25	.61	.65	.47	.26	.42	.45	.65	**.47**	.46	.25	.65
Wave Focus Styles	.12	.48	.55	.45	.34	.32	.37	.53	**.39**	.41	.12	.55
Saville PP	.13	.34	.53	.58	.31	.25	.35	.66	**.39**	.35	.13	.66
OPQ32i	.22	.37	.38	.52	.29	.25	.37	.51	**.36**	.37	.22	.52
NEO	.13	.09	.46	.61	.31	.42	.37	.57	**.37**	.40	.09	.61
HPI	.35	.31	.34	.52	.13	.25	.21	.44	**.32**	.32	.13	.52
16PF	.22	.12	.46	.50	.18	.30	.21	.29	**.28**	.25	.12	.50

Validities have been adjusted for attenuation based on the reliability of the criteria (based on 263 pairs of criterion ratings). No further corrections were applied (e.g., restriction of range, predictor unreliability).

Graph 16.3 Average (mean) concurrent validity of personality assessments based on external ratings of 'Great Eight' work performance criteria, adjusted for criterion unreliability. (N=308)

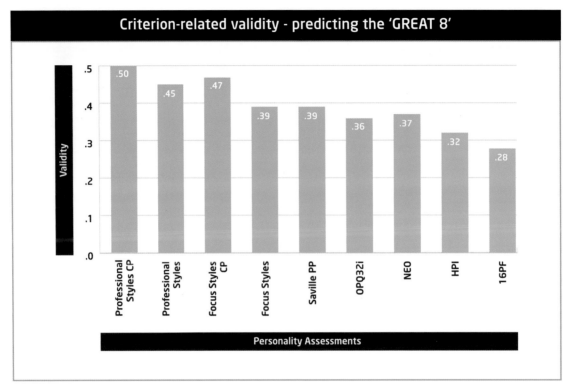

CP stands for Competency Potential. N=308.

savilleconsulting
wave

16.4 Predictive Validity

Predictive Validity: Wave Professional Styles and Job Performance

In order to assess predictive validity of Wave Professional Styles, a criterion measure must be completed at a later point in time than the predictor measure. In this study, 108 participants completed Wave Professional Styles at Time 1 and at Time 2, six months later, were rated on their work performance by external raters. For the rating task, external raters completed the 'Wave Performance 360' questionnaire, a tool for assessing an individual's job performance across a number of work domains.

The predictive validity of the 12 sections of Wave Professional Styles against their related job performance criteria can be seen in Table 16.51. Wave's Competency Potential 12 sections were also compared to their related job performance criteria. The predictive validity of the 12 sections of Wave's Competency Potentials scores can be found in Table 16.52.

Table 16.51 Predictive validity of Wave Professional Styles 12 Sections against independent criteria (external ratings of work performance competencies), both unadjusted and adjusted for criterion unreliability. (N=108)

Professional Styles Section (Predictor)	Work Performance Competency (Criterion)	Criterion Mean	Criterion SD	r*	r$_c$*
Evaluative	Evaluating Problems	16.62	2.74	.05	**.11**
Investigative	Investigating Issues	16.79	2.64	.11	**.23**
Imaginative	Creating Innovation	15.56	2.91	.12	**.26**
Sociable	Building Relationships	16.89	2.79	.28	**.50**
Impactful	Communicating Information	15.98	2.82	.28	**.54**
Assertive	Providing Leadership	16.14	2.83	.14	**.25**
Resilient	Showing Resilience	15.66	2.96	.19	**.34**
Flexible	Adjusting to Change	15.71	2.89	.17	**.36**
Supportive	Giving Support	16.61	2.89	.12	**.22**
Conscientious	Processing Details	17.03	2.77	.20	**.35**
Structured	Structuring Tasks	17.53	2.24	.16	**.38**
Driven	Driving Success	16.36	2.51	.17	**.31**
	Mean	16.41	2.75	.17	.32
	Median	16.49	2.81	.17	.33
	Min	15.56	2.24	.05	.11
	Max	17.53	2.96	.28	.54

*r is the unadjusted validity coefficient. r$_c$ validities have been adjusted for attenuation based on the reliability of the criteria (based on 263 pairs of criterion ratings). No further corrections were applied (e.g., restriction of range, predictor unreliability).

Note: Any raw correlation higher than .19 is statistically significant at the p<.05 level (two tailed) and any raw correlation higher than .16 is statistically significant at the p<.05 level (one tailed). N=108.

Table 16.52 *Predictive validity of Wave derived Competency Potential scores (12 Section level) against independent criteria (external ratings of work performance competencies), both unadjusted and adjusted for criterion unreliability.* (N=108)

Professional Styles Competency Potential (Predictor)	Work Performance Competency (Criterion)	Criterion Mean	Criterion SD	r*	r$_c$*
Evaluating Problems	Evaluating Problems	16.62	2.74	.10	.22
Investigating Issues	Investigating Issues	16.79	2.64	.05	.10
Creating Innovation	Creating Innovation	15.56	2.91	.11	.24
Building Relationships	Building Relationships	16.89	2.79	.30	.53
Communicating Information	Communicating Information	15.98	2.82	.26	.50
Providing Leadership	Providing Leadership	16.14	2.83	.12	.20
Showing Resilience	Showing Resilience	15.66	2.96	.24	.42
Adjusting to Change	Adjusting to Change	15.71	2.89	.18	.38
Giving Support	Giving Support	16.61	2.89	.15	.28
Processing Details	Processing Details	17.03	2.77	.20	.35
Structuring Tasks	Structuring Tasks	17.53	2.24	.21	.49
Driving Success	Driving Success	16.36	2.51	.18	.34
	Mean	16.41	2.75	.17	.34
	Median	16.49	2.81	.18	.35
	Min	15.56	2.24	.05	.10
	Max	17.53	2.96	.30	.53

*r is the unadjusted validity coefficient. r$_c$ validities have been adjusted for attenuation based on the reliability of the criteria (based on 263 pairs of criterion ratings). No further corrections were applied (e.g., restriction of range, predictor unreliability).

Note: Any raw correlation higher than .19 is statistically significant at the p<.05 level (two tailed) and any raw correlation higher than .16 is statistically significant at the p<.05 level (one tailed). N=108.

16.5 US Validity Data

Table 16.53 Concurrent validity of Wave Professional Styles 36 Dimensions against 36 level Job Performance criteria, both unadjusted and adjusted for criterion unreliability.
(N=399)

Wave Professional Styles Dimension	Work Performance Competency (Criterion)	r*	r$_c$*
Analytical	Examining Information	.16	.32
Factual	Documenting Facts	.13	.26
Rational	Interpreting Data	.27	.54
Learning Oriented	Developing Expertise	.12	.24
Practically Minded	Adopting Practical Approaches	-.01	-.02
Insightful	Providing Insights	.16	.32
Inventive	Generating Ideas	.26	.52
Abstract	Exploring Possibilities	.18	.36
Strategic	Developing Strategies	.19	.38
Interactive	Interacting with People	.14	.25
Engaging	Establishing Rapport	.20	.35
Self-promoting	Impressing People	.13	.26
Convincing	Convincing People	.05	.10
Articulate	Articulating Information	.11	.19
Challenging	Challenging Ideas	.17	.34
Purposeful	Making Decisions	.09	.18
Directing	Directing People	.18	.32
Empowering	Empowering Individuals	.17	.31
Self-assured	Conveying Self Confidence	.04	.08
Composed	Showing Composure	.19	.36
Resolving	Resolving Conflict	.16	.31
Positive	Thinking Positively	.25	.45
Change Oriented	Embracing Change	.24	.48
Receptive	Inviting Feedback	.12	.24
Attentive	Understanding People	.15	.30
Involving	Team Working	.18	.36
Accepting	Valuing Individuals	.24	.45
Reliable	Meeting Timescales	.25	.48
Meticulous	Checking Things	.21	.38
Conforming	Following Procedures	.16	.32
Organized	Managing Tasks	.26	.52
Principled	Upholding Standards	.02	.04
Activity Oriented	Producing Output	.16	.32
Dynamic	Taking Action	.18	.36
Enterprising	Seizing Opportunities	.19	.38
Striving	Pursuing Goals	.15	.30
	Mean	.16	.32
	Median	.17	.32
	Min	.01	-.02
	Max	.27	.54

r is the unadjusted validity coefficient. r$_c$ validities have been adjusted for attenuation based on the reliability of the criteria (based on 263 pairs of criterion ratings). As single item criteria were used - items with inter-rater reliabilities of .25 or less were set to .25 to limit the degree of adjustment. No further corrections were applied (e.g., restriction of range, predictor unreliability). Note: Any raw correlation higher than .10 is statistically significant at the p<.05 level (two tailed) and any raw correlation higher than .09 is statistically significant at the p<.05 level (one tailed).

Results based on 2008 validation study conducted in the United States with 399 study participants from the United States and Canada. Behavioral ratings were collected from a mixed group of managers, peers and colleagues.

411

16.6 Mexican Validity Data

Table 16.54 Concurrent validity of Wave Professional Styles 12 Sections against 12 level Job Performance criteria, both unadjusted and adjusted for criterion unreliability. (N=120)

Professional Styles Section (Predictor)	Work Performance Competency (Criterion)	r*	r$_c$*
Evaluative	Evaluating Problems	.20	.42
Investigative	Investigating Issues	.07	.15
Imaginative	Creating Innovation	.29	.65
Sociable	Building Relationships	-.01	-.02
Impactful	Communicating Information	.06	.11
Assertive	Providing Leadership	.16	.28
Resilient	Showing Resilience	-.05	-.09
Flexible	Adjusting to Change	.01	.02
Supportive	Giving Support	.19	.35
Conscientious	Processing Details	.23	.41
Structured	Structuring Tasks	.23	.54
Driven	Driving Success	-.04	-.07
	Mean	.11	.23
	Median	.12	.21
	Min	-.05	-.09
	Max	.29	.65

*r is the unadjusted validity coefficient. r$_c$ validities have been adjusted for attenuation based on the reliability of the criteria (based on 263 pairs of criterion ratings). No further corrections were applied (e.g., restriction of range, predictor unreliability. Behavioral ratings were collected from a mixed group of managers, peers and colleagues. N=120.

Note: Any raw correlation higher than .18 is statistically significant at the p<.05 level (two tailed) and any raw correlation higher than .16 is statistically significant at the p<.05 level (one tailed).

16.7 Criterion-Related Validity of Facet Scales

Concurrent validity of two item scales against their respective criteria averaged .28 if corrected for inter-rater reliability (.16 uncorrected) (N=500-632) at standardization. This compares to average corrected validity for the 36 broader styles dimensions (with six items) of .37 at standardization. This indicates that the main unit of analysis at the dimension level or higher is generally appropriate, although facet scales in and of themselves have acceptable criterion related validity (although they have more validity in combination as higher order dimensions).

Better average validity of facet scales has been achieved by selecting most valid facets and cross validating – Wave Focus Styles. Further technical information on Wave Focus can be found in the Saville Consulting Wave Focus Styles Handbook.

16.8 Validity Summary

This chapter advances a perspective on validation that emphasizes the importance of a criterion centric model of work performance which focuses on the effective forecasting of both individuals' overall effectiveness at work and behavioral effectiveness in terms of individual work competencies.

The chapter focuses first on the construct validity of Wave Professional Styles scores at dimension level. A central component of the construct validity section provides users of both Wave and other tools with a summary of how Wave Professional Styles relates to other measures of personality or style. This is supported by the correlation matrices in the appendices. Both the tables in the chapter against each Wave Styles dimension and the matrices are designed to aid users by allowing them to easily identify which dimensions of Wave Professional Styles directly relate (bivariate correlation) to other measures and which are unique to Wave (or unique to other measures).

In terms of Wave Professional Styles some dimensions such as Inventive, Interactive, Engaging, Convincing, Articulate, Directing, Conforming, Organized and Enterprising are frequently identified as having similar, related constructs in other measures i.e., they have clear scale counterparts in other questionnaires (correlations stronger than .40 or -.40). Some other dimensions of Wave Professional Styles such as Learning Oriented, Abstract, Strategic, Self-assured, Change Oriented, Activity Oriented and Striving more rarely have direct measures in scales of other tools. The scales of Factual, Practically Minded, Insightful, Empowering, Resolving, Receptive and Principled do not have direct scale counterparts in the other measures.

Wave Professional Styles was developed with the intention of increasing the validity of the assessments by writing questions or items based on a clear model of effectiveness in both behavioral and overall terms. The items were written with a view to predicting the behavioral components of effectiveness (competencies). Items were selected on the basis of their correlations with external ratings of overall measures of effectiveness as well as external ratings of behavioral effectiveness (work competencies). The use of both the criterion centric perspective and this performance driven methodology to select items was also supplemented by the use of the initial validation data to derive competency potential equations which were designed to maximize the prediction of the behavioral criterion model. Through this method Wave Professional Styles has been designed to maximize criterion related validity both in predicting overall effectiveness and individual behavioral effectiveness (competencies). The expectation was also that the criterion validity would generalize beyond the Wave criterion model to other competency criterion models such as the Great Eight (Bartram (2005)).

Wave has been specifically designed to align to and forecast the Behavior components of the BAG (Behavior, Ability and Global) Wave Performance Culture Framework and to forecast overall effectiveness (Global criteria). This allows the users of Wave Professional Styles a clear picture of what each scale is designed to forecast effectively, allowing them to receive a clearer picture of the validity of the tool and allow them to make better decisions. The clarity of this model also provides clear *a priori* hypotheses to be tested/validated and cross

413

The criterion related validity evidence presented in this chapter clearly supports the criterion-related validity of Wave Professional Styles and Competency Potential scores, both in measuring independent ratings of behavioral effectiveness and overall measures of effectiveness at work.

We refer to validity in a model being saturated if all the scales in the questionnaire show meaningful correlations with the performance criteria that they have been designed to predict (i.e., meaningful could for example be seen as statistically significant (non zero) correlations which when corrected for criterion unreliability are in the region of 0.20 and upwards)*.

The Wave Professional Styles scales show saturation across different validation studies at the dimension level. While a scale, such as Practically Minded, may not correlate positively with the respective aligned criterion in one validation study, it does in another.

After demonstrating that a model is saturated, we can then consider the overall validity of a questionnaire and secondly, how it compares to other questionnaires.

The original standardization provided evidence of Wave Professional Styles criterion related validity against overall performance and individual behavioral effectiveness criteria. However it did not provide the mechanism to compare the validity levels achieved with the levels found in other established instruments which were constructed with different approaches.

Project Epsom was designed to compare the criterion related validity of different tools.

As well as providing evidence supporting the saturation of the scales in the Wave Professional Styles questionnaires and the criterion related validity of behavioral competencies both from the Wave model and from independent competency models, Project Epsom provided evidence that Wave Professional Styles Competency Potential scales were more valid in combination in measuring overall effectiveness at work in a mixed occupational group. An important finding from across the different tools is that it is possible to create a mapping to competencies and use this to create an overall composite score from each of the established measures to effectively forecast overall effectiveness in a mixed occupational group.

This raises an important consideration in understanding the validity of personality and styles measures in forecasting effectiveness in mixed occupational groups. As it is possible to construct an *a priori* overall personality composite by summing different competencies together (on each personality measure) which provides a valid forecast of an individual's overall effectiveness at work. This overall composite or superordinate work related personality or 'Big One' of work personality is a potentially important finding which we believe merits further investigation. It indicates that some individuals are lower across competencies and they will tend to be less effective overall in work. By contrast, some individuals are likely to be superlative performers overall who are stronger across the competencies forecast by the personality and styles questionnaires.

Validity is not simply something that a questionnaire possesses, but it is an ongoing process. A central part of that process is equipping users of Wave Professional Styles to make their application more effective, by helping them make valid inferences.

*In an ideal world we could argue for confidence interval not to include r=0.20 rather than non zero, although in practice very large samples may be required to do this (or the use of meta-analyses across validation studies). While this level of .20 is to an extent arbitrary, this minimum figure provides a benchmark to illustrate that the model shows criterion validity across its scales and that there are not scales within the model which lack validation evidence and hence do not support a meaningful inference being made by the interpreter to forecast an individual's effectiveness at work. Of course, the higher the validity beyond this level the better.

17.0 Fairness

17.1 Overview

This chapter focuses on the issue of fairness in the use of Saville Consulting Wave and in particular presents data on group trends across different groups.

Key features and steps taken to increase fairness of Saville Consulting Wave Professional Styles and their application included:

Criterion Related Validity – If tests are forecasting what they are designed to forecast this allows the assessment to select on merit rather than using predictor measures that are unrelated to performance and potential at work. The validation-centric approach to development and the subsequent cross validations of the aligned model provide a basis for this (refer to Validity and Construction chapters). In particular, the aligned model is designed to make the validity in Wave Styles more transparent and allow for improved merit based decision making which will lead to improved effectiveness of individuals at work.

Work Related Content – The content of Wave Styles was specifically designed to be work relevant and to focus on attributes (motives and talents) which underpin behavioral and overall effectiveness at work.

Writing and Review - The items were specifically reviewed, for example to avoid content which was clinical, idiomatic, or requiring specific knowledge which would be available to one subgroup such as gender, age or ethnic subgroup and not to another (see Construction chapter for further information).

Job Analysis and Mapping Capability - Another aim of the Wave aligned model has been to increase the fairness and benefit attained in performance in application by creating mechanisms to increase the alignment between Wave Styles and what job analysis identifies as characteristics underpinning success (either for a particular job specification or for an organizational competency, capability or values framework). The Saville Consulting Wave Job Profiler and the Saville Consulting Performance Culture Framework which has the capacity to map to the 147 components of the underpinning Behavior, Ability, Global (BAG) model are designed to supplement job analysis and provide a precise and detailed mapping to organizational frameworks.

Local Validation Studies - The mechanism is also available using the Saville Consulting Wave Performance 360 to quickly conduct online validation studies for particular jobs. The 10 minute online questionnaire provides a fast and effective mechanism for collecting data on the effectiveness of employees in terms of behavioral, ability and global (overall effectiveness) by different raters.

Monitoring – Saville Consulting has an ongoing process of monitoring differences in data from different subgroups.

Training and Guidance for Users – Saville Consulting Wave has a program of training, accreditation and master classes to support users.

Fairness in Use

It is one thing for an assessment to be designed to be fair and valid and another for it to be used fairly. The more consistent the process created to align Wave to the job the better. Criteria for decision making based on job analysis and where possible validation data are more likely to result in the assessments being fairly applied using consistent and appropriate standards for candidates across different groups.

415

Group Trends

The rest of this chapter is devoted to presenting group trends on Saville Consulting Wave Professional Styles, including age, gender, ethnicity, geographical region and level of management responsibility.

Trends are presented for mean scores and internal consistency reliabilities.

Mean Scores

The information presented here is from actual usage data of Wave Professional Styles and as a result the differences may reflect differences in composition for the different groups on other variables. For example the age differences, as well as maturational effects could be related to longer tenure in organizations and generational differences as well as having a different composition in other variables including gender and job type. Similarly, gender and ethnic differences could reflect other biographical differences in the composition of these groups.

When looking at differences it is useful to remind ourselves of the scale of the differences and the impact, if any, there should be on profile interpretation.

In the following graphs and supporting text, Cohen's d is referred to, where .20 of an SD (.40 of a Sten) is a small effect, .50 of an SD (1 Sten) is a medium or moderate effect size and .80 of an SD (1.60 Stens) is a large effect size.

It should be remembered that differences whether small, moderate or large do not by themselves indicate bias in a test or a questionnaire that could lead to an individual from one protected or minority group being treated less favorably than others.

The first thing to consider is the direction and size of the difference. As can be seen for example in the UK ethnic data where there is small or even moderate differences with the Black and Asian groups tending to score slightly higher. Such differences in scores on the predictor assessments may or may not be reflected in the performance domain (how well an individual is performing in the job or a particular aspect of a job, such as a competency).

To establish whether differences are demonstrated in actual performance, ideally we would have matched criterion data to understand the relationship between test and questionnaires and external criterion data. In the absence of this data on large samples we have to rely on looking at differences between mean scores between groups and considering the size of these differences, the direction of these differences and whether the differences are likely to provide an underestimate or overestimate of an individual's performance at work for that particular group, given what we know about known differences (if any) in effectiveness of these groups.

Internal Consistency

As indicated in the Reliability chapter, Alternate form, reliability estimates given the design of Wave Professional Styles in particular, provide a more appropriate and realistic estimate of the questionnaires' reliability than internal consistency. Unfortunately, in actual usage data, it is the exception rather than the rule that both forms are taken by the same group, so internal consistency is used as, though less than ideal in that it provides an underestimate for Wave Styles, it never the less allows for a comparsion of the reliability of the assessment in different groups.

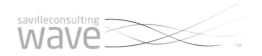

17.2 Age Trends UK

Age Trends UK (N=16,941)

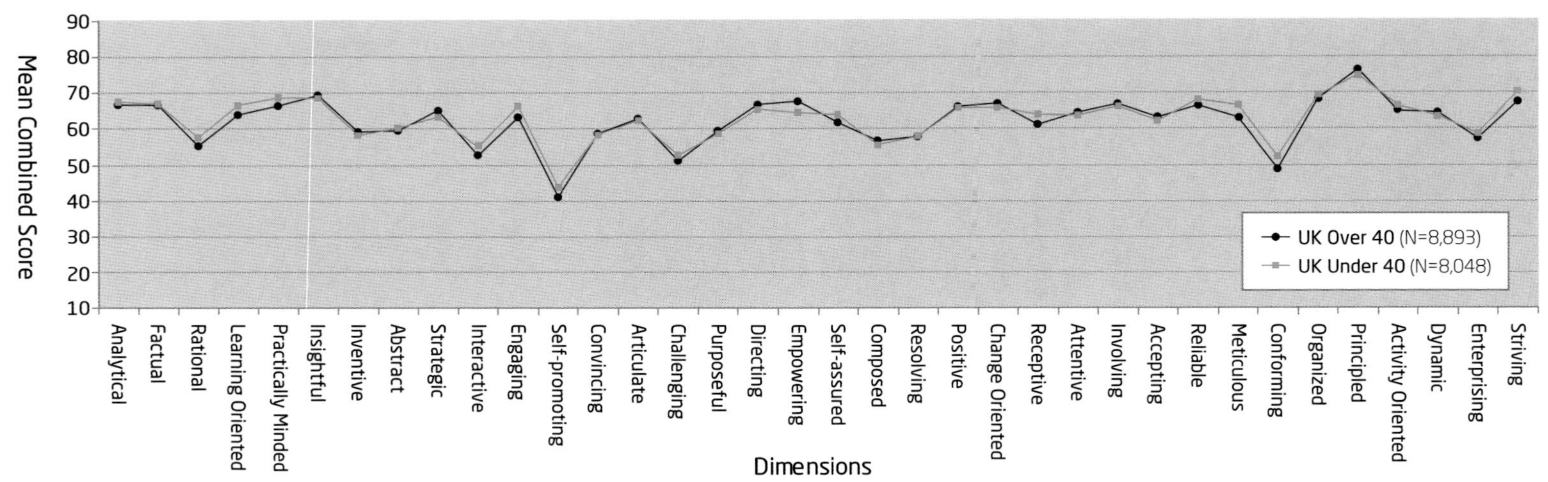
Mean Combined Score
90
80
70
60
50
40
30
20
10
UK Over 40 (N=8,893)
UK Under 40 (N=8,048)
Analytical
Factual
Rational
Learning Oriented
Practically Minded
Insightful
Inventive
Abstract
Strategic
Interactive
Engaging
Self-promoting
Convincing
Articulate
Challenging
Purposeful
Directing
Empowering
Self-assured
Composed
Resolving
Positive
Change Oriented
Receptive
Attentive
Involving
Accepting
Reliable
Meticulous
Conforming
Organized
Principled
Activity Oriented
Dynamic
Enterprising
Striving
Dimensions

17.3 Age Trends UK - Sten Profile

Age Trends UK - Sten Profile (N=16,941)

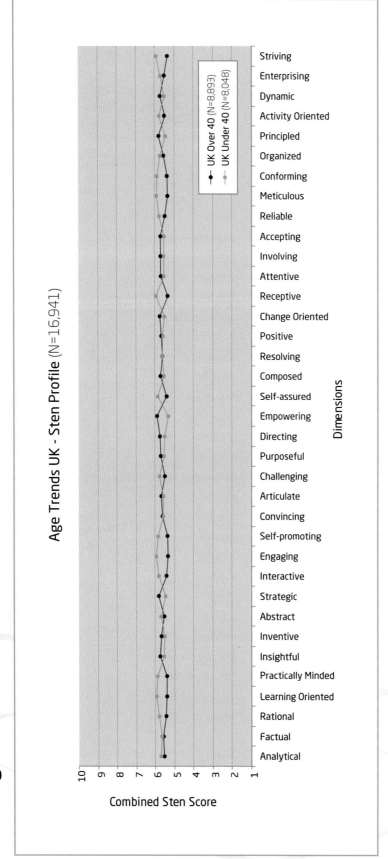

Legend:
- UK Over 40 (N=8,893)
- UK Under 40 (N=8,048)

Dimensions (top to bottom): Striving, Enterprising, Dynamic, Activity Oriented, Principled, Organized, Conforming, Meticulous, Reliable, Accepting, Involving, Attentive, Receptive, Change Oriented, Positive, Resolving, Composed, Self-assured, Empowering, Directing, Purposeful, Challenging, Articulate, Convincing, Self-promoting, Engaging, Interactive, Strategic, Abstract, Inventive, Insightful, Practically Minded, Learning Oriented, Rational, Factual, Analytical

Combined Sten Score (axis: 10, 9, 8, 7, 6, 5, 4, 3, 2, 1)

People under the age of 40 (N=8,048) were compared to people over 40 (N=8,893). Differences ranged from non-existent to small; no moderate or large differences were found.

17.4 Age Trends UK - Alpha

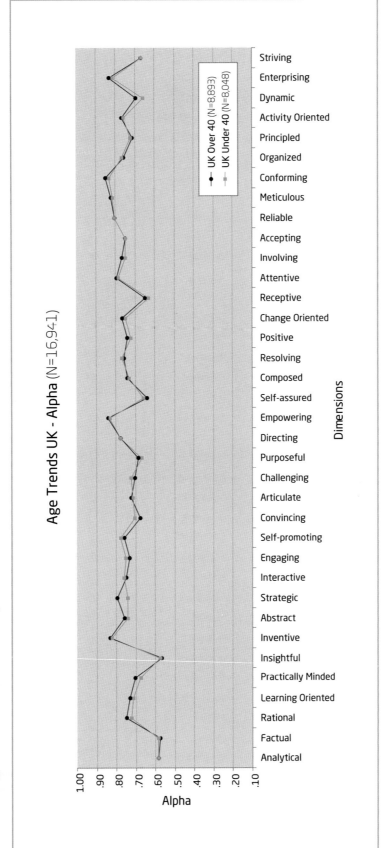

Age Trends UK - Alpha (N=16,941)

People under the age of 40 (N=8,048) were compared to people over 40 (N=8,893).

With a mean alpha of .71 for both groups, differences in internal consistency reliabilities on the 36 dimensions were mostly found to be negligible.

17.5 Gender Trends UK

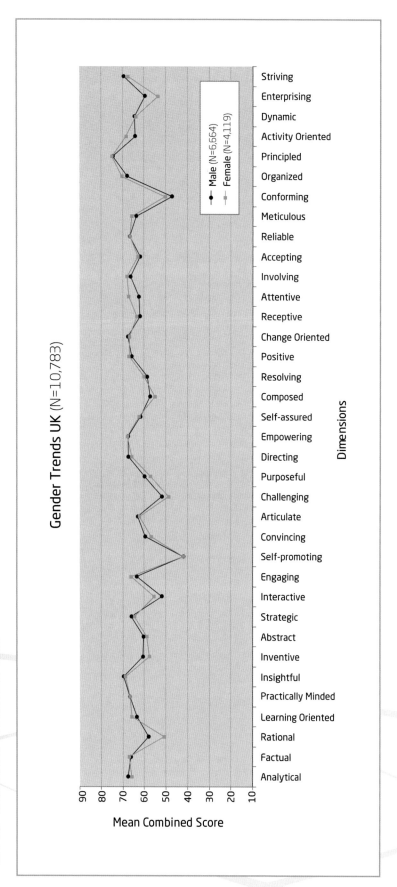

Gender Trends UK (N=10,783)

Dimensions

Mean Combined Score

Male (N=6,664)
Female (N=4,119)

Striving
Enterprising
Dynamic
Activity Oriented
Principled
Organized
Conforming
Meticulous
Reliable
Accepting
Involving
Attentive
Receptive
Change Oriented
Positive
Resolving
Composed
Self-assured
Empowering
Directing
Purposeful
Challenging
Articulate
Convincing
Self-promoting
Engaging
Interactive
Strategic
Abstract
Inventive
Insightful
Practically Minded
Learning Oriented
Rational
Factual
Analytical

17.6 Gender Trends UK - Sten Profile

Gender Trends UK - Sten Profile (N=10,783)

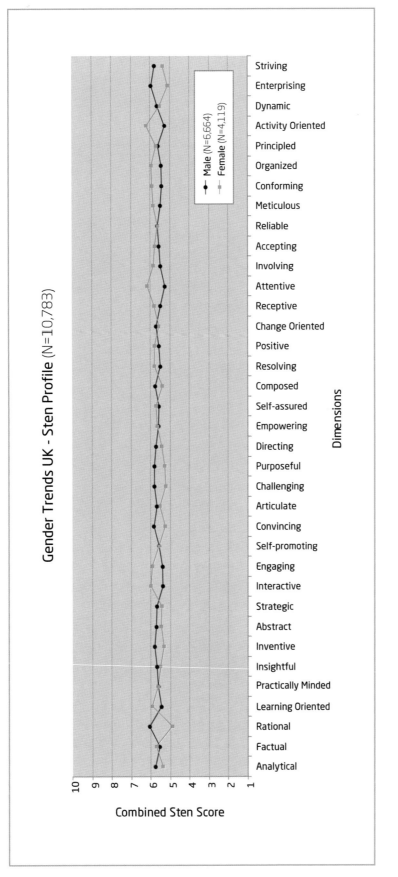

Mean scores for male individuals (N=6,664) were compared to mean scores for female individuals (N=4,119). 35 of the 36 dimensions showed no appreciable mean differences between men and women. The one dimension where a moderate difference was observed be·ween men and women was *Rational*, with men rating themselves higher than women. No large differences were found.

17.7 Gender Trends UK - Alpha

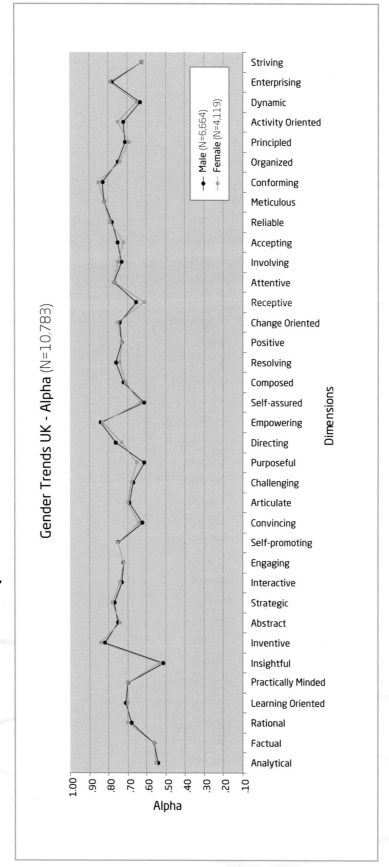

Gender Trends UK - Alpha (N=10,783)

Internal consistency reliabilities on the 36 dimensions for male individuals (N=6,664) were compared to those for female individuals (N=4,119).

With a mean alpha of .71 for both groups, differences in internal consistency reliabilities on the 36 dimensions were mostly found to be negligible.

17.8 Ethnic Background Trends UK

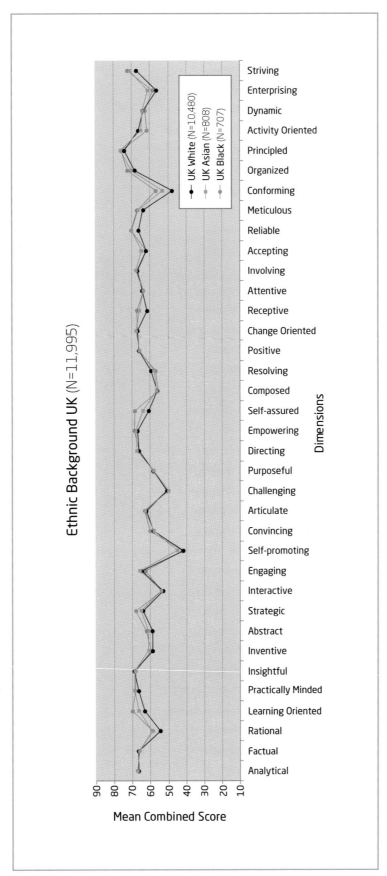

Ethnic Background UK (N=11,995)

17.9 Ethnic Background Trends UK – Sten Profile

Ethnic Background UK - Sten Profile (N=11,995)

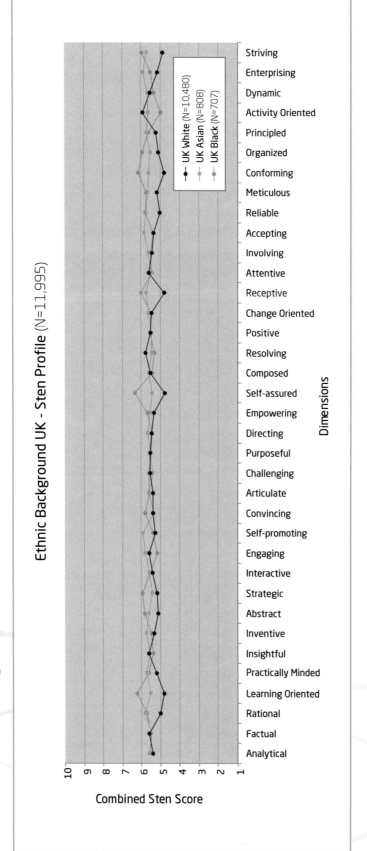

The White group (N=10,480) was compared to the Black (N=707) and Asian (N=808) groups in terms of their mean scores. On dimensions where there was a difference, it was more commonly found that the Black and Asian groups tended to rate themselves a little higher than the White group. Given that the evidence does not favor Black and Asian groups outperforming white groups in job performance, this provides support that Wave would not give a biased underestimate of Black and Asian individuals' likely performance and potential.

In particular, it was found that 30 of the 36 dimensions displayed no notable mean differences between the three ethnic subgroups. Five dimensions (*Learning Oriented, Self-assured, Receptive, Conforming and Striving*) showed a difference of 1 Sten or more, with the Black group rating themselves higher than the White group. On *Activity Oriented*, the Black group achieved a lower mean Sten than the White and Asian groups (difference is just below 1 Sten).

Note: Due to the large differences of sample sizes for these groups, the groups were weighted to be of equal size.

17.10 Ethnic Background Trends UK - Alpha

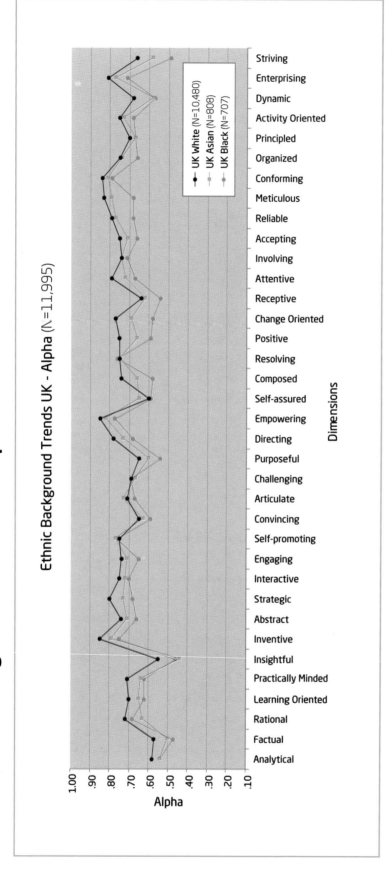

Ethnic Background Trends UK - Alpha (N=11,995)

The White group (N=10,480) was compared to the Black (N=707) and Asian (N=808) groups in terms of the 36 dimensions' Cronbach's alphas.

Generally, internal consistency reliability was highest for the White group (mean of .73, highest on 32 of the 36 dimensions). The Asian group tended to have the next highest reliabilities on most dimensions and the Black group slightly lower overall as a general trend. On Three of the 36 dimensions (Self-promoting, Articulate, Self-assured), a higher internal consistency was found for the Asian group than for the White and Black groups; on the dimension Resolving, the Black group had a very similar alpha to the White and Asian groups (.01 higher).

17.11 Age Trends US

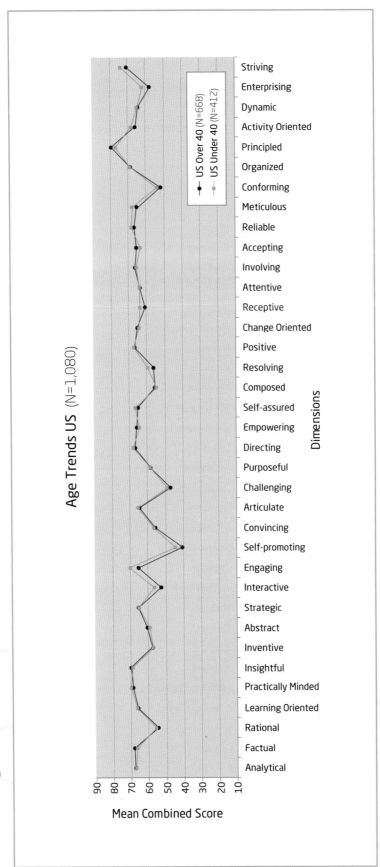

Age Trends US (N=1,080)

Dimensions

Mean Combined Score

Legend: US Over 40 (N=668), US Under 40 (N=412)

Dimensions (top to bottom): Striving, Enterprising, Dynamic, Activity Oriented, Principled, Organized, Conforming, Meticulous, Reliable, Accepting, Involving, Attentive, Receptive, Change Oriented, Positive, Resolving, Composed, Self-assured, Empowering, Directing, Purposeful, Challenging, Articulate, Convincing, Self-promoting, Engaging, Interactive, Strategic, Abstract, Inventive, Insightful, Practically Minded, Learning Oriented, Rational, Factual, Analytical

17.12 Age Trends US - Sten Profile

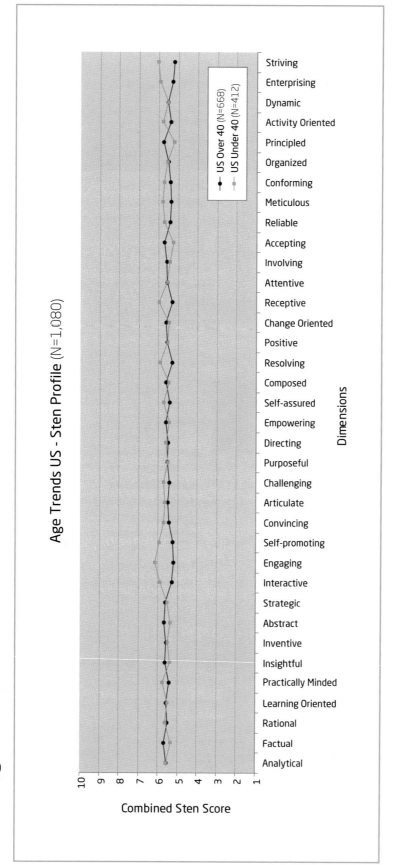

Age Trends US - Sten Profile (N=1,080)

No group trends are greater than one Sten.

The most notable group difference for age group is on *Engaging*, with the 'Under 40' age group reporting, on average, scores of .92 of a Sten (.46 of an SD) higher than the 'Over 40' age group. The other dimensions which show smaller group trends for age group are *Self-promoting* (.66 of a Sten) and *Striving* (.76 of a Sten), both of which show higher mean scores on average for the 'Under 40' group. All other age group trends by dimension are well below .66 of a Sten.

17.13 Gender Trends US

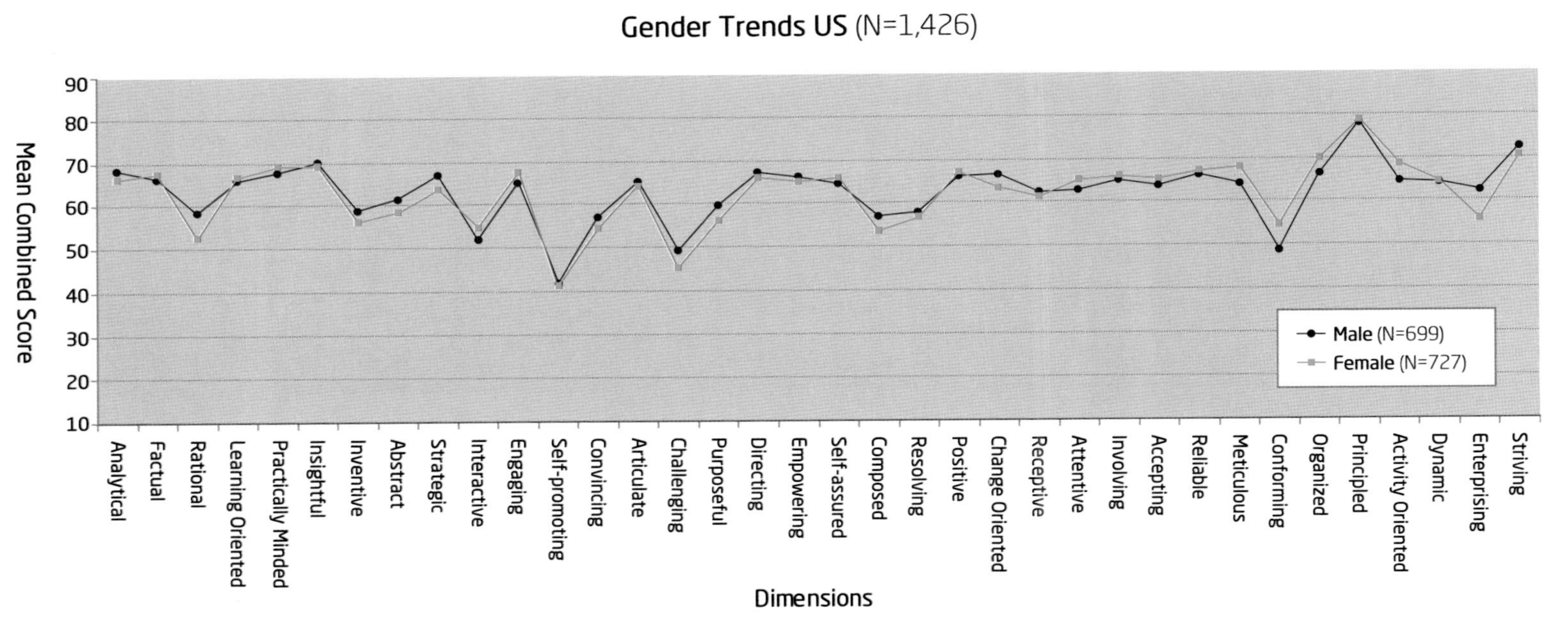

Gender Trends US (N=1,426)
Mean Combined Score
90
80
70
60
50
40
30
20
10
Male (N=699)
Female (N=727)
Analytical
Factual
Rational
Learning Oriented
Practically Minded
Insightful
Inventive
Abstract
Strategic
Interactive
Engaging
Self-promoting
Convincing
Articulate
Challenging
Purposeful
Directing
Empowering
Self-assured
Composed
Resolving
Positive
Change Oriented
Receptive
Attentive
Involving
Accepting
Reliable
Meticulous
Conforming
Organized
Principled
Activity Oriented
Dynamic
Enterprising
Striving
Dimensions

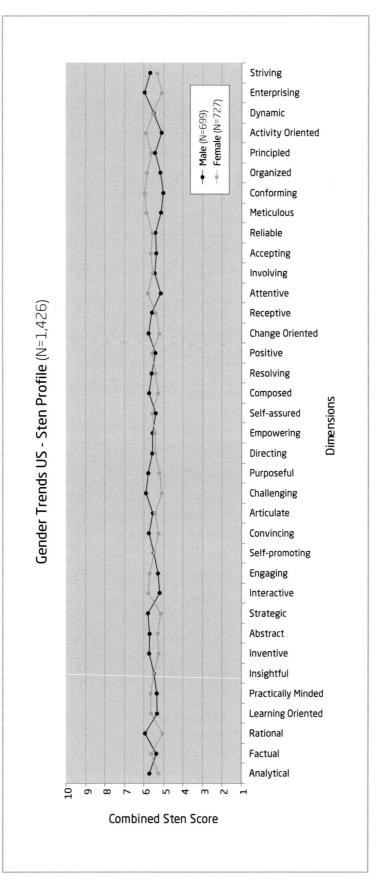

17.14 Gender Trends US – Sten Profile

No group trends are greater than one Sten.

The greatest group trends are on the dimensions *Conforming, Rational* and *Enterprising*. On *Rational* and *Enterprising* males demonstrate, on average, .90 of a Sten (.45 of an SD) higher than females, whereas females give .92 of a Sten higher than males on *Conforming*. Females also report notably higher combined scores than males on *Activity Oriented* (.84 of a Sten), *Meticulous* (.74 of a Sten) and *Organized* (.68 of a Sten). Males report higher combined scores than females on the dimension *Challenging* (.70 of a Sten). All other gender trends by dimension are below .66 of a Sten.

17.15 Ethnicity Trends US

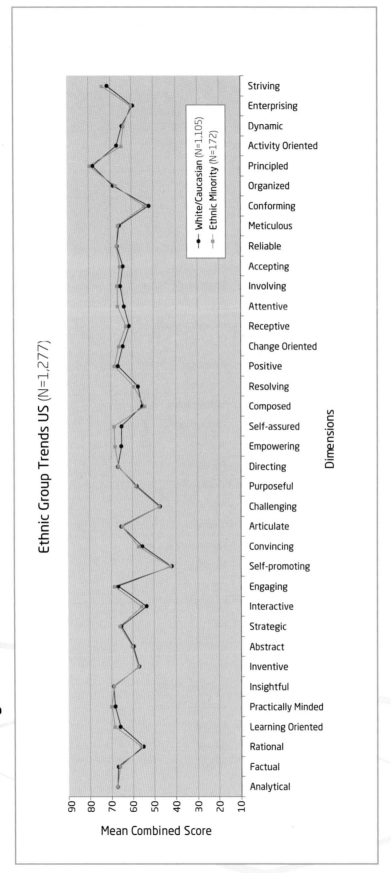

Ethnic Group Trends US (N=1,277)

Dimensions

Striving
Enterprising
Dynamic
Activity Oriented
Principled
Organized
Conforming
Meticulous
Reliable
Accepting
Involving
Attentive
Receptive
Change Oriented
Positive
Resolving
Composed
Self-assured
Empowering
Directing
Purposeful
Challenging
Articulate
Convincing
Self-promoting
Engaging
Interactive
Strategic
Abstract
Inventive
Insightful
Practically Minded
Learning Oriented
Rational
Factual
Analytical

Mean Combined Score

90 80 70 60 50 40 30 20 10

Legend:
— White/Caucasian (N=1,105)
— Ethnic Minority (N=172)

N.B. For the purposes of the analysis, because of small sample sizes, those from ethnic groups other than White/Caucasian were included as one group in the analysis. For a full breakdown of Ethnic Group in this sample, please refer to Table 17.1.

17.16 Ethnicity Trends US – Sten Profile

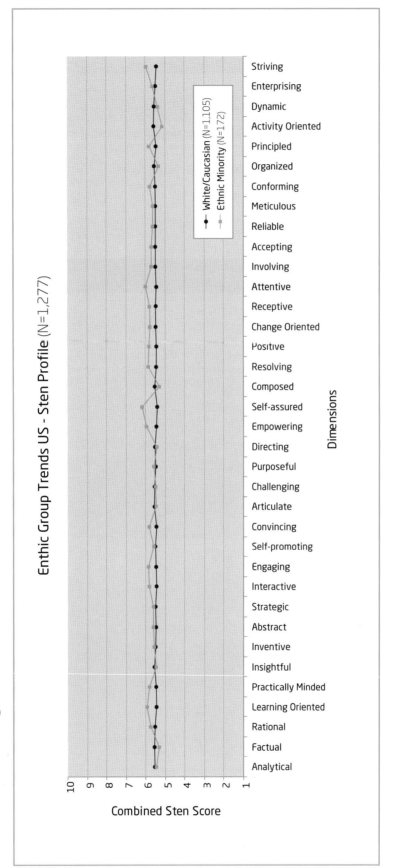

Ethnic Group Trends US – Sten Profile (N=1,277)

No group trends are greater than one Sten.

The largest difference is on *Self-assured* (.76 of a Sten/.38 SD difference), where the Ethnic Minority group scored, on average, .76 of a Sten higher than the White/Caucasian group. All other ethnic group trends by dimension are well below .66 of a Sten.

431

Table 17.1 Breakdown of Ethnic Group in US sample (N=1,277)

Ethnic Group Composition	N	%
Asian/Pacific Islander	37	3%
Black/African American	57	4%
Hispanic	71	6%
Native American/Alaskan Native	4	0%
Other	3	0%
White/Caucasian	1,105	87%
Total	**1,277**	**100%**

17.17 Group Trends - Occupational Levels of Management Responsibility

International Trends for Wave Professional Styles (IA)

Comparing Levels of Management Responsibility: Senior Managers & Executives (N=5,826) vs. Professionals & Managers (N=14,333) vs. Mixed Occupational Group (N=16,191) vs. Graduates (N=6,129)

Observations made here are based on data gathered internationally (including UK, US, Bulgaria, Germany, Australia, South Africa, Spain, Mexico, France, Brazil, Canada, Denmark, Netherlands, Italy and Sweden) and refer to the 36 Wave Professional Styles dimensions. The data is representative of actual usage data of Wave Professional Styles.

Mean scores of the 36 dimensions for four groups of varying levels of management responsibility (Senior Managers & Executives (N=5,826) vs. Professionals & Managers (N=14,333) vs. Mixed Occupational Group (N=16,191) vs. Graduates (N=6,129)) were compared. Differences have been calculated in terms of standardized effect sizes of the means (Cohen's d), whereby a small difference equals an effect size of $d=.20$, a medium difference equals an effect size of $d=.50$ and a large difference equals an effect size of $d=.80$ (Cohen, 1988). The majority of the observed differences between the four groups' means ranged from non-existent to small. A few were classified as small to medium ($d=.21-.50$); general trends are listed as follows on page 435.

17.18 Group Trends

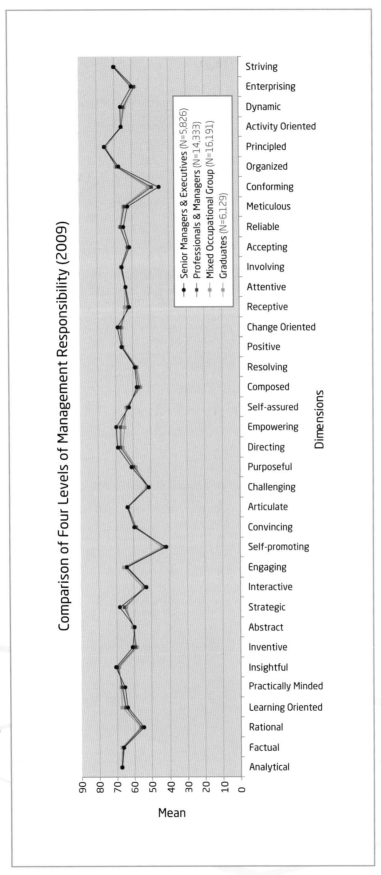

Comparison of Four Levels of Management Responsibility (2009)

- The majority of small to medium effect sizes were found when comparing the Senior Managers & Executives group to the group of Graduates. In particular, those two groups differed on the 12 dimensions *Learning Oriented, Practically Minded, Insightful, Strategic, Purposeful, Directing, Empowering, Change Oriented, Receptive, Meticulous, Conforming* and *Dynamic*. Senior Managers & Executives had higher means on *Insightful, Strategic, Purposeful, Directing, Empowering, Change Oriented* and *Dynamic*. Graduates were higher on *Learning Oriented, Practically Minded, Receptive, Meticulous* and *Conforming*.

  These results are backed up by previous research by Saville Consulting that found higher ratings on the dimensions *Strategic, Purposeful, Directing* and *Empowering* to be associated with higher levels of management responsibility.

- Overall, it was found that for most dimensions, either the Senior Managers & Executives group or the group of Graduates rated themselves higher than the other groups. Only for a few dimensions was this not the case: On *Involving, Accepting, Reliable, Organized* and *Principled*, the Mixed Occupational group had the highest means – but please be aware that effect sizes here were very small.

- The Mixed Occupational group was found to be very similar to the Professionals & Managers group as well as to the group of Graduates, with effect sizes mostly ranging around *d*=.00.

435

17.19 UK Management Responsibility Mean Scores

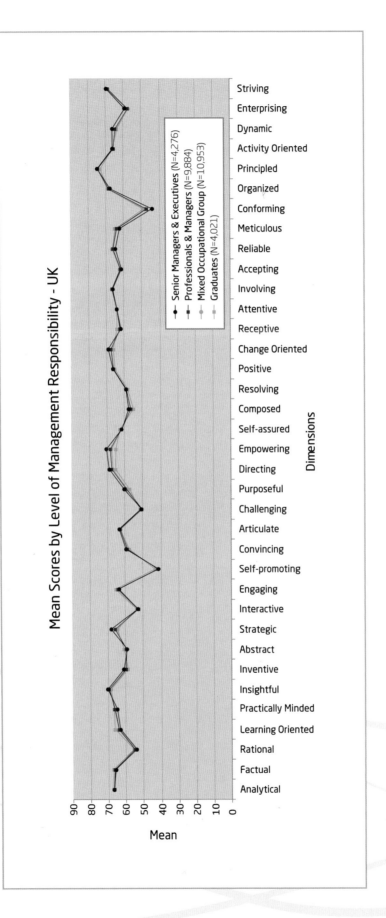

Mean Scores by Level of Management Responsibility - UK

Table 17.2 Level of Management Responsibility Differences - UK Alpha

Dimensions	Senior Managers & Executives (N=4,276)	Professionals & Managers (N=9,884)	Mixed Occupational Group (N=10,953)	Graduates (N=4,021)
Analytical	.56	.55	.55	.56
Factual	.57	.56	.56	.56
Rational	.71	.71	.71	.71
Learning Oriented	.70	.71	.71	.67
Practically Minded	.71	.70	.70	.69
Insightful	.52	.51	.52	.53
Inventive	.84	.83	.83	.84
Abstract	.75	.75	.74	.74
Strategic	.77	.77	.77	.75
Interactive	.74	.74	.74	.75
Engaging	.72	.72	.73	.74
Self-promoting	.76	.75	.75	.75
Convincing	.63	.63	.63	.65
Articulate	.68	.69	.69	.70
Challenging	.68	.67	.68	.71
Purposeful	.61	.63	.63	.65
Directing	.70	.74	.75	.76
Empowering	.82	.83	.84	.83
Self-assured	.61	.61	.62	.62
Composed	.73	.72	.71	.71
Resolving	.73	.75	.75	.75
Positive	.75	.73	.73	.73
Change Oriented	.75	.74	.74	.74
Receptive	.64	.64	.64	.63
Attentive	.78	.78	.78	.79
Involving	.74	.74	.74	.75
Accepting	.74	.74	.74	.74
Reliable	.78	.78	.79	.79
Meticulous	.83	.82	.82	.82
Conforming	.83	.84	.84	.84
Organized	.75	.75	.75	.76
Principled	.71	.71	.70	.72
Activity Oriented	.72	.73	.74	.74
Dynamic	.65	.64	.64	.63
Enterprising	.79	.79	.79	.79
Striving	.61	.62	.63	.64
Mean	.71	.71	.71	.72
Median	.72	.73	.74	.74
Min	.52	.51	.52	.53
Max	.84	.84	.84	.84

17.20 UK Management Responsibility - Alpha

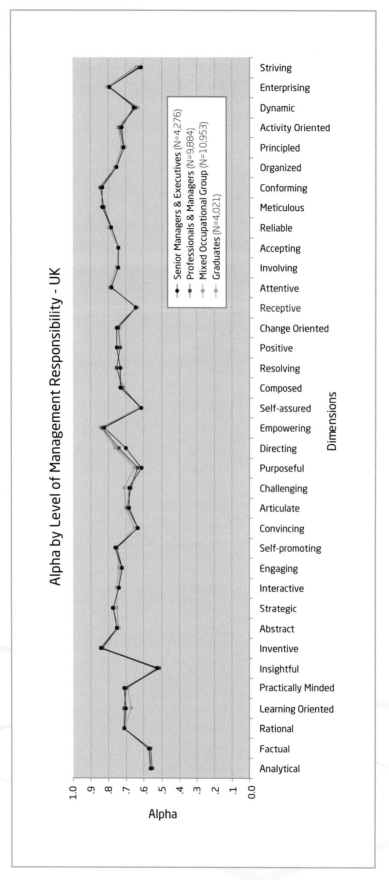

Alpha by Level of Management Responsibility - UK

17.21 US Management Responsibility Mean Scores

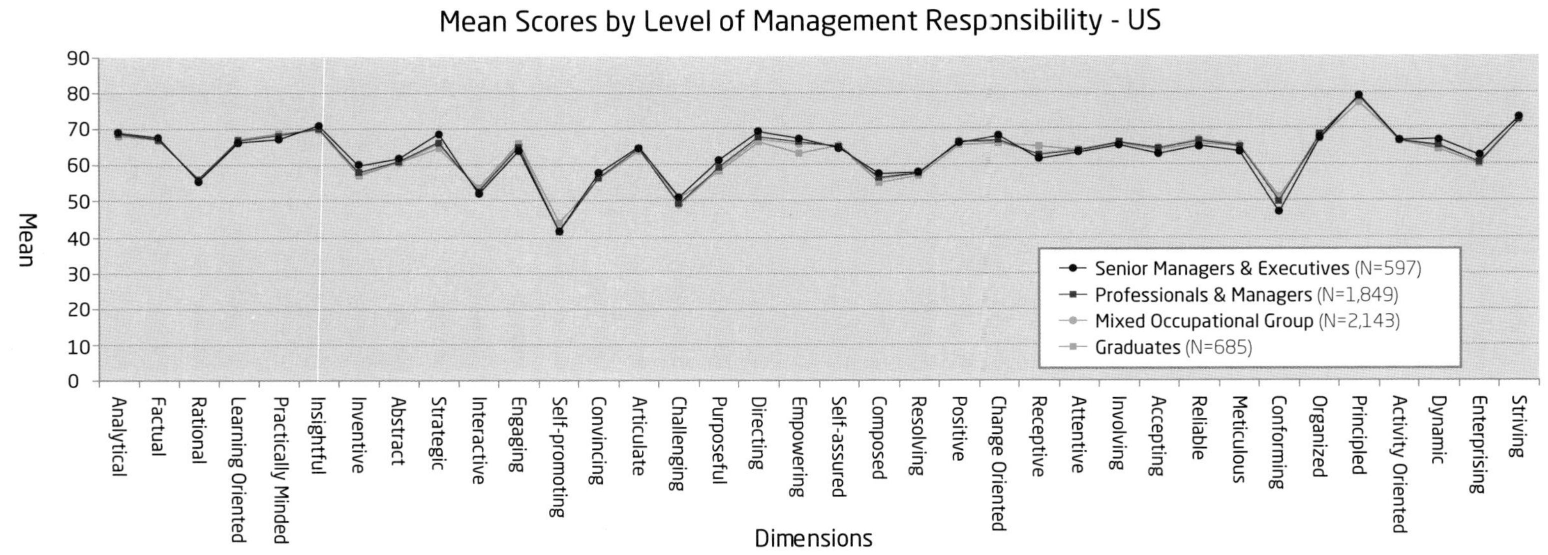

Mean Scores by Level of Management Responsibility - US
Mean
90
80
70
60
50
40
30
20
10
0
Analytical
Factual
Rational
Learning Oriented
Practically Minded
Insightful
Inventive
Abstract
Strategic
Interactive
Engaging
Self-promoting
Convincing
Articulate
Challenging
Purposeful
Directing
Empowering
Self-assured
Composed
Resolving
Positive
Change Oriented
Receptive
Attentive
Involving
Accepting
Reliable
Meticulous
Conforming
Organized
Principled
Activity Oriented
Dynamic
Enterprising
Striving
Dimensions
Senior Managers & Executives (N=597)
Professionals & Managers (N=1,849)
Mixed Occupational Group (N=2,143)
Graduates (N=685)

Table 17.3 Level of Management Responsibility Differences - US Alpha

Dimensions	Senior Managers & Executives (N=597)	Professionals & Managers (N=1,849)	Mixed Occupational Group (N=2,143)	Graduates (N=685)
Analytical	.52	.56	.57	.62
Factual	.60	.59	.59	.60
Rational	.68	.68	.69	.72
Learning Oriented	.71	.71	.71	.74
Practically Minded	.65	.64	.64	.63
Insightful	.46	.50	.52	.57
Inventive	.78	.80	.81	.82
Abstract	.77	.75	.76	.77
Strategic	.72	.72	.72	.73
Interactive	.74	.75	.75	.78
Engaging	.73	.76	.76	.78
Self-promoting	.77	.77	.79	.80
Convincing	.63	.63	.64	.63
Articulate	.68	.70	.71	.67
Challenging	.71	.73	.74	.75
Purposeful	.65	.63	.63	.64
Directing	.69	.71	.73	.75
Empowering	.82	.82	.82	.81
Self-assured	.57	.54	.55	.59
Composed	.70	.72	.72	.74
Resolving	.77	.76	.76	.76
Positive	.72	.71	.72	.73
Change Oriented	.72	.74	.75	.76
Receptive	.60	.62	.62	.62
Attentive	.80	.77	.77	.79
Involving	.79	.76	.76	.73
Accepting	.79	.74	.73	.72
Reliable	.78	.79	.79	.79
Meticulous	.83	.81	.81	.80
Conforming	.80	.81	.82	.84
Organized	.75	.75	.75	.78
Principled	.69	.68	.70	.71
Activity Oriented	.76	.76	.77	.76
Dynamic	.63	.65	.65	.65
Enterprising	.79	.81	.82	.83
Striving	.63	.59	.61	.60
Mean	.71	.71	.71	.72
Median	.72	.72	.73	.74
Min	.46	.50	.52	.57
Max	.83	.82	.82	.84

17.22 US Management Responsibility - Alpha

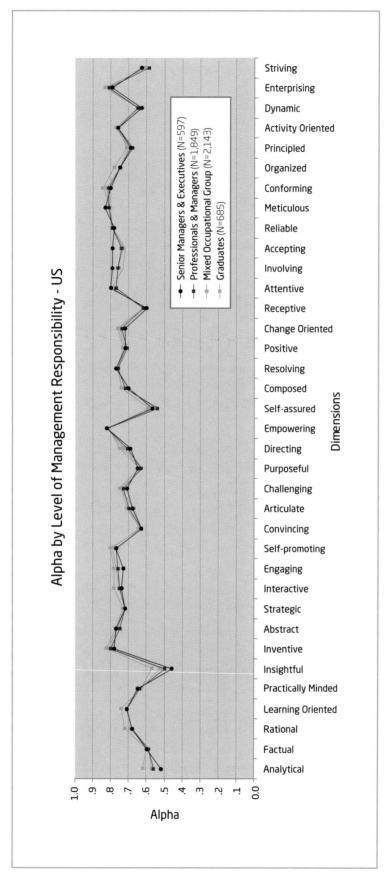

Alpha by Level of Management Responsibility - US

Dimensions

Striving
Enterprising
Dynamic
Activity Oriented
Principled
Organized
Conforming
Meticulous
Reliable
Accepting
Involving
Attentive
Receptive
Change Oriented
Positive
Resolving
Composed
Self-assured
Empowering
Directing
Purposeful
Challenging
Articulate
Convincing
Self-promoting
Engaging
Interactive
Strategic
Abstract
Inventive
Insightful
Practically Minded
Learning Oriented
Rational
Factual
Analytical

Alpha

1.0 .9 .8 .7 .6 .5 .4 .3 .2 .1 0.0

Senior Managers & Executives (N=597)
Professionals & Managers (N=1,849)
Mixed Occupational Group (N=2,143)
Graduates (N=685)

17.23 International Management Responsibility Mean Scores

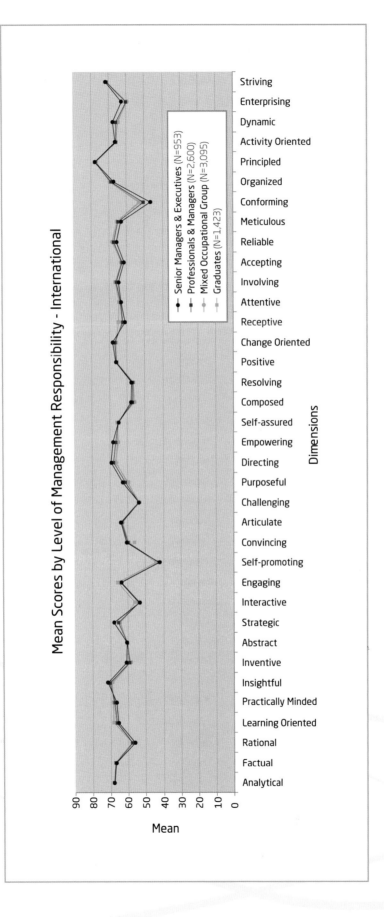

Mean Scores by Level of Management Responsibility - International

Dimensions

Striving
Enterprising
Dynamic
Activity Oriented
Principled
Organized
Conforming
Meticulous
Reliable
Accepting
Involving
Attentive
Receptive
Change Oriented
Positive
Resolving
Composed
Self-assured
Empowering
Directing
Purposeful
Challenging
Articulate
Convincing
Self-promoting
Engaging
Interactive
Strategic
Abstract
Inventive
Insightful
Practically Minded
Learning Oriented
Rational
Factual
Analytical

Mean

Senior Managers & Executives (N=953)
Professionals & Managers (N=2,600)
Mixed Occupational Group (N=3,095)
Graduates (N=1,423)

Table 17.4 Level of Management Responsibility Differences - International Alpha

Dimensions	Senior Managers & Executives (N=953)	Professionals & Managers (N=2,600)	Mixed Occupational Group (N=3,095)	Graduates (N=1,423)
Analytical	.53	.52	.53	.54
Factual	.54	.55	.54	.51
Rational	.71	.71	.71	.74
Learning Oriented	.72	.70	.70	.70
Practically Minded	.67	.64	.65	.65
Insightful	.53	.50	.53	.52
Inventive	.80	.79	.79	.79
Abstract	.74	.71	.70	.70
Strategic	.72	.72	.72	.71
Interactive	.74	.75	.75	.75
Engaging	.72	.73	.72	.74
Self-promoting	.77	.75	.76	.78
Convincing	.63	.65	.66	.66
Articulate	.65	.68	.69	.70
Challenging	.69	.69	.69	.67
Purposeful	.63	.64	.63	.61
Directing	.71	.73	.76	.74
Empowering	.82	.82	.83	.82
Self-assured	.60	.58	.60	.62
Composed	.67	.68	.68	.68
Resolving	.74	.72	.73	.73
Positive	.66	.68	.67	.69
Change Oriented	.71	.73	.72	.71
Receptive	.59	.61	.60	.61
Attentive	.79	.77	.76	.77
Involving	.75	.74	.73	.73
Accepting	.74	.72	.71	.68
Reliable	.78	.79	.79	.80
Meticulous	.81	.79	.79	.79
Conforming	.82	.82	.82	.83
Organized	.76	.74	.74	.75
Principled	.70	.67	.68	.67
Activity Oriented	.75	.76	.75	.73
Dynamic	.63	.64	.64	.63
Enterprising	.77	.80	.80	.80
Striving	.59	.59	.60	.59
Mean	.70	.70	.70	.70
Median	.71	.71	.71	.71
Min	.53	.50	.53	.51
Max	.82	.82	.83	.83

© 2009 Saville Consulting. All rights reserved. Version 1.0.

17.24 International Management Responsibility - Alpha

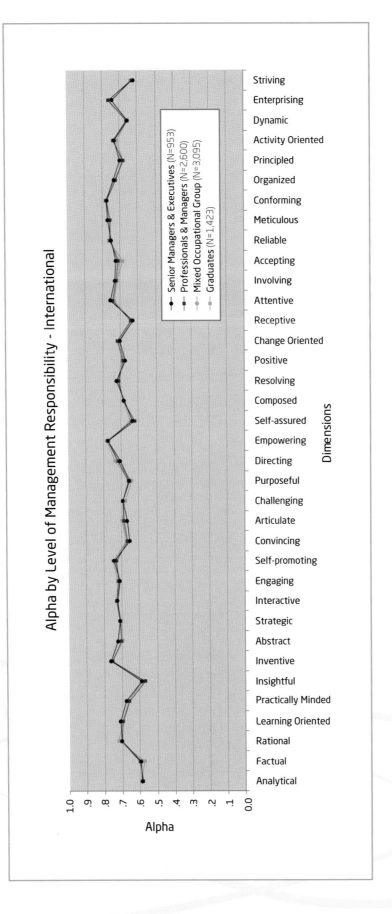

Alpha by Level of Management Responsibility - International

444

17.25 International Trends - Occupational Levels for Regions

International Trends for Wave Professional Styles (IA)

Comparing Regions: UK (N=29,143) vs. US (N=5,274) vs. International (N=8,071) completions

Observations made here are based on data gathered internationally (including UK, US, Bulgaria, Germany, Australia, South Africa, Spain, Mexico, France, Brazil, Canada, Denmark, Netherlands, Italy and Sweden) and refer to the 36 Wave Professional Styles dimensions. The data is representative of actual usage data of Wave Professional Styles.

Mean scores of the 36 dimensions for three regional groups (UK (N=29,143) vs. US (N=5,274) vs. International (N=8,071)) were compared. Differences have been calculated in terms of standardized effect sizes of the means (Cohen's d), whereby a small difference equals an effect size of $d=.20$, a medium difference equals an effect size of $d=.50$ and a large difference equals an effect size of $d=.80$ (Cohen, 1988). The majority of the observed differences between the three groups' means ranged from non-existent to small. A few were classified as small to medium see over page.

17.26 International Trends

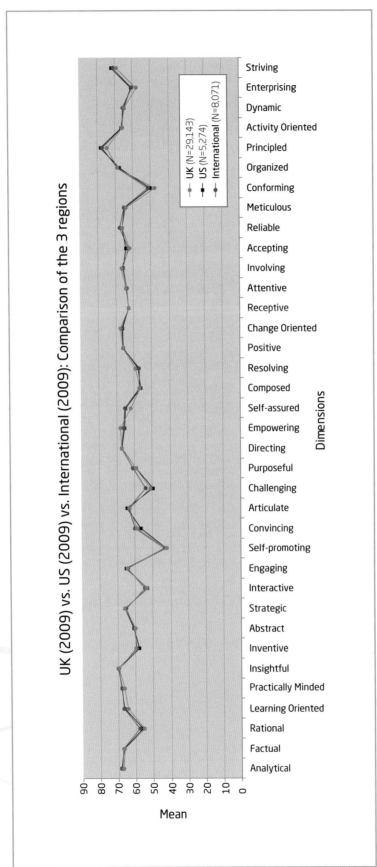

UK (2009) vs. US (2009) vs. International (2009): Comparison of the 3 regions

- UK vs. US: For 7 out of 36 dimensions, small to medium effect sizes of the means (d=.21-.50) were observed: *Learning Oriented, Convincing, Empowering, Self-assured, Principled, Enterprising* and *Striving*. The UK group had higher means on *Convincing* and *Empowering*. The US group was higher on *Learning Oriented, Self-assured, Principled, Enterprising* and *Striving*.

- UK vs. International: Small to medium effect sizes of the means were observed for 8 dimensions: *Rational, Learning Oriented, Challenging, Self-assured, Resolving, Conforming, Principled* and *Striving*. The UK group showed a higher mean on 1 dimension only, Resolving. The International group was higher on *Rational, Learning Oriented, Challenging, Self-assured, Conforming, Principled* and *Striving*.

- US vs. International: Small to medium effect sizes were observed merely for 2 dimensions, namely *Convincing* and *Challenging*, where the International group was higher than the US group.

In summary, it was observed that for the majority of dimensions where a difference in means was found, the UK group had rated themselves lower than the US and International groups. There was also a slight trend for the International group to have higher dimension means than the other two groups, although most of the differences found were very small. Please bear in mind that any regional subgroup variances observed here could also partly reflect the influence of factors such as age, gender, ethnicity, occupation and seniority (tenure).

17.27 Senior Managers & Executives by Region Mean Scores

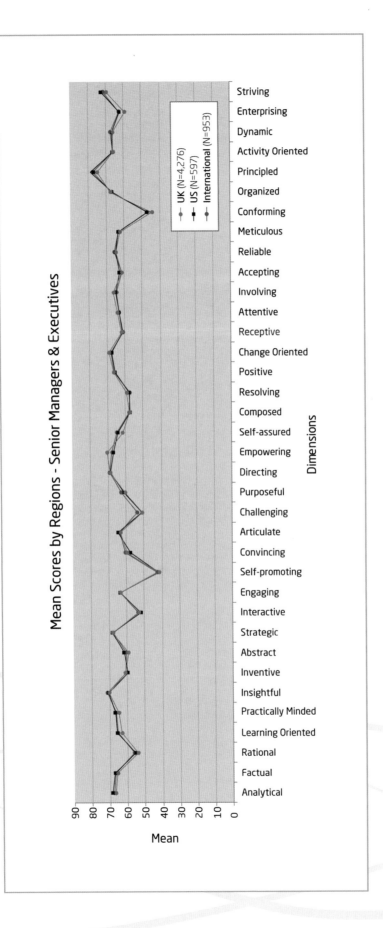

Mean Scores by Regions - Senior Managers & Executives

UK (N=4,276)
US (N=597)
International (N=953)

Dimensions: Striving, Enterprising, Dynamic, Activity Oriented, Principled, Organized, Conforming, Meticulous, Reliable, Accepting, Involving, Attentive, Receptive, Change Oriented, Positive, Resolving, Composed, Self-assured, Empowering, Directing, Purposeful, Challenging, Articulate, Convincing, Self-promoting, Engaging, Interactive, Strategic, Abstract, Inventive, Insightful, Practically Minded, Learning Oriented, Rational, Factual, Analytical

Mean

Table 17.5 Regional Differences - Senior Managers & Executives - Alpha

Dimensions	UK (N=4,276)	US (N=597)	International (N=953)
Analytical	.56	.52	.53
Factual	.57	.60	.54
Rational	.71	.68	.71
Learning Oriented	.70	.71	.72
Practically Minded	.71	.65	.67
Insightful	.52	.46	.53
Inventive	.84	.78	.80
Abstract	.75	.77	.74
Strategic	.77	.72	.72
Interactive	.74	.74	.74
Engaging	.72	.73	.72
Self-promoting	.76	.77	.77
Convincing	.63	.63	.63
Articulate	.68	.68	.65
Challenging	.68	.71	.69
Purposeful	.61	.65	.63
Directing	.70	.69	.71
Empowering	.82	.82	.82
Self-assured	.61	.57	.60
Composed	.73	.70	.67
Resolving	.73	.77	.74
Positive	.75	.72	.66
Change Oriented	.75	.72	.71
Receptive	.64	.60	.59
Attentive	.78	.80	.79
Involving	.74	.79	.75
Accepting	.74	.79	.74
Reliable	.78	.78	.78
Meticulous	.83	.83	.81
Conforming	.83	.80	.82
Organized	.75	.75	.76
Principled	.71	.69	.70
Activity Oriented	.72	.76	.75
Dynamic	.65	.63	.63
Enterprising	.79	.79	.77
Striving	.61	.63	.59
Mean	.71	.71	.70
Median	.72	.72	.71
Min	.52	.46	.53
Max	.84	.83	.82

17.28 Senior Managers & Executives by Region - Alpha

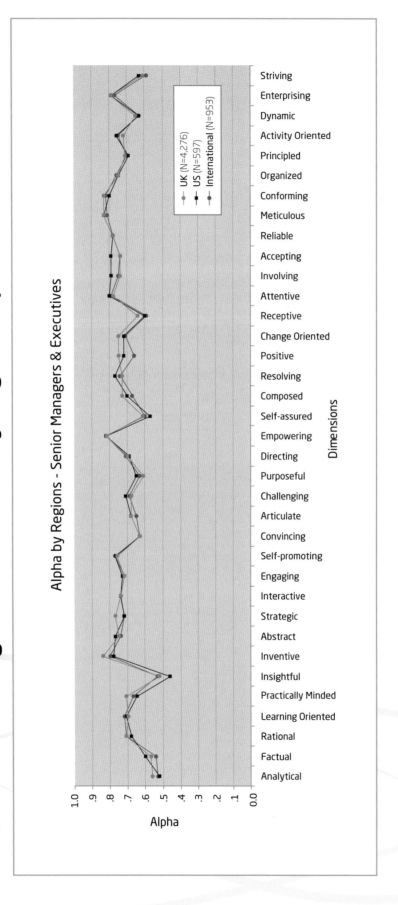

Alpha by Regions - Senior Managers & Executives

17.29 Professionals & Managers by Region Mean Scores

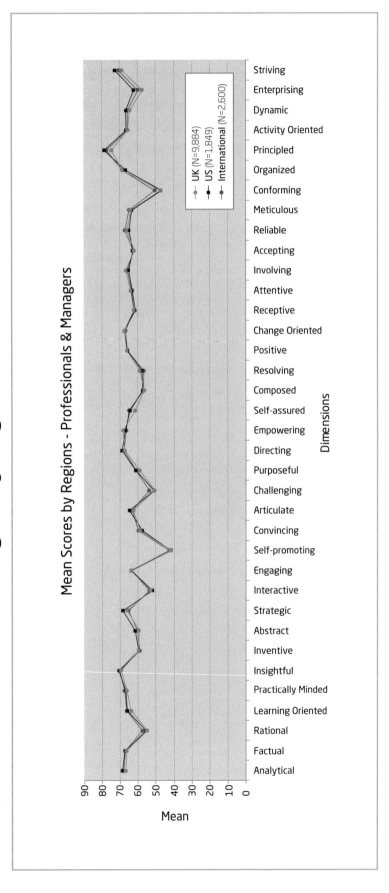

Table 17.6 Regional Differences - Professionals & Managers - Alpha

Dimensions	UK (N=9,884)	US (N=1,849)	International (N=2,600)
Analytical	.55	.56	.52
Factual	.56	.59	.55
Rational	.71	.68	.71
Learning Oriented	.71	.71	.70
Practically Minded	.70	.64	.64
Insightful	.51	.50	.50
Inventive	.83	.80	.79
Abstract	.75	.75	.71
Strategic	.77	.72	.72
Interactive	.74	.75	.75
Engaging	.72	.76	.73
Self-promoting	.75	.77	.75
Convincing	.63	.63	.65
Articulate	.69	.70	.68
Challenging	.67	.73	.69
Purposeful	.63	.63	.64
Directing	.74	.71	.73
Empowering	.83	.82	.82
Self-assured	.61	.54	.58
Composed	.72	.72	.68
Resolving	.75	.76	.72
Positive	.73	.71	.68
Change Oriented	.74	.74	.73
Receptive	.64	.62	.61
Attentive	.78	.77	.77
Involving	.74	.76	.74
Accepting	.74	.74	.72
Reliable	.78	.79	.79
Meticulous	.82	.81	.79
Conforming	.84	.81	.82
Organized	.75	.75	.74
Principled	.71	.68	.67
Activity Oriented	.73	.76	.76
Dynamic	.64	.65	.64
Enterprising	.79	.81	.80
Striving	.62	.59	.59
Mean	.71	.71	.70
Median	.73	.72	.71
Min	.51	.50	.50
Max	.84	.82	.82

17.30 Professionals & Managers by Region - Alpha

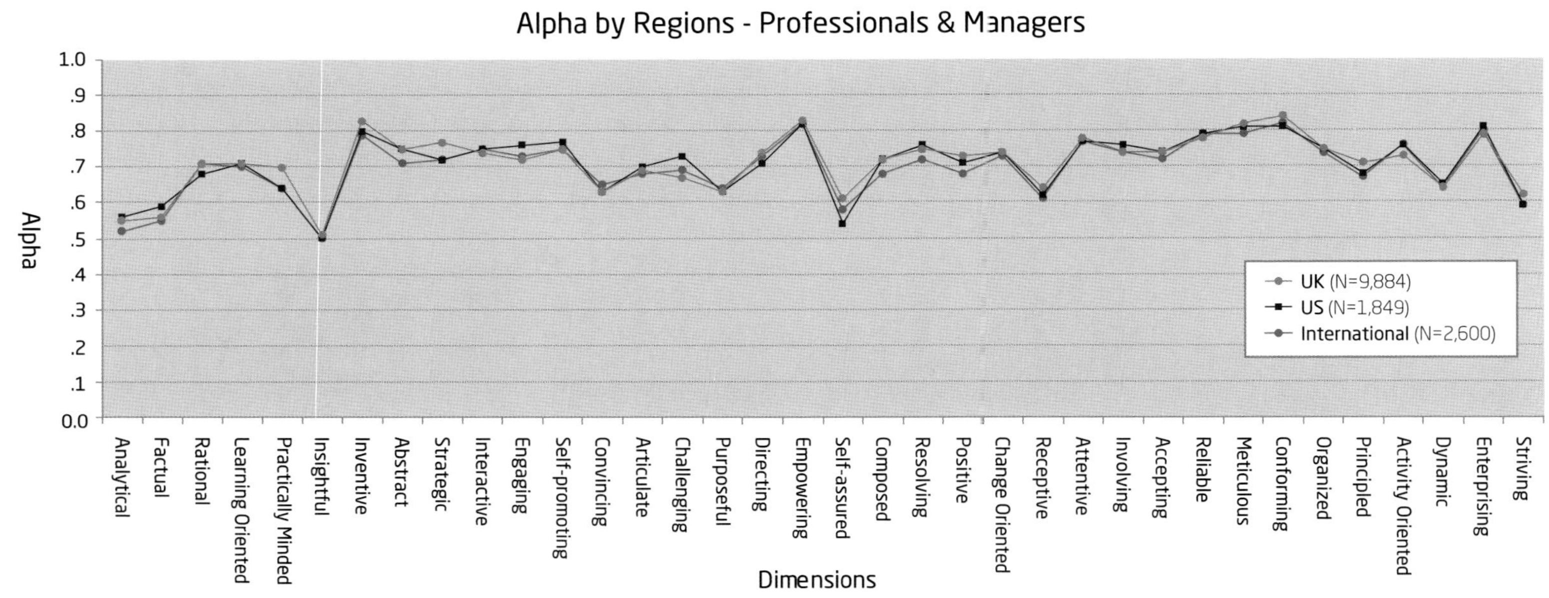
Alpha by Regions - Professionals & Managers
Alpha
1.0
.9
.8
.7
.6
.5
.4
.3
.2
.1
0.0
Analytical
Factual
Rational
Learning Oriented
Practically Minded
Insightful
Inventive
Abstract
Strategic
Interactive
Engaging
Self-promoting
Convincing
Articulate
Challenging
Purposeful
Directing
Empowering
Self-assured
Composed
Resolving
Positive
Change Oriented
Receptive
Attentive
Involving
Accepting
Reliable
Meticulous
Conforming
Organized
Principled
Activity Oriented
Dynamic
Enterprising
Striving
Dimensions
UK (N=9,884)
US (N=1,849)
International (N=2,600)

17.31 Mixed Occupational Group by Region Mean Scores

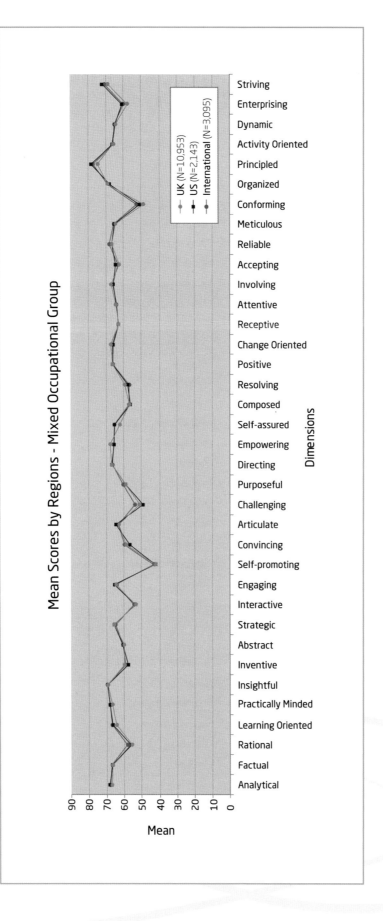

Mean Scores by Regions - Mixed Occupational Group

Table 17.7 Regional Differences - Mixed Occupational Group - Alpha

Dimensions	UK (N=10,953)	US (N=2,143)	International (N=3,095)
Analytical	.55	.57	.53
Factual	.56	.59	.54
Rational	.71	.69	.71
Learning Oriented	.71	.71	.70
Practically Minded	.70	.64	.65
Insightful	.52	.52	.53
Inventive	.83	.81	.79
Abstract	.74	.76	.70
Strategic	.77	.72	.72
Interactive	.74	.75	.75
Engaging	.73	.77	.72
Self-promoting	.75	.79	.76
Convincing	.63	.64	.66
Articulate	.69	.71	.69
Challenging	.68	.74	.69
Purposeful	.63	.63	.63
Directing	.75	.73	.76
Empowering	.84	.82	.83
Self-assured	.62	.55	.60
Composed	.71	.72	.68
Resolving	.75	.76	.73
Positive	.73	.72	.67
Change Oriented	.74	.75	.72
Receptive	.64	.62	.60
Attentive	.78	.77	.76
Involving	.74	.76	.73
Accepting	.74	.73	.71
Reliable	.79	.79	.79
Meticulous	.82	.81	.79
Conforming	.84	.82	.82
Organized	.75	.75	.74
Principled	.70	.70	.68
Activity Oriented	.74	.77	.75
Dynamic	.64	.65	.64
Enterprising	.80	.82	.80
Striving	.63	.61	.60
Mean	.71	.71	.70
Median	.74	.73	.71
Min	.52	.52	.53
Max	.84	.82	.83

17.32 Mixed Occupational Group by Region - Alpha

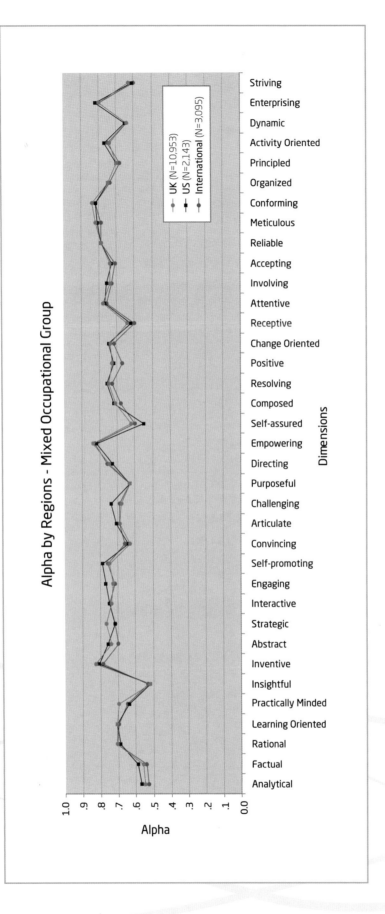

Alpha by Regions - Mixed Occupational Group

Legend:
UK (N=10,953)
US (N=2,143)
International (N=3,095)

Dimensions (top to bottom): Striving, Enterprising, Dynamic, Activity Oriented, Principled, Organized, Conforming, Meticulous, Reliable, Accepting, Involving, Attentive, Receptive, Change Oriented, Positive, Resolving, Composed, Self-assured, Empowering, Directing, Purposeful, Challenging, Articulate, Convincing, Self-promoting, Engaging, Interactive, Strategic, Abstract, Inventive, Insightful, Practically Minded, Learning Oriented, Rational, Factual, Analytical

Alpha axis: 0.0, .1, .2, .3, .4, .5, .6, .7, .8, .9, 1.0

17.33 Graduates by Region Mean Scores

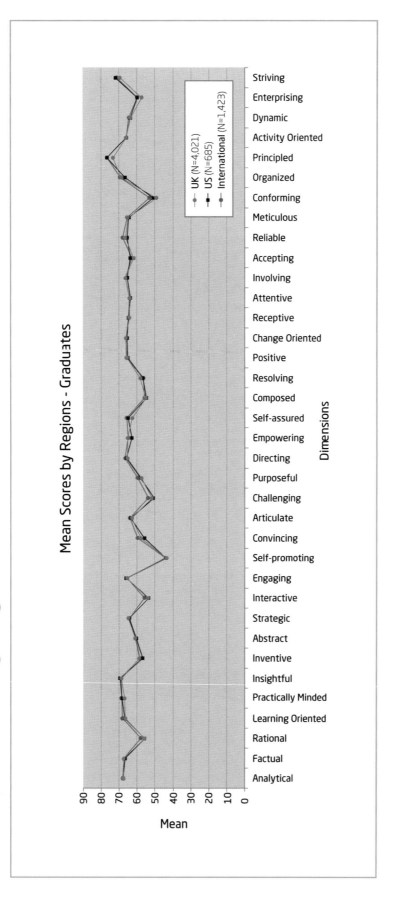

Table 17.8 Regional Differences - Graduates - Alpha

Dimensions	UK (N=4,021)	US (N=685)	International (N=1,423)
Analytical	.56	.62	.54
Factual	.56	.60	.51
Rational	.71	.72	.74
Learning Oriented	.67	.74	.70
Practically Minded	.69	.63	.65
Insightful	.53	.57	.52
Inventive	.84	.82	.79
Abstract	.74	.77	.70
Strategic	.75	.73	.71
Interactive	.75	.78	.75
Engaging	.74	.78	.74
Self-promoting	.75	.80	.78
Convincing	.65	.63	.66
Articulate	.70	.67	.70
Challenging	.71	.75	.67
Purposeful	.65	.64	.61
Directing	.76	.75	.74
Empowering	.83	.81	.82
Self-assured	.62	.59	.62
Composed	.71	.74	.68
Resolving	.75	.76	.73
Positive	.73	.73	.69
Change Oriented	.74	.76	.71
Receptive	.63	.62	.61
Attentive	.79	.79	.77
Involving	.75	.73	.73
Accepting	.74	.72	.68
Reliable	.79	.79	.80
Meticulous	.82	.80	.79
Conforming	.84	.84	.83
Organized	.76	.78	.75
Principled	.72	.71	.67
Activity Oriented	.74	.76	.73
Dynamic	.63	.65	.63
Enterprising	.80	.83	.80
Striving	.64	.60	.59
Mean	.72	.72	.70
Median	.74	.74	.71
Min	.53	.57	.51
Max	.84	.84	.83

458

17.34 Graduates by Region - Alpha

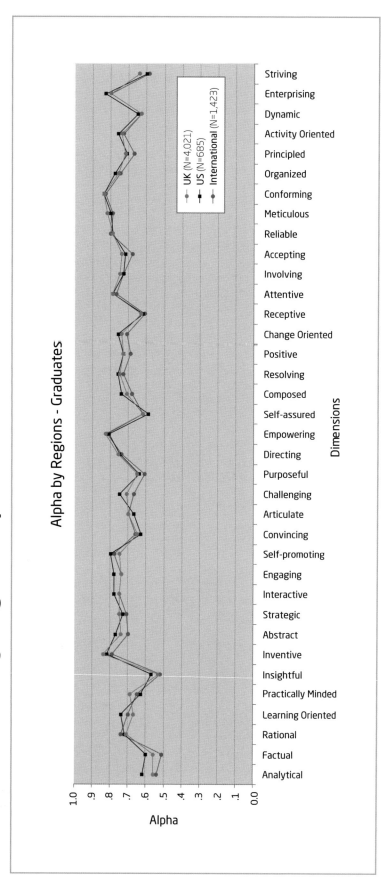

Alpha by Regions - Graduates

17.35 Fairness Summary

This chapter provides information on the fair application of Wave Professional Styles. To be applied fairly we give examples of appropriate and inappropriate uses of Wave in the Applications chapter. At the beginning of the chapter the key steps and features of Wave are highlighted that contribute to it being applied as a performance driven tool which can be used fairly for the selection and development of staff in the workplace.

The data presented on the differences between the means for different groups generally show no, small or moderate differences between groups. In each case, whether these differences are attributable to differences in the population means of these groups or are reflective of other variables is not readily discernable. However, some interesting observations can be drawn from the data.

The generally no appreciable or small differences of the size demonstrated here, do not justify treating age, gender or ethnic subgroups differently, and we do not as a result recommend using different separate norms for these age, gender or ethnic groups. On the contrary, they reinforce the case for using Wave Professional Styles fairly by using one group and consistent method for a particular job across age, gender and ethnicity. As a result no such norms are available on Oasys for these separate groups.

One notable difference in Ethnicity that has some consistency in appearing in US and UK minority groups is on Self-assured, where the minority groups are higher than the majority white group in both cases. This raises an interesting question as to whether, for example, the work and wider environment tends to make ethnic minorities become more Self-assured in the face of having to deal with more challenges.

The differences between age, gender and ethnicity are not such that we advise that they should impact on profile interpretation. On ethnicity in the UK, for example, the size and direction of the general trends make it unlikely that the scales of Wave Professional Styles will underestimate the performance and potential of the Black and Asian groups and therefore will avoid disadvantaging these groups in the selection or development at work. In fact the addition of Wave Professional Styles to a selection procedure is likely to increase the fairness of the selection procedure and reduce adverse impact against minority groups.

We advise that the choice of norm group should be appropriate to the level of management of the role being considered.

18.0 Lifestyles

18.1 Other Wave Styles Group Differences

This chapter provides additional background information about one major sample of people who form part of the ongoing validation of the Wave Styles questionnaires.

Participants who completed the Wave Styles questionnaires in the recent Project Epsom were also invited to complete a range of other questionnaires. One of these questionnaires, the Lifestyle Survey, asked participants about various aspect s of their lifestyle including their interests outside of work and their biographical details. The Lifestyle Survey formed an optional part of that research project. Another questionnaire, the Wave Performance 360 questionnaire, asked participants to indicate their level of effectiveness in a number of behavioral, ability and global areas of work performance. These areas of performance match to the scales in the Wave Styles questionnaires.

This chapter presents results associated with these questionnaires in three main sections:

1. Group Differences in Wave Styles profiles, based on Lifestyle Survey grouping variables
2. Group Differences In Wave Styles profiles, based on Wave Performance 360 grouping variables
3. Additional normative lifestyle information about the sample of people who participated in Project Epsom

Because several hundred people who completed the Wave Styles questionnaires in Project Epsom also completed the Lifestyle Survey, it is possible to compare different groups of individuals who have completed the Lifestyle Survey along the major scales of the Wave Professional Styles questionnaire. This allows us to look at how a person's preferred work styles relate to their wider preferences and interests.

Group difference graphs are presented, showing mean sten score group comparisons across the different Wave Styles scales. The average of the sten scale is 5.5 so group means tend to fluctuate close to this value.

Group differences have been calculated in terms of standardized effect sizes of the means (Cohen's d), whereby a small difference equals an effect size of d=.20, a medium difference equals an effect size of d=.50 and a large difference equals an effect size of d=.80 (Cohen, 1988). With the sten scores compared here, a small to moderate effect size was classified as a group difference of .40-1.00 Sten. A moderate to large effect was seen with differences of 1.00-1.59 stens and any difference in sten scores which equalled or exceeded 1.60 was classified as a large group difference.

It should be stated that because of the inherent limitations of the accuracy of any method of measurement, it is possible that the findings presented in this chapter are due to factors associated with our particular sample. The findings presented in this chapter do not fulfill criteria to demonstrate any causal links between the Wave Styles scales and those lifestyle variables considered. Cross-replication of these results in other samples should be sought before making claims about work performance and lifestyle. For example, whether these findings would be replicated in a different cultural group remains to be seen. Gender differences have been investigated where feasible and where group differences which arise may actually be due to gender differences, this is documented. Saville Consulting are continuing to investigative further the influence of a wide range of factors on performance at work.

461

Group differences are presented here for readers, not to confirm differences between people's preferred work performance styles and lifestyle choices, but rather for the purpose of general interest and in response to questions that Wave users sometimes ask. Another reason for providing this evidence is to demystify some assumptions and stereotypes people may associate with particular characteristics.

Introducing the Lifestyle Survey

Every participant who took part in Project Epsom received an email invitation to complete the Lifestyle Survey. This is an optional questionnaire with an average completion time of 15 minutes. In total, 654 participants chose to complete the Lifestyle Survey. The Lifestyle Survey contained a range of questions about attitudes and practices regarding health, leisure, work, social background and physical characteristics.

Because every question in the Lifestyle Survey was also optional, the number of responses given to each question varied. The highest response rate for a Lifestyle Survey question was 652; the lowest response rate was 564 responses. The number of responses for some questions was also reduced at the analysis stage because many of the questions in the survey were open-ended. Where a respondent had given an unexpected response or it was not clear what they had intended by their answer, this response was not counted in the final total.

Every time a question from the Lifestyle Survey is discussed in this chapter, the reader is made aware of how many responses this particular result is based on.

18.2 Section 1. Group Differences in Wave Styles profiles, based on Lifestyle Survey grouping variables

HOURS SPENT WORKING PER WEEK

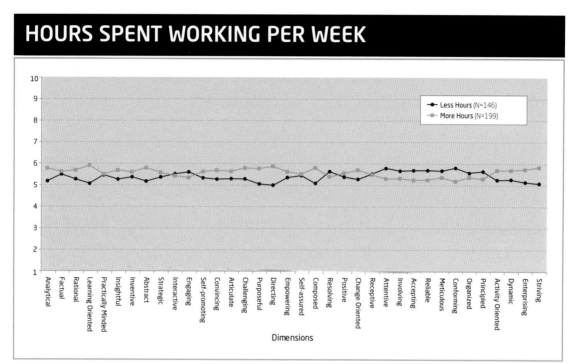

Hours Worked groups are created by converting raw scores into sten scores and splitting the group at 38 hours. The "Less Hours" group consists of participants who work 38 hours or less per week, and the "More Hours" group consists of participants who work more than 38 hours per week. ("Less Hours" N=146, "More Hours" N=199. Total Group = 345).

Summary

- For 19 out of 36 dimensions, the effect sizes of the group differences were found to be small to moderate. The More Hours group was higher on the *Analytical, Rational, Learning Oriented, Insightful, Abstract, Convincing, Challenging, Purposeful, Directing, Composed, Change Oriented, Activity Oriented, Dynamic, Enterprising* and *Striving* scales. The Less Hours group was higher on the *Attentive, Accepting, Reliable* and *Conforming* scales

- The high number of Wave scales associated with work hours suggests that it may be a "higher-order" factor or "marker", reflecting a number of other sub-factors and factor associations. It is possible that the differences seen here between people who work more or fewer hours may relate to the two major subfactors of the Big Five measure of "conscientiousness". People who work more hours seem to be demonstrating high "achievement", whereas people who work fewer hours seem to be demonstrating high "dependability". Of course, further research would need to be undertaken in order to seek support for this hypothesis

463

SALARY

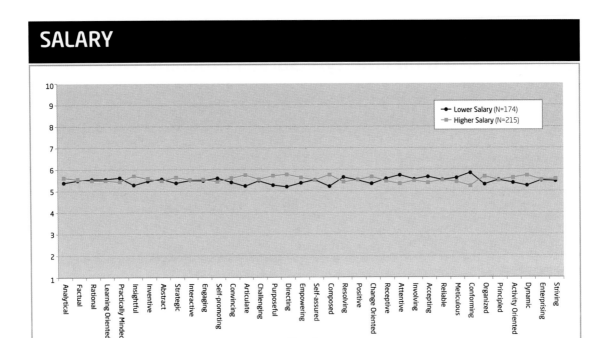

Salary groups are created by converting raw scores into sten scores and splitting the group at the median of £25,850. The "Lower Salary" group consists of participants who earn £25,850 or less per year, and the "Higher Salary" group consists of participants who earn more than this. ("Lower Salary" N=174, "Higher Salary" N=215. Total Group = 389).

Summary

- For 8 out of 36 dimensions, the effect sizes of the group differences were found to be small to moderate. The Higher Salary group was higher on the *Insightful, Articulate, Purposeful, Directing, Composed* and *Dynamic* scales. The Lower Salary group was higher on the *Attentive* and *Conforming* scales

- It is possible that the differences on the *Conforming* and *Composed* dimensions reflect gender differences, as women reported being more *Conforming* and less *Composed* than men did

BIRTH ORDER

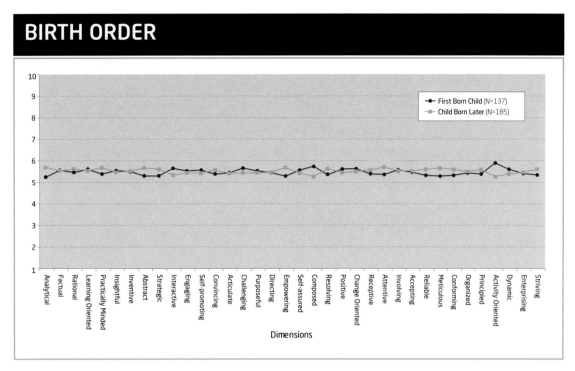

Birth Order groups are created by converting raw scores into sten scores and splitting the group so that those who were the first child born in a family are separated from those who were not the first born child. Fifty-one individuals who described themselves as an only child were removed from the analysis. ("First Born Child" N=137, "Child Born Later" N=185. Total Group = 322).

Summary

- For 4 out of 36 dimensions, the effect sizes of the group differences were found to be small to moderate. The First Born Child group was higher on the *Composed* and *Activity Oriented* scales. The Child Born Later group was higher on the *Analytical* and *Empowering* scales

- The authors do not expect the results to cross validate into other samples

COMMITMENT TO PROFESSION

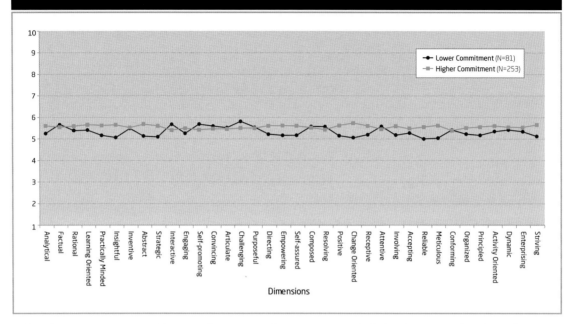

Commitment groups are created by converting raw scores into sten scores and splitting the group so that those who agree that they are committed are separated from those who disagree that they are committed. The "Lower Commitment" group consists of participants who disagreed or strongly disagreed that they were committed to their profession, plus those who were unsure about their level of commitment. The "Higher Commitment" group consists of participants who agreed or strongly agreed that they were committed to their profession. ("Lower Commitment" N=81, "Higher Commitment" N=253. Total Group = 334).

Summary

- For 13 out of 36 dimensions, the effect sizes of the group differences were found to be small to moderate. The Higher Commitment group was higher on the *Practically Minded, Insightful, Abstract, Strategic, Empowering, Self-assured, Positive, Change Oriented, Receptive, Involving, Reliable, Meticulous* and *Striving* scales

AVERAGE HAPPINESS

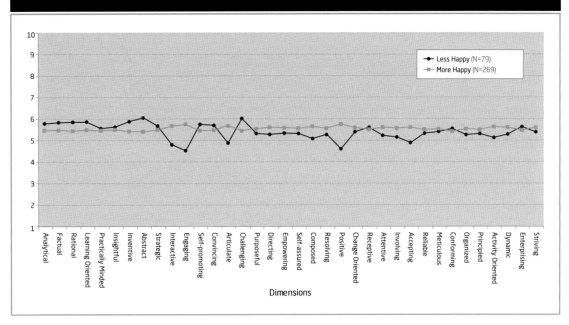

Happiness groups are created by converting raw scores into sten scores and splitting the groups so that those who reported that they are less happy were separated from those who reported that they are more happy. The Less Happy group consists of those who said that on average they are "slightly happy" at most. The More Happy group consists of individuals who are at least "generally happy", on average. The inequality of group sizes is due to the fact that there was a large tendency to report that one was "generally happy". ("Less Happy" N=79, "More Happy" N=269. Total Group = 348).

Summary

- For 10 out of 36 dimensions, the effect sizes of the group differences were found to be small to moderate. The More Happy group was higher on the *Interactive, Articulate, Composed, Involving, Accepting* and *Activity Oriented* scales. The Less Happy group was higher on the *Rational, Inventive, Abstract* and *Challenging* scales

- 2 out of 36 dimensions showed medium to large effect sizes - *Engaging* and *Positive* – with the More Happy group being higher on these dimensions

- The group differences on the *Composed* and *Challenging* dimensions may reflect gender differences, as men reported being more *Composed* and *Challenging* than women. These gender difference have relatively small effect sizes

467

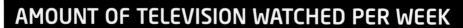

AMOUNT OF TELEVISION WATCHED PER WEEK

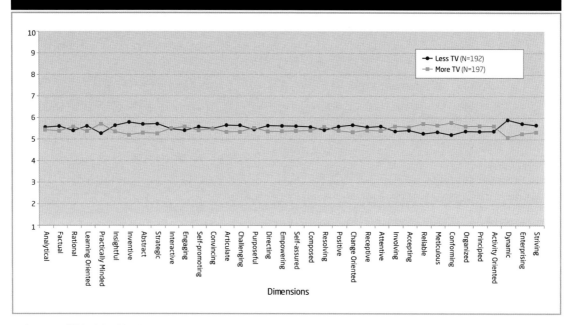

Amount of Television Watched groups are created by converting raw scores into sten scores and splitting the groups at the mean response, 12.36 hours per week. Individuals who watched TV for 12.36 hours or less per week formed the "Less TV" group. Those who watched TV for more than 12.36 hours per week formed the "More TV" group. ("Less TV" N=192, "More TV" N=197. Total Group = 389).

Summary

- For 7 out of 36 dimensions, the effect sizes of the group differences were found to be small to moderate. The More TV group was higher on the *Practically Minded, Reliable* and *Conforming* scales. The Less TV group was higher on the *Inventive, Strategic, Dynamic* and *Enterprising* scales

- It is possible that the group difference on the *Conforming* dimension is due to a gender difference, as women reported being more *Conforming* than men did. The size of this gender effect is small

TIME SPENT READING PER WEEK

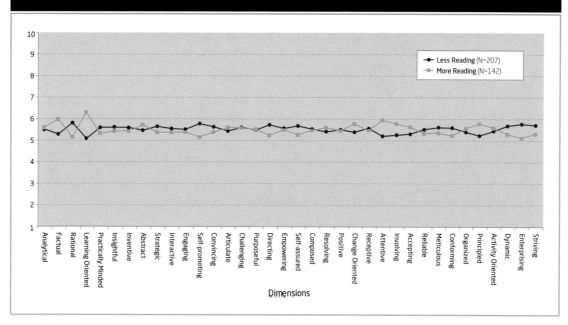

Time Spent Reading per week groups are created by converting raw scores into sten scores and splitting the groups at the mean response, 3.84 hours per week. Individuals who read for 3.84 hours or less per week formed the "Less Reading" group. Those who read for more than 3.84 hours per week formed the "More Reading" group. ("Less Reading" N=207, "More Reading" N=142. Total Group = 349).

Summary

- For 10 out of 36 dimensions, the effect sizes of the group differences were found to be small to moderate. The More Reading group was higher on the *Factual, Attentive, Involving* and *Principled* scales. The Less Reading group was higher on the *Rational, Self-promoting, Directing, Self-assured, Enterprising* and *Striving* scales

- 1 out of 36 dimensions showed a medium to large effect size - *Learning Oriented* – with the More Reading group being higher on this dimension

- The group difference on the *Attentive* dimension may actually be influenced by a gender difference, as women reported being more *Attentive* than men did. The size of this gender effect is small

- Contrastingly, the group difference on the *Rational* dimension may reflect a gender difference as men reported being more *Rational* than women did. The size of this gender effect is moderate

469

PORTIONS OF FRUIT AND VEGETABLES EATEN PER WEEK

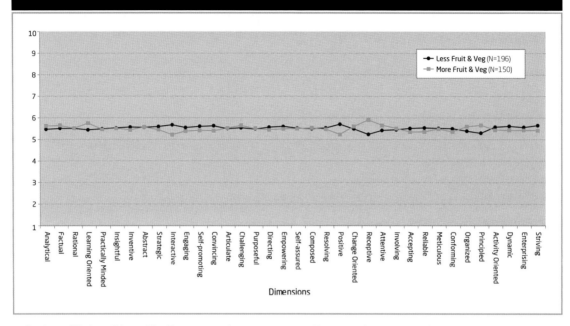

Portions of Fruit and Vegetables Eaten per week groups are created by converting raw scores into sten scores and splitting the groups at the mean response of 20.14 portions per week. Individuals who eat 20 or fewer portions of fruit and vegetables per week formed the "Less Fruit and Veg" group. Those who eat more than 20 portions of fruit and vegetables per week formed the "More Fruit and Veg" group. ("Less Fruit and Veg" N=196, "More Fruit and Veg" N=150. Total Group = 346).

Summary

- For 3 out of 36 dimensions, the effect sizes of the group differences were found to be small to moderate. The More Fruit and Veg group was higher on the *Receptive* scale and the Less Fruit and Veg group was higher on the *Interactive* and *Positive* scales

- Although the advantages of eating more fruit and vegetables are frequently reinforced, this sample saw practically no personality group differences between people who eat more fruit and vegetables and people who eat less fruit and vegetables. Those that do exist may be particular to this sample of individuals

- It would be interesting to split the groups at 35 portions of fruit and vegetables per week, a figure recommended by many experts, in order to see if there are any notable group differences along the Wave scales. Unfortunately, less than 10% of this sample eats 35 or more portions of fruit and vegetables per week and the available group size from this particular sample would not be sufficient for such comparisons

18.3 Section 2. Group Differences in Wave Styles profiles, based on Wave Performance 360 grouping variables

Comparisons are now presented based on groups split according to a selection of ability and global performance scales from the Wave Performance 360 questionnaire.

WORKING WITH NUMBERS

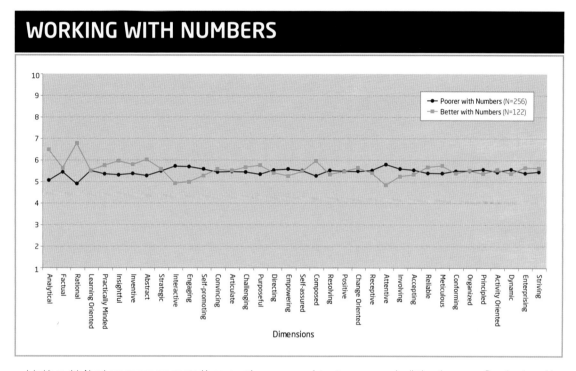

Working with Numbers groups are created by converting raw scores into sten scores and splitting the groups. People who said they were at most "Fairly Effective" at working with numbers were grouped "Poorer With Numbers" and were separated from those who said they were at least "Very Effective" at working with numbers, who were grouped "Better With Numbers". ("Poorer With Numbers" N=256, "Better With Numbers" N=122. Total Group = 378).

Summary

- For 8 out of 36 dimensions, the effect sizes of the group differences were found to be small to moderate. The Better With Numbers group was higher on the *Insightful, Inventive, Abstract, Purposeful* and *Composed* scales. The Poorer With Numbers group was higher on the *Interactive, Engaging* and *Attentive* scales

- 1 out of 36 dimensions showed a medium to large effect size - *Analytical* – with the Better With Numbers group being higher on this dimension

- 1 out of 36 dimensions showed a large effect size - *Rational* – with the Better With Numbers group being higher on this dimension

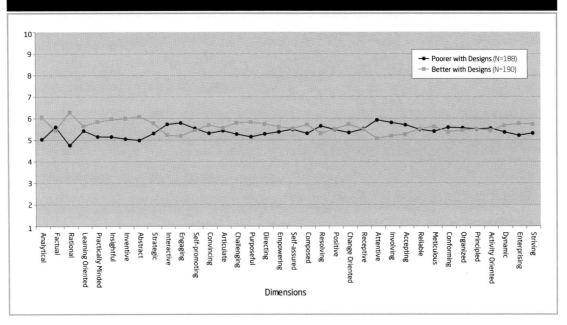

Working with Designs groups are created by converting raw scores into sten scores and splitting the groups. People who said they were at most "Unsure" of their effectiveness working with designs were grouped "Poorer With Designs" and were separated from those who said they were at least "Fairly Effective" at working with designs, who were grouped "Better With Designs". ("Poorer With Designs" N=188, "Better With Designs" N=190. Total Group = 378).

Summary

- For 15 out of 36 dimensions, the effect sizes of the group differences were found to be small to moderate. The Better With Designs group was higher on the *Practically Minded, Insightful, Inventive, Strategic, Challenging, Purposeful, Directing, Composed, Enterprising* and *Striving* scales. The Poorer With Designs group was higher on the *Interactive, Engaging, Attentive, Involving* and *Accepting* scales

- 3 out of 36 dimensions showed a medium to large effect size – *Analytical, Rational* and *Abstract* – with the Better With Designs group being higher on these dimensions

- In the case of the group differences for the *Challenging, Purposeful* and *Enterprising* dimensions, these may reflect underlying gender differences. On all three dimensions, men reported being higher than women did, although these gender effects remained small

WORKING WITH EQUIPMENT

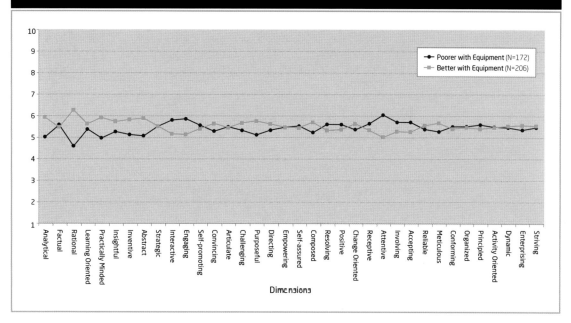

Working with Equipment groups are created by converting raw scores into sten scores and splitting the groups. People who said they were at most "Unsure" of their effectiveness working with equipment were grouped "Poorer With Equipment" and were separated from those who said they were at least "Fairly Effective" at working with equipment, who were grouped "Better With Equipment". ("Poorer With Equipment" N=172, "Better With Equipment" N=206. Total Group = 378).

Summary

- For 11 out of 36 dimensions, the effect sizes of the group differences were found to be small to moderate. The Better With Equipment group was higher on the *Analytical, Practically Minded, Insightful, Inventive, Abstract, Purposeful* and *Composed* scales. The Poorer With Equipment group was higher on the *Interactive, Engaging, Involving* and *Accepting* scales

- 1 out of 36 dimensions showed a medium to large effect size – *Attentive* – with the Poorer With Equipment group being higher on this dimension

- 1 out of 36 dimensions showed a large effect size – *Rational* – with the Better With Equipment group being higher on this dimension

- For the *Purposeful* dimension, this may reflect a gender difference, as men reported being more *Purposeful* than women did. This gender effect size is small nevertheless

DEMONSTRATING POTENTIAL

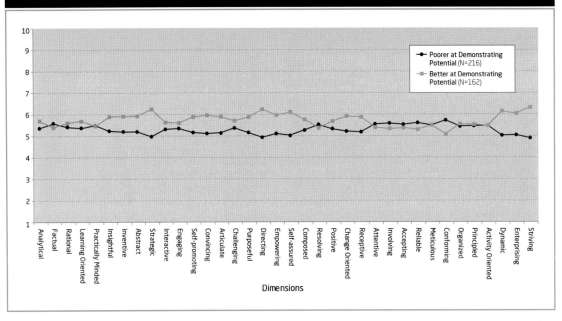

Demonstrating Potential groups are created by converting raw scores into sten scores and splitting the groups so that people who said they were at most "Fairly Effective" at demonstrating potential are separated from those who said they were at least "Very Effective" at demonstrating potential. ("Poorer At Demonstrating Potential" N=216, "Better At Demonstrating Potential" N=162. Total Group = 378).

Summary

- For 13 out of 36 dimensions, the effect sizes of the group differences were found to be small to moderate. The Better At Demonstrating Potential group was higher on the *Insightful, Inventive, Abstract, Self-promoting, Convincing, Articulate, Purposeful, Empowering, Composed, Change Oriented, Receptive* and *Enterprising* scales. The Poorer At Demonstrating Potential group was higher on the *Conforming* scale

- 5 out of 36 dimensions showed a medium to large effect size – *Strategic, Directing, Self-assured, Dynamic* and *Striving* – with the Poorer at demonstrating potential

- The group difference on the *Conforming* dimension may actually reflect a gender effect as women reported being more Conforming than men did. The gender effect size here is small

18.4 Section 3. Additional normative lifestyle information about the sample of people who participated in Project Epsom

The remainder of this chapter refers to the specific sample of individuals who chose to complete the Lifestyle Survey and does not compare the results to Wave scales. This means that sample sizes considered below are a good deal larger than those in the group comparisons. This section is included merely to provide additional normative information about the sample of individuals involved in the Project Epsom research.

Gender

Of these respondents, 63% indicated that they were female and 37% were male [1]. Follow-up research is being carried out to equalize the gender composition of this sample. This follow-up study will be published separately.

Height and Weight

When responses are split by gender, the average female in this sample stands 5'5" (165cm) tall [2] and weighs 67kg (147lbs) [3]. The average man is 5'10" (178cm) tall and weighs 83kg (182lbs) [4].

Leisure

Outside of work, in a typical week the average person spends just under six and a half hours using the internet [5], over twelve hours in front of the television [6] and nearly four hours reading a book [7].

People shop for an average of two and a half hours per week and housework typically takes up four and a half hours of a person's week [8].

Just fewer than 20% of people gamble at least once a month [9].

Diet

Although 7% of the sample is vegetarian [10], less than 1% of people are vegan [11].

On average, a person in this sample eats two takeaway meals per month, although 1% of people eat 15 or more per month. One-fifth of people reported that they never eat takeaway food [12].

It seems that most people do not get the five portions of fruit and vegetables per day which is recommended by many health experts. People typically reported eating 20 portions of fruit and vegetables per week [13].

People eat oily fish, on average, once a week [14] and 49% of people eat red meat more than once a week [15].

In this sample, 69% of people drink tea at least once a day and 13% said that they drink tea five times a day or more [16].

[1] Based on 651 responses	[5] Based on 652 responses	[9] Based on 650 responses	[13] Based on 647 responses
[2] Based on 403 responses	[6] Based on 651 responses	[10] Based on 649 responses	[14] Based on 647 responses
[3] Based on 392 responses	[7] Based on 651 responses	[11] Based on 640 responses	[15] Based on 645 responses
[4] Based on 235 responses	[8] Based on 650 responses	[12] Based on 646 responses	[16] Based on 646 responses

475

Health and Well-Being

The average person sleeps for 7 hours per night [17], but over one-fifth of people (21%) say that they sleep poorly [18].

A smoking ban in covered or enclosed public places is supported by 83% of people [19]. A similar percentage of people (82%) reports that they do not smoke. Less than 1% of people smoke 20 or more cigarettes per day [20].

The typical person claims to exercise for just under four hours every week, although nearly 14% of people do not do any form of exercise [21]. Nearly nine out of every ten people (89%) agreed or strongly agreed that their health is generally good [22].

Most people agreed that they are happy at least 75% of the time. Nearly a quarter of people surveyed (23%) said that they are happy more than 90% of the time [23]. Only 11% of the sample said that they were not generally happy [24].

At work

The mean annual salary of this sample is £32,000, but around 4% of people annually earn £100,000 or more [25]. Only 40% of people said that they are satisfied with their pay [26] and two-thirds of people (67%) believe that they should be paid more [27].

Careers in the arts (e.g. culture, design, entertainment, etc.) were generally seen as the most interesting area to work in and careers in operations (e.g. production, security, transport) were viewed as the least interesting area in which to work [28].

Over a quarter of people (29%) stated that they intended to leave their current organization within the next two years [29], and less than half (48%) plan to stay with their current organization for "a long time" [30].

On the other hand, 70% of people say that they are proud to work for their organization [31] and nearly three-quarters of people (72%) would recommend their organization to others as a good place to work [32].

Over three-quarters of people (77%) said that they are committed to their profession [33] and nearly a quarter of people (22%) would describe themselves as a workaholic [34].

In this sample, 16% of people said that they had been bullied at work [35], and nearly one quarter (24%) were not satisfied with the level of recognition that they currently receive for achieving good results [36].

[17] Based on 651 responses
[18] Based on 647 responses
[19] Based on 644 responses
[20] Based on 639 responses
[21] Based on 652 responses
[22] Based on 645 responses
[23] Based on 635 responses
[24] Based on 649 responses
[25] Based on 564 responses
[26] Based on 615 responses
[27] Based on 614 responses
[28] Based on 640 responses
[29] Based on 610 responses
[30] Based on 608 responses
[31] Based on 611 responses
[32] Based on 615 responses
[33] Based on 616 responses
[34] Based on 645 responses
[35] Based on 640 responses
[36] Based on 623 responses

Appendix A

Saville Consulting Wave Professional® Styles
The Development Sample Group Description

This sample consisted of 1,011 participants, employed in a range of job functions across a wide range of industry sectors. Of these, 60% worked in the following industry sectors: financial and legal services, IT, human resources, consumer and retail services, leisure and hospitality, arts and media, government and public services and health and community services. The remaining 40% worked in other industry sectors including transport and logistics, manufacturing & production, environment and sciences, property development, promotions, or described their industry sector as 'other'.

The breakdown of the development sample is provided below (with response rates for each biographical section given in the foot notes):

Gender[1]

57% of the sample were female and 43% were male.

Age[2]

The age of the group ranged from 17 to 75 years, with a mean age of 34 years.

Language[3]

87% of the group had English as a first language.

Education (highest qualification)[4]

25% had a post-graduate degree as their highest qualification, 41% of the group had a degree, 25% had school level qualifications (including A Level, GCSE or equivalent), with 8% having 'other' qualifications with the remaining 1% of the group having no formal qualifications.

Work Experience[5]

23% of the group had more than 20 years' work experience, 21% had between 10 and 20 years, 13% between 6 and 9 years, 18% between 3 and 5 years, 11% 1 to 2 years, 5% 6-12 months and 9% had less than 6 months experience.

Cultural Background[6]

70% of the sample described themselves as white British and 16% as other white backgrounds (including Irish, European, American, Canadian, New Zealander)[7], with the remaining 14% coming from a wide range of other backgrounds .

[1] Based on 100% sample response
[2] Based on 100% sample response
[3] Based on 97% sample response
[4] Based on 100% sample response
[5] Based on 100% sample response
[6] Based on 100% sample response
[7] Other backgrounds given included Armenia, Argentina, Australia, Austria, Barbados, Belgium , Bulgaria, Caribbean, Channel Islands, China, Colombia, Cyprus, Denmark, Egypt, Finland, France, Germany, Greece, Hungary, Iceland, India, Indonesia, Iran, Italy, Japan, Kashmir, Korea, Kuwait, Lebanon, Netherlands, Oman, Philippines, Poland, Portugal, Saudi Arabia, Scotland, South Africa, South America, Spain, Sweden, Switzerland, Trinidad, USA, Vietnam, Wales, West Africa.

Appendix B

Saville Consulting Wave Professional® Styles
The Standardization Sample

This sample consisted of 1153 participants, 96% of whom were currently employed in a range of job functions across a wide range of industry sectors. Of these, 75% worked in the following industry sectors: banking, financial services, oil/gas & utilities, hospitality, recruitment, and insurance. The remaining 25% worked in other industry sectors including consulting services, manufacturing & production, healthcare, engineering, education & training and HR.

The breakdown of the standardization sample is provided below (with response rates for each biographical section given in the foot notes):

Gender[1]

53% of the sample were female and 47% were male.

Age[2]

The age of the group ranged from 17 to 65 years, with a mean age of 36 years.

Cultural Background[3]

83% of the sample described themselves as white British, 12% as other white backgrounds (including Irish, European, American, Canadian, New Zealander and white Caribbean) with the remaining 5% of the sample describing themselves as either Indian, Pakistani, Chinese, Asian Other, Black Caribbean, Black African, or as mixed origin (e.g. White and Black Caribbean).

Language[4]

98% of the group described their understanding of written English either 'as a first language speaker' or 'fluently'.

Education (highest qualification)[5]

12% of the group had a postgraduate degree as their highest qualification, 25% of the group had a degree, 15% had a professional qualification (e.g. Chartership), 35% had school level qualifications (including A Level, GCSE or equivalent), 7% had an HNC, HND or equivalent, with 4% having 'other' qualifications (e.g. NVQ) with the remaining 2% of the group having no formal qualifications.

Work Function[6]

The participants worked in a range of job functions and areas. 77% of the group worked in the following functions/areas: HR, Customer Service, Accounts and Finance, Sales and Administration. The remaining 23% worked in a range of other functions/areas including Engineering, IT, Marketing, Executive, Office Management, Production, R&D and Catering.

478

Work Experience[7]

36% of the group had more than 20 years' work experience, 33% had between 10 and 20 years, 13% between 6 and 9 years, 11% between 3 and 5 years, 5% between 6 months and 3 years and 1% had less than 6 months' work experience.

[1] Based on 100% sample response
[2] Based on 94% sample response
[3] Based on 90% sample response
[4] Based on 88% sample response
[5] Based on 86% sample response
[6] Based on 86% sample response
[7] Based on 94% sample response

Appendix C

Saville Consulting Wave Professional® Styles
Epsom Sample Group Description

The matched sample used within this analysis consisted of 308 participants, 94% of whom were currently employed in a range of job functions across a wide range of industry sectors. 69% were employed as permanent staff and worked full time, 13% worked as permanent part-time staff, 6% worked as temporary staff, and 7% were self-employed. The remaining 6% were either retired, students, or currently unemployed.

The breakdown of the sample is provided below (with response rates for each biographical section given in the foot notes):

Gender[1]

69% of the sample were female and 31% were male.

Age[2]

The age of the group ranged from 18 to 64 years, with a mean age of 36 years.

Cultural Background[3]

84% of the sample described themselves as white or white British, 11% as other white backgrounds (including Irish, European, American, Canadian, New Zealander and white Caribbean) with the remaining 5% of the sample describing themselves as either Indian, Other Asian, Black Caribbean, Other Black, South African, Hispanic, or as mixed origin (e.g. White and Asian).

Education (highest qualification)[4]

19% had a postgraduate degree (including a masters or a post graduate certificate/diploma) as their highest qualification, 26% of the group had a first degree, 22% had a professional qualification, 25% had school level qualifications (e.g. GCSE, O Level or equivalent), 6% obtained higher education qualifications (e.g. A Level, BTEC, HNC, HND or equivalent) with the remaining 2% of the group having no formal qualifications.

Work Function[5]

The participants worked in a range of job functions and areas. 16% worked in the area of health and education, 12% in HR, training/development, 10% in sales and marketing, 8% in finance and law, 7% in customer services (including public relations, call centers and communications) 6% in IT and data processing, 6% in administrative roles, 6% in public safety and welfare/social services and 4 % in engineering and construction. The remaining 25% worked in a range of other functions/areas including the arts/entertainment, hospitality, leisure, research, insurance, etc.

Work Experience[6]

34% of the group had more than 20 years' experience, 30% had between 10 and 20 years work experience, 12% had between 6 and 9 years, 13% had between 3 and 5 years, 6% had between 1 and 2 years, 2% had between 6 months and one year, and 2% had less than 6 months' experience.1% had stated that this was not applicable.

[1] Based on 75% sample response   [2] Based on 66% sample response
[3] Based on 78% sample response   [4] Based on 75% sample response
[5] Based on 75% sample response   [6] Based on 77% sample response

Appendix D

Saville Consulting Wave Professional® Styles
UK Senior Managers & Executives Group Description

This sample consisted of 4,276 participants, employed in a range of job functions across a wide range of industry sectors. Of these, 70% worked in the following industry sectors: local government, healthcare, financial services, telecommunications, education/training, consultancy, construction, information technology and insurance. The remaining 30% worked in other industry sectors including manufacturing and production, consumer and retail services, arts and entertainment, property development, environment and sciences, leisure and hospitality, social services, tourism and travel or described their industry sector as 'other'.

The breakdown of the group is provided below (with response rates for each biographical section given in the foot notes):

Gender[1]

34% of the sample were female and 66% were male.

Age[2]

The age of the group ranged from 20 to 81 years, with a mean age of 43 years.

Education (highest qualification)[3]

33% had a postgraduate degree as their highest qualification, 20% had a first/undergraduate degree, 38% had a professional qualification, 7% had school level or some college qualifications, with the remaining 2% of the group having 'Other' or no formal qualifications.

Work Experience[4]

63% of the group had more than 20 years' experience, 31% had between 10 and 20 years work experience, 5% had between 6 and 9 years and 1% had less than 5 years' work experience.

Cultural Background[5]

61% of the sample described themselves as white or white British, 30% as other white backgrounds (including European, American, South African, Canadian, New Zealander and white Caribbean) with the remaining 9% coming from a wide range of other backgrounds[6].

---

[1] Based on 98% sample response
[2] Based on 81% sample response
[3] Based on 97% sample response
[4] Based on 97% sample response
[5] Based on 88% sample response
[6] Other backgrounds included India, Africa, China, Pakistan, Korea, Bangladesh, Iran, Oman, Malaysia, Cyprus and Japan.

Appendix E

Saville Consulting Wave Professional® Styles
UK Professionals & Managers Group Description

This sample consisted of 9,884 participants, employed in a range of job functions across a wide range of industry sectors. Of these, 80% worked in the following industry sectors: local government, telecommunications, healthcare, education/training, financial services, construction, information technology, consultancy and manufacturing and production. The remaining 20% worked in other industry sectors including consumer and retail services, insurance, tourism and travel, arts and entertainment, human resources, environment and sciences, leisure and hospitality, property development and social services or described their industry sector as 'other'.

The breakdown of the group is provided below (with response rates for each biographical section given in the foot notes):

Gender[1]

36% of the sample were female and 64% were male.

Age[2]

The age of the group ranged from 19 to 81 years, with a mean age of 41 years.

Education (highest qualification)[3]

30% had a postgraduate degree as their highest qualification, 24% had a first/undergraduate degree, 35% had a professional qualification, 8% had school level or some college qualifications, with the remaining 3% of the group having 'Other' or no formal qualifications.

Work Experience[4]

53% of the group had more than 20 years' experience, 34% had between 10 and 20 years' work experience, 9% had between 6 and 9 years, 3% had between 3 and 5 years and the remaining 1% had less than 3 years' work experience.

Cultural Background[5]

79% of the sample described themselves as white or white British, 8% as other white backgrounds (including European, American, Canadian, Australian, New Zealander and white Caribbean) with the remaining 13% coming from a wide range of other backgrounds[6].

---

[1] Based on 98% sample response
[2] Based on 82% sample response
[3] Based on 96% sample response
[4] Based on 98% sample response
[5] Based on 88% sample response
[6] Other backgrounds included Other Caribbean, India, Africa, Pakistan, China, Bangladesh, Korea, Malaysia, Cyprus, Japan, Iran and Oman.

482

Appendix F

Saville Consulting Wave Professional® Styles
UK Mixed Occupational Group Description

This sample consisted of 10,953 participants, employed in a range of job functions across a wide range of industry sectors. Of these, 80% worked in the following industry sectors: local government, telecommunications, healthcare, financial services, education/training, construction, information technology, consultancy and manufacturing and production. The remaining 20% worked in other industry sectors including community/social services, consumer and retail services, insurance, tourism and travel, human resources, environment and sciences, arts and entertainment and property development or described their industry sector as 'other'.

The breakdown of the group is provided below (with response rates for each biographical section given in the foot notes):

Gender[1]

38% of the sample were female and 62% were male.

Age[2]

The age of the group ranged from 16 to 81 years, with a mean age of 40 years.

Education (highest qualification)[3]

29% had a postgraduate degree as their highest qualification, 25% had a first/undergraduate degree, 34% had a professional qualification, 9% had school level or some college qualifications, with 2% having 'Other' qualifications and the remaining 1% of the group having no formal qualifications.

Work Experience[4]

50% of the group had more than 20 years' experience, 33% had between 10 and 20 years' work experience, 10% had between 6 and 9 years, 5% had between 3 and 5 years and 2% had less than 3 years' work experience.

Cultural Background[5]

77% of the sample described themselves as white or white British, 8% as other white backgrounds (including European, American, Canadian, Australian, New Zealander and white Caribbean) with the remaining 15% coming from a wide range of other backgrounds[6].

---

[1] Based on 98% sample response
[2] Based on 98% sample response
[3] Based on 96% sample response
[4] Based on 97% sample response
[5] Based on 87% sample response
[6] Other backgrounds included India, Other Caribbean, Africa, Pakistan, China, Bangladesh, Malaysia, Korea, Iran, Oman, Japan and Cyprus.

483

Appendix G

Saville Consulting Wave Professional® Styles
UK Graduates Group Description

This sample consisted of 4,021 participants, employed in a range of job functions across a wide range of industry sectors. Of these, 60% worked in the following industry sectors: telecommunications, local government, healthcare, consumer and retail services, information technology, education and training, financial and legal services, community and social services, manufacturing and production, consulting and arts and entertainment. The remaining 40% worked in other industry sectors including engineering, insurance, human resources, customer service, tourism and travel and environment and sciences, or described their industry sector as 'other'.

The breakdown of the group is provided below (with response rates for each biographical section given in the foot notes):

Gender[1]

44% of the sample were female and 56% were male.

Age[2]

The age of the group ranged from 19 to 62 years, with a mean age of 33 years.

Education (highest qualification)[3]

48% had a postgraduate degree as their highest qualification, while 52% had a first/undergraduate degree.

Work Experience[4]

58% of the group had between 10 and 20 years' work experience, 21% had between 6 and 9 years, 13% had between 3 and 5 years, 5% had between 1 and 2 years, 1% had between 6 months and one year, and 2% had less than 6 months' experience.

Cultural Background[5]

56% of the sample described themselves as white or white British, 9% as other white backgrounds (including European, American, Canadian, Australian, New Zealander, white Chinese and white Caribbean) with the remaining 35% coming from a wide range of other backgrounds[6].

---

[1] Based on 99% sample response
[2] Based on 78% sample response
[3] Based on 100% sample response
[4] Based on 100% sample response
[5] Based on 100% sample response
[6] Other backgrounds included India, Africa, China, Other Caribbean, Pakistan, Bangladesh, Oman, Korea, Japan and Iran.

484

Appendix H

Saville Consulting Wave Professional® Styles
US Senior Managers & Executives Group Description

This sample consisted of 597 participants, employed in a range of job functions across a wide range of industry sectors. Of these, 60% worked in the following industry sectors: financial and legal services, consulting, leisure and hospitality, constructing, operations, human resources, information technology, marketing and administration. The remaining 40% worked in other industry sectors including arts and media, security, healthcare, transport and logistics, manufacturing & production, environment and sciences, or described their industry sector as 'other'.

The breakdown of the group is provided below (with response rates for each biographical section given in the foot notes):

Gender[1]

31% of the sample were female and 69% were male.

Age[2]

The age of the group ranged from 23 to 78 years, with a mean age of 46 years.

Education (highest qualification)[3]

63% had a postgraduate degree as their highest qualification, 27% had a first/undergraduate degree, 6% had a professional qualification, 3% had school level or some college qualifications, with the remaining 1% of the group having 'Other' qualifications.

Work Experience[4]

65% of the group had more than 20 years' experience, 32% had between 10 and 20 years' work experience and the remaining 3% had less than 10 years' work experience.

Cultural Background[5]

85% of the sample described themselves as white/Caucasian (including European, Australian and white Caribbean), 9% as Hispanic with the remaining 6% of the sample coming from a range of other backgrounds[6].

[1] Based on 99% sample response
[2] Based on 84% sample response
[3] Based on 67% sample response
[4] Based on 99% sample response
[5] Based on 52% sample response
[6] Other backgrounds included Black/African American, Asian/Pacific Islander, African-Caribbean and Chinese.

485

Appendix I

Saville Consulting Wave Professional® Styles
US Professionals & Managers Group Description

This sample consisted of 1,849 participants, employed in a range of job functions across a wide range of industry sectors. Of these, 60% worked in the following industry sectors: financial and legal services, human resources, consulting, leisure and hospitality, operation, marketing and information technology. The remaining 40% worked in other industry sectors including administration, engineering, customer services, education and training, construction, arts and media, healthcare, transport and logistics, manufacturing and production and environment and sciences, or described their industry sector as 'other'.

The breakdown of the group is provided below (with response rates for each biographical section given in the foot notes):

Gender[1]

39% of the sample were female and 61% were male.

Age[2]

The age of the group ranged from 21 to 78 years, with a mean age of 44 years.

Education (highest qualification)[3]

58% had a postgraduate degree as their highest qualification, 32% had a first/undergraduate degree, 7% had a professional qualification, 2% had school level or some college qualifications, with the remaining 1% of the group having 'Other' qualifications.

Work Experience[4]

54% of the group had more than 20 years' experience, 35% had between 10 and 20 years' work experience, 9% had between 6 and 9 years and 2% had less than 6 years' work experience.

Cultural Background[5]

83% of the sample described themselves as white/Caucasian (including European, American, Australian and white Caribbean), 9% as Hispanic, 3% as Black/African American with the remaining 5% of the sample coming from a range of other backgrounds[6].

[1] Based on 99% sample response
[2] Based on 81% sample response
[3] Based on 67% sample response
[4] Based on 99% sample response
[5] Based on 48% sample response
[6] Other backgrounds included Asian/Pacific Islander, Indian, African-Caribbean, Chinese, Native American, Afghan and Korean.

Appendix J

Saville Consulting Wave Professional® Styles
US Mixed Occupational Group Description

This sample consisted of 2,143 participants, employed in a range of job functions across a wide range of industry sectors. Of these, 60% worked in the following industry sectors: sales, financial services, operations, human resources, consulting, leisure and hospitality, administration, marketing and engineering. The remaining 40% worked in other industry sectors including information technology, education and training, legal services, construction, arts and media, healthcare, transport and logistics, manufacturing and production, or described their industry sector as 'other'.

The breakdown of the group is provided below (with response rates for each biographical section given in the foot notes):

Gender[1]

42% of the sample were female and 58% were male.

Age[2]

The age of the group ranged from 20 to 78 years, with a mean age of 43 years.

Education (highest qualification)[3]

55% had a postgraduate degree as their highest qualification, 34% had a first/undergraduate degree, 8% had a professional qualification, 2% had school level or some college qualifications, with the remaining 1% of the group having 'Other' qualifications.

Work Experience[4]

52% of the group had more than 20 years' experience, 35% had between 10 and 20 years' work experience, 9% had between 6 and 9 years, 3% had between 3 and 5 years with the remaining 1% having had less than 3 years' work experience.

Cultural Background[5]

84% of the sample described themselves as white/Caucasian (including European, American, Australian and white Caribbean), 9% as Hispanic, 3% as Black/African American, 2% as Asian/Pacific Islander, with the remaining 2% of the sample coming from a range of other backgrounds[6].

---

[1] Based on 98% sample response
[2] Based on 81% sample response
[3] Based on 70% sample response
[4] Based on 99% sample response
[5] Based on 49% sample response
[6] Other backgrounds included Indian, African-Caribbean, Chinese, Native America, Afghan and Korean.

487

Appendix K

Saville Consulting Wave Professional® Styles
US Graduates Group Description

This sample consisted of 685 participants, employed in a range of job functions across a wide range of industry sectors. Of these, 60% worked in the following industry sectors: sales, consulting, financial services, education and training, operations, human resources, marketing, administration and customer service. The remaining 40% worked in other industry sectors including leisure and hospitality, arts and media, engineering, information technology, healthcare, tourism and travel, manufacturing and production, environment and sciences, or described their industry sector as 'other'.

The breakdown of the group is provided below (with response rates for each biographical section given in the foot notes):

Gender[1]

43% of the sample were female and 57% were male.

Age[2]

The age of the group ranged from 22 to 57 years, with a mean age of 36 years.

Education (highest qualification)[3]

57% had a postgraduate degree as their highest qualification, 43% had a first/undergraduate degree.

Work Experience[4]

70% of the group had between 10 and 20 years' work experience, 20% had between 6 and 9 years', 6% had between 3 and 5 years', 1% had between 1 and 2 years', with the remaining 3% having had less than 12 months' work experience.

Cultural Background[5]

80% of the sample described themselves as white/Caucasian (European and American), 12% as Hispanic, 3% as Black/African American, 2% as Asian/Pacific Islander, with the remaining 3% of the sample coming from a range of other backgrounds[6].

---

[1] Based on 99% sample response
[2] Based on 83% sample response
[3] Based on 100% sample response
[4] Based on 100% sample response
[5] Based on 76% sample response
[6] Other backgrounds included Caribbean, Indian, Chinese, Native American and Korean.

488

Appendix L

Saville Consulting Wave Professional® Styles
International Senior Managers & Executives Group Description

This sample consisted of 953 participants, employed in a range of job functions across a wide range of industry sectors. Of these, 60% worked in the following industry sectors: financial and legal services, insurance, healthcare, government and public services and consulting. The remaining 40% worked in other industry sectors including information technology, construction, manufacturing & production, consumer products, retail, education and training and electronics, or described their industry sector as 'other'.

The breakdown of the group is provided below (with response rates for each biographical section given in the foot notes):

Gender[1]

34% of the sample were female and 66% were male.

Age[2]

The age of the group ranged from 21 to 69 years, with a mean age of 43 years.

Education (highest qualification)[3]

41% had a postgraduate degree as their highest qualification, 22% had a first/undergraduate degree, 28% had a professional qualification, 7% had school level or some college qualifications, with the remaining 2% of the group having 'Other' or no formal qualifications.

Work Experience [4]

50% of the group had more than 20 years' experience, 42% had between 10 and 20 years' work experience, 7% had between 6 and 9 years, with the remaining 1% having had less than 6 years' work experience.

Cultural Background[5]

80% of the sample described themselves as white/Caucasian (including European, Asian, American, Australian and white Caribbean), 6% as Black, 6% as Hispanic, with the remaining 8% of the sample coming from a range of other backgrounds[6].

Country of Completion[7]

20% of respondents completed Professional Styles in the UK, 20% in the US, 20% in South Africa, 17% in Mexico, 13% in Australia, 3% in Canada, 3% in France, with the remaining 4% having completed the questionnaire in various other countries (namely Bulgaria, Denmark, Germany, Spain, Italy, Netherlands and Brazil).

---

[1] Based on 99% sample response   [2] Based on 83% sample response
[3] Based on 86% sample response   [4] Based on 98% sample response
[5] Based on 61% sample response   [6] Other backgrounds included Indian, Caribbean, Pakistani, and Chinese.
[7] Based on 100% sample response

489

Appendix M

Saville Consulting Wave Professional® Styles
International Professionals & Managers Group Description

This sample consisted of 2,600 participants, employed in a range of job functions across a wide range of industry sectors. Of these, 70% worked in the following industry sectors: financial and legal services, insurance, telecommunications, consulting, healthcare, government and public services and engineering. The remaining 30% worked in other industry sectors including information technology, manufacturing and production, education and training, consulting, oil/gas/utilities, consumer products, retail and tourism and travel, or described their industry sector as 'other'.

The breakdown of the group is provided below (with response rates for each biographical section given in the foot notes):

Gender[1]

40% of the sample were female and 60% were male.

Age[2]

The age of the group ranged from 21 to 69 years, with a mean age of 40 years.

Education (highest qualification)[3]

37% had a postgraduate degree as their highest qualification, 25% had a first/undergraduate degree, 28% had a professional qualification, 8% had school level or some college qualifications, with 2% of the group having 'Other' or no formal qualifications.

Work Experience[4]

40% of the group had more than 20 years' experience, 42% had between 10 and 20 years' work experience, 11% had between 6 and 9 years, 5% had between 3 and 5 years, with the remaining 2% having had less than 3 years' work experience.

Cultural Background[5]

73% of the sample described themselves as white/Caucasian (including European, Asian, American, Australian and white Caribbean), 9% as Black, 8% as Hispanic, 3% as Indian, with the remaining 7% of the sample coming from a range of other backgrounds[6].

Country of Completion[7]

20% of respondents completed Professional Styles in the UK, 20% in the US, 20% in South Africa, 19% in Mexico, 8% in Australia, 3% in Bulgaria, 3% in Denmark, 2% in France, 2% in Spain, with the remaining 3% having completed the questionnaire in various other countries (namely Germany, Canada, Italy, Netherlands, Brazil and Sweden).

[1] Based on 99% sample response
[2] Based on 79% sample response
[3] Based on 85% sample response
[4] Based on 99% sample response
[5] Based on 62% sample response
[6] Other backgrounds included Asian/Pacific Islander, Native American, Chinese, Pakistani, Other Caribbean, Japanese and Afghan.
[7] Based on 100% sample response

Appendix N

Saville Consulting Wave Professional® Styles
International Mixed Occupational Group Description

This sample consisted of 3,095 participants, employed in a range of job functions across a wide range of industry sectors. Of these, 70% worked in the following industry sectors: insurance, financial and legal services, healthcare, telecommunications, government and public services, consulting, information technology, education/training and engineering. The remaining 30% worked in other industry sectors including manufacturing and production, oil/gas/utilities, construction, administration, community and social services, consumer products, retail, customer services, sales, tourism and travel, human resources and electronics, or described their industry sector as 'other'.

The breakdown of the group is provided below (with response rates for each biographical section given in the foot notes):

Gender[1]

43% of the sample were female and 57% were male.

Age[2]

The age of the group ranged from 19 to 69 years, with a mean age of 39 years.

Education (highest qualification)[3]

33% had a postgraduate degree as their highest qualification, 27% had a first/undergraduate degree, 25% had a professional qualification, 12% had school level or some college qualifications, with 3% of the group having 'Other' or no formal qualifications.

Work Experience[4]

37% of the group had more than 20 years' experience, 38% had between 10 and 20 years' work experience, 12% had between 6 and 9 years, 7% had between 3 and 5 years, 3% had between 1 and 2 years', with the remaining 3% having had less than 12 months' work experience.

Cultural Background[5]

68% of the sample described themselves as white/Caucasian (including European, Asian, American, Australian, New Zealand and white Caribbean), 14% as Black, 7% as Hispanic, 4% as Indian, with the remaining 7% of the sample coming from a range of other backgrounds[6].

Country of Completion[7]

20% of respondents completed Professional Styles in the UK, 20% in the US, 22% in South Africa, 16% in Mexico, 8% in Australia, 4% in Denmark, 3% in Bulgaria, 2% in Spain, 2% in France, with the remaining 3% having completed the questionnaire in various other countries (namely Germany, Canada, Italy, Netherlands, Brazil and Sweden).

491

[1] Based on 99% sample response   [2] Based on 78% sample response
[3] Based on 86% sample response   [4] Based on 98% sample response
[5] Based on 63% sample response
[6] Other backgrounds included Asian/Pacific Islander, Caribbean, Chinese, Native American, Pakistani, Afghan and Japanese.
[7] Based on 100% sample response

Appendix O

Saville Consulting Wave Professional® Styles
International Graduates Group Description

This sample consisted of 1,423 participants, employed in a range of job functions across a wide range of industry sectors. Of these, 60% worked in the following industry sectors: financial and legal services, insurance, consulting, and telecommunications. The remaining 40% worked in other industry sectors including education/training, healthcare, government and public services, manufacturing and production, retail, information technology, consumer products, agriculture, construction, oil/gas/utilities and community and social services, or described their industry sector as 'other'.

The breakdown of the group is provided below (with response rates for each biographical section given in the foot notes):

Gender[1]

49% of the sample were female and 51% were male.

Age[2]

The age of the group ranged from 19 to 59 years, with a mean age of 33 years.

Education (highest qualification)[3]

51% had a postgraduate degree as their highest qualification, 49% had a first/undergraduate degree.

Work Experience[4]

53% of the group had between 10 and 20 years' work experience, 18% had between 6 and 9 years, 14% had between 3 and 5 years, 7% had between 1 and 2 years, 4% had between 6 and 12 months, with the remaining 4% having had less than 6 months' work experience.

Cultural Background[5]

59% of the sample described themselves as white/Caucasian (including European, American, Australian and white Caribbean), 21% as Black, 8% as Hispanic, 6% as Indian, with the remaining 6% of the sample coming from a range of other backgrounds[6].

Country of Completion[7]

18% of respondents completed Professional Styles in the UK, 17% in the US, 26% in South Africa, 16% in Mexico, 7% in Australia, 5% in Germany, 3% in Spain, 2% in France, 2% in Denmark, 2% in Bulgaria, with the remaining 2% having completed the questionnaire in various other countries (namely Canada, Italy, Netherlands and Brazil).

---

[1] Based on 99% sample response
[2] Based on 80% sample response
[3] Based on 100% sample response
[4] Based on 100% sample response
[5] Based on 72% sample response
[6] Other backgrounds included Chinese, Asian/Pacific Islander, Native American, Pakistani, Bangladeshi, Korean, Caribbean and Arab/Middle Eastern.
[7] Based on 100% sample response

Appendix P

Saville Consulting Wave Professional® Styles
Australian Professionals & Managers Group Description

This sample consisted of 474 participants, employed in a range of job functions across a wide range of industry sectors. Of these, 70% worked in the following industry sectors: financial and legal services, insurance and oil/gas/utilities. The remaining 30% worked in other industry sectors including information technology, healthcare, manufacturing and production, consultancy, local government, property development, community/social services, aerospace/aviation, education/training, and leisure and hospitality or described their industry sector as 'other'.

The breakdown of the group is provided below (with response rates for each biographical section given in the foot notes):

Gender[1]

55% of the sample were female and 45% were male.

Age[2]

The age of the group ranged from 21 to 61 years, with a mean age of 39 years.

Education (highest qualification)[3]

30% had a postgraduate degree as their highest qualification, 38% had a first/undergraduate degree, 25% had a professional qualification, 5% had school level or some college qualifications, with the remaining 2% of the group having 'Other' or no formal qualifications.

Work Experience[4]

40% of the group had more than 20 years' experience, 38% had between 10 and 20 years' work experience, 9% had between 6 and 9 years, 7% between 3 and 5 years, 3% between 1 and 2 years, with the remaining 3% having had less than 5 years' work experience.

[1] Based on 99% sample response
[2] Based on 75% sample response
[3] Based on 96% sample response
[4] Based on 55% sample response

493

494

References

Allison, D. B., Faith, M. S., & Gorman, B. S. (1996). Publication bias in obesity treatment trials? *International Journal of Obesity*, 20, 931-937.

American Psychological Association. (1999). *Standards for Educational and Psychological Measurement.* Washington DC, USA: American Educational Research Association.

Anderson, N. and Salgado, J. (2002). Cognitive and GMA Testing in the European Community: Issues and Evidence, *Human Performance*, 15 (1), 75-96.

Angleitner, A., J., O. P., & Lö, F. J. (1986). It's what you ask and how you ask it: An item-metric analysis of personality questionnaires. In A. Angleitner and J. S. Wiggins (Eds.), *Personality assessment via questionnaires* (pp. 61–107). Berlin, Germany: Springer-Verlag.

Baron, H. (1996). Strengths and limitations of ipsative measurement. Journal of Occupational and Organizational Psychology, 69, 49-56.

Barrick, M.R. & Mount, M.K. (1991). The Big Five personality dimensions and job performance: A meta-analysis. *Personnel Psychology*, 44, 1-25.

Bartram, D (2002, 2004). *The SHL Corporate Leadership Model.* SHL Research White Paper. Thames Ditton: SHL Group plc.

Bartram D., Robertson, I.T., & Callinan, M. (2002). A framework for examining organizational effectiveness. In Robertson, Callinan & Bartram, *Organisational Effectiveness: The Role of Psychology.* London: Wiley.

Bartram, D, Baron, H, & Kurz, R (2003). *Let's turn validation on its head.* Proceedings of the BPS DOP Conference, pp75-78. Leicester: BPS.

Bartram, D, Kurz, R, & Baron, H (2003). *The Great Eight Competencies: Meta-analysis using a criterion-centric approach to validation.* Paper presented at SIOP, Orlando, May 2003.

Bartram, D. (2005). The Great Eight Competencies: A criterion-centric approach to validation. *Journal of Applied Psychology*, 90, 1185-1203.

Bauchau, V. (1997). Is there a "file drawer problem" in biological research? *OIKOS*, 19, 407–409.

Burisch, M. (1984). Approaches to Personality-Inventory Construction – A comparison of merits. *American Psychologist*, 39 (3), 214-227.

Burisch, M. (1997). Test length and validity revisited. *European Journal of Personality*, 11, 303-315.

Campbell, J.P. (1990). Modeling the performance prediction problem in Industrial and Organizational Psychology. In M. Dunnette and L.M. Hough (Eds.), *Handbook of Industrial and Organizational Psychology*, Vol. 1, 2nd edition, pp. 697–731. Palo Alto, CA: Consulting Psychologists Press.

Campbell, J.P., McHenry, J.J. & Wise, L.L. (1990). Modeling job performance in a population of jobs. *Personnel Psychology*, 43, 313–333.

Campbell, J.P., McCloy, R.A., Oppler, S.H. & Sager, C.E. (1993). A theory of performance. In N. Schmitt, W.C. Bormann et al. (Eds), *Personnel Selection in Organizations*, pp. 35–70. San Francisco: Jossey-Bass.

Cattell, R. B. (1965). *The Scientific Analysis of Personality.* London: Penguin.

Costa, P. T., Jr., & McCrae, R. R. (1992). Normal personality assessment in clinical practice: The NEO Personality Inventory. *Psychological Assessment*, 4, 5-13.

Cronbach, L. J. (1970). *The Essentials of Psychological Testing (3rd Ed.).* New York: Harper & Row.

Digman, J. M. (1997). Higher-order factors of the big five. *Journal of Personality and Social Psychology*, 73, 1246-1256.

Ellingson, J. E., & Sakett, P. R. (2001). *Consistency of personality scale scores across selection and development contexts.* Poster presented at the Society for Industrial and Occupational Psychology, San Diego, California. USA.

Ferguson, E., Payne, T., & Anderson, N. (1994). Occupational personality assessment: Theory, structure and psychometrics of the OPQ FMX5- student. *Personality and Individual Differences,* 17(2), 217-225.

Foster, J., Johnson, C. & Gaddis, B (2008). *The predictive validity of personality: New methods produce new results.* Presented at the 23rd annual conference of the Society for Industrial-Organizational Psychology, April 2008.

Fullman, C. (2005). *An Empirical Investigation of the Criterion-Related Validity of the Professional Styles Personality Questionnaire.* Unpublished MSc dissertation. Goldsmiths College, University of London.

Goldacre, B. (2008). *Bad Science.* Harper-Collins.

Grove, W., H., Zald, D. H., Lebow, S.B., Snitz, B. E., & Nelson, C. (2000) Clinical versus Mechanical Prediction: A Meta-Analysis. Psychological Assessment, 12, 1,19-30.

Hogan, J., Davies, S. & Hogan, R. (2008). Generalizing Personality-Based Validity Evidence. In S. Morton McPhail (Ed.), *Alternative Validation Strategies: Developing New and Leveraging Existing Validity Evidence* (181-233). Jossey Bass: San Francisco, California.

Hough, L., Eaton, N. K., Dunnette, M. K., Kemp, J. D., & McCloy R. A. (1990). Criterion related validities of personality constructs and the effect of response distortion on those validities. *Journal of Applied Psychology,* 75(5), 581-595.

Hough, L.M. (1992) The Big Five personality variables – construct confusion. Description versus prediction. *Human Performance,* 5, 139-155.

Hurtz, G. M., & Donovan, J. J. (2000). Personality and job performance: The big five revisited. *Journal of Applied Psychology,* 85, 869-879.

Huxley, A. (1954). *The Doors of Perception.* New York: Harper & Row.

Judge, T. A, Bono, J. E., Ilies, R. & Gerhardt, M. W. (2002). Personality and leadership: A qualitative and quantitative review. *Journal of Applied Psychology,* 87(4), 765-780.

Kurz, R. (1999). Automated prediction of management competencies from personality and ability variables. *Proceedings of the Test User Conference* pp. 96-101. Leicester: BPS.

Kurz, R. & Bartram, D. (2002). Competency and individual performance: Modelling the world of work. In I. T. Robertson, M. Callinen and D. Bartram (Eds.), *Organizational Effectiveness: The Role of Psychology.* Chichester: Wiley.

Kurz, R (2005). *Convivence of Personality, Motivation, Interest & Ability Theories in Competency.* Paper presented at EAWOP Congress, Istanbul, May 2005.

Kurz, R (2006). *Personality, Motivation and Culture Preference.* Paper at the Work Psychology Congress, Leipzig, Germany, 2006.

Kurz, R. MacIver R. & Saville, P. (2008). *Coaching with Saville Consulting Wave™.* In Passmore. J. (Ed): Psychometrics in Coaching. Kogan Page, London.

Kurz, R., Saville, P., MacIver, R., Mitchener, A., Parry, G., Oxley, H., Small, C., Herridge, K. & Hopton, T. (2009). *The structure of work effectiveness as measured through the Saville Consulting Wave® Performance 360 'B-A-G' Model of Behavior, Ability and Global Performance.* (In press).

Landy, F. (1985). Stamp Collecting Versus Science: Validation as Hypothesis Testing. *American Psychologist* 41(11),1183-1192.

Landy, F. (2007). *Employment Discrimination Litigation.* In S. M. McPhail (Ed). Alternative Validation Strategies: Developing New and Leveraging Existing Validity Evidence. San Francisco, USA: Jossey-Bass.

Lie, D. (2008). A Single Subjective Question May Help Screen for Excessive Daytime Sleepiness. *Journal of Clinical Sleep Medicine,* 4,143-148.

MacIver, R., Saville, P., Kurz, R., Mitchener, A., Mariscal, K., Parry, G., Becker, S., Saville, W., O'Connor, K., Patterson R., Oxley, H. (2006a). Making Waves: Saville Consulting Wave Styles questionnaires. *Selection and Development Review,* 22(2), 17-23.

MacIver, R., Saville, P., Kurz, R., Henley, S., Mitchener, A., Mariscal, K., Parry, G., Becker, S., Hurst, E., Saville, W., O'Connor, K, Patterson R., McLellan, S. & Blakesley, M. (2006b). *The Validation Centric Development of the Professional Styles Questionnaires.* Presented at the BPS Occupational Psychology Conference, Glasgow, UK.

MacIver, R., Saville, P. Kurz, R. and Anderson, N. (2008). *New Aspects of Validity: User Available and User Received Validity.* Poster presented at the 6th Annual International Test Commission (ITC) Conference, Liverpool, UK, July 2008.

MacIver, R., Saville, P., Kurz, R., Oxley, H., Feindt, S., Beaujouan, Y.-M., McDowall, A.(2009) *Effectiveness at Work: Investigating the Structure and Prediction of Performance Based on a Co-validation of Seven Personality and Three Aptitude Assessments.* Symposium presented at European Association of Work and Organizational Psychology Conference, Santiago, Spain.

Miles, A. (2006). Issues surrounding the engagement of new starters. *Proceedings of the British Psychological Society Division of Occupational Psychology Conference,* Glasgow, UK, January 2006.

Morgeson, F. P., Campion, M. A., Dipboye, R. L., Hollenbeck, J. R., Murphy, K. & Schmitt, N. (2007). Reconsidering the use of personality tests in personnel selection contexts. *Personnel Psychology,* 60(3), 683-729.

Musek, J. (2007). A general factor of personality: Evidence for the Big One in the five factor model. *Journal of Research in Personality,* 41, 1213 - 1233.

Norman, W. T. (1963). Personality measurement, faking, and detection: An assessment method for use in personnel selection. *Journal of Applied Psychology,* 47 (4), 225-241.

Nyfield, G., Gibbons, P. J., Baron H, & Robertson, I. (1995). *The Cross Cultural Validity of Management Assessment Methods.* Paper presented at the 10th Annual SIOP Conference Orlando, USA, May 1995.

Ones, D. S., Viswesvaran, C., & Reiss, A. D. (1996). The role of social desirability in personality testing for personnel selection: The Red Herring. *Journal of Applied Psychology,* 81, 660-679.

Plake, B. S. & Impara, J. C. (Eds.) (2001). *The Mental Measurements Yearbook,* University of Nebraska Press, Lincoln: USA.

Robertson, I.T. & Kinder, A. (1993). Personality and job competencies: the criterion related validity of some personality variables. *Journal of Occupational and Organisational Psychology,* 66, 225-244.

Robertson, I. T. & Smith, M. (2001). Personnel selection. *Journal of Occupational and Organizational Psychology,* 74(4), 441-472.

Salgado, J. F. (1997). The five factor model of personality and job performance in the European Community. *Journal of Applied Psychology,* 82, 30-43.

Salgado J. F. (1998). The Big Five personality dimensions and job performance in army and civil service occupations: A European perspective. *Human Performance,* 11, 271-278.

Saville, P. (1975). *Occupational Testing.* HTS Management Consultants, London.

Saville, P., Holdsworth, R., Nyfield, G., Cramp, L., & Mabey, W. (1984). *Occupational Personality Questionnaire Manual.* Thames Ditton: Saville-Holdsworth Ltd.

Saville, P. (2008). *Personality Questionnaires – Valid Inferences, False Prophecies.* Presented at the Division of Occupational Psychology of the British Psychological Society Annual Conference, UK, January 2008.

Saville, P. (2008b). Does Your Test Work? Presented at the Psychological Society of South Africa Annual Conference, Johannesburg, August 2008.

Saville, P. (2008c). A Comparison of Leadership in Business and Elite Athletes. Presented at the A&DC Conference, Institute of Directors, London, November 2008.

Saville, P., Holdsworth, R., Nyfield, G., Cramp, L., & Mabey, W. (1984). *Occupational Personality Questionnaire Manual.* Thames Ditton: Saville-Holdsworth, Ltd.

Saville, P, MacIver, R., Kurz, R. & Hopton, T. (2008a). *Saville Personality Questionnaire Manual and User Guide.* Saville Consulting Group: Jersey. (In press).

Saville, P., MacIver, R. and Kurz, R. (2008b). *Saville Consulting Wave Professional Styles Manual and User Guide.* Saville Consulting Group: Jersey. (In press).

Saville, P., MacIver, R. and Kurz, R. (2008c). *Saville Consulting Wave Focus Styles Manual and User Guide.* Saville Consulting Group: Jersey. (In press).

497

Saville, P., MacIver, R. and Kurz, R. (2009c).Handbook to Saville Consulting Wave Focus Styles. Saville Consulting Group: Jersey. (In press).

Saville, P. & Wilson, E. (1991). The reliability and validity of normative and ipsative approaches in the measurement of personality. *Journal of Occupational Psychology*, 64, 219-238.

Scargle, J. D. (2000). Publication bias: The "file-drawer" problem in scientific inference. *Journal of Scientific Exploration*, 14(1), 91-106.

Schmidt, F. L., & Hunter, J. E. (1998). The validity and utility of selection methods in personnel psychology: Practical and theoretical implications of 85 years of research. *Psychological Bulletin*, 124(2), 262-274.

Schmitt, N., Gooding, R. Z., Noe, R. A., & Kirsch, M. (1984). Meta-analyses of validity studies. *Journal of Applied Psychology*, 70, 280-289.

Schmitt, N. & Oswald, F. L. (2006). The impact of correction for faking on the validity of non-cognitive measures in selection settings. *Journal of Applied Psychology*, 91(3), 613-621.

SHL (2000). *OPQ32 Technical Manual*. Thames Ditton, England: SHL Group plc.

Stagner, R. (1958). The gullibility of personnel managers. *Personnel Psychology*, 11, 347-352.

Tett, R. P., Jackson, D. N., & Rothstein, M. (1991). Personality measures as predictors of job performance. A meta-analytic review. *Personnel Psychology*, 44, 704-742.

Timmons, J.A. and Spinelli, S. (2003). *New Venture Creation: Entrepreneurship for the 21st Century*. London: McGraw-Hill / Irwin.

Wiggins, J. S. (1973). *Personality and prediction: Principles of personality assessment*. Reading, MA: Addison-Wesley.

Saville Consulting UK Ltd

Harley House
94 Hare Lane
Claygate
Surrey KT10 0RB
United Kingdom

Tel   +44 (0)1372 475700
Fax   +44 (0)1372 475701

info.uk@savilleconsulting.com

Saville Consulting Group

1st Floor, Anley House
Anley Street
St Helier
Jersey JE2 3QE
British Channel Islands

Tel   +44(0)1534 726820

info.group@savilleconsulting.com

Saville Consulting Asia Pacific

P O Box 1855
North Sydney
NSW 2060
Australia

Tel   +612 8004 2941
Mobile   +61 408 55 66 77
Fax   +612 9904 4750

info.ap@savilleconsulting.com

Contact Us

UK, USA, France, Denmark, Spain, Caribbean, South Africa, Poland, Sweden, Bulgaria, Netherlands, Germany, Italy, Dubai, Brazil, Turkey, Mexico, Canada, Australia, New Zealand, Hong Kong, Ireland, Singapore

20.0 Index

A

A Priori Hypotheses
85-286, 288, 297-298, 301, 303, 353, 356, 363-364, 402, 413-414

Ability
2-13, 29, 121, 143-144, 149-151, 153-156, 160, 285, 306, 361, 402, 413, 415, 461, 471

Accomplishing Objectives
3, 122, 397, 402, 404

Administration
3, 35-37, 133, 283, 296, 304, 342, 344

Administrators
5-36

Aligned Model
4-15, 183, 287, 305, 360, 400, 415

Applications
5-16, 27, 29, 121, 121, 129, 167, 183, 314

Applying Specialist Expertise
97, 402

Assessment Goal
27, 29, 37, 128, 185, 283, 319-320, 341, 353-355, 358-362, 415-416

Assessment Purpose
11, 35-36, 121, 130, 309, 311, 316, 342, 351, 353-357, 359, 363

Average Happiness
467

B

BAG Work Criterion Model
12-13, 16, 19, 398, 402, 413, 415

Behavior
12-13, 16, 19, 23-24, 29, 121, 124-126, 129, 131, 146, 154, 156, 285-286, 288-290, 293, 305, 307, 311, 315, 317, 319, 355, 357, 359-364, 402, 413-414, 461

Benchmark
27-28, 166, 320, 354, 414

The Big Five
11, 18, 289, 305, 307, 314, 463

Birth Order
465

C

Career Counseling
11, 24, 27, 29, 316, 317, 360

Case Studies
135-161

Ronald J. Stouffer	135
Bob Wilson	141
Ajaz Ahmed	148
Kathryn McCusker	155

Clusters
13, 16, 19-20, 43, 128-129, 133, 179-183, 293, 298, 301, 306-307

Commitment to Profession
169, 466

Competency Model
14, 16, 24, 35, 121, 182-183, 287, 289-290, 293, 298, 303, 355, 358-360, 364, 414

Competency Potential
11, 15, 166, 183, 303, 316, 357, 359-360, 362-363, 390, 392, 396, 398, 400-401, 404-406, 409-410, 414

Competency Development
27, 360, 362, 397, 402

Construction
283, 287, 306

Correlations with other questionnaires
313, 369

Criterion
11, 14, 16, 35, 124, 182, 284-287, 289-290, 296-299, 302, 315-316, 353-356, 357-364, 369, 390, 394-396, 399-402, 404-416

Criterion Centric
11, 12, 24, 36, 361, 388, 402, 413

Criterion Model
14, 19, 284, 293-296, 299, 304-305, 357-359, 361-362, 364, 388, 413

Cross Validation
15, 183, 285-286, 298, 302-303, 357, 359, 363-364, 398, 413-415, 465

Culture Prediction
25, 27

D

Deep Dives
124-125

Demonstrating Potential
13, 344, 397, 402, 474

499

Development
11-12, 15, 22, 24-25, 27-28, 31, 35-36, 122, 166, 167-168, 182-185, 283-289, 292-294, 296, 298, 301-306, 314, 316-317, 320, 341-342, 351, 353, 355-356, 360-361, 363, 369, 397-398, 402, 415, 460

Matrix 1: Intercorrelations of Wave Professional Styles

Invited Access \ Supervised Access	Analytical	Factual	Rational	Learning Oriented	Practically Minded	Insightful	Inventive	Abstract	Strategic	Interactive	Engaging	Self-promoting	Convincing	Articulate	Challenging	Purposeful
Analytical		.36	.50	.37	.07	.41	.31	.53	.25	-.15	-.28	-.07	.27	.04	.27	.17
Factual	.39		.18	.28	-.01	.18	-.04	.29	.01	-.22	-.13	-.10	-.02	-.05	.09	-.14
Rational	.48	.25		.30	.24	.15	.07	.33	.02	-.21	-.25	-.13	.01	-.13	.07	.01
Learning Oriented	.38	.27	.26		.05	.20	.22	.49	.19	-.07	-.12	-.03	.03	.12	.14	.09
Practically Minded	.06	-.05	.23	-.01		.05	-.10	-.02	-.19	-.08	.02	-.09	-.02	-.13	-.07	.02
Insightful	.36	.14	.16	.27	.01		.41	.37	.47	-.11	-.16	.04	.26	.02	.19	.39
Inventive	.30	-.04	.09	.31	-.08	.41		.44	.49	.14	-.05	.14	.31	.12	.28	.29
Abstract	.48	.36	.33	.51	-.06	.28	.52		.38	-.15	-.26	-.05	.06	.02	.18	-.02
Strategic	.21	.00	-.02	.23	-.19	.44	.56	.52		.08	-.03	.16	.35	.27	.20	.32
Interactive	-.10	-.22	-.21	-.09	-.10	-.13	.15	-.10	.05		.58	.41	.31	.39	.14	.10
Engaging	-.24	-.14	-.25	-.12	-.02	-.18	-.06	-.26	-.07	.60		.30	.11	.40	-.02	.00
Self-promoting	-.07	-.08	-.14	-.04	-.12	-.06	.14	-.02	.11	.43	.29		.29	.28	.21	.13
Convincing	.25	-.04	-.02	-.01	-.06	.22	.31	.13	.31	.27	.09	.26		.31	.55	.46
Articulate	.07	.01	-.10	.10	-.12	.03	.14	.06	.23	.38	.37	.24	.31		.20	.18
Challenging	.30	.07	.05	.11	-.06	.16	.24	.20	.19	.15	-.06	.22	.56	.20		.29
Purposeful	.19	-.15	-.01	.04	-.03	.39	.32	.07	.33	.11	.01	.15	.45	.19	.28	
Directing	.06	-.23	-.14	-.11	-.07	.29	.21	-.02	.33	.22	.14	.22	.42	.34	.22	.54
Empowering	-.03	-.17	-.23	-.06	-.17	.26	.34	.11	.41	.28	.18	.22	.33	.38	.10	.29
Self-assured	-.08	-.12	-.11	.02	-.03	.13	.10	-.04	.25	.19	.24	.20	.12	.23	.07	.18
Composed	.06	-.15	-.01	.08	-.02	.13	.14	-.01	.21	.08	.04	-.05	.19	.38	.12	.38
Resolving	.02	.04	-.15	-.04	-.05	-.01	-.02	-.01	.02	.08	.17	-.05	.18	.13	.11	.08
Positive	-.14	-.17	-.15	-.02	-.04	.03	.06	-.12	.07	.31	.36	.06	.02	.14	-.10	.10
Change Oriented	.15	-.17	.07	.29	-.03	.28	.35	.23	.33	-.01	-.04	-.14	.07	.13	.08	.27
Receptive	.01	.09	.04	.13	.03	.05	.04	.11	.07	-.01	.08	.20	-.03	.03	.05	-.13
Attentive	-.05	.09	-.25	.04	.00	-.05	-.02	.05	-.04	.05	.17	-.05	-.08	.10	-.03	-.23
Involving	-.15	.02	-.08	-.07	.06	-.12	-.12	-.06	-.15	.03	.18	-.08	-.13	.02	-.12	-.28
Accepting	-.19	-.01	-.13	-.12	.10	-.12	-.14	-.08	-.18	.00	.16	-.10	-.25	.00	-.25	-.23
Reliable	-.16	.02	.13	-.07	.15	-.07	-.30	-.17	-.24	-.18	.00	-.17	-.17	-.23	-.25	-.04
Meticulous	.14	.30	.22	.00	.13	.05	-.17	.03	-.17	-.21	-.07	-.16	-.10	-.20	-.17	-.13
Conforming	-.21	.12	.10	-.19	.22	-.31	-.53	-.27	-.44	-.14	-.02	-.04	-.30	-.27	-.32	-.45
Organized	.01	.11	.04	-.11	.06	.11	-.26	-.05	.01	-.17	-.04	-.12	-.09	-.14	-.18	-.01
Principled	.00	.12	.00	.05	.05	.05	-.08	.00	-.07	-.13	.00	-.24	-.11	-.03	-.17	-.05
Activity Oriented	.04	-.09	.05	.18	.09	.13	-.04	-.05	-.02	.00	.02	-.09	.01	-.15	-.07	.22
Dynamic	.13	-.21	-.10	.01	-.08	.36	.37	.08	.39	.31	.10	.23	.39	.21	.18	.45
Enterprising	.07	-.09	-.02	-.10	-.09	.20	.34	.05	.33	.29	.24	.29	.52	.28	.17	.40
Striving	.15	-.08	.08	.06	-.09	.27	.29	.14	.40	.16	.17	.23	.37	.18	.15	.40

Correlations between dimensions of the same cluster are shaded in their cluster colour

504

Dimensions

Directing	Empowering	Self-assured	Composed	Resolving	Positive	Change oriented	Receptive	Attentive	Involving	Accepting	Reliable	Meticulous	Conforming	Organized	Principled	Activity Oriented	Dynamic	Enterprising
.04	-.05	-.06	.06	-.02	-.16	.14	.03	-.12	-.21	-.18	-.07	.20	-.19	.01	.01	.05	.11	.09
-.24	-.19	-.19	-.17	.04	-.17	-.17	.02	.09	.06	.06	.01	.29	.11	.10	.10	-.07	-.20	-.14
-.11	-.21	-.07	.00	-.19	-.11	.10	.00	-.27	-.13	-.13	.11	.20	.06	.04	.01	.04	-.06	.01
-.06	.00	.05	.09	-.04	-.03	.30	.18	.02	-.10	-.11	-.06	.02	-.21	-.12	.06	.19	.04	-.05
-.05	-.16	-.03	-.01	-.03	-.02	-.01	.01	-.01	.08	.06	.18	.12	.21	.08	.07	.13	-.05	-.09
.27	.24	.14	.09	-.02	.01	.25	.08	-.07	-.17	-.17	-.09	.01	-.29	.03	-.01	.12	.38	.19
.19	.34	.13	.12	-.04	.03	.36	.06	-.03	-.14	-.15	-.27	-.16	-.50	-.24	-.03	-.02	.34	.29
-.08	.03	-.07	-.06	-.06	-.16	.17	.14	.05	-.08	-.04	-.12	.09	-.17	-.03	.04	-.08	-.01	-.01
.37	.40	.35	.22	.01	.10	.31	.13	-.08	-.17	-.20	-.18	-.16	-.38	.06	-.04	-.01	.41	.35
.23	.25	.21	.05	.09	.28	.03	.01	.07	.03	-.04	-.17	-.24	-.14	-.18	-.09	.01	.29	.28
.15	.17	.26	.07	.24	.31	-.02	.06	.18	.22	.13	.03	-.10	-.01	-.02	.04	.05	.12	.22
.25	.18	.28	-.11	-.06	.00	-.13	.17	-.05	-.10	-.15	-.19	-.11	-.02	-.09	-.21	-.08	.21	.33
.43	.29	.16	.18	.16	-.02	.09	-.03	-.09	-.16	-.28	-.18	-.09	-.30	-.08	-.06	.01	.36	.47
.31	.35	.26	.35	.16	.10	.13	.03	.08	-.02	-.04	-.21	-.18	-.26	-.13	-.02	-.11	.23	.28
.20	.09	.07	.09	.04	-.16	.08	.02	-.10	-.19	-.28	-.24	-.13	-.31	-.19	-.16	-.05	.17	.19
.50	.28	.21	.36	.03	.06	.26	-.10	-.26	-.30	-.27	-.03	-.13	-.40	-.03	-.05	.21	.45	.39
	.55	.25	.28	.14	.06	.21	.01	-.07	-.07	-.16	-.06	-.11	-.31	.12	-.06	.14	.47	.40
.55		.18	.20	.26	.14	.16	.09	.22	.12	.09	-.16	-.17	-.30	-.07	.01	-.05	.34	.37
.22	.15		.24	.01	.35	.20	.12	.03	-.09	.01	-.03	-.13	-.17	.03	-.06	.03	.28	.24
.24	.15	.22		.09	.31	.43	-.01	-.08	-.11	-.06	-.10	-.21	-.39	-.13	.03	.20	.22	.16
.12	.26	.05	.15		.13	.00	.07	.47	.28	.27	-.01	-.02	-.02	-.03	.14	.03	-.06	.02
.05	.13	.40	.23	.08		.35	.07	.07	.05	.15	-.01	-.22	-.14	-.11	.07	.08	.23	.09
.13	.15	.18	.45	.00	.33		.09	-.11	-.04	-.07	-.11	-.19	-.44	-.19	.00	.25	.33	.12
-.06	.04	.10	-.07	.04	.07	.14		.12	.28	.14	.02	.02	.06	.05	.09	.06	-.01	.03
-.07	.24	.02	-.05	.46	.08	-.11	.10		.51	.53	-.09	-.07	.09	-.08	.20	-.12	-.17	-.20
-.06	.16	-.09	-.08	.30	.10	-.05	.24	.51		.53	.08	.01	.25	.03	.23	-.08	-.20	-.22
-.11	.13	-.05	-.02	.33	.19	-.08	.10	.50	.54		.10	.02	.25	.01	.31	-.08	-.23	-.28
-.06	-.17	-.05	-.13	-.06	-.06	-.14	.04	-.16	.05	.11		.49	.47	.59	.26	.29	-.08	-.10
-.10	-.19	-.13	-.20	-.02	-.17	-.18	.09	-.10	.05	.05	.48		.42	.50	.17	.19	-.16	-.06
-.28	-.33	-.15	-.38	-.06	-.13	-.44	.12	.03	.21	.24	.47	.45		.40	.15	.01	-.38	-.32
.17	-.04	-.01	-.13	-.10	-.12	-.18	.05	-.14	-.02	-.01	.60	.50	.42		.17	.20	-.01	-.05
-.09	.02	-.06	-.05	.12	.06	.02	.07	.15	.25	.37	.28	.18	.17	.15		.08	-.05	-.04
.13	-.08	-.01	.21	-.02	.03	.22	.01	-.14	-.09	-.08	.30	.17	-.03	.27	.03		.25	.04
.50	.35	.26	.24	-.06	.26	.31	-.01	-.16	-.15	-.19	-.05	-.16	-.37	.02	-.07	.23		.42
.41	.36	.17	.16	.04	.11	.12	.00	-.17	-.17	-.23	-.08	-.06	-.30	-.07	-.07	.00	.41	
.41	.29	.29	.15	.02	.16	.23	.11	-.19	-.16	-.17	.08	.09	-.22	.09	.01	.15	.43	.53

Any correlations between dimensions that are .4 or above and are not within their own section are shaded green

Any correlations between dimensions that are -.4 or below and are not within their own section are shaded orange

505

Matrix 2: Wave PS 36 level against OPQ32i

WAVE DIMENSIONS / OPQ	Persuasive	Controlling	Outspoken	Independent Minded	Outgoing	Affiliative	Socially Confident	Modest	Democratic	Caring	Data Rational	Evaluative	Behavioral	Conventional	Conceptual
Analytical	-.02	.15	.19	.12	-.24	-.29	-.16	-.07	-.09	-.24	.40	.42	.06	-.04	.29
Factual	-.16	-.08	.09	.02	-.08	-.06	-.04	.03	.07	-.04	.12	.39	.10	.05	.31
Rational	-.09	.05	-.01	-.07	-.23	-.28	-.18	-.02	-.21	-.27	.61	.15	-.27	.16	.03
Learning Oriented	-.13	.04	.04	.02	-.12	-.17	.03	.07	-.09	-.18	.13	.21	.11	-.08	.38
Practically Minded	-.13	.03	.04	-.03	-.11	-.16	-.14	.14	.00	-.04	.09	.03	-.21	.23	-.14
Insightful	-.08	.20	.15	.17	-.21	-.34	-.12	-.08	-.15	-.29	.05	.28	-.05	-.15	.02
Inventive	.18	.25	.22	.36	-.03	-.20	-.05	-.16	-.16	-.33	-.07	.09	-.07	-.46	.27
Abstract	-.03	.06	.02	.13	-.23	-.24	-.16	-.08	.00	-.24	.19	.35	.14	-.22	.61
Strategic	.03	.24	.03	.13	-.09	-.20	-.03	-.20	-.08	-.26	-.08	.08	.08	-.36	.13
Interactive	.16	.07	.08	-.15	.73	.41	.47	-.32	.14	.18	-.29	-.28	.06	-.24	-.11
Engaging	.15	.04	-.05	-.30	.48	.41	.55	-.22	.15	.31	-.28	-.29	.05	-.07	-.25
Self-promoting	.17	.17	.12	.12	.45	.28	.22	-.49	.00	-.06	-.15	-.11	.08	-.24	.01
Convincing	.43	.43	.49	.30	.19	-.18	.05	-.31	-.13	-.33	-.03	.13	-.15	-.23	.14
Articulate	.24	.32	.20	-.13	.40	.12	.59	-.26	.09	.00	-.10	-.07	.07	-.26	.06
Challenging	.23	.37	.56	.35	.15	-.15	.03	-.22	-.09	-.31	-.03	.26	-.03	-.26	.23
Purposeful	.19	.43	.35	.16	.00	-.22	.08	-.13	-.28	-.39	.00	.12	-.17	-.25	.05
Directing	.20	.78	.28	.03	.17	-.09	.22	-.31	-.05	-.28	-.09	.02	-.07	-.31	-.02
Empowering	.22	.30	.16	.04	.24	.02	.20	-.19	.17	.08	-.24	-.10	.14	-.35	.12
Self-assured	.09	.11	.04	.09	.08	-.08	.08	-.23	-.23	-.21	-.07	-.17	-.09	-.18	-.09
Composed	.09	.30	.24	-.02	.06	-.15	.29	-.10	-.21	-.24	.08	.00	-.13	-.23	-.03
Resolving	.12	.00	.06	-.16	.11	.13	.25	-.05	.12	.37	-.15	-.12	.23	-.09	.04
Positive	.02	-.08	-.09	-.14	.13	.07	.24	-.13	-.11	.03	-.17	-.33	-.03	-.10	-.18
Change Oriented	.00	.18	.01	-.03	-.08	-.19	.11	-.07	-.11	-.21	-.02	-.02	.03	-.29	.04
Receptive	.02	.05	.03	-.06	.05	.06	-.06	-.14	.26	.09	-.04	.08	.20	-.16	.11
Attentive	-.16	-.28	-.21	-.20	.08	.38	.15	.09	.41	.58	-.29	-.09	.66	-.07	.09
Involving	-.08	-.18	-.20	-.43	.04	.24	.01	.12	.53	.46	-.05	-.08	.21	.12	-.04
Accepting	-.16	-.31	-.32	-.37	.00	.27	.08	.10	.28	.50	-.08	-.18	.19	.10	-.16
Reliable	-.07	-.12	-.09	-.31	-.17	-.11	-.08	.12	-.06	.12	.03	-.07	-.24	.28	-.22
Meticulous	-.18	-.07	-.08	-.12	-.26	-.14	-.22	.06	.02	.01	.10	.16	-.15	.36	-.14
Conforming	-.26	-.33	-.28	-.24	-.10	.08	-.19	.12	.15	.25	.16	-.05	-.08	.61	-.21
Organized	-.15	-.02	-.10	-.21	-.22	-.13	-.14	.03	.02	.07	.08	.04	-.07	.27	-.18
Principled	-.18	-.13	-.13	-.24	-.25	-.03	-.12	.16	.16	.20	-.07	.07	.08	.18	-.05
Activity Oriented	-.12	.04	-.04	-.11	-.07	.03	-.08	.05	-.16	-.10	-.07	-.14	-.07	.01	-.16
Dynamic	.14	.39	.20	.22	.19	-.05	.16	-.38	-.17	-.34	-.15	-.10	-.02	-.44	-.02
Enterprising	.53	.32	.25	.18	.10	-.14	.08	-.26	-.20	-.38	-.05	-.08	-.20	-.27	-.04
Striving	.10	.21	.06	.14	-.02	-.15	.00	-.24	-.12	-.30	-.09	.01	-.09	-.28	.06

a. Listwise N=308

Innovative	Variety Seeking	Adaptable	Forward Thinking	Detail Conscious	Conscientious	Rule Following	Relaxed	Worrying	Tough Minded	Optimistic	Trusting	Emotionally Controlled	Vigorous	Competitive	Achieving	Decisive	Consistency
.16	-.09	-.08	.02	.02	-.07	-.09	.02	-.26	-.07	-.15	-.17	-.03	-.08	.11	.14	.11	-.04
.02	-.05	.08	-.01	.19	.00	-.03	-.13	-.05	-.14	-.22	-.08	-.01	-.12	-.12	-.02	-.04	.20
.00	-.16	-.13	-.06	.20	.17	.12	.17	-.15	.11	-.05	-.09	.20	.02	.11	-.02	.05	-.17
.08	.14	-.06	-.03	-.04	-.08	-.17	-.02	-.17	.05	-.02	-.11	.08	-.02	.01	.10	.08	.11
.00	-.07	-.02	-.10	.25	.14	.06	.08	-.01	.05	-.08	-.04	.16	.18	-.02	-.10	.01	-.06
.26	.11	.08	.13	.09	.10	-.26	-.02	-.22	-.08	.03	-.22	.06	.02	.16	.13	.24	.01
.76	.31	-.07	.06	-.35	-.24	-.49	-.01	-.12	.04	.04	-.28	-.03	-.07	.20	.15	.23	-.14
.37	.16	-.01	.08	-.06	-.13	-.18	-.12	-.07	-.04	-.07	-.25	-.06	-.11	.05	.14	.02	-.07
.36	.19	.05	.47	-.18	-.09	-.28	-.10	-.10	-.10	.17	-.20	-.17	-.07	.12	.37	.10	-.09
.09	.03	-.02	-.13	-.28	-.21	-.09	-.03	-.10	-.07	.09	.07	-.37	.10	.04	.10	-.07	-.07
-.16	-.10	-.03	-.12	-.09	.00	-.01	.04	-.06	-.01	.09	.12	-.32	.08	-.07	.08	-.15	-.04
.10	.10	.10	-.04	-.29	-.26	-.09	-.10	-.07	-.13	.07	-.07	-.31	-.12	.25	.15	-.09	-.04
.22	.08	-.01	-.03	-.31	-.14	-.27	-.11	-.22	-.01	-.16	-.37	-.12	-.14	.33	.19	.16	-.11
.08	-.01	-.08	-.16	-.27	-.19	-.19	.05	-.43	.07	.08	-.02	-.33	-.04	-.01	.05	-.02	-.04
.21	.09	-.05	-.09	-.26	-.19	-.32	-.08	-.18	.00	-.20	-.34	-.12	-.16	.34	.13	.05	-.07
.17	.09	-.02	.01	-.15	-.04	-.39	.03	-.34	.07	-.02	-.31	-.05	-.02	.21	.21	.54	-.09
.12	-.03	-.02	.03	-.11	-.02	-.22	-.07	-.31	-.03	-.04	-.30	-.29	.03	.18	.26	.15	-.16
.28	.06	.06	-.02	-.26	-.25	-.19	-.16	-.09	-.02	.02	-.10	-.25	-.13	.00	.12	.01	-.07
.05	.15	-.01	.25	-.20	-.05	-.12	.09	-.19	.06	.43	-.14	-.12	.08	.22	.34	.01	-.09
.11	.07	-.17	-.10	-.18	-.11	-.31	.44	-.65	.33	.13	-.05	.04	.13	.10	.02	.24	-.10
-.03	-.12	.05	-.10	-.06	-.11	-.11	.07	-.10	.07	.03	.08	-.10	-.04	-.21	-.06	-.04	-.05
.02	.08	-.15	.05	-.17	-.04	-.18	.34	-.19	.26	.57	.15	-.10	.15	-.03	.07	.07	-.01
.22	.31	-.07	.05	-.24	-.14	-.39	.27	-.31	.19	.29	-.07	.02	.11	.09	.16	.25	-.05
.00	.03	.10	.06	-.01	-.10	.02	-.17	.06	-.08	-.09	-.01	-.17	-.03	.00	.21	-.20	-.09
-.09	-.01	.14	-.03	-.07	-.20	-.04	-.13	.16	-.10	.00	.26	-.18	-.06	-.32	-.11	-.15	.12
-.21	-.22	.03	-.13	.13	.04	.24	-.01	.15	.01	-.10	.33	-.09	-.08	-.31	-.10	-.28	.02
-.15	-.16	-.01	-.05	.08	.02	.19	.16	.07	.12	.18	.54	-.13	-.04	-.36	-.11	-.20	.00
-.28	-.31	-.03	.08	.46	.61	.31	.10	.08	-.02	-.02	-.01	.12	.13	-.20	-.03	-.01	-.09
-.17	-.30	.03	.06	.60	.44	.40	-.11	.14	-.17	-.17	-.08	.01	.07	-.08	.10	-.16	-.06
-.46	-.47	.08	.03	.53	.35	.75	-.07	.30	-.14	-.13	.20	.12	-.06	-.24	-.20	-.26	.00
-.26	-.28	.05	.24	.61	.54	.37	-.17	.12	-.25	-.11	-.06	-.04	.12	-.18	.07	-.10	.00
-.16	-.07	-.04	.03	.28	.30	.20	.01	.13	-.06	-.04	.19	.00	.02	-.20	-.08	-.11	.06
-.04	.00	-.05	.00	.18	.17	-.02	.07	-.01	.01	.00	-.01	.12	.51	-.06	.09	.14	.02
.27	.23	-.01	.17	-.29	-.10	-.37	-.09	-.24	.00	.18	-.27	-.20	.18	.34	.34	.15	-.16
.19	.12	-.04	.07	-.35	-.12	-.21	-.08	-.17	-.02	.09	-.35	-.13	-.04	.54	.34	.10	-.18
.12	.10	.00	.20	-.20	.08	-.16	-.14	-.12	-.01	.17	-.24	-.15	.03	.37	.59	.02	-.09

Any correlations between dimensions that are .4 or above are shaded green

Any correlations between dimensions that are -.4 or below are shaded orange

Matrix 3: Wave PS 36 level against NEO-PI-R

CORRELATIONS[a] NEO / WAVE DIMENSIONS	GLOBAL FACTORS					(N1) Anxiety	(N2) Angry Hostility	(N3) Depression	(N4) Self-Consciousness	(N5) Impulsiveness	(N6) Vulnerability	(E1) Warmth	(E2) Gregariousness	(E3) Assertiveness	(E4) Activity	(E5) Excitement-Seeking
	(N) Neuroticism	(E) Extraversion	(O) Openness	(A) Agreeableness	(C) Conscientiousness											
Analytical	-.09	-.18	.20	-.15	.11	-.19	-.04	-.07	-.06	-.05	-.15	-.21	-.19	.11	.02	.09
Factual	.07	-.11	.19	-.02	.01	.02	.05	.11	.03	.09	.04	-.04	-.06	-.07	-.04	.00
Rational	-.10	-.18	-.12	-.07	.18	-.18	-.06	-.08	-.08	-.20	-.14	-.25	-.14	-.03	-.01	.14
Learning Oriented	-.08	-.11	.32	-.07	-.03	-.11	-.01	-.04	-.05	.01	-.12	-.08	-.07	-.02	.07	.02
Practically Minded	-.01	-.03	-.13	.05	.11	-.05	.01	.02	.05	-.08	-.12	.04	-.11	.02	-.06	.00
Insightful	-.11	-.10	.10	-.21	.21	-.22	.02	-.10	-.11	.02	-.25	-.18	-.23	.20	.13	.02
Inventive	.00	-.03	.39	-.21	-.09	-.10	.03	.05	.01	.13	-.06	-.16	-.13	.22	.22	.20
Abstract	.09	-.21	.40	-.08	.05	-.01	.02	.10	.05	.02	.02	-.21	-.15	-.02	.07	.16
Strategic	-.03	.05	.24	-.28	.16	-.07	.04	-.10	-.05	.06	-.13	-.11	-.02	.29	.30	.12
Interactive	-.11	.54	.00	-.06	-.22	.00	.04	-.08	-.19	.12	.02	.46	.52	.30	.23	.17
Engaging	-.11	.59	-.09	.13	-.04	.03	-.10	-.13	-.23	.04	-.07	.62	.54	.24	.17	.12
Self-promoting	.09	.28	.09	-.33	-.18	.09	.27	.05	-.03	.24	.22	.11	.30	.18	.15	.20
Convincing	-.02	.08	.09	-.53	.00	-.10	.25	-.03	-.09	.16	-.09	-.17	.03	.47	.19	.15
Articulate	-.28	.35	.20	-.08	-.07	-.24	-.09	-.23	-.39	-.04	-.16	.32	.34	.45	.19	.13
Challenging	.09	.00	.21	-.51	-.09	-.06	.34	.09	-.01	.22	.00	-.22	-.06	.28	.09	.20
Purposeful	-.16	.11	.09	-.36	.09	-.25	.06	-.13	-.18	.04	-.34	-.13	-.01	.48	.22	.14
Directing	-.20	.28	.08	-.33	.19	-.21	.03	-.20	-.25	.04	-.33	.11	.13	.68	.33	.15
Empowering	-.02	.24	.21	-.07	-.05	.03	.01	.02	-.09	.09	-.06	.17	.12	.35	.18	.11
Self-assured	-.30	.28	.04	-.21	.02	-.25	-.12	-.38	-.29	-.09	-.23	.09	.20	.25	.28	.13
Composed	-.47	.10	.11	-.09	-.11	-.54	-.22	-.32	-.40	-.15	-.40	.01	.04	.31	.11	.09
Resolving	-.07	.20	.09	.08	-.05	-.01	-.08	-.05	-.11	-.01	-.08	.18	.19	.09	.01	.11
Positive	-.49	.37	.04	.22	-.09	-.42	-.43	-.51	-.37	-.15	-.40	.35	.21	.13	.21	.03
Change Oriented	-.44	.12	.20	-.03	-.14	-.43	-.29	-.30	-.33	-.12	-.40	.04	.05	.22	.15	.12
Receptive	.11	.08	.13	.02	.02	.14	.04	.07	.01	.10	.12	.11	.08	.03	.08	.11
Attentive	.16	.08	.28	.34	-.18	.23	-.04	.16	.17	.07	.18	.29	.16	-.25	-.14	-.07
Involving	.04	.05	-.02	.44	-.01	.11	-.18	.08	.07	-.10	.09	.23	.19	-.17	-.18	-.07
Accepting	-.14	.09	-.01	.62	-.13	-.04	-.34	-.11	-.04	-.19	-.02	.29	.13	-.27	-.18	-.15
Reliable	.06	-.06	-.29	.18	.49	.07	-.10	-.02	.01	-.18	-.14	.04	-.08	-.04	-.03	-.09
Meticulous	.20	-.08	-.24	.09	.49	.20	.01	.06	.12	-.07	-.02	.02	-.09	-.09	.00	-.09
Conforming	.25	-.18	-.45	.26	.25	.31	.03	.15	.25	-.13	.26	.01	-.06	-.37	-.27	-.2
Organized	.16	-.10	-.26	.03	.61	.16	.04	.01	.08	-.08	-.03	.01	-.10	-.02	.03	-.1
Principled	.06	-.09	.01	.28	.30	.02	-.10	-.04	.05	-.14	-.08	.03	-.04	-.08	-.04	-.1
Activity Oriented	-.05	.08	.00	-.01	.24	-.05	-.06	-.06	-.05	.02	-.19	.10	.04	.11	.25	.0
Dynamic	-.08	.31	.17	-.35	.09	-.12	.09	-.08	-.17	.11	-.18	.06	.08	.45	.54	.2
Enterprising	-.06	.23	-.02	-.42	.07	-.06	.13	-.14	-.16	.08	-.08	-.04	.14	.37	.33	.2
Striving	-.03	.23	.02	-.33	.23	-.02	.04	-.12	-.13	.08	-.15	-.02	.14	.30	.39	.2

a. Listwise N=308

508

(E6) Positive Emotions	(O1) Fantasy	(O2) Aesthetics	(O3) Feelings	(O4) Actions	(O5) Ideas	(O6) Values	(A1) Trust	(A2) Straightforwardness	(A3) Altruism	(A4) Compliance	(A5) Modesty	(A6) Tender-Mindedness	(C1) Competence	(C2) Order	(C3) Dutifulness	(C4) Achievement Striving	(C5) Self-Discipline	(C6) Deliberation
-.11	.06	.02	-.04	.00	.42	-.01	-.07	-.05	-.15	-.11	-.19	-.09	.18	.03	.05	.13	-.01	.05
-.08	.10	.08	.16	.03	.16	.19	.00	.00	-.04	-.04	-.02	-.07	.07	.02	.00	-.05	-.10	.08
-.10	-.20	-.12	-.36	-.10	.18	-.13	-.10	.04	-.13	-.03	-.12	-.19	.15	.21	.11	.03	.14	.21
-.01	.14	.16	.06	.20	.34	.13	.02	.00	-.17	-.08	-.08	-.02	.08	-.06	-.06	.02	-.06	-.08
-.07	-.20	-.05	-.12	.01	-.11	-.05	-.01	.03	.09	-.06	.14	.05	.17	.08	.10	-.03	.13	.06
-.05	-.04	.07	-.02	.10	.11	-.06	-.07	-.12	-.12	-.15	-.12	-.11	.27	.13	.09	.20	.12	.03
-.01	.33	.27	.00	.28	.38	.03	-.12	-.17	-.17	-.13	-.19	.00	-.01	-.18	-.12	.07	-.13	-.24
-.08	.22	.26	.03	.15	.48	.07	-.05	-.03	-.18	-.07	-.12	-.08	.13	-.03	-.01	.07	-.09	.06
.10	.15	.18	.06	.20	.23	.01	-.04	-.19	-.16	-.18	-.24	-.11	.13	.05	-.02	.34	.07	-.02
.34	.09	.01	.16	.08	-.02	.07	.07	-.09	.19	-.03	-.12	.11	-.10	-.19	-.17	.01	-.09	-.26
.37	-.04	.00	.21	.08	-.14	.02	.19	.01	.39	.08	-.08	.13	.05	-.02	-.01	.07	.09	-.04
.17	.25	.12	.19	-.07	.02	.00	-.14	-.29	-.09	-.20	-.51	-.06	-.15	-.14	-.25	-.02	-.26	-.16
-.05	.12	.05	.03	-.01	.15	-.08	-.28	-.40	-.32	-.48	-.36	-.14	.02	-.12	-.12	.15	-.10	-.18
.22	.11	.12	.15	.19	.19	.08	.18	-.12	.06	.00	-.30	.00	.14	-.07	-.04	.11	.00	-.08
-.08	.22	.16	.11	.00	.22	.01	-.27	-.41	-.38	-.52	-.31	-.16	-.06	-.15	-.20	.02	-.22	-.24
-.01	.04	.01	.02	.09	.17	-.04	-.13	-.22	-.17	-.30	-.21	-.17	.20	-.04	.01	.24	.07	-.21
.16	.03	.07	.04	.08	.12	-.04	.00	-.22	-.04	-.21	-.28	-.09	.27	.09	.07	.35	.14	-.10
.16	.15	.20	.13	.16	.13	.04	.06	-.13	.07	-.06	-.11	.15	.03	-.16	-.07	.14	-.03	-.21
.29	.02	-.01	.06	.13	.01	.10	.03	-.20	-.03	-.07	-.36	-.08	.16	-.01	-.05	.26	.11	-.05
.05	-.03	.00	-.14	.21	.17	.10	.10	-.08	-.06	-.01	-.17	-.02	.16	-.08	.00	.05	.02	-.17
.14	.04	.08	.18	.10	.03	.17	.09	-.03	.17	.07	.06	.08	-.01	-.02	-.02	.00	.06	-.01
.44	-.01	.00	-.03	.22	-.01	.11	.35	.15	.26	.24	-.08	.11	.17	-.08	.06	.14	.15	-.10
.13	.07	.05	-.05	.40	.13	.19	.12	.00	-.07	.05	-.07	.00	.06	-.11	-.04	.08	.09	-.19
.05	.06	.11	.14	.03	.11	.06	.09	.05	.03	.02	.00	.09	-.07	-.01	.00	.11	-.02	-.01
.08	.22	.22	.42	.17	.05	.21	.24	.10	.28	.19	.24	.31	-.09	-.13	-.11	-.17	-.16	.01
-.04	-.11	.03	.09	.03	-.07	.08	.31	.30	.30	.27	.28	.25	-.02	.00	.11	-.06	.06	.15
.09	-.06	.00	.02	.01	-.11	.09	.56	.38	.39	.44	.26	.40	-.01	-.09	.08	-.11	.04	.14
.00	-.32	-.10	-.15	-.17	-.17	-.17	.02	.21	.21	.12	.24	.06	.23	.46	.43	.21	.56	.30
-.06	-.22	-.07	-.02	-.23	-.13	-.20	-.03	.17	.20	.03	.14	-.01	.25	.46	.38	.22	.34	.32
-.09	-.32	-.20	-.13	-.46	-.35	-.26	.02	.26	.16	.17	.21	.06	.01	.33	.21	-.11	.15	.39
-.01	-.33	-.10	.01	-.22	-.15	-.14	.00	.14	.14	.07	.12	-.05	.31	.63	.38	.29	.53	.41
-.01	-.15	.13	.12	-.02	-.02	-.10	.22	.28	.20	.11	.23	.14	.24	.19	.38	.11	.21	.24
.00	-.08	.04	.05	.08	.04	-.01	.03	.09	.19	.03	.13	-.03	.22	.20	.20	.19	.23	-.03
.24	.18	.10	.14	.19	.13	.06	-.09	-.21	-.06	-.21	-.25	-.06	.08	-.02	-.01	.29	.06	-.25
.11	.04	.00	-.03	.04	.04	-.14	-.21	-.29	-.19	-.29	-.38	-.16	.04	-.06	-.06	.28	.04	-.16
.16	.02	-.01	.06	.07	.09	-.07	-.15	-.16	-.08	-.21	-.25	-.15	.14	.00	.09	.48	.19	-.08

Any correlations between dimensions that are .4 or above are shaded green

Any correlations between dimensions that are -.4 or below are shaded orange

Matrix 4: Wave PS 36 level against 16PF5

CORRELATIONS[a] 16PF5 / WAVE DIMENSIONS	Warmth	Reasoning	Emotional Stability	Dominance	Liveliness	Rule Conscious	Social Boldness	Sensitivity
Analytical	-.28	.33	.02	.22	-.19	-.02	-.07	-.25
Factual	-.13	.29	-.11	.04	-.09	-.04	-.04	.17
Rational	-.40	.05	.10	.13	-.08	.07	-.07	-.50
Learning Oriented	-.20	.20	-.01	.04	-.07	-.18	.01	.14
Practically Minded	-.18	-.07	.03	.04	-.05	.08	-.07	-.28
Insightful	-.29	.08	.05	.24	-.16	-.06	-.03	-.18
Inventive	-.16	.10	-.06	.24	.10	-.26	.10	-.07
Abstract	-.26	.19	-.12	.09	-.07	-.17	-.07	-.05
Strategic	-.04	.08	.10	.22	.00	-.16	.14	-.03
Interactive	.45	-.13	.10	.11	.50	-.01	.57	.10
Engaging	.48	-.13	.19	.00	.48	.13	.52	.10
Self-promoting	.20	-.01	-.08	.19	.29	-.11	.35	.11
Convincing	-.05	-.03	-.02	.50	.03	-.15	.29	-.12
Articulate	.22	.11	.21	.29	.27	-.01	.65	.02
Challenging	-.12	.16	-.12	.45	.04	-.23	.18	-.09
Purposeful	-.12	.05	.12	.39	.00	-.11	.20	-.22
Directing	.10	-.01	.15	.46	.13	.03	.44	-.18
Empowering	.25	-.02	.01	.24	.17	.01	.30	.08
Self-assured	.03	-.05	.27	.22	.15	-.07	.23	-.11
Composed	-.08	.12	.28	.24	.07	-.16	.30	-.22
Resolving	.32	-.14	.07	.10	.18	-.02	.14	.08
Positive	.16	.01	.48	.01	.24	.03	.22	-.05
Change Oriented	.00	.09	.29	.17	.08	-.23	.18	-.11
Receptive	.21	.00	-.11	.10	.03	-.01	.00	.13
Attentive	.43	-.02	-.10	-.22	.14	.01	-.06	.35
Involving	.27	-.06	-.03	-.15	.03	.21	-.03	.08
Accepting	.29	-.05	.13	-.33	.04	.21	-.07	.13
Reliable	-.01	-.21	.12	-.13	-.12	.35	-.15	.00
Meticulous	-.12	-.07	.01	-.02	-.14	.35	-.22	-.02
Conforming	.03	-.19	-.12	-.31	-.17	.47	-.29	.03
Organized	-.01	-.08	.02	-.05	-.23	.32	-.16	.06
Principled	.05	.01	.10	-.11	-.12	.34	-.20	.15
Activity Oriented	.03	-.04	.07	.08	.03	.02	-.05	.09
Dynamic	.02	-.07	.11	.35	.18	-.19	.33	-.06
Enterprising	.01	-.10	.12	.40	.17	-.06	.27	-.21
Striving	-.04	-.03	.15	.24	.14	-.07	.15	-.13

510

a. Listwise N=308

Vigilance	Abstractedness	Privateness	Apprehension	Openess to Change	Self Reliance	Perfectionism	Tension	IM PFRS
.09	.11	.16	-.11	.15	.19	-.09	.07	-.02
.03	.04	.01	.05	.15	.12	.00	.06	-.08
.03	-.13	.20	-.14	-.10	.10	.15	.02	.06
.06	.16	.11	-.06	.25	.10	-.16	.01	-.01
.08	-.29	.10	-.07	-.07	.06	.11	-.07	.05
.08	.02	.24	-.14	.24	.27	.10	.11	-.07
.14	.45	.15	-.07	.45	.20	-.19	.04	-.11
.11	.30	.15	-.01	.37	.18	-.08	.06	-.08
.05	.19	.07	-.07	.35	.07	-.04	.10	-.06
-.03	.06	-.42	.02	.04	-.41	-.14	-.09	.04
-.17	-.16	-.39	.01	.11	.42	.02	-.26	.13
.15	.25	-.28	.16	.09	-.14	-.12	.21	-.21
.27	.26	.05	-.13	.30	.04	-.11	.25	-.16
-.12	.01	-.23	-.17	.20	-.27	-.12	-.20	.11
.30	.33	.11	-.08	.36	.12	-.16	.24	-.24
.16	.09	.16	-.26	.28	.11	-.11	.09	-.04
.09	.00	-.05	-.17	.21	-.09	.09	.00	.00
.03	.22	-.09	.01	.26	-.05	-.11	-.14	-.03
.04	.02	-.02	-.25	.13	-.06	-.01	-.03	.04
-.06	.01	.04	-.38	.16	-.09	-.19	-.19	.16
-.05	.00	-.09	.02	.06	-.20	-.02	-.28	.10
-.25	-.04	-.17	-.33	.02	-.16	-.08	-.37	.35
-.08	.08	.11	-.30	.35	-.07	-.24	-.26	.16
.03	.04	-.14	.20	.16	-.14	.03	-.03	-.08
-.17	.10	-.21	.23	.09	-.14	-.12	-.21	.03
-.23	-.21	-.16	.14	-.12	-.35	.02	-.28	.12
-.39	-.15	-.26	.00	-.15	-.20	-.02	-.39	.28
-.01	-.44	.05	.04	-.25	.01	.49	-.06	.13
.03	-.32	.03	.12	-.24	.09	.58	.06	.03
-.01	-.41	-.03	.25	-.55	.01	.42	.04	.04
.02	-.41	.02	.17	-.17	.09	.61	.07	.04
-.16	-.22	.03	.02	-.05	-.04	.13	-.09	.17
.05	-.19	.02	.01	.02	-.04	.16	-.10	.07
.15	.20	-.01	-.09	.35	-.03	-.05	.17	-.08
.14	.19	.07	-.19	.18	-.01	.00	.10	-.04
.09	.08	.04	-.13	.16	.00	.09	.06	-.01

Any correlations between dimensions that are .4 or above are shaded green

Any correlations between dimensions that are -.4 or below are shaded orange

Matrix 5: Wave PS 36 level against Hogan Personality

CORRELATIONS[a] HPI / WAVE DIMENSIONS	Empathy	Not Anxious	No Guilt	Calmness	Even Tempered	No Somatic Complaint	Trusting	Good Attachment	Competitive	Self Confidence	No Depression	Leadership	Identity	No Social Anxiety	Likes Parties	Likes Crowds	Experience Seeking	Exhibitionistic	Entertaining	Easy To Live With
Analytical	-.09	.11	.05	.15	.00	.14	-.09	-.03	.13	.15	.08	.10	.01	.07	-.07	-.08	.11	-.04	.07	-.14
Factual	-.14	-.04	-.07	-.08	-.17	.02	.00	-.06	-.10	-.06	-.10	-.07	-.06	-.02	-.10	-.03	.03	-.02	.05	-.16
Rational	.09	.18	.07	.24	.06	.09	-.14	.15	.06	.09	-.01	.01	-.01	-.01	.05	-.03	.04	-.10	.03	.02
Learning Oriented	-.03	.08	-.04	.02	-.04	.04	-.08	-.09	.08	.11	-.01	.05	-.06	.07	-.08	.03	.13	-.09	.04	-.16
Practically Minded	.06	.11	-.02	.16	.03	.06	-.13	.01	-.06	-.03	-.05	-.04	-.06	-.03	-.02	-.10	-.02	-.18	-.05	.03
Insightful	-.06	.13	.07	.11	-.03	.07	-.11	.00	.21	.20	.08	.24	.07	.05	-.16	-.17	.15	.02	-.04	-.12
Inventive	-.07	.00	-.04	-.01	-.01	.06	-.12	-.10	.25	.20	-.04	.26	.02	.12	.09	.04	.33	.17	.18	-.08
Abstract	-.11	-.04	-.03	.04	-.07	.05	-.10	-.07	.17	.05	-.10	.09	-.09	.01	-.01	.02	.19	.04	.03	-.06
Strategic	-.05	.00	.04	.00	-.01	.07	.03	-.11	.37	.24	.09	.33	.12	.11	.03	.01	.20	.12	.04	-.07
Interactive	.10	-.05	.04	-.14	-.02	.09	.06	-.09	.06	.19	.17	.18	.08	.36	.39	.25	.11	.41	.34	.22
Engaging	.27	.03	.10	.00	.10	.12	.18	.09	.03	.23	.20	.11	.07	.29	.37	.29	.07	.23	.27	.38
Self-promoting	-.18	-.17	-.09	-.21	-.21	-.08	-.06	-.07	.13	.15	.08	.28	-.04	.22	.31	.15	.07	.57	.40	-.03
Convincing	-.23	.06	.01	-.04	-.11	.03	-.20	-.11	.28	.23	.03	.46	.06	.25	.15	.06	.18	.31	.24	-.14
Articulate	.11	.16	.19	.09	.08	.18	.11	.02	.18	.41	.26	.39	.14	.63	.22	.22	.25	.37	.34	.17
Challenging	-.30	.01	-.07	-.12	-.20	.00	-.18	-.12	.24	.09	.00	.40	.00	.16	.09	.09	.26	.28	.21	-.19
Purposeful	-.09	.15	.05	.07	-.01	.15	-.18	-.09	.36	.31	.12	.48	.08	.26	.11	.10	.20	.09	.09	-.07
Directing	.00	.08	.14	.03	.07	.16	-.03	-.03	.38	.35	.18	.73	.08	.40	.17	.10	.20	.25	.17	.01
Empowering	.00	-.05	-.03	-.11	-.02	.00	-.01	-.13	.20	.14	.05	.30	.06	.18	.13	.14	.16	.27	.19	.05
Self-assured	.20	.17	.24	.14	.08	.23	.01	.02	.33	.36	.28	.26	.14	.17	.12	.04	.15	.24	.15	.01
Composed	.21	.44	.17	.25	.24	.21	.02	.01	.16	.31	.20	.25	.11	.45	.11	.11	.26	.05	.09	.09
Resolving	.14	.03	.03	.06	.05	.10	.06	.14	-.02	.00	.07	.01	.05	.10	.10	.19	.07	.02	.08	.19
Positive	.48	.37	.36	.27	.39	.29	.26	.12	.11	.28	.40	.03	.24	.27	.13	.11	.11	.01	.11	.34
Change Oriented	.24	.29	.16	.25	.22	.24	.01	-.10	.21	.22	.22	.17	.09	.27	.05	.10	.35	-.01	-.07	.12
Receptive	.01	-.14	-.05	-.13	-.07	-.13	-.01	-.02	.12	-.10	-.05	.06	-.03	-.01	.10	.11	.05	.09	.01	-.01
Attentive	.12	-.18	-.09	-.10	-.02	-.02	.19	-.03	-.18	-.21	-.03	-.24	-.09	-.13	.04	.10	-.03	-.01	-.08	.17
Involving	.20	-.03	-.02	.04	.06	.04	.18	.05	-.19	-.26	-.06	-.27	.01	-.12	.00	.12	-.15	-.14	-.10	.21
Accepting	.39	.15	.11	.13	.23	.06	.40	.12	-.27	-.14	.07	-.33	.06	-.10	-.05	.01	-.16	-.14	-.06	.35
Reliable	.10	.10	-.01	.11	.15	-.01	.00	.11	.01	-.10	-.05	-.13	-.04	-.13	-.05	-.06	-.24	-.25	-.13	.08
Meticulous	-.08	-.09	.01	-.01	-.06	-.11	-.03	.12	.03	-.09	-.07	-.09	-.01	-.24	-.08	-.12	-.21	-.20	-.14	-.01
Conforming	-.04	-.17	-.09	-.03	-.10	-.15	.03	.14	-.33	-.30	-.15	-.42	-.11	-.35	-.13	-.14	-.46	-.23	-.16	.02
Organized	-.07	-.13	.09	.03	-.03	-.06	.07	.14	.06	-.07	.03	-.04	.05	-.19	-.15	-.16	-.23	-.16	-.17	-.02
Principled	.03	.06	.05	.10	.09	.07	.08	.05	-.08	-.12	-.03	-.17	.07	-.18	-.05	-.03	-.16	-.22	-.12	.03
Activity Oriented	.09	.03	-.03	.06	.00	-.04	-.01	-.12	.07	-.01	.02	.04	-.01	-.03	.02	.04	-.01	-.12	-.20	.06
Dynamic	-.09	-.01	.03	-.10	-.02	.10	-.11	-.18	.43	.33	.15	.51	.05	.27	.19	.02	.35	.33	.16	-.06
Enterprising	-.09	.01	.08	-.02	.01	.08	-.13	-.06	.44	.31	.13	.39	.08	.19	.20	.14	.26	.25	.17	-.03
Striving	-.02	.02	.07	-.05	-.01	.06	-.08	-.05	.55	.27	.07	.32	.12	.12	.21	.14	.17	.15	.12	-.06

a. Listwise N=305

Inventory (HPI)

Sensitive	Caring	Likes People	No Hostility	Moralistic	Mastery	Virtuous	Not Autonomous	Not Spontaneous	Impulse Control	Avoids Trouble	Science Ability	Curiosity	Thrill Seeking	Intellectual Games	Generates Ideas	Culture	Education	Math Ability	Good Memory	Reading	Self Focus	Impression Management
-.14	-.16	-.26	-.14	.02	-.11	-.05	-.11	-.06	-.07	-.08	.29	.41	.23	.22	.18	.06	.08	.29	.11	.05	.10	-.07
.03	-.10	-.20	-.11	-.07	-.04	-.16	-.09	.00	.03	-.01	.08	.07	.06	.09	.04	.14	.28	.05	.24	.27	.07	-.01
-.09	-.11	-.23	-.05	.15	.04	.00	-.19	-.03	.04	-.06	.29	.41	.22	.17	.08	-.05	-.02	.44	.06	-.14	.02	.05
-.17	-.23	-.16	-.12	-.01	-.09	-.18	-.14	-.12	-.08	-.01	.23	.15	.10	.12	.13	.18	.23	.09	.26	.45	.09	.05
.05	.06	-.05	.02	.12	.15	.11	-.08	-.12	-.01	-.06	.10	.16	.12	.01	-.08	-.07	-.19	.02	-.16	-.18	-.07	.03
-.04	-.10	-.15	-.14	.09	.09	-.06	-.12	-.15	-.20	-.13	.19	.28	.22	-.02	.17	.05	-.01	.06	.02	-.01	.04	-.04
-.10	-.08	-.07	-.11	.00	-.15	-.03	-.16	-.30	-.43	-.31	.26	.33	.21	.03	.52	.12	-.02	.00	-.01	-.03	.10	-.15
-.07	-.15	-.21	-.09	-.03	-.17	-.05	-.18	-.21	-.17	-.10	.39	.37	.23	.08	.29	.22	.05	.11	.08	.00	.27	-.05
-.08	-.05	-.07	.02	-.05	-.04	-.04	-.03	-.05	-.20	-.10	.18	.14	.13	-.01	.26	.07	.06	.00	.07	-.07	.14	-.12
.12	.22	.51	.08	-.13	-.07	.01	.17	-.09	-.16	-.03	-.06	-.05	-.01	-.03	.12	-.05	.11	-.06	.09	-.05	.06	-.09
.19	.33	.58	.22	-.01	.13	.13	.23	.06	.00	.09	-.13	-.12	-.03	-.06	.07	-.05	.09	-.00	.10	-.03	-.07	-.05
.03	.05	.18	-.14	-.17	-.16	-.15	.17	-.06	-.19	-.19	.00	.03	.02	-.11	.23	.01	.12	-.01	.12	-.13	.20	-.26
-.22	-.07	-.01	-.30	-.11	-.14	-.15	-.09	-.01	-.21	-.32	.13	.22	.14	.00	.26	.00	.01	.01	.02	-.10	.10	-.13
.01	.06	.35	.04	-.01	-.04	.05	.07	-.01	-.09	.04	.21	.08	.11	.06	.26	.16	.20	.11	.20	.05	-.02	-.07
-.24	-.18	-.06	-.36	-.18	-.21	-.24	-.13	-.08	-.28	-.33	.20	.27	.29	-.02	.22	.11	.06	.04	.06	-.01	.18	-.13
-.19	-.04	-.06	-.26	-.01	-.02	-.04	-.17	-.09	-.29	-.16	.18	.18	.12	-.01	.23	.03	.07	.08	.16	.01	-.02	-.09
-.06	.03	.14	-.09	.00	.03	.05	-.01	.02	-.17	-.06	.14	.13	.13	-.05	.22	.03	.04	.05	.06	-.13	.07	-.11
.05	.09	.23	.00	-.08	.00	.09	.05	-.06	-.19	-.12	.13	.06	.08	.00	.25	.15	.03	-.04	.06	-.05	.18	-.13
.07	.01	.08	.04	.02	.01	.05	-.01	-.07	-.16	-.04	.08	.05	.14	-.03	.11	-.02	.12	.07	.06	-.16	.02	-.02
-.21	-.19	.08	-.01	.07	-.08	.05	-.20	-.23	-.16	.01	.13	.20	.22	.10	.16	-.03	.06	.19	.16	.06	-.13	.06
.16	.21	.19	.16	.06	-.01	.18	-.02	.01	-.06	-.04	.05	.01	.09	.06	.07	-.01	-.01	-.08	.03	-.04	.04	.02
.08	.14	.23	.22	.19	.17	.30	-.05	-.16	-.10	.13	.07	.00	.09	-.01	.07	-.03	.03	.03	-.02	.02	-.21	.17
-.10	-.06	.05	.10	.13	-.09	.10	-.16	-.34	-.29	.03	.20	.17	.25	-.02	.13	-.01	-.03	.07	.04	-.03	.00	.09
.08	.00	.03	.02	.06	-.01	.04	.09	-.09	-.08	-.06	.05	.06	.04	-.04	.05	.04	-.02	-.06	.07	-.04	.25	-.05
.35	.32	.25	.18	-.05	-.05	.17	.21	-.02	-.03	.12	-.06	-.15	-.09	-.07	-.01	.16	.04	-.20	.02	.09	.20	-.04
.18	.13	.20	.28	.08	.09	.17	.11	.09	.22	.20	-.05	-.12	-.11	.04	-.20	.01	-.03	-.07	-.10	-.02	.04	.12
.26	.19	.20	.37	.18	.09	.38	.19	.06	.16	.28	-.14	-.19	-.17	.00	-.14	-.05	-.09	-.11	-.08	-.02	-.06	.12
.02	.04	-.04	.10	.20	.39	.13	.00	.21	.25	.07	-.16	-.12	-.17	.10	-.21	-.07	-.14	.02	.00	.02	-.12	.07
.17	.13	-.09	-.02	.12	.41	.07	.01	.16	.22	.07	-.15	-.02	-.12	.04	-.08	-.06	-.04	.01	.06	-.03	-.02	.01
.20	.10	-.08	.12	.06	.25	-.03	.12	.30	.45	.21	-.26	-.24	-.29	.01	-.40	-.12	-.03	.01	-.07	-.09	.00	.07
.10	.05	-.05	.04	.12	.40	-.03	.08	.33	.29	.14	-.16	-.18	-.24	.00	-.22	-.06	-.03	.00	.03	.07	.05	-.02
.04	.06	-.06	.08	.18	.19	.12	-.01	.14	.19	.15	-.03	-.11	-.14	-.01	-.14	.11	-.08	-.12	-.07	.10	-.14	.17
.00	-.04	.06	.04	.15	.17	.07	.02	-.11	-.03	.10	-.09	-.03	-.03	.08	-.06	-.07	.03	.06	.08	.19	-.05	.02
-.03	-.02	.09	-.12	.00	-.07	-.02	-.03	-.25	-.38	-.18	.10	.15	.24	-.09	.28	-.02	-.01	-.06	.05	-.06	.14	-.16
-.05	.00	.08	-.10	.01	.02	-.10	-.06	-.13	-.25	-.21	.10	.20	.19	-.02	.27	-.06	-.01	.07	.04	-.16	.10	-.09
.00	.01	.06	-.05	.07	.16	-.07	-.03	-.06	-.17	-.11	.03	.13	.18	-.02	.19	-.11	.09	.00	.09	-.13	.11	-.07

513

Any correlations between dimensions that are .4 or above are shaded green

Any correlations between dimensions that are -.4 or below are shaded orange

Matrix 6: Wave PS 36 level against Hogan Development

CORRELATIONS[a] HDS / WAVE DIMENSIONS	HDS Excitable	HDS Skeptical	HDS Cautious	HDS Reserved	HDS Leisurely
Analytical	-.04	.05	-.09	.23	.12
Factual	.07	-.02	.05	.09	-.06
Rational	-.14	.10	-.06	.22	.07
Learning Oriented	.01	.00	-.07	.13	.03
Practically Minded	-.03	.05	.04	.04	-.02
Insightful	-.04	.12	-.09	.21	.09
Inventive	-.02	.10	-.19	.16	.14
Abstract	.04	.05	.03	.24	.11
Strategic	-.10	.06	-.16	.06	.02
Interactive	-.09	-.07	-.26	-.43	-.15
Engaging	-.21	-.15	-.23	-.61	-.22
Self-promoting	.10	.14	-.09	-.18	.05
Convincing	.10	.26	-.30	.10	.12
Articulate	-.21	-.11	-.44	-.25	-.13
Challenging	.23	.27	-.19	.19	.11
Purposeful	-.10	.14	-.39	.09	.08
Directing	-.12	.10	-.41	-.12	.00
Empowering	-.02	.02	-.17	-.20	.06
Self-assured	-.20	.02	-.26	-.02	-.08
Composed	-.25	-.11	-.48	.03	-.04
Resolving	-.07	-.05	-.17	-.21	-.04
Positive	-.49	-.30	-.33	-.23	-.19
Change Oriented	-.27	-.08	-.37	.05	-.04
Receptive	.01	.01	.07	-.12	-.11
Attentive	.05	-.16	.21	-.25	-.10
Involving	-.08	-.22	.13	-.28	-.23
Accepting	-.24	-.40	.07	-.27	-.18
Reliable	-.16	-.01	.08	-.08	-.04
Meticulous	-.02	.06	.20	.00	.05
Conforming	.06	-.05	.40	-.05	-.04
Organized	-.10	.00	.14	-.06	-.05
Principled	-.12	-.14	.15	-.03	-.17
Activity Oriented	-.12	-.07	-.09	-.12	-.02
Dynamic	-.05	.11	-.29	-.04	.08
Enterprising	-.04	.19	-.34	-.02	.05
Striving	-.12	.13	-.22	.00	.09

a. Listwise N=368

Survey (HDS)

HDS Bold	HDS Mischievous	HDS Colorful	HDS Imaginative	HDS Diligent	HDS Dutiful
.17	.19	-.01	.20	.06	-.23
-.07	-.08	-.16	.02	.01	-.09
.15	.14	-.08	.00	.22	-.13
.04	.07	-.07	.13	-.02	-.21
.03	.05	-.16	-.10	.16	.03
.26	.26	.00	.13	.14	-.31
.28	.37	.28	.48	-.13	-.27
.13	.16	.00	.27	.08	-.15
.31	.19	.23	.27	.00	-.19
.09	.11	.44	.11	-.15	.12
-.02	-.04	.32	-.13	.00	.14
.34	.22	.51	.25	-.09	.11
.38	.30	.38	.33	-.06	-.30
.21	.14	.46	.08	-.08	-.18
.36	.30	.26	.39	-.15	-.30
.31	.36	.28	.20	-.02	-.40
.43	.25	.39	.20	.11	-.30
.25	.18	.37	.30	-.10	-.08
.34	.24	.31	.14	-.07	-.13
.16	.31	.27	.06	-.18	-.30
.09	.12	.15	.08	-.07	.06
-.02	.14	.19	.01	-.15	-.01
.15	.36	.18	.12	-.21	-.26
.07	.01	.09	.06	.11	.09
-.12	-.14	-.06	.00	-.10	.26
-.20	-.28	-.13	-.19	.00	.32
-.27	-.26	-.17	-.18	-.07	.36
-.11	-.22	-.22	-.27	.46	.10
-.02	-.19	-.32	-.17	.62	.06
-.27	-.48	-.36	-.40	.38	.49
-.05	-.26	-.23	-.31	.55	.08
-.20	-.30	-.24	-.18	.19	.04
-.01	.04	-.02	-.11	.21	-.05
.35	.39	.36	.34	.01	-.27
.39	.39	.49	.29	-.01	-.22
.36	.24	.26	.24	.14	-.19

Matrix 7: Wave PS 36 level against FIRO B

CORRELATIONS[a] FIRO B — WAVE DIMENSIONS	Firo Need for Inclusion	Firo Need for Control	Firo Need for Openness	Firo A Including People (do)	Firo B Including People (want to)	Firo C Others Include me (do)	Firo D Others Include me (want others to)
Analytical	.06	.26	-.15	.05	.09	.00	.09
Factual	.09	.01	.05	.09	.12	.02	.10
Rational	-.09	.17	-.14	-.11	-.05	-.09	-.06
Learning Oriented	.02	.02	-.06	.10	.02	-.01	-.02
Practically Minded	.00	-.11	.02	-.10	-.03	.07	.03
Insightful	.04	.15	.00	.04	.01	.06	.02
Inventive	.11	.26	-.06	.08	.07	.09	.10
Abstract	.02	.23	-.13	.04	.02	-.01	.04
Strategic	.19	.27	.01	.20	.20	.10	.15
Interactive	.29	.08	.22	.33	.26	.29	.10
Engaging	.34	-.08	.31	.38	.29	.35	.10
Self-promoting	.28	.37	.13	.23	.29	.17	.24
Convincing	.14	.42	-.03	.09	.15	.10	.12
Articulate	.23	.18	.03	.30	.17	.23	.09
Challenging	.12	.29	-.08	.08	.14	.05	.12
Purposeful	.08	.19	-.07	.08	.05	.06	.06
Directing	.17	.31	.04	.20	.15	.13	.08
Empowering	.22	.25	.05	.21	.22	.21	.09
Self-assured	.17	.14	.06	.15	.20	.07	.14
Composed	.01	.09	-.08	.00	-.05	.02	.03
Resolving	.10	.05	.16	.13	.09	.13	-.01
Positive	.17	-.16	.13	.18	.08	.17	.11
Change Oriented	.04	-.02	-.09	.13	.00	.04	-.02
Receptive	.14	.16	.15	.13	.18	.07	.10
Attentive	.24	-.13	.22	.24	.25	.16	.15
Involving	.12	-.10	.14	.16	.15	.12	.00
Accepting	.11	-.14	.11	.10	.12	.08	.06
Reliable	-.05	-.16	.08	-.08	-.10	.06	-.07
Meticulous	-.01	-.05	.18	-.08	.02	.00	.00
Conforming	-.08	-.07	.07	-.13	-.01	-.08	-.04
Organized	.00	.01	.08	.01	.01	.03	-.05
Principled	.01	-.17	.11	-.06	-.03	.04	.05
Activity Oriented	.04	-.08	.10	.01	-.01	.05	.05
Dynamic	.23	.25	.07	.22	.23	.17	.15
Enterprising	.13	.30	-.03	.12	.11	.14	.06
Striving	.21	.20	.09	.18	.20	.14	.17

a. Listwise N=301

Firo E Controlling People (do)	Firo F Controlling People (want to)	Firo G People control me (do)	Firo H People control me (want them to)	Firo I Open with People (am)	Firo J Open with People (want to be)	Firo K People open control me (are)	Firo L People open with me (want them to be)
.27	.20	.10	.11	-.16	-.12	-.16	-.06
-.01	.05	.02	-.03	-.03	-.04	.04	.16
.10	.18	.06	.11	-.07	-.08	-.16	-.12
.10	.06	-.08	-.04	-.12	-.06	-.04	.01
-.08	-.07	-.10	-.03	.01	-.03	.06	.03
.34	.22	-.13	-.05	-.03	-.07	.02	.07
.39	.33	-.09	.04	-.06	-.12	-.01	-.01
.23	.22	.05	.10	-.08	-.14	-.13	-.08
.37	.28	-.02	.07	-.01	-.06	.03	.05
.11	.02	.04	.05	.23	.18	.16	.13
-.04	-.07	-.06	-.04	.25	.26	.29	.19
.34	.34	.15	.15	.12	.12	.06	.12
.58	.46	-.02	.05	-.03	-.04	-.04	.02
.35	.20	-.06	-.02	.05	.02	.04	.00
.44	.37	-.07	.02	-.07	-.07	-.13	.00
.44	.34	-.20	-.12	-.08	-.10	-.03	-.02
.61	.42	-.18	-.08	.01	-.03	.07	.06
.34	.23	.00	.08	.04	-.03	.10	.03
.22	.22	-.06	-.02	.02	.07	.01	.10
.27	.11	-.14	-.02	-.03	-.01	-.10	-.11
.04	.00	.01	.09	.13	.09	.17	.11
-.01	-.08	-.20	-.13	.08	.10	.14	.09
.14	.08	-.17	-.11	-.08	-.05	-.10	-.08
.12	.03	.13	.14	.16	.15	.08	.12
-.28	-.21	.10	.07	.15	.18	.17	.20
-.26	-.22	.14	.12	.17	.10	.15	.04
-.34	-.27	.17	.12	.13	.11	.10	.04
-.20	-.12	-.04	-.05	.09	.04	.14	.00
-.08	.02	-.03	-.05	.14	.12	.18	.14
-.35	-.19	.23	.15	.08	.09	.05	.03
-.01	.03	.01	.01	.06	.02	.12	.05
-.16	-.16	-.06	-.06	.06	.04	.15	.10
-.02	-.07	-.08	-.05	.03	.05	.13	.11
.47	.30	-.12	-.02	.05	.03	.06	.08
.47	.41	-.11	-.02	.00	.00	-.04	-.06
.36	.27	-.13	-.01	.04	.01	.10	.13

Any correlations between dimensions that are .4 or above are shaded green

Any correlations between dimensions that are -.4 or below are shaded orange

Matrix 8: Wave PS 36 level against Myers-Briggs

CORRELATIONS[a] MBTI / WAVE DIMENSIONS	MBTI Extraversion	MBTI Introversion	MBTI Sensing	MBTI Intuition
Analytical	-.21	.21	-.11	.11
Factual	-.13	.13	-.15	.15
Rational	-.13	.13	.18	-.18
Learning Oriented	-.08	.08	-.21	.21
Practically Minded	-.05	.05	.24	-.24
Insightful	-.16	.16	-.07	.07
Inventive	.02	-.02	-.51	.51
Abstract	-.20	.20	-.35	.35
Strategic	.05	-.05	-.25	.25
Interactive	.71	-.71	-.02	.02
Engaging	.65	-.65	.11	-.11
Self-promoting	.36	-.36	-.13	.13
Convincing	.12	-.12	-.13	.13
Articulate	.47	-.47	-.18	.18
Challenging	.06	-.06	-.24	.24
Purposeful	.00	.00	-.08	.08
Directing	.26	-.26	-.04	.04
Empowering	.26	-.26	-.24	.24
Self-assured	.15	-.15	-.05	.05
Composed	.13	-.13	-.07	.07
Resolving	.14	-.14	-.03	.03
Positive	.28	-.28	-.06	.06
Change Oriented	.08	-.08	-.18	.18
Receptive	.07	-.07	-.12	.12
Attentive	.08	-.08	-.10	.10
Involving	.17	-.17	.12	-.12
Accepting	.09	-.09	.08	-.08
Reliable	-.09	.09	.35	-.35
Meticulous	-.17	.17	.22	-.22
Conforming	-.08	.08	.49	-.49
Organized	-.07	.07	.33	-.33
Principled	-.11	.11	.08	-.08
Activity Oriented	.03	-.03	.10	-.10
Dynamic	.23	-.23	-.18	.18
Enterprising	.17	-.17	-.11	.11
Striving	.08	-.08	-.15	.15

a. Listwise N=337

Type Indicator (MBTI)

MBTI Thinking	MBTI Feeling	MBTI Judging	MBTI Perceiving
.41	-.41	-.06	.06
.06	-.06	-.01	.01
.38	-.38	.12	-.12
.15	-.15	-.07	.07
.07	-.07	-.04	.04
.29	-.29	-.02	.02
.14	-.14	-.35	.35
.21	-.21	-.06	.06
.16	-.16	.01	-.01
-.26	.26	-.19	.19
-.35	.35	-.01	.01
-.09	.09	-.12	.12
.29	-.29	-.05	.05
.00	.00	-.11	.11
.34	-.34	-.15	.15
.32	-.32	-.12	.12
.15	-.15	.04	-.04
-.15	.15	-.13	.13
.06	-.06	-.05	.05
.23	-.23	-.25	.25
-.17	.17	-.02	.02
-.09	.09	-.22	.22
.12	-.12	-.33	.33
-.14	.14	.06	-.06
-.47	.47	-.04	.04
-.33	.33	.05	-.05
-.37	.37	-.03	.03
-.04	.04	.48	-.48
.02	-.02	.35	-.35
-.19	.19	.48	-.48
-.01	.01	.64	-.64
-.10	.10	.18	-.18
-.02	.02	.06	-.06
.12	-.12	-.13	.13
.18	-.18	-.11	.11
.16	-.16	-.04	.04

519

Any correlations between dimensions that are .4 or above are shaded green
Any correlations between dimensions that are -.4 or below are shaded orange

520